Money, Finance, Political Economy

Deena Khatkhate, alumnus of the University of Bombay and Manchester University, a reputed economist held senior positions at the Reserve Bank of India, and the International Monetary Fund and also was a senior consultant at the World Bank, the United Nations and the Asian and African Development Banks. He wrote extensively on economics in leading academic journals like The Quarterly Journal of Economics, The Review of Economics and Statistics, The Oxford Economic Papers, The Oxford Bulletin of Economics and Statistics, The Journal of Post Keynesian Economics, Economic Development and Cultural Change, The Journal of Development Studies, The Economic and Political Weekly, Social Research, World Development, Economia Internazionale, IMF Staff Papers etc., was a member of the editorial board of the IMF Staff Papers, an associate editor of the Encyclopedia of India, (of which Professor Stanley Wolpert was the chief editor), and Managing Editor of World Development. He co-edited with Warren L. Coats Jr., *Money and Monetary Policy in Less Developed Countries* (1980, Pergamon Press, London), edited *National and International Aspects of Financial Policies in the Less Developed Countries* (1981, Pergamon Press, London), and *Money and Finance: Issues, Institutions and Policies* (1998, Orient Longman, Bombay for the Sameeksha Trust). He authored several papers on financial liberalisation in the World Bank's Economic Discussion Paper Series and co-authored its pioneering study on the Asian Bond Market. A book of his non-economic writings, *Ruminations of a Gadfly*, was published by Academic Foundation, New Delhi.

Deena Khatkhate lives in Chevy Chase, Maryland, USA.

MONEY, FINANCE, POLITICAL ECONOMY

GETTING IT RIGHT

Deena Khatkhate

ACADEMIC FOUNDATION

NEW DELHI

First published in 2009
by

ACADEMIC FOUNDATION
4772-73 / 23 Bharat Ram Road, (23 Ansari Road),
Darya Ganj, New Delhi - 110 002 (India).
Phones : 23245001 / 02 / 03 / 04.
Fax : +91-11-23245005.
E-mail : academic@vsnl.com
www. academicfoundation.com

Cataloging in Publication Data--DK
  Courtesy: D.K. Agencies (P) Ltd. <docinfo@dkagencies.com>

Khatkhate, Deena
  Money, finance, political economy: getting it right/
Deena Khatkhate.
  p.   cm.
  Articles; previously published.
  With reference to India.
  Includes index.
  ISBN 13: 9788171887156
  ISBN 10: 8171887155

  1. Economic development--India. 2. India--Economic policy-
-1991- 3. Monetary policy--Developing countries. 4.
Monetary policy--India. 5. Finance--Developing countries. 6.
Finance--India. 7. International economic relations.   I. Title.

DDC 338.954   22

Typeset by Italics India, New Delhi.
Printed and bound in India.

10 9 8 7 6 5 4 3 2 1

Anil

IN EVER LOVING MEMORY

Contents

I
Money

II
Finance

III
National Economy

List of Tables

Prelude

The aim of science is not to open the door to infinite wisdom,
but to set a limit to infinite error.

— Bertolt Brecht

This book consists mainly of assorted articles published in the *Economic and Political Weekly, World Development, Asian Survey, and Finance and Development*; there are some unpublished ones too, written over a decade ago. These articles cover a wide swath of national and international aspects of money, finance and exchange rates and the political economy of development. The purpose of this prelude is first to persuade readers to reprise those articles on the political economy of development in India, brain drain, and reshaping of the international monetary system, which appeared to be unconventional in approach, analysis and policies at the time when they were written or published but are no longer so in the transformed world of today, while at the same time admitting where I went wrong as, for example, in regard to the impact of fiscal deficit on real interest rates. Second, the prelude is intended to appraise the readers with the dynamics of monetary theory and finance from the perspective of developing countries and the constraints of political economy on the issues of economic development.

Chapter 18, "Restructuring the political process in India", was published in 1977 in the aftermath of a crushing electoral defeat of the Congress party under Indira Gandhi.[1] It argued that:

> something more fundamental is at stake in India than a mere eye-washing economic programme, that commitments and implementation are invariable concomitants of governance of the country, that social justice and economic growth are not correlates of economic policy which gyrate between public ownership of the means of production and unbridled private enterprise but are deeply embedded in the political process. Without transforming the political process, therefore, nothing worthwhile can be attained in the sphere of economic policy.

This mode of going beyond purely economic factors was caught on later by leading economists like Pranab Bardhan (1984) and Jagdish Bhagwati (1988). Bardhan focused on the political constraints on the efficiency of the public sector and agricultural and industrial investment. He traced these constraints

---

1. A pseudonym, "Kautilya", as the author was used because of denial of permission to publish the article by the International Monetary Fund, where I worked at the time.

to the existence of a proprietary coalition of the industrial-capitalist class: white-collar bureaucrats and rich farmers, all of whom belong to the top percentile of the population. There are continuing conflicts among these proprietary classes, which resulted in deceleration of public investment and rise in the capital-output ratio in the economy, thereby slowing down economic growth. In the name of social welfare, the proprietary groups have created a semi-autonomous government that protects the administrative power of a literati bureaucracy power group, a business class that is insulated from foreign and domestic competition and most easily manipulates its way through the maze of regulatory controls, and the rich farmers who benefit from massive agricultural subsidies. This configuration of power derives its legitimacy from populist rhetoric of national self-reliance, the role of the benign state in providing distributive justice, and the need for protection from the greed and rapacity of the unbridled private sector. In such a conjuncture, the policies evolved only eventuate in economic waste on a larger scale, a loss-making public sector, a decline in saving, and even atrophy of the private sector.

Bhagwati offered a slightly different perspective. According to him, the state bred proliferating rent-seeking activities through the paraphernalia of its control instruments:

> The entire society it yielded with entrepreneurs enjoying squatters' rights, created a business class that wanted liberalisation in the sense of less hassles, not genuine competition. The bureaucrats, however idealistic at the outset, could not but have noticed that this regime gave them the enormous power that the ability to confer rents generates. The politics of corruption also followed as politicians became addicted to the use of licensing illegal funds for election and then for themselves (Bhagwati, 1988: 541).

Bhagwati's thesis of a linkage between ideology and interests has much power to explain the slow growth of the Indian economy covering both the public and private sectors.

A common thread running through the political economy models of economic policy by Bardhan and Bhagwati is the arbitrariness of power wielded by the political authorities in India. But these models do not explain why the state became autonomous, why the proprietary classes could use the state machinery with impunity for their parochial interests, and why the ideology and ideas detrimental to macroeconomic efficiency emerged in the first place (Khatkhate, 1991). An answer to some of these questions was sought in the structure of the Indian political process (Chapter 18). Paradoxically, the Indian political system operates in such a way that, at one extreme, economic policy has punishment as its basis, but without any sanction for enforcing it and, at the other, incentive as its basis without any built-in mechanism to reward for success. It is this ambivalent nature of economic policy which inclines politicians whether in power or out of power to opportunism. When they need votes on the eve of elections, they proclaim a turn to the left in economic policy. But once they are entrenched in power, the pay-off of leftism in policy posture slowly begins to dwindle. Anxiety to perpetuate themselves in power seizes them and the search is on for funds to meet the expenses of the next elections. The time is ripe then for a swing to the right in policy stance, which lasts until the coffers of the political party in power are filled. The reason for these political business cycles lies in the concentration of political power at the centre in a federal polity. The situation can be changed only with a radical transformation of the political process, that can ensure diffusion of political power among state units or even lower down the ladder among the district units.

In India today, there has been a distinct move towards decentralisation of power, not so much policy-induced as by happenstance. The end of party hegemony at the centre as well as in the states, growing number of small-sized states, strengthening of the bargaining power of the state governments *vis-à-vis* the centre, and economic liberalisation providing more space for the power of the states, have resulted in greater decentralisation of power. This has paved the way for increased competition among states with consequent benefits and, in the process, both economic efficiency and growth have accelerated. However, diffusion of power and the restructuring of the political process have still many miles to go. Despite the fact that India made a "travesty of planning"—in I.M.D. Little's telling phrase (Little, 1982 and Chapter 9, "Oeirolysis of development?")—it continued the *effete quango*—the Indian Planning Commission—as the political class across all political parties is not ready to allow a smooth transition to decentralisation of power. One of the ex-planners was brutally frank on this issue. "The Planning Commission works on the unspoken assumption that a quasi-federal constitution must in practice be worked as a unitary one in the interest of planning" (Chelliah, 1991). Even the leftists are loath to purchase the Planning Commission, as one of them derided the Planning Commission, on the ground that:

> ...the economies to be reaped from the indivisibilities and centralised decision making had been exaggerated by Indian economists who had not taken into account adequately the diseconomies of economic centralisation including its political consequences of stifling local or regional initiatives (Mitra 1975: 1705–10).

Maybe with the efflux of time, when the states assert themselves even more than at present for economic policy autonomy, the Planning Commission would fade away, as the Tariff Commission did a few decades ago.

The importance of the political element in economic policymaking is also thrown into bold relief by the glib discourse in countries like India on the so-called antithetical relationship between growth and income distribution. This debate is false, as I tried to explain in Chapter 10, "Economic growth *versus* income distribution: A perennial charade", written in 1978. As Robert Solow (whom I quoted there) said long ago,

> If economic growth is a good thing, it does not follow that economic growth with a lot of pious talk about equality is a good thing. In principle, we can have growth with or without equity; and we can have stagnation with or without equity. An argument about first principles should keep these things separate.

Since 1951, with the ushering in of a deliberate policy of economic development, there has been a constant refrain about the conflict between growth and income distribution (and poverty alleviation to boot), and yet India, until it pursued a strong economic liberalisation policy in 1991, achieved neither growth nor equity in income distribution and decline in poverty level. Now the poverty level has sharply declined (Chapter 14, "Indian economic reform: A philosopher's stone"), though income distribution has not improved as much as desired. But this consequence is due not so much to the growth strategy adopted that succeeded beyond initial expectations as to the government's failure to translate growth into more equal income distribution. But this is a political problem which requires a political solution. As argued in Chapter 10,

> the implementation [of the programme of income transfer] implies a certain transmission process—a channel through which ideas and ideals which the politicians profess and the administrators articulate, move up from the political parties to the political government, and move down from the latter to the bureaucracy and further down to the people. It also subsumes a feedback from the lower layer to the political parties via the political government.

Unless these political issues are confronted boldly, "to set aside economic growth as an objective of policy on the ground that equal income distribution is a prior condition to be met is to lose something tangible on the swing without getting anything by way of equality in income distribution on the roundabout."

However, to change the political process is no easy task when populism and vote-bank politics run rampant across the spectrum of different ideologies. It calls for a "transforming type of leadership as distinct from the transactional type" (Chapter 16, "Profile of leadership in a developing society"). The transactional type defines common "interests as separate interests of individuals or groups comprising society rather than its collective welfare." The transforming type of leadership on the other hand is "imbued with a vision of how society should evolve. It is not exogenously planted but grows from within". In India, the political leadership is of the transactional kind, catering to special interest groups and pliable to be moulded according to the direction in which the wind is blowing. Until the transforming leadership evolves with its benign impact on the political process, Indian politicians and bureaucrats would continue to indulge in hoary, futile and wordy debate on equality and growth, as they have been doing of yore.

The absence of a transforming kind of leadership has its counterpart in the failure of the intelligentsia to be the 'public intellectual' in the vanguard of ideas which can navigate a dispassionate, non-ideological and in the end creative discourse on the political, economic and social issues confronting the polity. Not that India has been lacking in

> ...a highly educated class but it consists more of "intellectual workers" as distinguished from intellectuals as defined by Paul Baran. This class made many notable contributions in social and natural sciences, but it fell short of that signal distinction of being public intellectuals who could influence the extent and nature of social and political change in the country (see Chapter 17, "Intellectuals and Indian polity").

To be the public intellectual, they have to "perceive prevailing social and political reality in its interconnectedness or as a part of historical process." The absence of such a class in India is a consequence of the limited employment opportunities which made

> ...the best minds gravitate to a few centres of excellence or non-academic but remunerative positions in the government, leaving academia in general bereft of the cream of talent. Those who remained continued their miserable existence without any real interest in scholarship or knowledge, constantly humiliated by the treatment they received from the intellectual "Brahmins".... The brightest and the best looked for approbation of their contributions to knowledge either towards institutions of learning abroad or to the authorities rather than to their own tribe which was large and growing but also intellectually diminishing.

Whatever space was left for the genuine intellectuals was pre-empted by the leftist ideologues, who had their glory-days of influence during the interventionist regime of post-independence India. They appropriated squatter's rights for want of opposition from others in the social milieu. Despite a startling performance of the Indian economy since 1991 with unprecedented growth rate both in the aggregate and per capita, amazing rise in domestic saving and investment, and lower trajectory of poverty, these tub-thumping intellectuals continued with their siren song of the impending doom of the Indian economy, misguiding the venal politicians and perpetuating the deeply rooted malady of the intellectual class. They obfuscated informed debate and tried to revive discredited policy nostrums of the communist countries which are consigned to the dump-hill of history. And yet they tend, paradoxically, to touch chords among the politicians, perpetually disposed to populism, rent-seeking and vote-bank politics. This shows that my ruminations in the article on the Indian intellectuals, written in 1977, still have resonance in India of the present, despite a sea-change it has undergone since then.

Chapter 26, "Brain drain as a social safety valve", written in 1971, has a chequered background.[2] This article took a contrarian's view of the brain drain from developing countries to the industrial countries. The prevailing widely held belief, except that of neo-classical economists like Harry Johnson, for whom "...the brain drain becomes no more than an aspect of labor mobility, which, if anything, should contribute to the world output and welfare" (Johnson, 1968), was that "...such a migration not only sets back the growth of the less developed countries, but also leads to a back-flow of aid to the very countries normally considered as donors of aid." My position on this issue was that "The brain drain provides a safety valve for the less developed countries which possess surplus university graduates. So long as the tendency to produce these persists—and it is likely to be so for a variety of factors, the brain drain is inevitable." The reasons I cited were:

> ...migration tends to bring about, after a time, a certain desirable social, political, and economic transformation, which not only helps to raise the social product of the educated but also facilitates its quicker realization. The employment possibilities within the national boundaries limit the opportunity cost of graduates but once the employers in the outside world are free to absorb them, the opportunity cost of the educated tends to be determined not only by domestic circumstances but also by the international market, and is therefore higher than before.

I referred in support of this to P.C. Mahalanobis, who said that the productivity of statisticians in Indian conditions is low because they operate in a social, political and institutional environment which stultified their initiative and creativity. Besides, emigration leads to more invisible earnings and also a spread of technology and new ideas to the developing countries.

Now the debate on brain drain has taken a U-turn. There is greater recognition than before that brain drain actually results in brain gain and is also referred to as "brain circulation" and "brain exchange" (United Nations,

---

2. When Finance and Development (F&D) of the IMF published this article, Le Monde, a leading French newspaper, wrote an editorial castigating the IMF, mistaking views in the article as representing the official policy of the IMF. The Managing Director of the IMF, Pier-Paul Schwaitzer passed on Le Monde's editorial to the editor for comments, who explained that he published my article in order to present the other side of the on-going controversy to encourage informed public debate, while drawing his attention to the journal's usual rider that views expressed therein are those of the author.

2001) because of the impact of brain drain such as increased trade between emigrating and host countries, foreign direct investment, and spread of technology (Doequier and Rapoport, 2004). Most of the underlying logic and analytics of the new awakening about the benign effects of brain drain were fully anticipated in my article. Looking at this from the perspective of India in particular, the brain drain from it which started in the 1970s has proved to be a blessing. Most of the educated emigrants are the pioneers in the Silicon Valley technology revolution, which has reverberations in the Indian economy of the 1990s onward in the form of rapid development of information technology not only transforming India in a major way but also impacting significantly leading industrial countries like the United States.

Last, I would like to draw the attention of readers to chapters 20 and 21 on the international monetary system. When I wrote on this subject in 1987, while in the employment of the IMF, I received some flak for propounding something so profane. "International monetary system: Which way?" was published in *World Development* soon after I retired from the IMF. "Conflict and cooperation in the international monetary system" languished in my files by default. In retrospect, it seems now that I was ahead of the curve in thinking on the issues dealt with in those articles. The ideas I put forth are no longer idiosyncratic but are now being seriously debated in the international fora. These institutions are at the crossroads, in search of a new mission and in search of a *raison d'être* for their very existence. The emerging countries, until recently habitual borrowers from these institutions, have acquired new clout. I had visualised that:

> There is a possibility that the evolving international monetary system may in future take a different track than the one to which it has become habituated over the years. There is a loud message in the on-going developments in the international arena that a distinction between the pure monetary character of the IMF and the developmental character of the World Bank may not remain as clearly definable as in the past. The juridical distinction between the IMF and the World Bank, though narrowed over the years, may tend to be further reduced to a point of almost complete fusion of their functions. (Chapter 21).

Today, the number of borrowers from the World Bank and the IMF is dwindling, with the need for resources being concentrated mainly in the extremely poor countries in the Africa region. The reports of the Meltzer Commission and also think-tanks are straws in the wind and a major thrust for the reform of these institutions will soon gather momentum.

Equally pertinent is the idea of decentralisation of IMF operations in the context of emerging monetary unions or organisations, which I argued for in Chapter 20:

> At present, international monetary policy is implemented by the International Monetary Fund and its achievements over the years are rather remarkable, but its structure is premised on the belief that international monetary cooperation is world-wide in scope. This belief is overtaken by recent events. The European Monetary System (EMS) has emerged with a bang, with its own sub-regional cooperative framework, exchange rate arrangements and its own currency unit.... The time may soon come for similarly formed regional monetary blocks, not only among the industrial countries but also among developing or emerging ones. If such regional groups come into existence, there will be a need to decentralise the structure of the monetary system by allowing a fuller play to regional bodies to explore wider potential for cooperation and to facilitate the International Monetary Fund to focus more than before on those issues which cannot be solved efficiently on a regional scale.

This foreboding seems to be borne out by recent developments in Latin America and particularly in Asia, where swap facilities against speculative attacks, called the Chiang Mai Initiative, are being established. This has led some perceptive observers and economists to plead for the Federal Reserve System type of organisational structure for the IMF (Kapur and Webb, 2007), which is not different in essence from what I proposed in Chapter 20.

In Chapter 8, "Fiscal deficit and real interest rates", I have now recanted my views on justification of fiscal deficit for financing economic development. I had argued earlier, perhaps being in an age of innocence, that fiscal deficit, in the presence of a large amount of unemployment and excess capacity in the producing sectors, would result in new investment without inflationary pressures. The basic assumption underlying this argument was that the interventionist policies of a benign state would be effective. This assumption is naïve and devoid of any economic rationale, as the experience of emerging countries, including India, has demonstrated during the last five decades.

Turning to the second purpose of the prelude, there is a common thread running through Parts I and II, which connects adaptation of monetary theory and policy developments in recent years along with the associated financial sector strategies with the developmental issues that dominated the practical policies in developing countries in general. The central theme in money and finance is that a country's monetary policy and its monetary system are critical to the pace and nature of the development process (Chapters 1 to 4). These issues, important as they are for the national economies, have close links with changes in the international monetary system, which are elaborated in Chapters 5, 6 and 20 to 24.

In bringing out this volume, I have benefited by my long association with Vinoo Bhatt and Anand Chandavarkar as intellectual soulmates, which started when we worked together in the Research Department of the Reserve

Bank of India and continues even today in Washington, D.C. Most of the essays are a product of the way of thinking germinated by these two fellow economists, whose benchmarks for standard of scholarship are derived from the edict of Professor Edward Shills of Chicago University that good quality research stems from a peer review process and avoidance of path dependency. They, in particular, persuaded me to include in the volume those few articles which proved to be prescient. My special debt is to John Williamson of the Peterson Institute for International Economics, Washington D.C., Govinda Rao of the National Institute of Public Finance and Policy, New Delhi and Anand Chandavarkar for significant suggestions to improve the chapter scheme, which clarified the unifying theme of the book.

I express my gratitude to the editors of the *Economic and Political Weekly, World Development, Asian Survey and Finance and Development* for permitting me to reproduce the articles first published there. Likewise, I thank the Saraswat Co-operative Bank, Mumbai for allowing me to include the key-note address I gave at the 16th Bank Economists Conference held in Mumbai on 28–30 January 1993. In preparation of this volume, both Ms. Southamini Borlo and Chet Ninoo-Quarcoo of the World Bank-IMF Library helped me to trace numerous references far beyond their call of duty and Arthur Monteiro prepared the manuscript for publication with admirable proficiency.

REFERENCES

Acharya, S. (2006). "Indian economic reform: A philosopher's stone", *Economic and Political Weekly* XLI (22): 2203-5, 3 June.

Bardhan, P. (1984). *The Political Economy of Development in India*. Oxford: Basil Blackwell.

Bhagwati, J. (1988). "Poverty and public policy", *World Development* 16(5): 539–55.

Chelliah, R. (1991). *Towards a Decentralised Polity*. New Delhi: Fiscal Research Foundation.

Doequier, F. and H. Rapoport (2004). *Skilled Migration and Human Capital Formation in Developing Countries: A Survey*. December.

Johnson, H.G. (1968). "An international model", in W. Adams (ed.), *Brain Drain*. New York: Random House.

Kapur, D. and R. Webb, (2007). "Beyond the IMF", *Economic and Political Weekly* XLII(7): 581–9, 17 February.

Khatkhate, D. (1991). "National economic policy in India", in D. Salvatore (ed.), *National Economic Policies, Handbook of Comparative Economic Policies* 1: 231–75. New York: Greenwood Press.

Little, I.M.D. (1982). *Economic Development and International Relations, A Twentieth Century Fund Book*. New York: Basic Books.

Meltzer, A. (2000). *The Report of the International Financial Institutions Advisory Commission*. Washington D.C.: International Financial institutions Advisory Commission.

Mitra, A. (1975). "Will growth and centralised financial arrangements do?'" *Economic and Political Weekly* X(43): 1705–10, 9 October.

United Nations (2001). *Human Development Report 2001*. New York: United Nations.

I

MONEY

1 | Money and Monetary Policy in LDCs in the 1990s*

Twelve years ago, the key issues concerning money's role in economic development were summarised in an introductory chapter to a collection of articles on that topic.[1] The central theme was that a country's monetary policy and its monetary system are very important to the pace and nature of its economic development. At that time there was a newly developing consensus that inflation is primarily a monetary phenomenon, and that inflation and macroeconomic instability are generally harmful to growth. Of particular relevance for LDCs, it was argued, is the role played by money (and the financial system) in allocating saving to its most productive uses. It was also argued that both low or negative real rates of interest and directed credit policies interfered with the functioning of the financial system and thus with the efficient allocation of saving.

These views have now become the conventional wisdom of the 1990s. However, the focus of the debate has changed in several respects over the intervening decade in response to new objectives, institutional and political developments, new analytical insights, and further experiences across countries at different stages of development.

In this article an attempt is made to expand on and update the earlier review by treating more extensively topics touched on in the original article that, with the benefit of hindsight, deserved much fuller discussion, and by adding several topics that intervening developments and experience have brought to the fore. In the former category this paper discusses:

(a) the information gathering and processing, and risk assessment and management aspects of the financial system;

(b) the insights of public choice theory into the difficulties of actually obtaining welfare enhancing policies in highly centralised economic

---

* Co-written with Warren L. Coats, Jr.

1. This chapter was first published in the Economic and Political Weekly XIV(46), 17 November 1979. The book Money and Monetary Policy in Less Developed Countries was published by Pergamon Press in 1980.

systems and the related problems of rent-seeking behaviour associated with several types of government intervention in economic activities; and

(c) the implications of openness and capital mobility for monetary and interest rate policies.

In the category of new issues this paper discusses:

(a) increased interest in "buffer stock" models of the demand for money;

(b) the renewed debate over the most appropriate monetary anchor; and

(c) problems associated with liberalisation of repressed financial systems.

ROLE OF THE FINANCIAL SECTOR

The earlier review stressed the importance of macroeconomic stability because it was needed for money to perform its vital role as a unit of account and a means of payment. It also stressed the importance of positive real rates of interest on financial assets (e.g. deposits) because they encouraged a larger share of saving to flow to investments via the financial system. Macroeconomic stability and positive real rates of interest contribute to the financial system's ability to allocate saving to the most productive investments at the lowest possible cost, thereby raising the level of income and its rate of growth associated with a given rate of saving. The efficiency of investment generally has been more important for a country's economic growth than has been its rate of saving (or investment). However, macroeconomic stability and positive real rates of interest probably raise the rate of saving as well.

The above explanation of the financial system's contribution to growth, though correct, now seems to be overly simplified and unlikely to convey the full extent of the financial sector's role. The extent of economic specialisation, the foundation of economic development, is limited both by the (information and transaction) costs of trading and by the limited availability of investment financing. An efficient financial system reduces the information and transaction costs of trading, and extends the availability of finance and lowers its cost. Market allocation of resources, including savings, has almost always been more efficient than government allocation. This reflects more than the differences in incentives facing decision-makers in private enterprises and government bureaucracies discussed in the next section. It also reflects the inability of centralised decision-making to effectively utilise the complex mass of information on individual preferences and capabilities that can only be known in small part by any individual. Decentralised decision-making of market economies has evolved to better capture and utilise such information (Hayek, 1945; 1988).

More indirect, impersonal, and complex economic arrangements and relationships are more risky, however. An agreement to repay in the future is more difficult to enforce than is an agreement to exchange assets now. The expertise and the contractual forms and arrangements that develop in the financial sector (e.g. the nature of specific financial instruments) are meant to reduce costs and to evaluate, allocate, monitor, and minimise risk.[2] In addition to providing an efficient pricing and payments mechanism, one of the most important contributions banks make to economic growth is to develop expertise in assessing creditworthiness. By collecting and analysing the information needed to determine the most profitable loans, including the prospects for repayment, and by monitoring the activities of borrowers, financial intermediaries increase the efficiency of resource use. In addition, access to a variety of financial instruments enables economic agents to pool, price, and exchange risk.

When bank credit is allocated at below market clearing interest rate, the allocative and risk management expertise of banks is replaced by political and bureaucratic mechanisms. Over time, the development of project and risk assessment expertise and mechanisms by lending institutions is discouraged, the lack of which can be a serious problem for financially repressed economies attempting to liberalise. In addition to lowering the productivity of investment, these policies have generally weakened the financial viability of the affected financial institutions to the extent that a staggeringly large number of them are now insolvent. These insolvencies reflect a tragic amount of economic waste.[3]

LESSONS OF PUBLIC CHOICE THEORY

The below-market-clearing interest rates and associated directed credit policies discussed in the earlier review, and common in many LDCs, interfere with the financial sector's ability to allocate saving to its most productive uses in obvious

---

2. These aspects of the financial sector's contribution to economic growth were expanded upon in the World Development Report, 1989: Financial Systems and Development, to which both authors contributed.

3. The Savings and Loan and banking insolvencies in the United States have other causes. These are primarily consequences of excessive risk taking without effective supervision, encouraged by deposit insurance (moral hazard), regional (state) limitations on the activities of individual banks, and other restrictions on the nature of the financial services bank may provide.

ways. The adverse consequences of rent-seeking opportunities created by those policies, however, were only hinted at in that review. Directed credit policies, like other non-market allocation mechanisms, create opportunities for personal gain that do not contribute to the social good.[4] Rent-seeking behaviour tends to reduce output in several ways. The labour resources expended might have been more productive in other uses. The existence in some areas of rent-seeking and the corruption it sometimes encourages might contribute to the toleration of corruption in other areas and/or a general decline in public trust in government.

Rent-seeking opportunities also create constituencies both within and outside of government against their elimination. The interests of these beneficiaries of the present arrangements are often more direct, focused, and intense than those of the 'general' public that would benefit from reform. This fact can make the adoption and execution of reform difficult. It requires that a government be willing and able to reform itself. The most dramatic examples of the difficulties of self-reform are currently in progress in the Soviet Union and Eastern Europe. Soviet president Gorbachev has demonstrated amazing skill at developing, encouraging, and then managing internal political competition between ideological and interest groups as the engine to force reform of the Soviet system.

Refinement and clarification of economic theory, and especially the accumulation of evidence from years of experience with various policy approaches, have been essential and often decisive factors behind political support for economic reform. They provide an understanding of the consequences of policies from which a consensus can be formed on what is in the general public interest. Such consensus can then be used to oppose the often better-placed special interests that are protecting the status quo. The recently expressed desire of the majority of the citizens of centrally planned economies to convert their economies to market-based systems has a great deal to do with the failure of centrally planned economies to deliver what was expected of them even over a long period of time and the current intellectual consensus on the superiority of market over centrally planned systems. One of the many dangers of partial reform is that the remaining rent-seeking opportunities continue to support and encourage the special interests that benefit from them, which then tend to resist or even reverse further reform.

---

4. If the objectives of directed credit policy were ill advised in the first place, activities that circumvent and thwart those objectives might improve social welfare, but to a more limited extent and at a higher social cost than would unrestricted market allocation. See Tullock (1967) and Bhagwati (1982).

Increased Economic and Financial Integration

Along with the intellectual and political forces discussed above, growing economic and financial integration has been an increasingly important force behind economic and financial liberalisation over the last few decades. Technological advances in information processing and dissemination (computers and telecommunications), increased freedom of trade, and financial liberalisation in the industrial countries have made policies based on autarky virtually impossible. Efforts to maintain and fortify the insulation required to enforce non-competitive prices, such as below-market interest rates, have become increasingly hard to implement and to justify.

The increased worldwide integration of markets has improved resource allocation and economic efficiency, but, as indicated above, has limited the policy options available to authorities in both developed and developing countries. The significant increase in international capital mobility, for example, has reduced the ability of national monetary authorities to conduct domestic monetary and fiscal policies independently of external considerations, even with flexible exchange rates.[5] The increased ease with which capital flows internationally means that it is now more difficult and costly than it once was to attempt direct controls of interest rates and the allocation of credit, even in the short run. Capital flight to external assets must be added to the existing domestic forces (informal financial markets, on-lending, and corruption) tending to undercut such policies. These developments suggest that domestic interest rates now need to conform more closely than before to international levels. It is worth reviewing here the implications of capital mobility for domestic monetary and fiscal policies under both fixed and floating exchange rates.

Perfectly mobile capital renders domestic money supply endogenous in nominal as well as real terms for (relatively small) countries that fix the exchange rates of their currencies in terms of some other currency. Fixed exchange rate makes domestic price level exogenous, while freely mobile capital makes domestic interest rate exogenous. This makes it impossible for the monetary authorities to change permanently domestic money supply from the nominal quantity the public wishes to hold at the exogenously determined price level and interest rate.[6]

---

5.   For evidence that there is considerable capital mobility even for many countries generally considered relatively closed, see Haque and Montiel (1990).

6.   The real quantity of money is basically demand-determined, in any event. This observation is not meant to deny that the rate of growth of nominal money supply, by determining the rate of inflation, influences the cost of holding money, and hence is an important determinant of the demand for real money balances.

Given output growth, an increase in the quantity of money will depress domestic interest rates, leading to capital outflow. If capital is perfectly mobile, no interest rate differential can persist across national boundaries, and capital outflow will continue until the initial interest differential is eliminated, i.e. until the domestic increase in money supply is exactly reversed.

Allowing exchange rates to float restores to the central bank the ability to control domestic nominal money supply, because the domestic price level becomes independent of the world price level. With highly mobile capital, however, floating exchange rates cannot restore domestic policy independence from the foreign sector because domestic policies that create a demand by foreigners for domestic assets (or *vice versa*) affect exchange rates, which affect the allocation of domestic resources.

Perfect capital mobility ties the level of domestic real interest rates to those of the world. Temporary differences in the level of domestic and international interest rates, such as might result from an unexpected change in domestic money supply, cause exchange rate changes that lead to real resource transfers, which in turn will eventually eliminate any real interest rate differential. Exchange rate changes imply changes in the relative prices of tradable and non-tradable goods, which helps establish (or preserve) external and overall balance but can also cause a reallocation of resources between these sectors.

The mechanism by which capital mobility links interest rates and exchange rates may be summarised as follows. Capital flows internationally to the extent that savings are invested across national boundaries as a result of current account deficits or surpluses, i.e. to the extent there are net transfers of real resources across national borders. With freely floating exchange rates, the inducement for capital to flow internationally as a result of a change in relative interest rates is offset by exchange rate movements; capital flows will accrue only after exchange rate changes have brought about current account adjustments.[7]

An increase in domestic money supply that reduces domestic interest rates relative to foreign rates, for example, would raise the premia in the forward exchange market of the domestic currency in terms of other currencies sufficiently to eliminate any financial gain from investing in foreign assets with higher interest rates. As a result of this increase in forward premia, the spot purchase and investment of foreign exchange, and the forward repurchase

---

7. Borrowing abroad for financing the purchase of foreign goods, of course, results in an immediate current account adjustment (and therefore capital flow) with no effect on exchange rates (except as might result from changing foreign perceptions of creditworthiness, etc).

of the domestic currency would result in the same yield as would investing in domestic assets at the lower interest rate. However, investors prepared to take the risk could buy the foreign exchange spot and hold foreign assets uncovered by future commitments to reacquire the domestic currency, if they believed that the forward premia overstated the likely appreciation in the future spot exchange rates of the domestic currency. If this were the market's general view, speculation would immediately lower the spot exchange rate until it was expected to appreciate to the same extent as implied by the forward premia.[8]

Through these channels, market forces would tend to eliminate any net advantage from shifting financial assets across national borders, so that the public would be satisfied holding the existing stock of assets at the new interest rates. The depreciation of the spot exchange rate in the low-interest-rate country, however, would result over time in the current account surplus needed to realise the desired net capital outflow.

It can be seen in this simplified account that while floating exchange rates with capital mobility allow divergent inflation rates and nominal interest rates and therefore domestic control of the nominal money stock by the central bank, they do not isolate the domestic economy from the world economy, nor allow domestic monetary policy to operate without regard for the foreign sector. The freer capital is to respond to interest rate differences, the more efficient long-run resource allocation will tend to be, but the larger will be the exchange rate effects (and hence real economy effects) of such differentials. If these interest differentials and exchange rate effects are in fact temporary, but are not correctly perceived as such by market participants, they could impede the efficient allocation of resources by causing unnecessary and costly short-term reallocations between tradable and non-tradable goods sectors.

Resource reallocations resulting from exchange rate changes are costly, often involving a temporary increase in unemployment, idling of capital equipment, and heightened political strains that are associated with any redistribution of costs and benefits in a society. Moreover, frequent changes in exchange rates can cloud resource allocation decisions and lead to reallocations that prove to be mistaken; exchange rate movements that are expected to be temporary can lead to political support for protection in the form of trade and capital controls. These costs of resource reallocation in response to exchange rate changes are the basis of the often expressed desire for exchange

---

8. This is the overshooting phenomenon in the Dornbusch sense. See Dornbusch (1976).

rate stability, and are simply a specific example of the general case against macroeconomic instability.

Artificially low real interest rates require capital controls to restrain the capital flight (in search of higher yielding and/or less risky investments) that normally accompany them. While capital mobility is not perfect in developing countries, the authorities' ability to control capital movements is increasingly limited by the proliferation of financial instruments internationally and the ease with which they can be obtained or traded. This, and an increased understanding of the shortcomings of 'low interest rate' policies and of the repressed financial sectors that result from the more extreme versions of such policies, have diminished the interest of authorities in adhering to them.

Fortunately, the policies needed to avoid capital flight, e.g. realistic exchange rates, acceptable fiscal deficits, attractive domestic financial assets, a healthy, competitive financial sector and economic and political stability are the same policies that are needed for efficient resource allocation in general. Authorities wishing to liberalise their domestic economy's financial sector and the international movement of capital should liberalise their domestic financial sector first in order to minimise the prospects of capital flight (Edwards, 1984).

ESTIMATING DEMAND FOR MONEY

A major theme of the earlier review was the recent move away from many of the conclusions of earlier short-run-focused Keynesian models. The attack on Keynesian theory by Milton Friedman and others in the 1960s was further refined in the 1970s, primarily by efforts to incorporate behavioural assumptions into macroeconomic models consistent with those used elsewhere in economics (microeconomic foundations). Studies of earlier hyper-inflations, as well as an increasing number of contemporary ones in Latin America and elsewhere, supported monetarist models and revealed that Keynesian theory had little of interest to say about inflation. A growing understanding of the role of expectations in macroeconomic models advanced by Friedman (1968) and Ed Phelps (1967 and 1970) helped explain (in fact they predicted) the empirical failure of the alleged trade-off in industrial economies between inflation and unemployment (the "Phillips Curve").

Major theoretical developments during this period resulted from refinements of the implications of forming expectations of the future values of important economic magnitudes in ways consistent with the information available to agents and their understanding of how the economy works (rational expectations). In some respects, however, the important insights and theoretical refinements derived from the assumption that agents form expectations rationally have gone too far, especially but not exclusively in the underdeveloped economy context. While present treatments of rational expectations focus attention on the importance of information, they tend to abstract from the costs of obtaining it. In fact, the key functions of money (and of financial systems) of reducing the costs of transacting (including those of obtaining information on market opportunities) tend to be overlooked or downplayed by current treatments of rational expectations (Laidler, 1990).

The "buffer stock" view of money and its implications for empirical estimates of the short-run demand for money (Coats, 1982b and Laidler, 1990) attempt to correct the tendency of rational aspects models to ignore the role of money in reducing transaction costs. It has particular relevance to underdeveloped economies where market integration is incomplete, financial assets other than money are rather limited, and transaction costs are relatively high. The approach says that changes in the quantity of money (that are not themselves induced by changes in money demand) will to some extent be willingly absorbed into money holdings, which serve as a buffer stock to reduce the cost of transacting, including the costs of adjusting to changed circumstances. If the increased money stock proves permanent, then money demand will ultimately adjust fully.

In most models, money demand adjusts via changes in income, interest rate and the price level. The long-run independence of income and (real) interest rates from the quantity of money implies, however, that a permanent change in the quantity of money ultimately is fully reflected in adjustments in the price level. The long-run properties of buffer stock models are no different from those of traditional money demand models, but in the short-run they imply smaller adjustments of interest rates (and income) to changes in the money stock (Coats, 1982b). As noted above, this result assumes that the change in the quantity of money was independent of the demand for it.

Money supply is 'independent' of its demand as a result of the relationship between the extension of credit and the creation of money by the banking system. An increase in bank reserves (e.g. as a result of a foreign capital inflow or of central bank financing of the government) leads banks to increase their lending (or purchases of financial assets). Lending rates may need to be adjusted to encourage the public to borrow what banks wish to lend. Additional deposits (money) are created as a by-product of bank lending. Interest rates that clear the credit market will not generally also clear the money market in the long run, i.e. the increase in money supply that results from increases in bank loans and the associated interest rate will not generally be the same as the increase in long-run money demand from that interest rate. The buffer stock approach reconciles the discrepancy in money and credit demand in the short-run and assigns the determination of the interest rate primarily to credit markets. Some of the apparent shifts in money demand over the last two decades found in conventionally estimated money demand functions for the US have been explained by the buffer stock approach.

MONETARY ANCHORS

The establishment of price stability has become an unquestioned objective of macroeconomic policy virtually everywhere. This is in sharp contrast to the views held by many economists and policymakers in earlier decades, and is welcome. There remains considerable uncertainty, however, over how best to achieve and preserve price stability.

At the time the first review was written, the use of money growth rate rules or targets to anchor the price level had not yet come into vogue. Money growth rules of one sort or another were embraced in the very early 1980s by many industrial countries for several compelling reasons:

(a) the link between inflation and money growth (the long-run stability of the demand for money) had been empirically established beyond a reasonable doubt for a wide range of developed and developing countries;

(b) the short-run variability of money demand made the outcome of monetary fine-tuning unreliable;

(c) the experience of the 1960s and 70s suggested that discretionary monetary policy tended to have a rather strong inflationary bias for 'public choice' reasons, which could be avoided by replacing discretion with rules (the time inconsistency problem);[9] and

(d) the adoption of monetary rules meant the abandonment of exchange rate rules or targets, and the grudging acceptance of floating exchange rates was relatively widespread by the early 1980s.

---

9. A so-called political business cycle could be observed in many industrial countries as a result of governments' attempts to exploit the short-run Phillips curve to increase employment in periods preceding major elections. The long-run effect of these increases in aggregate demand was an increase in inflation. See Kydland and Prescott (1977).

Several things have led to the more recent abandonment of monetary rules in many countries and the search for alternative monetary anchors. One is that the demand for money proved less stable than some had expected. Monetarists, such as Friedman, had always focused on the long-run stability of the demand for money and had warned that the unusually close relationship between money and the arguments in its demand function during the 1960s and early 70s was fortuitous and not likely to last. Contrary to the impression given by some critics, the long-run stability of money's demand has remained pretty much intact though some predictable drifts have occurred in response to the very dramatic growth in the range and nature of financial instruments that resulted from technical advances in information processing and dissemination and from regulatory liberalisation. Unpredictable short-run variations in the demand for money, however, can be relatively large and troublesome for overly rigid monetary rules.

There is a special problem in adhering to monetary growth rules in developing countries, reflected in the use of government deficit limits as performance criteria in adjustment programmes financed by the IMF. In LDCs, which typically lack well-developed financial markets, governments are limited to borrowing from their central banks to finance their deficits. In this context monetary policy and fiscal policy merge. Monetary growth rates cannot be kept to non-inflationary rates unless the government's borrowing requirements are kept to low levels.

The short-run instability in the demand for money, combined with a growing disillusionment with floating exchange rates, has increased interest in a fixed exchange rate as the monetary anchor. The phenomenon of exchange rate overshooting, described above in Section 1.3, explains why real effective exchange rates have been more volatile than was originally expected. Fixed rates are probably more conducive to freer trade, more rapid growth and greater efficiency in worldwide resource allocation than are floating rates. The rub, of course, is that fixed exchange rates require subordinating domestic monetary and fiscal policy to external balance and most countries simply are unwilling or unable to do so. Under these conditions floating exchange rates are clearly preferable to fixed ones.

For countries prepared to play by the rules of a fixed exchange rate regime (sometimes called the gold standard rules), however, the fixed rate becomes the monetary anchor of the system. A country's money supply must be allowed to match whatever amount is demanded at the price level implied and imposed by the value of whatever the domestic currency has been fixed to. This makes any instability in the demand for money irrelevant. It is no longer necessary even to estimate it. Simply supplying or redeeming domestic money for foreign currency at rates implied by their values in terms of the one to which the domestic currency is fixed will ensure that the economy has whatever amount of money it wants at that rate.

Another reason for interest in fixed exchange rates as monetary anchor is the potential for a fixed rate monetary system to give quick credibility to anti-inflationary efforts. Renewed interest has arisen from the efforts of the centrally planned economies of Eastern Europe and the USSR to establish market-based economies and monetary systems that integrate their economies more closely with existing market economies and to establish the convertibility of their currencies needed to support that integration. Similar interest arises from countries attempting to re-establish macroeconomic and price stability after periods of high inflation.

Reducing monetary growth to rates consistent with stable prices causes very high real rates of interest and contraction of real output until the public is convinced that prices are and will remain stable. The ability to reduce inflationary expectations quickly depends on the credibility of a non-inflationary monetary (and fiscal) policy. It has been argued that a publicly announced monetary growth rule with a consistent fiscal policy would help establish credibility and reduce the expected rate of inflation more quickly than waiting for the development of a non-inflationary track record, which might take many years. Experience in this regard has been disappointing. The monetary rule embodied in a fixed exchange rate (or redeemability in terms of a commodity basket) with full convertibility supported by an adequate stock of reserves (or whatever the redemption asset might be) and a consistent fiscal policy, potentially could establish credibility more quickly. If the policies and the commitment to the policies are credible, the prices of tradable goods will be known to be stable from the very first instance because they can always be imported at a relatively stable price in terms of the local currency. The use of fixed exchange rates in this way has been an important feature of most stabilisation programmes in Eastern Europe.

The choice of the currency to which the domestic money is fixed determines the behaviour of the domestic price level measured in terms of the domestic currencies. Countries generally fix their currencies to others that have low inflation rates and thereby 'import' relative price stability. A system of fixed exchange rates relies on the good behaviour of the central bank that issues the currency the country's money is fixed to. The US dollar and the German mark have frequently been selected for this purpose because of the track record of the Federal Reserve and the Bundesbank in keeping inflation of their currencies low. That record, however, has been far from perfect and the question has been raised whether countries could not do better.

Recent proposals to achieve zero inflation rate by fixing the value of money to a basket of commodities rather than to another currency answer the above question in the affirmative (Coats, 1989). In its broadest outlines such a system would work like a traditional fixed exchange rate system or the gold standard. Domestic money must be supplied and redeemed on demand at its fixed value in terms of an independently defined unit of account (an amount of foreign currency, a quantity of gold, a basket of commodities, etc.). The system would differ from these earlier systems in two important respects. While having a gold standard's advantage of protecting the value of the unit of account (and hence of the medium of exchange via the redeemability requirement) from political influences, the proposed system would not impose the relative price changes of a single commodity such as gold or silver on the price level. By defining the system's unit of account as a basket of goods, the quantities of which could be adjusted periodically to preserve their purchasing power against the broadest possible price index, as suggested by Irving Fisher at the turn of the century (Fisher 1913), the unit of account would have an almost constant real value day-to-day as well as in the long-run. The other major difference with earlier monetary systems based on commodity standards is that money would not be redeemed directly for its unit of account. It would be redeemable indirectly for the commodity basket; i.e. it would be redeemable for something (a commodity or financial instrument) equal in current market value to the basket. Indirect redeemability eliminates the need to hold expensive and cumbersome inventories of all of the items in the valuation basket.

This 'new' technique of indirect redeemability has actually been in use for many years. Two examples should suffice. If Austria's shilling is fixed in price to the German mark (DM), it is still possible, and in fact common, to exchange (redeem) shilling for US dollars (or some other currency). The amount of dollars received per shilling will have the same market value as the fixed amount of DM to which shilling holders are entitled, i.e. the amount of dollars received will just enable the redeemer of shilling to buy in the market the amount of DM implied by the fixed shilling price of DM. As indicated, this example of indirect redeemability has been practised for centuries. A more recent example is provided by the SDR and the ECU, the assets of the IMF and the EC valued on the basis of currency baskets. While exchanges (redemptions) of SDRs or ECUs may be, and sometimes are, made for the appropriate amounts of all of the currencies in their valuation baskets, they are more often exchanged for an amount of a single currency that will just buy in the market the appropriate number of units of the entire basket.

An important challenge for any monetary system is to strengthen the incentives for, or constraints on, the system to adhere to the rules of the system adopted (Coats, 1989). Failure to do so in the past has led to painful devaluations and the abandonment of fixed exchange rates (even, eventually, to the abandonment of the gold standard). No system is inured to this risk, but systems based on an independently defined unit of account, because they are more transparent and less subject to manipulation, are likely to be more resistant to violations of their rules than others.

PHASING OF FINANCIAL LIBERALISATION

The truly newest topic since the original review was written concerns how to get from a repressed to a basically free-market economy with the least damage and with political support intact. The totally unforeseen and considerably more difficult task of creating market economies out of centrally controlled ones is an extreme version of this topic. This is a vast and complex topic about which there is much yet to learn. In this update of the original review of monetary policy in developing countries, the reasons for and objectives of financial sector reform and the lessons for designing successful reforms gleaned from the experiences of countries that have attempted them are revisited.

It has been common for developing countries, especially those that rely heavily on central economic planning, to tap their financial systems' resources and to direct them in accordance with their development plans. Controlled interest rates and government-directed credit allocation are among the commonly used tools of central planners. Such policies have stunted the development of financial systems and invariably reduced the efficiency with which saving has been invested (to mention but one of the functions of financial institutions). The growing recognition that economic development requires greater scope for market allocation has its counterpart in the financial sector as well.

The superiority of market allocation of saving, which is the heart and soul of the financial system, and the basis for the financial sector's importance for economic development, is now well established. Many countries now recognise that their intervention in credit allocation has had an unfavourable impact on both financial and industrial development. The evidence from country experience also suggests that directed credit programmes have not been efficient tools for income redistribution or for overcoming imperfections in the real goods markets.

These lessons have prompted an increasing number of countries to liberalise their financial systems. Their experiences vary. Liberalisation of financial systems in some countries led to financial collapse and the return to controls. In some others it succeeded, though in varying degrees, in improving the quality and lowering the cost of financial services and in raising growth rates. Some preliminary lessons can be gleaned from recent experiences.

Financial reforms generally include, inter alia, the freeing of interest rates; elimination of directed credit allocations; removal of barriers to entry into the market of new, or departure of existing, financial institutions; elimination of restrictions on the activities into which any given institution may enter; removal of discriminatory taxes on financial transactions; improvement of information available to borrowers and lenders in the making of their financial decisions; and assurance of a supportive legal, regulatory and administrative structure, including the improvement of prudential regulation and supervision of financial institutions, an adequate bankruptcy law, and effective and efficient enforcement of debt contracts.

The cost of moving too slowly or not going far enough in implementing the above policies is continuation and further entrenchment of weak and/or inefficient financial institutions, continued misuse of resources, and slower growth and lower living standards than necessary. The cost of moving too quickly could be politically unsustainable levels of unemployment and loss of income, resulting in the failure to achieve lasting reform and regression to more controls. In short, the manner and pace of reform seem critical for its ultimate success. The lessons of experience with financial liberalisation are tentative, some lessons being clearer than others.[10]

---

10.   The following draws heavily on Khatkhate and Cho (1989) and Coats (1990).

Macroeconomic Environment

The first and strongest lesson is that financial liberalisation is very difficult, and unlikely to succeed, without a considerable degree of macroeconomic stability. The rocky liberalisations in Argentina, Brazil, Colombia, Mexico, and Uruguay and the temporarily derailed liberalisation in Chile in the mid-1970s through the early 1980s were undertaken in the midst of serious inflation (generally 100 per cent per annum or more), reflecting their governments' need to finance expenditures by borrowing from their central banks. Large government deficits, and rapid inflation invariably were accompanied by resource wasting, over-valued exchange rates.

Inflation has a number of pernicious effects. The informational content of prices is reduced so that the economy becomes less efficient. Investments, in fact long-term commitments of all types, become more risky and are therefore reduced. Additional resources are absorbed by efforts to overcome or adjust to the distorting effects of inflation. The real returns on financial assets are reduced and the profitability of financial institutions weakened. Both of these effects reduce the financialisation of saving, which further reduces economic efficiency and growth.

Financial reform itself involves changes in relative prices that need to be assessed and absorbed by economic agents. When they take place in an environment of general price instability it is much more difficult to determine appropriate interest rates and to interpret those that result. Experience suggests that without macroeconomic stability it is very difficult to achieve the level of interest rates that are well aligned with the real sector's productivity, whether interest rates are market determined or regulated. Successful financial liberalisation either began in an environment of relative macroeconomic stability or addressed macro instability first. In addition, the continued health and viability of a liberalised financial sector requires the continued maintenance of a reasonable degree of macroeconomic stability.

A related lesson, seen repeatedly all over Latin America, is that once monetary virtue is lost, it cannot be regained easily or without significant cost. The opiate of inflation, so seductive and pleasant in the beginning, loses its kick over time, requiring larger and larger doses just to continue its pleasurable stimulation. An addicted economy cannot function efficiently, but it cannot withdraw from its addiction without considerable pain. The failure to restrain government expenditures within the limits that can be financed without inflationary monetary growth, therefore, begins a very dangerous process. By reducing the attractiveness of financial assets, inflation reduces the tax base, particularly the base relevant for the inflation tax, and hence, reduces government revenue, which, in the absence of improved fiscal discipline, further increases the need to borrow from the central bank. This increases inflation further and further until fiscal discipline is rediscovered (or there is monetary collapse) at which point a terrible price is paid to re-establish price stability.

A government's rediscovered commitment to price stability is not quickly believed, hence inflationary expectations are slow to adjust—once lost, government's credibility is hard to re-establish. As a result, real interest rates rise to high levels, and aggregate demand falls more rapidly than prices, temporarily increasing unemployment. Investment and growth are therefore slow to recover after a period of inflation.

Insolvent Institutions

The second lesson is that liberalising insolvent financial institutions will not generally make them healthy again. Many financial institutions in developing countries are insolvent. Financial liberalisation generally reduces the earnings of financial institutions during the adjustment period. Until a restructured, healthier system establishes itself, financial liberalisation causes considerable strain for many banks and other financial institutions. To withstand these strains they need to be viable to begin with.

Insolvent institutions generally do not allocate resources in an efficient manner as the objective of their lending is to minimise or cover over their own portfolio losses in the hope that they can recoup them in the future. Experience shows that insolvent institutions generally continue to make losses and therefore continue to waste valuable resources. They should be closed or restructured at the very beginning of any reform and steps taken to reduce the prospects that the practices that lead to insolvency will re-emerge in the future. These steps include the elimination of excessive priority lending, unrealistic interest rate ceilings on loans, and excessive directed credit, and the establishment of adequate prudential regulation. Because insolvent financial institutions are often the victims of the arrears of insolvent borrowers, closing or restructuring the offending firms (often state owned enterprises) will also be necessary.

Real Sector Environment

This leads to the third lesson, which is that increased market allocation of credit will not generally improve the allocation of resources in countries with a distorted price structure. In fact, market allocation of credit under these circumstances may increase misallocation by allowing finance to respond to incorrect price signals. For example, the overvalued exchange rate in Chile in the early 1980s continued to favour the non-tradable sector, leading among other things to excessive real estate development. By postponing the adjustment of relative prices between tradable and non-tradable goods the ultimate adjustment was made larger and more disruptive. In the subsequent crisis, real estate was one of the sectors hit the hardest. This, in turn, contributed to widespread defaults on bank loans and the collapse of the banking system. Trade and other 'real' sector liberalisation should proceed or at least coincide with financial sector liberalisation.

Liberalisation of the real sector, however, creates additional stresses in the financial sector. Structural adjustment is meant to cause a reallocation of resources from the protected but less productive firms and activities to more productive uses and this often bankrupts or impairs the viability of these firms. Stress in the real sector can hardly avoid reflecting itself in the financial sector from which it has borrowed. Those countries that liberalised their financial systems during periods of rapid relative price changes, such as generally occur during stabilisation and structural adjustments, experienced actual (*ex post*) real interest rates often considerably in excess of the return to investment. Such excessively high real rates are symptomatic of distress borrowing.

Full liberalisation of bank interest rates and lending policies encounters two problems in this environment. One is that the bank management skills necessary to assess credit risks and properly control bank exposure in the new liberal environment generally take time to develop. This exposes banks to unfamiliar and difficult-to-assess risks if their activities are not limited. The other is that those banks that do encounter difficulties may be tempted to continue lending to bankrupt or overly risky customers in order to maintain the appearance that outstanding loans to distressed firms are still viable. For a bank that has already lost its capital, gambling on risky long shots (betting the bank) is the only hope left. In the environment of significant corporate distress encountered in Argentina, Chile, the Philippines, Turkey and Uruguay, real interest rates were raised to unsustainable levels, which distressed firms willingly paid in order to avoid admitting insolvency in the hope that things would improve in the future.

Thus, major structural reforms should be completed prior to complete financial liberalisation. Inefficient public enterprises and highly protected domestic firms that would not be viable without public subsidy and trade protection should be restructured before financial liberalisation. In these early phases of reform, interest rates should be set at modestly positive real rates (reflecting the rate of return on capital), but should not be left fully to the market.

Prudential Regulation

A fourth lesson is that when financial institutions are free to set interest rates and enter new lines of business, it becomes more important for investors, be they stockholders or depositors, to have accurate information on the condition and activities of these institutions. It may also be necessary to impose some prudential limits on their lending. In their effort to free the financial system of repressive economic regulation (and taxation), some governments failed to provide adequate prudential regulation (e.g. market value accounting, reporting, and capital standards; and lending and portfolio concentration limits) and were unprepared or unequipped to properly monitor bank behaviour on behalf of depositors. Liberalisation of the banking system in the absence of effective prudential regulation and supervision allowed banks to engage in imprudent lending and fraud, and facilitated widespread financial distress in the Southern Cone. Privatisation of banks in the Southern Cone without establishing adequate prudential regulatory framework also led to heavy concentration of bank loans to their affiliated firms when they became part of industrial groups after privatisation.

Pace of Reforms

A final lesson concerns the pace of reform. Although there are exceptions (e.g. New Zealand), most successful liberalisations were implemented gradually. Since financial reforms change the rules of the game, rapid implementation may impose losses on otherwise viable firms that entered into contracts and arrangements under the old rules with the expectation of their continuance. As already noted, a gradual liberalisation also allows time for financial institutions to develop the skills needed and to adapt to the new competitive environment. Undue delay, on the other hand, incurs the cost of perpetuating the inefficiencies of the repressed system. And the longer the period of government control, the more serious the shortcomings become. The lesson is that the authorities must anticipate how reforms and the consequent changes in relative prices will affect different groups. Both from the standpoint of equity and making change politically acceptable, it may be necessary to provide some form of transitional compensation to those most adversely affected while maintaining the incentive effects of the reforms. The appropriate balance among these considerations will depend on the initial degree of repression and other aspects of the economic environment already discussed.

The issue of the appropriate pace of reform has arisen again in the context of the conversion of centralised or command economics to market economies. The reforms under way in Eastern Europe and potentially in the Soviet Union have no historical counterparts from which to learn. It is clear that the expertise and infrastructure of capitalism will take many years to develop. However, the macroeconomic, legal and regulatory environment in which private enterprises are established and developed, could and probably should be reformed as quickly as possible.

Transitional Controls

As discussed above, complete liberalisation may not lead to equilibrium interest rates in countries with serious macroeconomic instability or in countries without adequate competition in financial markets. In countries in which these conditions have not been established, the government may need to manage interest rates to avoid serious misalignment and greater distortion in resource allocation. In those cases, the government should adjust the level of interest rates to reflect changes in inflation, cost of funds, and exchange rate movements. Countries with open economies need to pay close attention to the level of domestic rates as compared to international rates adjusted for expected exchange rate changes. Preferential interest rates should be phased out and the structure of interest rates should be set to allow different margins for loans of different maturity, risk, and administrative costs.

When substantial progress has been made in reforming industry and the financial system and when the economy is stable, the government can move toward more complete liberalisation of interest rates. Some countries have first set ranges on deposit and lending rates, allowing banks to set specific rates within the ranges. The ranges were widened and ultimately removed as liberalisation progressed. Unfortunately, very few countries have succeeded in controlling interest rates in the manner prescribed above. Successful examples are Korea, Japan, and Taiwan.

CONCLUSION

Over the period since the original review was written, a consensus has developed that money plays a very important role in facilitating economic development and efficiency. It is now clear that the importance of a well developed, healthy, competition and market-based financial system is even greater than suggested in the original review. Healthy and efficient financial institutions capable of allocating saving to the most productive investments and of prudently managing the risks involved cannot be built overnight and require a liberal but supportive environment. A supportive environment includes stable prices, accounting systems and standards that depict the true conditions of firms, legal systems that clearly establish and enforce lender's rights (e.g. for collateral and foreclosure), and 'regulatory' or supervisory agencies that focus on the soundness and honesty of financial firms rather than on where they allocate saving. An increasingly integrated world economy has made it more costly and difficult to shelter the allocation of resources from market forces. It is clearer than ever that all economies benefit from market-related interest rates, exchange rates and resource allocation. Establishing and maintaining a healthy, stable monetary system is not and will not be easy but it is important for the pace of development.

REFERENCES

Bhagwati, Jagdish (1982). "Directly unproductive profit-seeking activities", *Journal of Political Economy* XXX(5): 988–1002, October.

Coats, Warren (1990). "Experiences with financial liberalisation: The lessons for India", *Economic and Political Weekly* XXIX(1): 31–47, 5–12 May.

————. (1989). "In search of a monetary anchor: a new monetary standard", *Working Paper* XX(2): 223–39. International Monetary Fund. September.

————. (1982a). "Interest rate consequences of targeting money", *Staff Papers*, International Monetary Fund, 29(1), March.

————. (1982b). "Modeling the short-run demand for money with exogenous supply", *Economic Inquiry* X(2), April.

Dornbusch, R. (1976). "Expectations and exchange rate dynamics", *Journal of Political Economy* 84(6): 1151–76, December.

Edwards, S. (1984). "The order of liberalisation of the external sector in developing countries", *Essays in International Finance 156*. Princeton, N.J.: International Finance Section, Department of Economics, Princeton University.

Fisher, Irving (1913). *The Purchasing Power of Money.* New York: Macmillan, 2nd edn.

Friedman, M. (1968). "The role of monetary policy", *American Economic Review* 58(1): 1–17, March.

Haque, Nadeem U. and Peter Montiel (1990). "Capital mobility in developing countries: some empirical tests", *Working Paper*, International Monetary Fund, December.

Hayek, F.A. (1988). *The Fatal Conceit.* Chicago, Ill.: University of Chicago Press.

————. (1945). *The Use of Knowledge in Society*, Reprinted in *Individualism and Economic Order.* London: Routledge and Kegan Paul. 1948.

Khatkhate, Deena and Yon Je Cho (1989). "Lessons from financial liberalisation in Asia: A comparative study", *Discussion Papers*, No. 50. April. The World Bank.

Kydland, Finn and Edward Prescott (1977). "Rules rather than discretion: The inconsistency of optional plans", *Journal of Political Economy* 85(3).

Laidler, David (1990). *Taking Money Seriously and Other Essays.* Cambridge, Mass.: The MIT Press.

Phelps, E. (1967). "Phillips curves, expectations of inflation and optimal unemployment over time", *Economica* NS 34, August.

————. (1970). *Microeconomic Foundations of Employment and Inflation Theory.* New York: Norton.

Tullock, Gordon (1967). "The welfare cost of tariffs, monopolies and theft", *Western Economic Journal* 5(3): 224–32.

World Bank (1989). *World Development Report.* Oxford University Press.

Published in the Economic and Political Weekly XXVI(25): 1538-44 (1991).

2 | Money Illusion, Many Allusions

For a long time, money, both as a target and as an instrument variable in scientific discussion on economic growth, remained in limbo. Admittedly, in the early post-war years, there was a flood of literature on economic development in which loose and often obfuscating references were made to monetary policy, both along the lines of early versions of the quantity theory of money and the so-called Keynesian formats of monetary analysis. In the domain of practical policy, money was even taken as a surrogate for real capital. However, all this was devoid of any theoretical underpinning and the result was an unabashed pursuit of inflationary financing of developmental outlay. Development economics was not the only branch of economics guilty of this omission; beginning with the Harrod-Domar formulation, growth economics consistently ignored the role of money in the growth process on the dubious assumption that it was the real factors which dominated dynamic change and that money was no more than a veil or an illusion. For money and finance to be recognised as the crucial variable, it took many years until Patinkin, Levihari, Tobin, Johnson and the most influential of all, Gurley and Shaw, came on the scene with a variety of growth models which provided explicitly for the role of money. With all this rather dramatic transformation in the views about money, its influence remained confined to the pure growth theory and its ingredients, such as the saving and investment functions and technical change. It is only recently, again thanks to the extension of the basic Gurley-Shaw syndrome, that money, with all its attributes, has been brought directly into development economics.

Ronald McKinnon treats the subject[1] in all its ramifications; he enlarges not only upon what money should do in the development process but also upon its wide-ranging implications in trade, exchange rate, taxation and other economic policies. Then he proceeds to seek empirical validation of this hypothesis in the experience of Brazil, Korea, Taiwan, Mexico, etc. However, the main core of his theory is contained in Chapters 6 and 9 of the book. Assessment of McKinnon's contribution, both theoretical and operational,

---

1. McKinnon, Ronald I. (1973). Money and Capital in Economic Development. Washington DC: The Brookings Institution.

depends principally upon two things: first, whether his theoretical schema is internally consistent and sufficiently general; and secondly, whether the policy prescriptions it yields are novel enough to make a substantial difference to economic strategy in the less developed countries.

ASSUMPTIONS

McKinnon has basically three assumptions. First, that there is complete self-financing of economic activity in the producing units. This implies a total absence of any distinction between those who save and those who invest; both come to one and the same thing. This assumption also suggests that economic units neither borrow from each other nor lend to each other. Second, the average size of the saving-investment units is small so that what can be set aside as an investment fund from their own income at any point in time can meet only a fraction of the desired investment expenditure which, by its very nature, is lumpy. The third assumption, used more as a pedagogic device than as a reflection of reality, is that government does not participate directly in the process of capital accumulation either through the tax-expenditure process or by using seignorage from money issue. This assumption means that government revenues are used purely for current consumption purposes.

From these three basic assumptions the following conclusions emerge. Since complete self-financing is prevalent in all households, each would be inclined to hold a part of its income in one asset or another, which would normally be different from its own output. The exception to this rule is when the output of the household itself is used as a capital asset, as in a subsistence economy. Which one of the assets would be held by households would depend upon the relative rate of return on the available assets. Following the portfolio behaviour analysis, a household would hold that asset which would give the highest rate of return. The question then is whether the capital asset held is the real good, which may be real capital accumulation itself or a financial asset. This issue is, however, resolved in the McKinnon schema by the second assumption of the lumpiness of expenditure. A household accumulates financial assets gradually, but until the amount of financial assets reaches a level where it can finance all investment expenditure, capital accumulation would not take place. Another consideration is that the average lag between income and investment is longer than that between income and consumption. In other words, it is inevitable that real capital accumulation and money balance accumulation have to continue simultaneously. This complementary relationship lasts over the long haul and only after the development process reaches a certain advanced stage does the complementarity tend to get blurred. From then on, the accumulation of money balances and capital accumulation become competitive. McKinnon makes rather too much of this complementarity relationship, and goes even further to juxtapose it to the relationship postulated in the literature of neoclassical monetary theory. From this, the policy that McKinnon explicitly suggests is that real interest should be raised so that real monetary balances would tend to expand and this is healthy from the point of view of both resource allocation and growth.

Some explanation is necessary as regards money balances as well as the rate of return on them. The concept of money balances implies real money balances, that is to say, nominal money deflated by the price level (M/P) and the rate of return is given by the nominal money interest rate minus the rate of change in the price level (d − Px). So long as the real rate, i.e. d − Px is positive, the income units will tend to hold larger and larger money balances and this is conducive to the capital accumulation process. One question may arise: what is denoted by the rate of return on cash, and demand deposits on which no interest is paid in most countries? The holding of money has certain inherent advantages such as convenience, liquidity, etc., the imputed value of which would give the rate of return on these kinds of money balances. However, the rate of return so calculated would vary with the change in the price level. If prices were to change, the rate of return would turn negative, and *vice versa* if prices were to fall. It is natural to conclude from this that a depressionary situation is helpful in raising the rate of return on money balances, although McKinnon does not favour this over raising the nominal rate of interest, leaving the price level stable.

Let us examine a little more closely the main core of the McKinnon theory that accumulation of real money balances and real capital are complementary up to a certain stage and his strictures on the neoclassical monetary theory. The complementary relationship between real money balances and capital accumulation stems from the peculiarity of McKinnon's assumptions one and two, i.e. that there is complete self-financing of investment activity and that investment is lumpy. The saving of those who undertake investment is inadequate at any given time to finance that investment and this impels them to accumulate saving in money form to a level sufficient to finance the lumpy investment. In this situation, the higher the real rate of return on money balances, the greater is the accumulation of real money balances and, therefore, the larger is the real capital formation. This is, therefore, a case of implicit theorising par excellence. By the same logic, the 'competing asset effect', i.e. the substitutability between the real money balances and capital accumulation materialises when limits of self-financing are reached or when the amount of financing necessary to undertake investment equals the volume of investments.

Mere Illusion

However, the distinction between complementary and competing relationships is a mere illusion created by McKinnon's failure to segregate the class of savers from the class of entrepreneurs. It is now well accepted in monetary economics that savers are not necessarily those who undertake investment. In fact, the very distinction between them is lauded as the *raison d'être* of efficient resource allocation and consequent acceleration in economic growth. In the presence of such a distinction, the relationship between the real money balances and capital accumulation has to be necessarily one of complementarity. Savers are faced with a spectrum of assets to hold their savings in. They may choose real goods—durable, consumer, or capital goods—but if they are not entrepreneurs they will be left with surplus savings over and above their own self-financed investments, which find their way into some financial asset or other. In a relatively less sophisticated underdeveloped economy, such financial assets are more often than not money balances. Now the money balances are no more and not less a conduit for transferring real resources to those sectors where real capital formation takes place. In point of fact, it constitutes an indispensable condition for capital formation. Hence, both these processes— real money balance accumulation and capital formation—remain essentially complementary to each other.

It is in this context that McKinnon's strictures on the neoclassical monetary theory, which postulates substitutability between money balances and capital accumulation, have to be analysed. Superficially he is right in his attack, but if it is recognised that in the neoclassical framework of two assets, i.e. money and physical capital, there is no independent investment function, then much of his criticism should be deemed to be misdirected.[2] It has been

---

2. The neoclassical system is represented as follows:

$$S = I + \Delta M \rightarrow sY = I + \Delta f (r, Y)$$
$$S = sY \rightarrow sY = \Delta k + \Delta f (r,Y)$$
$$M = f(r, Y)$$
$$= \Delta k$$

contd...

demonstrated that if the investment function is envisaged as distinct from the saving function, competitive relationships just disappear.[3]

Apart from this theoretical chink in McKinnon's formulations, one may question its relevance to the real world of the less developed countries—countries which can be taken as representative of McKinnon's model or completely self-financed investment activity. In fact, there is no country which conforms to this model—not even the most undeveloped country in Africa which, of course, is not McKinnon's concern. As he categorically states on page 2, his analysis

> focuses on semi-industrial LDCs—those that have made more or less autonomous efforts to industrialise or to develop some commercial and agricultural activities, perhaps with the help of capital flows from abroad or foreign technical assistance. Brazil, Chile, Pakistan and Turkey will be covered more directly than will the pristine economies of Africa.

Surely these can hardly be the countries where completely self-financed investment is the prevailing rule.

The pity of it all is that while McKinnon's policy conclusions have a great deal of relevance in explaining the development problem in almost all the less developed countries, the analytical tools he has forged seem largely inappropriate to support them. In fact, the same conclusions can be validated by reference to the more generalised theory of Gurley and Shaw. As observed earlier, saving and investment activity are rarely concentrated in one category of households; those who save differ from those who invest and this dichotomy is often instrumental in bringing about a better allocation of savings. If this is conceded, then it follows that the accumulation of financial assets—whether they are money, bonds, or equity is an immaterial issue—provides a conduit for the transfer of excess savings of those whose own investment falls short of their savings to those whose investment exceeds their own savings. Note that in this framework there is no need for any economic units to be self-sufficient in financing. There is lending by one sector to another, even when it is a deficit-spending unit. Thus, both the capital accumulation and real

---

contd...

where

M denotes money demand; k, capital; S, saving; I, real investment; Y, income, and r, interest rate.

It is clear that once demand for M is determined and that aggregate saving as a proportion of income is given, investment is automatically determined. In other words, non-financial saving is identical with real investment.

3. For proof, see Villanueva Delano P. (1971). "A neoclassical monetary growth model with independent savings and investment functions", Journal of Money Credit and Banking, November.

money balances accumulation can coexist, as in the McKinnon schema. This is precisely the approach I have adopted elsewhere with exactly the same policy prescriptions.[4]

POLICY PRESCRIPTIONS

The other interesting question that comes to mind, while mulling over the policy implications of McKinnon's theory, is whether the policies he suggests are a logical follow-up to this theory. Here again the answer is in the negative. His policy prescriptions are mainly two—a high interest rate policy and steady growth in the quantum of real money balances (M/P). The former is sought to be justified not so much as a prop for raising the saving rate as for accelerating the financialisation of savings. The higher the rate of return on money balances, represented either by liquidity advantages or the interest rate, the greater is the incentive to transfer goods into money balances and hence the larger is the volume of investment. The process continues until the scattered financial markets are fully integrated into a homogeneous entity. There are, of course, indirect effects on the saving rate which are favourable, but they need to be attributed not to the high interest rate policy *per se*, but to the financial development which introduces a superior kind of allocative mechanism. The interest rate effects on saving have been increasingly questioned for a variety of reasons. For one thing, where the empirical investigations have a solid statistical base, it has been found that income is the main explanatory variable. In many less developed countries where positive correlation between saving and interest rates has been found, it is spurious either because the wrong proxy has been chosen for interest rate or because the saving function has been misspecified.

The second policy prescription ensuring a steady expansion of real money balances is consistent with the neo-quantity theories of the Chicago School. What passes off as a non-inflationary level of deficit financing—familiar to economists in India for well over a decade—is only an alias for the real money balances. In computation of the amount of deficit financing, either the price level is assumed to be constant or, if it is assumed to vary, a corresponding adjustment is made in the estimate of deficit financing, derived from given changes in real income and income velocity of money. This is only an alternative way of relating the desired real volume of money to the national income. It is clear, therefore, that for neither policy alternative is McKinnon's

---

4. Khatkhate, Deena (1972). "Analytic basis of the working of monetary policy in less developed countries", IMF Staff Papers. XIX(3): 533–57, November.

theoretical formulation essential and they can be derived, equally plausibly, from other sets of analytical apparatus.

Coming down from the theoretical propositions to the empiricism of McKinnon, one faces even more serious problems. Allusions to the countries where policies emerging from his model have been successfully applied are plentiful, but the conceptual issues involved in statistical mapping are of questionable validity and the statistical techniques used are of 'juxtapositioning' type. The first question is how to measure the real rate of return on financial assets. A generally accepted procedure is to rely on the difference between the nominal interest rate paid and the rate of inflation. However, on many grounds this does not seem to be a legitimate procedure. First of all, in what way can one confidently isolate the effect of the real rate of return on assets from that of the expected rate of inflation? The manner in which the real rate of return is calculated incorporates the effects of actual inflation. But the expected rate of inflation series is generated from the actual rates of inflation so that these two influences on financialisation of savings are intermingled. In that case, it is not possible to say with any degree of confidence whether the changes in the real money balances are due to the real rate of return or the expected rate of inflation. From the analytical point of view this distinction between the two variables is of great importance.

McKinnon uses the wholesale price index (WPI) for adjusting the nominal interest rate to arrive at a real rate of return. This is because it is an index which measures basically the changes in prices of commodities which compete with money. On the other hand, in the consumer price index (CPI) the service component has a larger weightage. This may perhaps hold true in respect of the developed countries where services form a larger proportion of GNP, but in the LDCs it need not matter whether one uses a WPI or CPI. Leaving aside this relatively minor point, the tables he has constructed on Taiwan and Korea do not unequivocally support his thesis that a higher real rate of return calculated on the basis of changes in WPI ensures real financial growth. In Taiwan, for instance, there are certain years, such as 1959, 1960, 1962, etc., when the fall in real return on bank deposits did not lead to a decline in the ratio of M_2 (broader definition of money) to GNP. A more careful look at these tables also bears out that changes in the M_2/GNP ratio are not significantly correlated (with a negative sign) with the changes in the WPI, which would have been proven if McKinnon had used regression techniques. In fairness, however, it has to be pointed out that McKinnon does not refer to Taiwan so much as one of the success stories as an empirical basis for his thesis. There is little difference between Taiwan on the one hand and Korea on the other insofar as the nature of financial policies is concerned. And yet if their experiences are divergent, something more than a simple-minded application of McKinnon's theories is necessary to explain it.

Finally, the question of what should constitute the money balances is left unresolved. McKinnon, in most of his case studies, defines money balances as broad money which includes saving and time deposits, though he makes an exception while dealing with Germany by including deposit certificates issued by the banks. But the real difficulty faced by empirical investigators is not whether to include this or that asset in the variable of money balances, but where to draw the line in regard to the choice of financial assets which embrace a wide spectrum of assets. In many LDCs even government bonds qualify as near money. If this is so, then the empirical analysis should go far beyond what McKinnon has attempted to derive support for his model. It is for these reasons that development economists as well as policymakers should focus their attention not so much on this theory or that, as on a more thorough and comprehensive enquiry into the monetary sector developments in the LDCs before being sold on any one of the new fangled theories being incessantly churned out of the academic mills.

Published in the Economic and Political Weekly XXIII(28): 1427–32 (1988).

3 | Inflation Targeting
Much Ado about Something

Inflation targeting as a framework for operating monetary policy has acquired almost a cult status ever since the Reserve Bank of New Zealand formulated it for the first time in the early 1990s. About 34 countries—21 industrialised and 13 emerging countries—have now become inflation targeters, with varying degrees of success in exercising their monetary policy directed at relative price stability without adversely affecting output and employment. There has been a considerable amount of empirical work on countries pursuing this framework to assess the impact of inflation targeting on their economies and the general verdict is by and large positive, though the impact varies according to the stage of development whether they are industrialised or emerging because certain preconditions essential for inflation targeting policy success may not be necessarily present.

The whole debate on inflation targeting has revolved around the possible shape of the so-called Phillips curve. Reactive inflation targeting owes its origin to the evaporation of the relationship between inflation and unemployment—the famous Phillips curve which explained, on the basis of UK unemployment and price data in the 1960s, that a percentage reduction in unemployment would lead to a certain rise of some magnitude in the inflation rate. Derived from this trade-off was an activist monetary policy—a policy well suited to political authorities and subservient central banks.

However, the relationship between inflation and unemployment broke down during the 1970s. Its place was taken by the concept of non-accelerating inflation rate of unemployment (NAIRU), introduced by Milton Friedman and Edmond Phelps, which ruled out reliance on the inflation–unemployment trade-off. Any expansionary monetary policy would trigger a pressure from the workers for raising their wages, and hence inflation, without any impact on the level of unemployment.

It was in the context of such a *desideratum* that the inflation targeting framework evolved. The rationale is that if a central bank sets an inflation target which is any point numerical value or a range of values, depending upon the monetary history of the country in question and its political economy, and then adjusts its monetary policy, principally the short-term interest rate, to keep prices near the target, the economic agents would conduct their profit-maximising productive activities without being distracted by relative price distortions. It is a sort of commitment and communicative device constructed with prior agreement with the government, thereby demarcating the fiscal and monetary policy domains. If the forecast inflation rate based on an implicit or explicit model of the central bank exceeds the targeted inflation rate, the central bank steps up the short-term interest rate, so that the forecast rate remains in a targeted zone and vice versa.

However, recent developments arising mainly from growing globalisation seem to have revived the inflation trade-off, indicating that the non-accelerating rate of unemployment is moving downward without any pressure on prices, thereby reviving a semblance of the Phillips curve. The only difference is that the newly invented Phillips curve is more flat than downward sloping (*The Economist,* 2006). However, the revival of the Phillips curve has not overshadowed the relevance of the inflation targeting framework. A headline inflation, which includes volatile commodity prices, is rising as a result of rapid globalisation, which suggests a need for a hike in interest rates. There is, however, one major difference. After the revival of a flattened Phillips curve, the measure of inflation rate target followed by most of the inflation targeters seems to have changed from core to headline inflation rate, as will be discussed later in this article.

In discussions on inflation targeting, its one important dimension is passed over. If stable prices are indispensable for raising growth and employment, what would be the consequences of an onset of deflation? The logic of inflation targeting might imply an expansionary monetary policy to reverse the deflationary forces but the Japanese experience in the 1990s belied this logic. There is a certain asymmetry—restrictive monetary policy can help to control inflation but expansionary monetary policy would not, in a situation of a liquidity trap.

There is a misconception about inflation targeting which needs to be clarified before proceeding to assess its empirical validation, or the inter-country comparisons of experiences in regard to the implementation of inflation targeting policy. It is argued that inflation targeting focuses on a narrow target of inflation to the exclusion of employment, growth, poverty alleviation and income distribution, which are dominant objectives in emerging or developing countries (Jalan, 2000; Jha, 2006). A little digression is warranted to show why stabilising inflation also helps employment and output growth. The modern theory of monetary policy is based on the premise that monopolistically competitive firms set their product prices at a mark-up over marginal production cost so that their profits are maximised over time. This implies that a monetary policy directed at low inflation ensures that the production costs rise at the targeted rate of inflation. As Goodfriend and Eshwar Prasad (2006) have put it well:

> The reasoning is as follows: First, an economy with a stable inflation rate must be one in which firms maintain their profit maximizing mark-ups on average, otherwise actual inflation would deviate from targeted inflation as firms attempt to restore their profit-maximizing mark-ups. Second, an economy in which monetary policy sustains the profit-maximizing mark-up would operate as if firms sustained the profit-maximizing mark-ups themselves, by adjusting product prices flexibly, and continuously. Third, targeting inflation thus makes actual output conform to potential output, i.e. the level of aggregate output determined by supply factors in an environment of perfectly flexible prices. Fourth, this reasoning implies that monetary policy geared to targeting inflation yields the best cyclical stabilization of employment.

This holds true when prices of production of the monopolistically competitive firms are relatively stable. However, there are some products like oil, food, etc. which are more flexible, being open to supply and demand shocks and this impacts heavily on the overall inflation. This suggests that the nominal anchor for monetary policy should be a core and not the headline inflation rate (Goodfriend and Prasad, 2006). On the basis of this rationale of monetary policy, inflation targeting stabilises not only the price level but also employment and output, thereby obviating a need for setting multiple targets for operating monetary policy.

There is a strong belief held that certain preconditions have to prevail in economies if they have to take recourse to inflation targeting framework. These are: institutional independence of the central bank, well-developed technical infrastructure, i.e. a capacity to devise a forecasting model, fully deregulated prices and exchange regime and a healthy financial system (Eichengreen et al., 1999). However, this is not supported by the survey results of the IMF for 21 inflation targeting and 10 non-inflation targeting countries. "No inflation targeter had all these preconditions in place prior to the adoption of inflation targeting although unsurprisingly, the industrial country inflation targeters were generally in better shape than the emerging country inflation targeters at least in some dimensions" (IMF, 2005: 176–7). Only one-fifth of the emerging market targeters had central bank independence; they also faced a wide variety of fiscal imbalances; they had a higher level of public debt; most of them had little or no forecasting capability and no forecasting models at all; they were all sensitive to the exchange rate and commodity prices volatility; most of them had weak financial systems at the time of adoption of inflation targeting, low risk-weighted capital adequacy ratio, low capital market capitalisation, small size of the bond market and banks foreign currency open position (IMF, 2005). Thus, the absence of the preconditions by itself did not appear to militate against their adopting inflation targeting. What is surprising is that once these countries adopted inflation targeting, there was also improvement in their institutional structure, data availability and forecasting capability. This raises a very interesting question: whether acceptance of inflation targeting framework itself was not instrumental in paving the way for a developed financial system and more autonomy for the central banks.

There is likewise considerable debate about how inflation targeting impacts on the outcome—inflation, output, employment and their variability. Until recently the most-cited empirical studies on this issue showed that for the industrial country targeters, inflation targeting on the whole has been beneficial in regard to inflation reduction and output expansion but the statistical significance is limited (Ball and Sheridan, 2003; Levin *et al.* 2004; Truman, 2003; Hyvonen, 2004). But no firm conclusions can be drawn because the number of comparators against which their performance was evaluated was limited, their inflation performance had improved not necessarily due to the monetary policy in the 1990s, and most importantly, many of the countries in the group had already contained inflationary pressures as a preparation to joining the European Economic and Monetary Union.

In order to get more reliable empirical results about the impact of inflation targeting, the IMF analysed the data for 13 emerging market inflation targeters, and compared them against the remaining 22 emerging market countries drawn from the J.P. Morgan EMBI Index plus seven additional countries (IMF, 2005). The conclusions are the following: (i) Though the inflation rate declined both in the inflation-targeting and non-targeting countries, the fall in the former was much sharper; (ii) transition of high and variable inflation that prevailed before adopting inflation targeting to low and stable prices was rapid and well sustained and this performance was superior to that of the non-inflation targeters; and (iii) there is no evidence that inflation targeters met their inflation objectives at the expense of real output.

Of course, all these results are subject to a caveat that it is very difficult to establish a firm causal relationship between inflation targeting and its final outcome in the absence of the counterfactual. But this shortcoming is universal in all statistical exercises and for that reason, the conclusions based on them should be interpreted with due caution and should be supported from other available sources.

This impact analysis differs, however, from the results of Fraga *et al.* (2003) for the emerging market inflation targeters, which are taken by some economists as more definitive proof of the inappropriateness of inflation targeting for the emerging market economies (Jha, 2006). However, the results of Fraga *et al.* are not comparable with those of the IMF. For one thing, the IMF compares the inflation targeting emerging countries with the non-inflation targeting emerging market economies, while Fraga and his co-authors have different comparator countries, i.e. the industrial country inflation targeters.

For all this sophisticated econometric analysis with allowance for nuances of data, institutional background and the financial system development and structure, one wonders whether the country experiences are really comparable. In the IMF study, the inflation anchor is the consumer price index (CPI) but nowhere is it clarified whether it is a core or the headline index. A comparison can be valid only if the countries concerned adopt the same monetary anchor. In fact, the practices vary among the inflation targeting countries. It is known that in the inflation targeting framework of monetary policy, it is crucial whether a headline or a core CPI is chosen for fixing a target and the forecast exercises. And if a country chooses one or the other or changes the measure of inflation midstream during the implementation of the inflation targeting-based monetary policy, the impact results will not be comparable, let alone the validity of the generalisations based on them.

Several of the inflation targeting countries have alternated between one or the other measure and sometimes even a combination of the two, as pointed out by Malan Rietveld (2006). The majority of inflation targeting central banks now target headline CPI. Some central banks, including those in Australia, New Zealand and the Czech Republic have switched from targeting a core measure to headline CPI. In practice, however, these central banks still make extensive use of various measures of core inflation as a tool in evaluating the monetary policy stance. Some, like the Bank of Canada, the Norges Bank and the Central Bank of Chile, even give core inflation central position in their communication framework. These groups can therefore be identified as: "pure headline targeters", "headline targeters with a focus on core indices for operational and communicative purposes", and "core targeters". Among the emerging market inflation targeters, Korea and Czech Republic switched from a headline to a core inflation target, but not fully. Chile does the same, Brazil adopts a headline inflation, Colombia sets an overall inflation target but pays attention to the core measure in its analysis. If the measures of inflation are so diverse and varying, how is it possible to get comparable empirical evidence about whether the inflation targeting based monetary policy succeeded or not?

There is also another conundrum. As observed earlier, the stabilisation of inflation is seen as a key to the stabilisation of employment and to economic growth. But this is based on the assumption that the nominal anchor for monetary policy is core and not headline CPI. When central banks move on to the headline inflation for fixing targets, what happens to the benign impact of inflation targeting on employment and output growth?

These are not purely academic questions in a country like India. It has been long recognized since the 1960s that the prices of food and other wage goods are the kingpin of the inflationary pressures (Khatkhate, 1959; Joshi and Little, 1994; Desai, 2006). But monetary policy is not a determinant of inflation in India. Furthermore, the political economy of Indian development is such that there is a low threshold for inflation tolerance, even though India is known to be a relatively low-inflation country. If inflation tends to rise even moderately by a percentage or two, there is often a reflexive hue and cry, and the political parties get into a frenzy.

Though the sources of inflation in India are non-monetary such as changes in food output, marketed surplus, lax fiscal policies and so on, the Reserve Bank of India has to be on the alert to maintain its credibility and authority. Added to this, is the onset of globalisation which has made the Indian economy more sensitive to price level changes, and therefore those of real interest rates. Any benign neglect on the part of the monetary authorities in regard to prices will accentuate volatility of capital flows—both portfolio and short-term—into and out of the country. The implications of this are clear. If India ever contemplates initiating inflation targeting as an operational strategy, it will have to rely on the headline and not the core CPI. Currently, there is no all-India CPI, which therefore has to be constructed. India therefore has to lean largely on non-monetary economic policies and only to a limited extent on monetary policy to stabilise the inflationary pressures and to ensure output growth.

REFERENCES

Ball, L. and N. Sheridan (2003). "Does inflation targeting matter?", *IMF Working Papers 03/129*.Washington DC: IMF.

Desai, M. (2006). "Why is India a low inflation country", *Development and Nationhood: Essays in the Political Economy of South Asia*. New Delhi: Oxford University Press.

Eichengreen B., P. Masson, M. Sevastano, and S. Sharma (1999). *Transition Strategies and Nominal Anchors on the Road to Greater Exchange-Rate Flexibility. Essays in International Finance*, No. 213. Princeton, NJ. pp.112-21.

Fraga A., I. Goldfajn, Minella (2003). "Inflation targeting in emerging market economies", *NBER Working Paper* 100019.

Goodfriend, M. and E. Prasad (2006). "A framework for independent monetary policy in China", (unpublished). Washington DC: IMF.

Hyvonen, M. (2004). "Inflation convergence across countries", *Research Discussion Paper No. 2–4*. Sydney: Economic Research Department, Reserve Bank of Australia (June).

IMF (2005). *World Economic Outlook*. Washington, DC: IMF. September. pp.127–43.

Jalan, B. (2000). "Welcome Remarks" at the *11th C.D. Deshmukh Memorial Lecture*, Mumbai: Reserve Bank of India.

Jha, R. (2006). *Inflation Targeting in India: Issues and Prospects*. Canberra: Australian National University, ASARC Division of Economics, Research School of Pacific Studies.

Joshi, V. and I.M.D. Little (1994). *India: Macroeconomics and Political Economy, 1964–1991*.Washington DC: The World Bank.

Khatkhate, D. (1959). "The impact of inflation on India's economic development", *Economic Development and Cultural Change* VII(3).

Levin, A., F. Nattalucci and J. Piger (2004). "The macroeconomic effects of inflation targeting", *Federal Reserve Bank of St Louis Review* 86(4).

Rietveld, M. (2006). "The difficult choice of an inflation target", *Central Banking* XVI(4): 41–50.

The Economist (2006). "Economics focus—curve ball", *The Economist*. London. 30 September.

Truman, E.M. (2003). *Inflation Targeting in the World Economy*. Washington DC: Institute for International Economics.

(The author thanks Anand Chandavarkar for his helpful comments on an earlier draft of this paper. Errors, if any, are mine.)

Published in the Economic and Political Weekly XLI(49):1531-33 (2006).

4 | Assessing the Level of Interest Rates

The problem of measurement assumes particular importance in deriving a time series for real interest rates from nominal interest rates because of scepticism about the suitability of available price indices for deflating nominal interest rates. Since empirical verification of interest rate effects depends crucially on the realism of the measure of level of real interest rates, it is necessary to search for an alternative measure, if the conceptual problems are found to be insurmountable. The purpose of this paper is to discuss briefly these conceptual issues as a background to suggest an alternative to approximate an appropriate level of interest rate in less developed countries (LDCs).

Some Conceptual Issues

The interest rate performs several functions in an economy. It is the relative price between present and future consumption. Interest is a reward for saving out of currently earned income and also for accumulating financial assets. The interest rate together with the rate of return on foreign financial assets and expected changes in exchange rates influence how the public allocates its wealth among domestic and foreign financial assets and goods. The interest rate also constitutes an element in the cost of borrowing and influences the allocation of borrowed funds.

A distinction between a real and nominal interest rate is important for economic analysis and policy. This distinction between the nominal and real interest rate was first emphasised by Irving Fisher during the 1930s (Fisher, 1930 [1980]), but was later neglected mainly because of the dominance of Keynesian thinking and the price stability in most industrial countries during much of that period. Since prices remain unchanged in the Keynesian system with its underlying assumption of unemployment of labour and under-utilisation of capital, a fall in the money interest rate following an expansion in money supply implies a fall in the real interest rate as well.[1] However, in the

---

1. For this and other related analytical issues in the context of a financially repressed economy, see Galbis (1982), where he clearly delineates the characteristics of Fisherian and Keynesian theories of interest rate, and Fry (1983).

wake of the high inflation experienced both in the developed and developing countries since the 1960s, the distinction between real and nominal interest rate has acquired fresh relevance. This is particularly so in LDCs, which have generally suffered from a high degree of financial repression, identified as the existence of negative real interest rates and a slower growth of real financial assets. Though it is recognized that it is imperative to maintain positive real interest rates in order to provide incentives to accumulate real money balances, increase financial intermediation, and to promote unification of financial markets, difficulties are often encountered in identifying what the real interest rate is, particularly in a large number of LDCs, where nominal interest rates are fixed through government intervention.

It will be helpful to explore the meaning of real interest rate and how it adjusts to its equilibrium level in market-oriented economies. Fisher defined the real interest rate as simply the percentage premium paid on present goods over future goods of the same kind. Essentials of this concept of the real interest rate are (1) definite and assured payments, (2) definite and assured repayments, and (3) definite dates (Fisher, 1930: 35). This Fisherian concept may be expressed in various ways, depending upon one's viewpoint as well as the purpose to be served. The real interest rate may, for example, be viewed as "the anticipated reduction in wealth that individuals face when they choose to consume goods now instead of saving and investing; in this sense, it represents the relative cost of current consumption in terms of forgone future consumption" (Alchian and Klein, 1973: 424–59).

It is necessary to bear in mind two clear implications of this particular definition of the real interest rate. For one thing, from the saver's point of view, present sacrifice is balanced by access to a stream of consumption goods and services at a future date. However, the nature of the future stream of consumption goods and services is determined by asset creation through investment that is financed by current savings. For another, the real interest rate determines the proportion of resources devoted to the production of durable goods, i.e. capital goods, as against production of goods available for immediate consumption. From both these points of view, the identification of the real interest rate is an indispensable precondition.

A further question is which one of the real interest rates is the most relevant. Real rates of interest vary according to the time horizon of the asset—long, medium, and short. It is the long-term interest rate that is most germane to the economic agents involved in saving-investment activities because capital goods have a long time span. It is, however, not the historical or current long-term interest rate but an expected long-term real interest rate that is important because investment decisions are dictated by what the investors or the entrepreneurs expect to happen in the future. Past occurrences may have their usefulness but only insofar as they provide signals about what is likely to happen in the foreseeable future.[2]

The expected real long-term interest rate is thus crucial to the behaviour of economic agents, and changes in its level have far-reaching repercussions. If the expected long-term real interest rate for some reason rises, the present value of future claims will decline, with a consequent fall in the wealth of individuals. The opposite occurs if the expected long-term rate declines. While the value of wealth of the community will change with every change in the real interest rates, its impact on the value of any particular asset will vary according to its durability. Individuals with more durable assets will suffer greater loss than those with less durable assets when the long-term real interest rate rises and gain more when it falls.

A change in the perceived expected long-term real interest rate can come about in two ways. First, real factors such as productivity and propensity to sacrifice current consumption for future consumption can affect the level of the expected real interest rate. Second, in a monetary economy the anticipated real interest rate can also change as a result of changes in the rate of inflation, even though there is no change in the real factors affecting the real interest rate (perhaps some kind of money illusion is implied). The nominal rate of interest is reckoned in terms of monetary units. When prices are stable, the money rate of interest and the real rate of interest coincide. If the assumption of stable prices does not hold good, the real interest rate will change unless the money interest rate changes in the same direction and to the same extent as the rate of change in prices.[3] However, even if the money interest rate changes

---

2. To recapitulate what Irving Fisher said succinctly:

   "The rate of interest is always based upon expectation, however little this may be justified by realisation. Man makes his guess of the future and stakes his acts upon it... Our present acts must be controlled by the future, not as it actually is, but as it appears to us through the veil of change" (as quoted in Santoni and Stone, 1982: 200).

3. The money interest rate is given by the expression $r^m = a + r_1 + ar_1$ where a is the relevant inflation rate, r_1 is the real interest and ar_1 the cross product of both, i.e. real interest rate and price level. The cross product can be ignored in a good approximation, when the compounding period is short or the compounding is continuous. Then the monetary rate of interest is equal to the real interest rate plus the rate of anticipated inflation (see Hirshleifer, 1970: 136).

   The difficulty of calculating the expected real interest rates is thrown into sharp relief when

with a change in the rate of change of prices, there are doubts about whether there is a full compensation in the monetary interest rate for the variation in prices.

It is sometimes argued that historically, real rates of interest have been unaffected by the inflationary process. This is on the basis that money interest rates reach high levels when inflationary expectations become established, as for example during a period of rapid inflation such as that experienced in the United States during 1978–1982, in the developed European countries in the late 1970s, and in the Latin American countries during most of the post–Second World War period. Fisher obtained a significantly high correlation between inflation and money interest rates for Britain and the United States during the first half of the 19th century. He arrived at this result only through the use of an index of anticipated price level changes based on a distributed lag expectation model with high weights being given to the more recent years. Despite his findings, even Fisher became doubtful about whether money interest rates tended to adjust to maintain the expected real interest rate unchanged. This was because an unanticipated change in prices would lead to only a partial adjustment in money interest rates, implying a fall in the real interest rate. He attributed this discrepancy to a 'trick played on the money market by "money illusion" when contracts are made in unstable money'.

Another argument for a relation between real interest rates and inflation was given by Robert Mundell (1963). He argued that in a period of rapid rise in prices following a marked expansion of money supply, a lag would occur between the increase in inflation and money interest rate because the reduction in the community's wealth (i.e. real money balances) resulting from inflation would cause individuals to replenish their wealth relative to income, thereby inducing a lower level of real interest rates.

It is necessary to point out at this stage that the relationship between the expected rate of inflation and nominal interest rates is discussed so far without any regard for the effect of taxation on this relationship. Theoretically, it should be expected that the higher the taxation is—the relevant tax in view is income

---

contd...

seen in comparison with the real wage rate. The money interest rate can be translated into a real interest rate or a goods rate by use of some index number in the same way as it is possible to convert money wage into real wage. But here the similarity ends. Unlike the case of wages, the process of estimating expected real rates of interest entails two points of time instead of only one. Hence, "we must translate from money into goods not only in the present, when the money is borrowed, but also in the future, when it is repaid" (Fisher, 1930: 42). It is this distinction which is of strategic importance in estimating real expected long-term interest rate.

tax—the greater should be the impact of expected inflation on the nominal interest rate. Thus the Fisher equation, i = r + π (where i is real interest rate, r is nominal interest rate, and π is the expected inflation) is transformed into

$$I = r + π/1 - T$$

where T stands for taxation.

However, the presence of income taxation does not necessarily raise the nominal interest rate beyond what it could be by the presence of inflation alone. As seen earlier in this section, nominal interest rates are not fully adjusted by expected inflation in a competitive economy and this applies as well to the impact of taxation on nominal interest rates via the changes in expected inflation. There are several reasons for it. For one thing, if the lenders' options are limited, they may be inclined to accept a lower rate of return on all their financial assets. This means that the impact of π on i would be smaller than π/1 − r as in the modified Fisher equation. For another, borrowers on their part may consider tax increases in the context of rising expected inflation as an additional burden and as a result may not be willing to pay higher nominal interest rate on their borrowed funds. Third, to the extent that numerous lenders do not pay taxes on interest received and on some financial instruments, there is no impact of taxation felt on nominal interest rate. Finally, with the increase in taxation, if the nominal interest rates go up in a given country, funds from countries where taxation is heavier will flow in and in consequence the level of money interest rate will in fact be lower. (For a comprehensive discussion of these and other related issues, see Tanzi, 1984.) The sum and substance of all this is that tax-related factors do not always lead to a rise in nominal interest rates via their impact on price level. This is supported by some empirical work in respect of eight industrial countries, demonstrating that taxation of interest income and interest expenses has only a negligible effect on nominal interest rates in those countries. For this reason, the analysis in the rest of this section has ignored the role taxation plays in the relationship between expected inflation and the real interest rate.

An important question is whether the rate of change of a price index can be used to approximate the real interest rate. As observed earlier, a critical real interest rate is the long-term expected real interest rate. However, the expected real interest rate cannot be observed in the nature of things, and has therefore to be estimated. The nominal interest rate is nearly equal to the sum of the real interest rate and the rate of price change. A consumer price index is generally employed to estimate the expected long-term real interest rate, though recourse is also taken at times to other price indices such as the wholesale price index and the gross national product deflator. It is now increasingly realised that none of these indices is suitable for estimating the expected real interest rate (see Alchian and Klein, 1973; Brown and Santoni, 1981). The basic reason is that use of these indices yields misleading results when the real interest rate itself changes in either direction. As Alchian and Klein have argued:

> price indices which represent measures of current consumption, service prices, and current output prices, are theoretically inappropriate for the purpose to which they are generally put. The analysis...bases a price index on the Fisherian tradition of a proper definition of inter-temporal consumption and leads to the conclusion that a price index used to measure inflation must include asset prices. A correct measure of changes in the nominal money cost of a given utility level is a price index for wealth. If monetary impulses are transmitted to the real sector of the economy by producing transient changes in the relative prices of service flows and assets (i.e. by producing short-run changes in the real rate of interest), then the commonly used, incomplete current flow price indices provide biased short-run measures of changes in the purchasing power of money (Alchian and Klein, 1973: 173).

The inadequacy of the commonly used price indices to capture the real interest rate is due to the fact that these indices do not reflect correctly the mix of goods available to individuals inasmuch as consumer goods have larger weight than capital goods and other long-term assets in the construction of these indices. This results in a biased estimate of real interest rates based on these price indices, when the real interest rate is changing either upward or downward only as a result of changes in the propensity to save (Brown and Santoni, 1981). If the real interest rate rises following a reduction in the rate of saving, other things (such as output, quantity of money and its velocity) remaining constant, the prices of consumer or non-durable goods will rise relative to the prices of long-lived or capital goods. The opposite situation would occur if the real interest rate falls when the amount of saving increases. Under these circumstances, the use of the usual price indices, in which excess weight is given to short-lived or consumer goods, will impart an upward bias to the general level of prices, when the real interest rate rises, and a downward bias when it declines. Thus, when the real interest is rising following a fall in saving rate, the expected real interest rate will be underestimated when approximated by using the usual price indices. Conversely, it will be overestimated when the real interest rate falls when the saving rate rises, thereby giving misleading signals to policymakers in competitive economies in pursuing their monetary-fiscal policies, as demonstrated by the experience in the United States during the late 1970s (Brown and Santoni, 1981).

This problem would not arise (although others might) if the real interest rate remained unchanged. In fact, the available evidence shows that real interest rates change. Wilcox (1983) has produced persuasive empirical evidence for the United States that real interest rates declined in the middle 1970s as a result of reduction in the supply of complementary factors of production, especially energy. As input prices rose, the profitability of capital fell. The lowered growth rate of the capital stock and concomitant decline of investment dragged down the real rate of interest. When the real interest rate declined, derivation of real interest level from nominal interest rate by using CPI may perhaps have exaggerated the extent to which real interest rates became negative during that period.

APPROXIMATING AN APPROPRIATE LEVEL OF INTEREST RATES IN LDCs

Since the estimation of real interest rates is beset with conceptual and statistical difficulties as observed earlier, an alternative approach to the determination of that level of domestic nominal interest rates in LDCs, which may broadly correspond to the level of estimated real interest rates, is explored in this Section.[4] The alternative approach is to judge the appropriateness or otherwise of the level of domestic nominal interest rates in LDCs in relation to the relevant foreign interest rate, adjusted for expected changes in exchange rates. It may be argued that such adjusted foreign interest rate may not be relevant for most of the LDCs which are closed (defined as having pervasive foreign exchange and trade controls). However, the so-called closed economies of LDCs are not really closed in any operational sense. Even in countries with severe exchange and trade controls, an illicit substitution of foreign currency and foreign financial assets or gold for domestic currency and domestic financial assets can and does take place when incentives for doing so are sufficiently strong (Bhagwati, 1978; Tanzi and Blejer, 1984). Therefore, it seems reasonable to judge the appropriateness of the level of domestic nominal interest rates in relation to the relevant foreign interest rate, after adjusting it for the expected change in the exchange rate. If the level of domestic nominal interest rates is lower than that of the adjusted foreign interest rate, then it could be taken as a signal for making an upward change in domestic nominal interest rate and *vice versa*, if domestic nominal interest rate exceeds the adjusted foreign interest rate.

---

4. Some other alternative is proposed by Brown and Santoni but it has many shortcomings, as discussed in Khatkhate (1982a).

A domestic nominal interest rate to be considered as appropriate is derived by adjusting the foreign interest rate for expected change in the exchange rate. Adjustment can be made by adopting the following rule:

$$rd_1 = r_f + e$$

where

rd_1 is domestic nominal interest rate considered to be appropriate in LDCs;

$r_f =$ London one-year inter-bank offer rate on US dollar deposits (LIBOR). Since data on this series are available only since 1977, the US treasury bill rate has been used for the years 1971–1976. There was little difference between these two rates in the later years.

$e =$ annual percentage change in actual exchange rate in LDCs during the period, defined as domestic currency per unit of foreign currency. Ideally, future (however defined) changes in exchange rate should be used, though current exchange rate changes are considered as the interest rate series is calculated over a 10-year period.[5]

LIBOR or the US treasury bill rate is chosen as a benchmark. The interest rate so derived is designated as Rd_2.

---

5. It would have been better to have adjusted for expected rather than actual changes in exchange rates but the generation of expected exchange rates is fraught with several conceptual and statistical difficulties. There are many approaches to the estimation of the future course of inflation but the familiar one, since the pioneering effort of Fisher (1930), is the distributed lag method by which expected inflation is related to past inflation rates with an identifying restriction that the weights on past inflation must sum up to unity. However, this identifying condition holds good only in a situation when the rate of inflation remains more or less unchanged or changes only marginally. The historical experience shows that the rate of inflation fluctuates widely from year to year or quarter to quarter (Feldstein and Summers, 1978). In general, however, expectations about future inflation are governed not only by the past experience of inflation but also by other factors. As Gordon pointed out,

> people do use outside information to evaluate recent experience. Before deciding whether to incorporate a recent burst of inflation into their expectation of the future, they ask whether there are any outside recent experiences either particularly relevant or irrelevant over the forecasting horizon. This is a process which mechanical weighting procedures, no matter how economically sophisticated, are unlikely to capture. (Gordon, 1973: 463)

Apart from this, whichever price index is selected is itself suspect in a large number of LDCs so that the index of expected inflation built on it tends to accentuate its inadequacies. For this and several other reasons, reliance is placed by many either on the current level of real interest rates (Chandavarkar, 1971; McKinnon, 1973; Khatkhate, Leite and Collyns, 1982; Lanyi and Saracoglu, 1983) or on the unweighted averages of real interest rates for some years in the immediate past as indicative of expected real interest rates (Galbis, 1979).

Table 4.1

Mean of Interest Rates: Rd_1, Rd_2, Rd_3 in LDCs, 1971–1980

		$Rd_1{}^a$	$Rd_2{}^b$	$Rd_3{}^c$	$Rd_1 - Rd_2$
Africa	Benin	3.97	12.45	−6.25	−8.48
	Botswana	3.91	12.45	−1.25	−8.54
	Cameroon	5.08	12.45	−8.05	−7.37
	Congo	5.28	12.45	−5.17	−7.17
	Gambia	6.91	11.28	−3.22	−4.37
	Gabon	5.25	12.45	−6.77	−7.00
	Ghana	5.29	33.76	−41.70	−28.47
	Ivory Coast	3.97	12.45	−12.90	−8.48
	Kenya	5.37	13.97	−4.97	−8.60
	Liberia	4.81	9.00	−3.73	−4.19
	Malawi	6.67	11.67	−5.56	−5.00
	Mauritania	5.91	9.54	−5.00	−3.63
	Morocco	6.00	12.08	−2.55	−7.15
	Niger	3.97	12.45	−8.28	−8.48
	Nigeria	5.54	9.28	−10.80	−3.74
	Senegal	3.97	12.45	−4.16	−8.48
	Sierra Leone	4.04	15.83	−6.53	−11.79
	Somalia	5.95	16.54	−12.90	−10.59
	Tanzania	3.79	12.45	−7.31	−8.66
	Togo	3.97	12.45	−5.80	−8.58
	Tunisia	4.00	11.30	−4.11	−7.30
	Upper Volta	3.97	12.45	−5.26	−8.48
	Zambia	4.76	13.57	−2.95	−8.81
	Zimbabwe	5.36	12.00	−4.38	−6.64
Asia	Bangladesh	8.14	20.50	−5.38	−12.36
	Burma	0.12	13.16	−6.83	−13.04
	Fiji	5.00	10.24	·4.98	−5.34
	India	6.79	11.25	−2.24	−4.46
	Indonesia	11.06	17.30	−7.86	−6.24
	Korea	15.46	16.61	−2.67	−1.15
	Malaysia	7.61	7.16	1.20	0.45
	Nepal	12.1	11.71	4.2	0.39
	Pakistan	8.39	18.21	−0.47	−9.82
	Philippines	9.45	13.20	−3.27	−3.75
	Singapore	6.99	6.47	1.49	0.52
	Sri Lanka	9.58	20.84	−2.48	−11.26

contd...

contd...

		$Rd_1{}^a$	$Rd_2{}^b$	$Rd_3{}^c$	$Rd_1 - Rd_2$
	Thailand	9.66	9.74	0.16	−0.08
Europe	Portugal	12.72	19.97	−6.40	−7.25
	Turkey	12.09	38.74	−21.56	−29.72
	Yugoslavia	9.91	26.51	−11.73	−16.60
Latin America	Antigua	4.12	11.30	−3.84	−6.18
	Argentina	58.95	154.53	−71.34	−95.58
	Barbados	7.49	9.05	−3.55	−1.56
	Bolivia	13.66	45.03	−21.01	−31.37
	Brazil	31.07	59.07	−13.25	−28.00
	Chile	60.31	158.25	−118.42	−97.94
	Colombia	20.98	20.54	1.23	0.44
	Costa Rica	13.58	27.83	−3.68	−14.25
	Dominica	3.10	11.30	−9.68	−8.20
	Dominican Republic	6.33	9.00	−0.32	−2.67
	Ecuador	8.29	16.33	−5.81	−8.04
	El Salvador	7.50	9.00	−2.06	−1.50
	Grenada	3.10	11.30	−8.33	−8.20
	Guatemala	8.75	9.00	0.28	0.25
	Haiti	8.29	9.00	0.05	0.71
	Honduras	9.58	9.00	0.93	0.58
	Jamaica	10.04	16.10	−4.68	−6.06
	Mexico	15.40	31.92	−3.65	−15.52
	Panama	4.79	9.00	−2.17	−5.21
	Paraguay	8.50	9.00	−4.05	−0.50
	Peru	22.96	44.37	−15.14	−21.41
	St Vincent	6.00	9.80	−4.50	−3.80
	Trinidad and Tobago	7.17	10.37	−10.11	−3.2
	Uruguay	44.10	55.95	−18.58	−11.85
	Venezuela	7.72	6.67	−4.54	−0.95
Middle East	Jordan	6.10	9.22	3.08	−3.12
	Yemen Arab Republic	8.04	9.48	−4.98	−1.44
	Yemen People's Dem. Rep.	3.91	7.71	−5.08	−3.80

Note: a. Interest rates chosen are those on time deposits of maturity of six months and above, and in some cases the saving deposits because of lack of data. Sources: Most of the Latin American countries' interest rates series up to 1976 are from Galbis' "Inflation and interest rate policies in Latin America, 1967–76", IMF Staff Papers, June 1979, and from respective central bank bulletins thereafter. For the rest, the sources are the IMF Central Banking Department's advisory reports and central bank bulletins.

b. Rd_2 is derived, as explained in the text, by adjusting the foreign interest rate for actual percentage change in exchange rate. Source: IMF, International Financial Statistics, 1986.

c. Rd_3 is calculated by correcting nominal interest rate (Rd1) for a percentage change in GDP deflator, i.e. $d = (1 + i) / (1 + p) - 1$, where i is the nominal interest rate and p is the GDP deflator.

Source: IMF, *International Financial Statistics*, 1986.

The means of nominal interest rate (Rd_1) and the two computed interest rate series for LDCs, i.e. foreign interest rate adjusted for actual changes in exchange rate (Rd_2) and real interest rate (Rd_3), i.e. actual nominal interest rate adjusted for percentage change in GDP deflator (or in some cases CPI) of LDCs in respect of selected LDCs are presented in Table 4.1. The last column of the table displays the difference between Rd_1, i.e. the nominal interest rates and Rd_2, i.e. foreign interest rates adjusted for exchange rate changes. Looking at the figures in that column and comparing them with real interest rates, i.e. Rd_3, it is clear that the countries which have negative real interest rates are also the countries in which domestic nominal interest rates are less than their corresponding Rd_2, i.e. the foreign interest rates adjusted for exchange rate changes. Likewise, the countries where the domestic nominal interest rates are higher than their Rd_2 are the countries having positive real interests. Such a close correspondence between internationally competitive interest rates and the positive real interest rates domestically may be attributed to the fact that the existence of positive domestic real interest rates which are internationally competitive stimulates domestic saving mobilisation effort by preventing leakages from whatever domestic saving takes place to foreign financial assets or goods and by inducing generation of varied types of remunerative financial assets internally (Guitian, 1981).

The conclusion derived from the data in Table 4.1, that the countries having negative real interest rates (Rd_3) are also the countries in respect of which relevant foreign exchange rate exceeds their domestic nominal interest rates (Rd_2) and vice versa, does not alter significantly even if LDCs are grouped by degree of inflation, degree of openness of their economies, or by region. Thus, it will be seen from Table 4.2 that the coefficient of correlation between Rd_3 and ($Rd_1 - Rd_2$) is highest (0.99) in respect of Europe, followed by Latin America (0.93), Africa (0.87) and Asia (0.67). Only for the Middle East the coefficient is low and negative. However, signs for Rd_3 and $Rd_1 - Rd_2$ are negative. The low and negative coefficient therefore has little significance. The same pattern more or less prevails in high- and low-inflation countries or LDCs with open and closed economies.

The question that assumes importance in this connection is whether LDCs, confronted with the problem of complexities in determining real interest rates on the basis of price indices, can derive useful guidance in setting the level of real domestic interest rates. On the face of it, the alternative appears to be legitimate because of a very high coefficient of correlation between Rd_2 and

($Rd_1 - Rd_2$). However, it raises a host of issues which need to be understood, if not resolved. First of all, since this alternative of looking at the relevant foreign interest rate plus the expected change in the exchange rate implicitly assigns very high weight to foreign factors in relation to domestic factors. However, the use of this alternative should not be taken to mean that LDCs should totally ignore the domestic imperatives. They need to balance the domestic considerations against the foreign factors. If, for instance, the real interest rates in industrial countries become negative, as happened in fact during much of the 1970s, and a given developing country is inflating at the industrial countries' rate of inflation, LDCs relying for guidance on the relevant foreign interest rate with exchange rate adjustment will have to decide what weight they have to give to the foreign influences in relation to the relevant domestic factors. If the rate of return to capital is high in relation to the real interest rates determined on the basis of foreign factors, the domestic considerations will require that real interest rates will have to be higher than what would ensue from the relevant foreign interest rate plus the expected exchange rate change. This means that a relatively higher weight should be assigned to the domestic factors in such a situation. In the opposite case also, where the rate of return to capital is lower than the market-determined real interest rate, following reliance on the foreign factors for guidance LDCs will have to give more weight to the domestic factors.

Table 4.2

Correlation Coefficients between Rd_3 and $Rd_1 - Rd_2$ for Selected LDCs Classified by Region, Degree of Inflation and Openness of Economy, 1971–80

		Rd_3 and $Rd_1 - Rd_2$
By region	Africa (25)	0.87
	Asia (13)	0.67
	Europe (3)	0.99
	Latin America (25)	0.93
	Middle East (3)	0.23
By degree of inflation	High inflation (41)	0.94
	Low inflation (28)	0.63
By degree of openness	Open economy (44)	0.93
	Closed economy (25)	0.84

Note: Parentheses contain number of countries.

Source: Table 4.1.

If on the other hand, LDCs determine their domestic real interest rates by deriving guidance from the interest rates in the industrial countries adjusted for exchange rate changes which are positive, as experienced in the first half of 1980s; if the inflation rates in LDCs are higher than in the industrial countries as generally prevailed during the last three decades, and if the marginal return to capital in LDCs is positive, the LDCs will be better served by giving more weight to the foreign factors. During 1971–1980, in respect of 48 out of 63 LDCs included in Table 4.3, the domestic interest rates if linked entirely with the foreign factors are lower on an average than the incremental output/capital ratio (IOCR). Countries where IOCR was lower than their corresponding Rd_2 included high-inflation countries like Argentina, Brazil, Chile, Peru, Uruguay, and Turkey. These countries should be treated as a special category.

The evidence on the marginal rate of return is more ambiguous. Thus, the marginal rate of return, which is less precise a measure than IOCR, is higher than the corresponding Rd_2 only in respect of 18 LDCs out of 50 for which the marginal rate of return is computed. Here again, the high-inflation countries form an exception. This means that in general domestic investment and growth in LDCs would not have been adversely impacted by the level of domestic interest rates determined on the basis of the foreign interest rate adjusted for the expected exchange rate change. Apart from this, assigning by LDCs a relatively high weight to the foreign factors in determining domestic real interest rates seems warranted on other ground as well. What is crucial from the point of view of domestic investment is the differential between the expected rate of interest and the expected rate of return on investment. If the domestic nominal interest rate is out of line with the foreign interest rate adjusted for the expected change in exchange rate, it will lead to an outflow of domestic capital; and the resulting foreign exchange shortages, by creating difficulties in the implementation of future investment projects, may well depress the expected rate of return (Lanyi and Saracoglu, 1983). In that case, the differential between the expected rate of interest and the expected rate of return will narrow, leading to lower investment. On the other hand, if domestic interest rates remain in rough parity with the relevant foreign interest rate (adjusted for the expected change in exchange rate), the general economic environment is likely to be more attractive, thereby raising the expected rate of return on present and future investment.

Table 4.3

*Mean of Foreign Interest Rate with Exchange Rate Adjustment (Rd₂),
Incremental Output-Capital Ratio and Marginal Rate of Return
to Capital in Selected LDCs, 1971–1980*

Country		Rd_2	Incremental/output capital ratio (IOCR)[a]	Marginal rate of return to capital[b]
Africa	Benin	12.45	17.10	7.29
	Botswana	12.45	31.00	1.24
	Cameroon	12.45	31.20	5.60
	Congo	12.45	22.40	—
	Gabon	12.45	11.40	5.51
	Gambia	11.28	44.60	—
	Ghana	33.76	−2.00	0.23
	Ivory Coast	12.45	23.50	10.78
	Kenya	13.97	26.10	13.33
	Malawi	11.67	24.60	20.53
	Mauritania	9.54	9.10	0.17
	Mauritius	14.80	18.50	8.21
	Niger	12.45	10.80	—
	Nigeria	9.28	32.10	22.11
	Senegal	12.45	13.80	7.71
	Sierra Leone	15.83	16.50	7.49
	Somalia	16.54	32.20	—
	Tanzania	12.45	30.80	13.41
	Togo	12.45	12.00	7.67
	Tunisia	11.30	30.70	26.25
	Upper Volta	12.45	15.80	4.47
	Zambia	13.57	−2.00	0.68
Asia	Bangladesh	20.50	18.10	—
	Burma	13.16	33.63	15.02
	Fiji	10.24	20.10	—
	India	11.25	16.90	17.46
	Indonesia	17.30	41.80	37.53
	Korea	16.61	31.70	16.18
	Malaysia	7.16	30.30	5.92
	Nepal	11.71	—	9.20
	Pakistan	18.21	28.40	28.82
	Philippines	13.20	22.09	18.73
	Singapore	6.47	24.00	—
	Sri Lanka	20.84	22.80	10.53
	Thailand	9.74	28.20	16.34

contd...

contd...

Country		Rd_2	Incremental/output capital ratio (IOCR)[a]	Marginal rate of return to capital[b]
Europe	Portugal	19.97	21.40	8.76
	Turkey	38.74	24.90	14.38
	Yugoslavia	26.51	17.00	—
Latin America	Antigua	11.30	18.20	—
	Argentina	154.53	12.40	—
	Barbados	9.05	16.70	0.07
	Bolivia	45.03	18.10	9.80
	Brazil	59.07	31.00	29.14
	Chile	158.25	12.00	2.64
	Colombia	20.54	25.90	13.47
	Costa Rica	27.83	21.90	8.55
	Dominica	11.30	4.10	—
	Dominican Republic	9.00	38.00	28.98
	Ecuador	16.33	36.30	23.05
	El Salvador	9.00	39.00	28.98
	Guatemala	9.00	32.00	—
	Haiti	9.00	20.00	3.79
	Honduras	9.00	16.90	17.46
	Jamaica	16.10	−2.00	−0.43
	Mexico	31.92	30.80	16.04
	Panama	9.00	16.90	4.66
	Paraguay	9.00	36.40	19.50
	Peru	44.37	20.20	10.42
	Trinidad and Tobago	10.37	16.80	—
	Uruguay	55.95	25.10	9.46
	Venezuela	8.67	13.80	7.34
Middle East	Jordan	9.22	27.90	13.16
	Yemen Arab Republic	9.48	47.50	37.03

Note: a. IOCR is calculated by dividing the rate of growth of real GDP by the investment/income ratio.

b. Marginal rate of return to capital is calculated by multiplying IOCR by the share of profit in GDP.

Source: Table 4.2 and statistics gathered by the author. The latter can be made available on request.

Thus, if the domestic conditions are what are specified above—and they reflect by and large the reality in LDCs—it appears that it would be at least a second-best policy that the monetary authorities in LDCs supplement their knowledge in determining the desired level of domestic nominal interest rates, by drawing on the relevant foreign interest rate and the expected change in exchange rate indicated by the differential between the domestic and foreign inflation rates (as reflected in respective GDP deflators)[6] without being much concerned with measurement problems involved in approximating the level of real interest rates. This policy rule may incidentally help to combine the imperatives of an interventionist approach to the determination of interest rate policy in LDCs, with some element of a free market mechanism.

SUMMARY AND CONCLUSIONS

The principal purpose of this paper has been to underscore the difficulties in measuring the level of real interest rates and to suggest an alternative to approximate real interest rates. The problem of measurement arises because real interest rates, not being observable, have to be estimated. Real interest rate can change as a result first, of a change in real factors such as productivity and thrift, and second, as a result of a change in the rate of change in prices. If the real factors remain constant, a change in real interest rate, following a change in rate of change in prices, can be estimated. But when a real interest rate changes due to real factors, complications arise in estimating real interest rate levels by correcting nominal interest rate for price changes. The inadequacy of the existing price indices to capture the real interest rate is due to the fact that these indices do not reflect correctly the mix of goods available to individual savers insofar as consumer goods have a larger weight than capital goods and other long-term assets in the construction of indices. If the real interest rate rises, the prices of consumer goods will rise relative to the prices of long-lived goods. Therefore, the use of price indices in which larger weight is assigned to short-lived goods will impart an upward bias to the general level of prices when the real interest rate increases and a downward bias when it declines. Thus, when the real interest rate is rising, the expected real interest rate will be underestimated. Conversely, it will be overestimated when the real interest rate falls.

For these reasons, an alternative interest rate series is constructed by adjusting the relevant foreign interest rate in advanced industrial countries for the actual changes in the exchange rates of LDCs. A rationale for preparing this series lies in the fact that there needs to be a reasonable relationship between domestic nominal interest rate and adjusted foreign interest rate, since even in LDCs with trade and exchange controls, domestic currency and financial assets

---

6. According to the Fund's 1984 Annual Report on Exchange Arrangements and Exchange Restrictions, several LDCs have increasingly used since 1983 inflation differentials either alone or in combination with other factors to adjust their exchange rates.

are always substituted, legally or otherwise, for foreign currency and financial assets. It may be noted that both series of interest rates are constructed with reference to the current and not expected rate of inflation, in view of the limitations both of the statistical techniques used and the data for LDCs.

It is quite clear that countries with negative real interest rates (Rd_3) are also the countries where domestic nominal interest rates (Rd_1) are less than the interest rates derived from the foreign interest rate adjusted for exchange rate changes (Rd_2). Likewise, countries where the domestic nominal interest rates are higher than their Rd_2 are the countries having positive real interest rates. This conclusion does not change even if the relationship between Rd_3 and $(Rd_1 - Rd_2)$ is observed for separate groups of LDCs classified by region, degree of inflation and the extent of openness of the economy. A policy implication suggested by this is that LDCs may in certain circumstances approximate desired level of interest rates domestically if they decide to determine the domestic nominal interest rates by observing (a) the domestic inflation rate as reflected in the GDP deflator and (b) foreign inflation rate as reflected in the GDP deflator in the industrial countries as a group, both of which give some idea about the direction in which LDCs' exchange rates may move, and (c) the foreign interest rate. However, they should also take care in assigning proper weights to the domestic factors such as rate of return to capital.

References

Agarwala, R.K. (1983). "Price distortions and growth in developing countries", *World Bank Staff Working Papers* No. 575.

Alchian, A. and B. Klein (1973). "On correct measure of inflation", *Journal of Money, Credit and Banking* III(1): 230-42, February.

Bhagwati, J. (1978). *Anatomy and Consequences of Trade Control Regimes.* National Bureau for Economic Research.

Brown, Gilbert T. (1973). *Korean Pricing: Policies and Economic Development in the 1960s.*Baltimore, MD: Johns Hopkins University Press.

Brown, W. and G. Santoni (1981). "Unreal estimates of the real rate of interest", *Federal Reserve Bank of St. Louis Review* 63(1) (January).

Chandavarkar, Anand G. (1971). "Some aspects of interest rate policies in less developed economies: The experience of selected Asian countries", *IMF Staff Papers* XVIII(1): 48–110, March.

Coats, Warren L. and Deena R. Khatkhate (1984). "Money and monetary policy in less developed countries: Main issues", Paper presented at a workshop on *Monetary and Fiscal Aspects of Economic Development,* 6–8 March. *Developing Economies* XXII(4): 329–48.

Elliot, Jon Walter (1977). "Measuring the expected real rate of interest: An exploration of macroeconomic alternatives", *American Economic Review* 89(2): 85–110.

Fama, Eugene F. (1975). "Short-term interest rates as predictors of inflation", *American Economic Review* 87(2): 120–38.

Feldstein, Martin and Otto Eckstein (1970). "The fundamental determinants of the interest rate", *The Review of Economics and Statistics* 81(3): 225–39.

Fisher, Irving (1930 [1980]). *The Theory of Interest (As Determined by Importance to Spend Income and Opportunity to Invest It)*. New York: Macmillan.

————. (1965). *The Theory of Interest and Capital*, New York: Augustus M Kelly.

Fry, Maxwell (1982). "Models of financially repressed developing economies", *World Development*, September; Reproduced in Deena Khatkhate (ed.) (1983). *National and International Aspects of Financial Development in LDCs*. Oxford: Pergamon Press.

Galbis, Vicente (1982). "Analytical aspects of interest rate policies in less developed countries", *Savings and Development* 6(2): 70–9.

————. (1981). "Interest rate management: the Latin American experience", *Savings and Development* 5(1): 17–29.

————. (1979). "Inflation and interest rate polices in Latin America, 1967–76", *IMF Staff Papers* 26(2): 334–65, June.

————. (1977). "Financial intermediation and economic growth in less developed countries: A theoretical approach", *Journal of Development Studies* 13(2): 91-105; Reproduced in Warren L. Coats, Jr., and Deena R. Khatkhate (eds.) (1980). *Money and Monetary Policy in Less Developed Countries: Survey of Issues and Evidence*. Oxford: Pergamon Press.

Giovannini, Alberto (1983). "The interest elasticity of savings in developing countries: The existing evidence", *World Development* 5(7): 230–43 .

Gordon, R.J. (1973). "Interest rates in the long run: a comment", *Journal of Money, Credit and Banking* Part II, III(1): 51–62.

Guitian, Manuel (1981). *Fund Conditionality: Evolution of Principles and Practices*. Washington DC: IMF.

Hirschman, A.O. (1958). *The Strategy of Economic Development*. New Haven: Yale University Press.

Hirshleifer, J. (1970). *Investment, Interest and Capital*. Englewood Cliffs, NJ: Prentice-Hall.

IMF, (1984). *Annual Report on Exchange Arrangements and Exchange Restrictions*.

Johnson, Omotunde (1984). "Financial policies and macroeconomic performance of developing countries". *(mimeo)*.

Keynes, J.M. (1936). *The General Theory of Employment, Interest and Money*. New York: Harcourt Brace and World.

Khan, Mohsin S. and Roberto Zahler (1984). "Trade and financial liberalisation in the context of external shocks and inconsistent domestic policies". *(mimeograph)*. IMF.

Khatkhate, Deena R. (1987). "Assessing the impact of interest rates in less developed countries", *World Development* 9(5): 410-22..

————. (1986). "Measuring expected real interest rates", in S. Guhan and M. Shroff (eds.), *Essays on Economic Progress and Welfare*. Bombay: Oxford University Press.

————. (1982). "National and international aspects of financial policies in LDCs: A prologue", *World Development* 4(9): 520–34.

————. (1980). "False issues in the debate on interest rate policies in less developed countries", *Banca Nazional del Lavoro Quarterly Review* 133 (June).

Khatkhate, Deena R., Warren L. Coats, Jr., and Klaus-Walter Riechel (1978). "The Sri Lanka financial system and a framework for monetary policy", Chapter II. *(mimeo)*. IMF.

Khatkhate, Deena R. and Delano Villanueva 1979. "Deposit substitutes and their monetary policy significance in developing countries", *Oxford Bulletin of Economics and Statistics* 39(1): 52–63.

Khatkhate, Deena R., Sergio Leite and Charles Collyns (1982). "A study of the financial system and policy in Fiji". *(mimeo)*. IMF.

Kornosky, D.S. (1969). "Interest rates and price level changes, 1952–69", *Federal Reserve Bank of St. Louis Review* 39(12): 189–212.

Lanyi, Anthony and Saracoglu R. (1983). "Interest rate policies in developing economies", *Occasional Paper No. 22*. IMF.

McKinnon, Ronald I. (1979). *Money in International Exchange: The Convertible Currency System*. New York: Oxford University Press.

—————. (1973). *Money and Capital in Economic Development*. Washington DC: Brookings Institution.

Mundell, Robert (1963). "The inflation and real interest", *Journal of Political Economy* LXXI (February–December).

Roe, Allan R. (1982). "High interest rates: A new conventional wisdom for development policy? Some conclusions from Sri Lankan experience", *World Development* 10(3): 143–56.

Santoni, G.J. and Courtney C. Stone (1982). "The Fed and the real rate of interest", *Federal Reserve Bank of St Louis Review* 64(10): 150–67.

Saracoglu, R., (1984). "Expectation of inflation and interest rate determination", *IMF Staff Papers* 31(1): 65–79, March.

Tanzi, Vitto (ed.), (1984). *Taxation, Inflation and Interest Rates*. Washington, DC: IMF.

Wilcox, James A. (1983). "Why real interest rates were so low in the 1970s", *American Economic Review* 73(1): 82–96.

Published in the Economic and Political Weekly VIII(45): 2005-7 (1973).

II

FINANCE

5 National and International Aspects of Financial Policies in LDCs

Speak in French when you cannot think of the English for a thing.
—Through the Looking Glass

After a period of animated controversy between Keynesians advocating policies of low interest rates and monetary expansion and monetarists who insisted on the importance of the distinction between nominal and real interest rates, economists have now almost reached a consensus on the role of money in the development process. This consensus has arisen because:

> it was increasingly felt that what was called for was not new concepts so much as new ways of looking at them. In LDCs, money's role need be neither denigrated nor exaggerated. Money's traditional functions as a medium of exchange and a store of value remain important in LDCs, but its function as a conduit of resources from savers to investors is more central to an understanding of its contributions to development (Coats and Khatkhate, 1980: 3).

The body of the consensus derives from the framework set up by McKinnon and Shaw, fleshed out by the earlier work of Goldsmith and Patrick (Goldsmith, 1969; Patrick, 1966), and extended by the theoretical and empirical output of a large number of younger economists (Fry, 1982). This analysis attached central importance to financial policies of higher real interest rates, which were supposed to encourage the build-up of real money balances, increased financial intermediation and unification of financial markets. Eventually, such a policy would lead to the efficient utilisation of resources and particularly of scarce capital. This new paradigm has contributed to an improved understanding and perception of the economies of LDCs, their problems, and how these problems are accentuated by distortions arising from interventionist policies.

For a while it was believed that the programme contained the secret of how to reconcile stabilisation objectives with those of development (Roe, 1982). However, the accumulation of empirical evidence on several developing countries where the prescribed set of policies was adopted has raised doubts about the validity of this conclusion. In the presence of distortions in the financial markets, it is no doubt a sensible policy to raise real interest rates. The problematic issue is how far to go. Raising real interest rates without any regard for the rates of return on investment may run counter to the requirements of development. To argue that once funds are generated through the accumulation of real balances, investment can take care of itself ignores the very dynamics of development. Thus, the hiatus between stabilisation and development has not really been bridged. This is evident from the recent concern with supply-side policies rather than demand management policies, a dichotomy which parallels the distinction between the stabilisation and development problems.

I

The difficulties involved in reconciling the stabilisation objectives with the developmental concerns can be clearly perceived in the rationale underlying the major policy prescription of the new paradigm, i.e. the raising of real interest rates first to arrest the financial retardation and then to accelerate the pace of financial development. The case for positive real interest rates is made by considering the choice between assets in the institutional context of LDCs (Khatkhate, 1980). Given the available assets and the rates of return corresponding to each, the asset holder tends to balance increasing yield from his wealth portfolio against increasing its liquidity characteristics and reducing the riskiness of returns. If, for example, consumer prices are expected to rise at a faster rate, the owners of wealth will tend to reshuffle their assets in favour of holding more consumer goods, at the expense of financial assets.

Essential to this rationale for maintaining a competitive yield on financial assets is the condition that build-up of the real money balances does not compete with real capital accumulation. While such a complementary relationship does prevail most of the time in LDCs for reasons explained elsewhere (Coates and Khatkhate, 1980), it is likely to be absent if real interest rates rise above the rates of return to capital. In other words, a rise in real interest rates will contribute to investment and hence development only so long as the resulting real interest rates remain lower than the rate of return on capital (Khatkhate, 1980).

The implications of complementarity for economic development are brought into bold relief when interest rate policy is considered in small, open developing economies in which savings accumulated can be channelled either into domestic physical capital or into foreign assets. The average real rate of interest on accumulated savings in such economies can exceed the rate of return on real physical capital only to the extent that the country holds net foreign assets (i.e. foreign financial assets net of foreign financial liabilities) bearing a higher yield. This means that the level of domestic real interest rates could be maintained above the real rate of return to capital but in such an eventuality the savings that are accumulated would find an outlet abroad. The country would be deprived of much needed investment finance. The dilemma posed by the desire to maintain positive real interest rates in such developing economies is thus real. In order to achieve rising real money balances the real interest rate will have to take into account the domestic inflation rate, foreign interest rates (adjusted for anticipated movements of the exchange rate) and the rate of return to domestic capital. However, these three criteria are not mutually consistent in open economies; the effort to adhere to one may thwart compliance with another. Suppose the adjusted interest rate differential is in favour of holding deposits abroad, then there will be an outflow of savings, while domestic investment would languish. Thus development may be sacrificed on the altar of stabilisation. Such consequences are not, however, limited to the most open of economies. Even in countries with severe exchange controls, an illicit substitution of foreign currency and financial assets for domestic currency and financial assets can take place when the incentives are sufficiently high. In this connection, Tanzi and Blejer draw attention to yet another problem of contradictory effects of interest rates on mobilisation of financial savings and the short-term capital flows and stress the inability of the interest rate policy to deal simultaneously with several objectives (Tanzi and Blejer, 1982).[1]

Though the rate of return to capital is of vital importance in the management of interest rates in LDCs, two reasons are commonly adduced for its exclusion from consideration. For one thing, a positive real interest rate implies a positive real return to capital in a growing economy (Galbis, 1979). For another, the rate of return to capital does not offer a simple operational guideline as it is conceptually confused and difficult to measure. Taking the first reason, even if the real rate of return to capital in an economy were positive, it would not follow that the growth of the economy would not be affected if the real interest rate happened to exceed the real rate of return to

---

1. Tanzi and Blejer (1982) have dealt with the very important issue of currency substitution, but they have left out a crucial factor, viz., the rate of return to capital, from their analysis.

capital. What is germane is not the absolute levels of real interest rates and real rates of return to capital, but the level of real interest rates in relation to the rate of return to capital. Tobin has emphasised this point time and again (e.g. Tobin, 1978). It is imperative, therefore, to consider the rate of return to capital along with other criteria in determining the level of interest rates if the domestic investment is not to become hostage to the foreign interest rate (Khatkhate, 1980; Roe, 1982; Leite, 1982).

The second argument for exclusion of the rate of return to capital is that it does not offer a simple operational guideline. Much of the scepticism about the rate of return to capital stems from the confusion between the marginal productivity of capital and the rate of return to capital. The former of these concepts is obviously highly abstract and not easy to translate into an operational guideline. It is true that defining a rate of return to capital is not straightforward, particularly when the prevailing rates of return on investment in LDCs vary across sectors. But several operational guidelines have been developed for calculation of the rate of return to capital, based on the work of Little and Mirrlees (1968) as well as Dasgupta et al. (1972). The World Bank in particular has now accumulated considerable evidence on economic and internal rates of return to capital for many LDCs, for use in project planning and evaluation.

In any case, the measurement of real interest rates is also not immune from criticism. Doubt has been cast on the procedure of arriving at real interest rates by deflating nominal interest rates by the consumer price index. Brown and Santoni (1981), for instance, argue that such estimates of real interest rates have a systematic bias because such indices give too little weight to the prices of capital goods. When the real interest rate rises the prices of consumer goods rise in relation to those of capital goods, and hence the consumer price index rises in relation to the general price index. Thus the method underestimates the true rise in the real interest rate. In truth, all the operational indicators used in the pursuit of economic policy should be regarded as approximations to the real magnitudes rather than precise measurements.

Several LDCs, particularly those with small open economies, face severe difficulties in raising real interest rates close to world market levels. The capacity of the domestic financial system to offer high real interest rates on deposits depends in the ultimate analysis on the opportunities available to utilize those funds at an equally high real loan rate. But the level of loan rates is governed in turn by the existence of bankable projects yielding a sufficiently high return. If such projects are not forthcoming due to lack of necessary technical expertise or infrastructure facilities, the financial system must perforce transmit its large accumulated financial liabilities abroad for investment in high-yielding foreign financial assets. Thus the high real interest rate policy, while helping to financialise savings, does not succeed in contributing to domestic investment and hence to development. A solution to such problems lies in instituting a machinery to identify and examine projects. High interest rates alone are not enough.

As pointed out by Roe (1982), imperfections of the financial markets have also to be considered in determining the appropriate level of the real interest rate. Lending operations of banks in LDCs are bedevilled by a variety of risks absent in perfect credit markets where there is full information about the borrowers. Lending rates include the cost involved in mediating a loan plus a premium for bearing risk. As a result, the spread between the rate paid to the owners of wealth on their savings (i.e. deposit rate) and the loan rate is often much wider in LDCs than in developed countries. Unless market imperfections are attenuated significantly, the financial system will not be in a position to offer a real interest rate on deposits which is near the rate of return to capital. McKinnon has underestimated the high transitional cost of his policy package arising from imperfections of the financial system, which have deferred, if not eliminated, the expected benefits (Roe, 1982). An assessment of the McKinnon type of liberalisation policies must therefore focus on the costs of liberalisation as well as on the costs of financial retardation (Khatkhate, 1982).

II

The tension between the objective of stability and developmental imperatives manifests itself even more starkly when dealing with the broader aspects of economic stabilisation policies in LDCs. As observed earlier, the financial policies emerging from the liberalists' perception of developing countries are concerned primarily with functioning of the financial sector and only at second remove with developments in the real economy, such as balance of payments, output and prices. But the financial policies associated with economic stabilisation cover a wider area and embrace measures directed toward reaching macroeconomic goals such as a sustained improvement in the balance of payments and containment of inflationary pressures.[2] The

---

2. In the words of one of the early designers of stabilisation programmes, stabilisation policies aim at "a suitable relationship between resource availability and needs that cause minimum strain on the internal price level and produces a desired balance of payments result" (Robichek, 1967: 1–2).

rationale for these policies stems from the macroeconomic theory of open economies developed over the period 1950–1970 (Khan and Knight, 1982). However, the relevance of these policies has been questioned by LDCs or their protagonists. LDCs, it is argued, are not in a position to escape in one leap from the problems of adverse balance of payments and inflation as they must readjust the structure of their economies through time. The gap in their balance of payments is due to the investment requirements of their economies which necessitate a deliberate shift in the composition of aggregate demand to promote fixed capital formation. In other words, balance-of-payments deficit is endemic to LDCs. If so, an important distinction has to be drawn between the level of aggregate demand and its composition (Khan and Knight, 1982; Guitian, 1981). Furthermore, the factors causing economic disturbances in LDCs which widen the balance-of-payments deficit are generally exogenous (Dell, 1980). All this implies that the stabilisation policies which aim at curtailing aggregate demand in fact accentuate rather than alleviate the problems of LDCs. Thus, again, the aims of stability and development conflict.

However, the evidence is mixed, neither leaning unequivocally toward the developmental lobby nor the stabilisation advocates. First of all, there is substantial truth in the arguments of those who attribute the current account deficits of developing countries to exogenous factors such as deterioration of terms of trade. Khan and Knight demonstrate this for the period 1973–1980 (Khan and Knight, 1982). At the same time, internal factors, such as distortion-accentuating interventionist policies, have contributed to worsening of the situation. Since stabilisation policies have adverse consequences for output growth and employment in the short run, as demonstrated again by Khan and Knight, it may be asked whether the use of familiar stabilisation policies can be considered to be misplaced. There are two strands of thought on this issue. One, espoused in the 1950s by the school of 'structuralists' and now appearing in a new form, is that conventional stabilisation policies with a full panoply of instruments—such as exchange rate variation, monetary restriction and other associated measures—tend to have perverse effects. This view is articulated by Porter and Ranney (1982). Tracing these effects to the distinguishing characteristics of LDC economies, Porter and Ranney state that:

> ... the traditional stabilisation policies have very different, and generally less desirable, effects in LDCs than in advanced country models. Most notably, contractionary policy is likely to fuel rather than dampen inflationary tendencies. But there are other awkwardnesses, three of which merit attention. First, it is difficult to attack balance-of-payments crises except through serious recession to cut back import demand. Second, all macro policies have effects on the government budget and the balance of payments,

which affect the monetary base. This, in turn, severely limits policymakers' ability to alter economic conditions in more than the very short run. Third, most restrictive policy is likely to worsen the income distribution.

The empirical evidence is not generally supportive of the "stabilisation pessimism" of Porter and Ranney.[3] Somewhat more encouraging conclusions, better reflecting the reality in LDCs, are reached by several 'stabilisation optimists", even though their formulation is not necessarily in the conventional mould. To the extent that external factors contribute to the disturbance in the economy, demand restraint should certainly have salutary effects on the economy, though it is necessary to know how short is the period during which adjustments have to be made. If developmental imperatives are strong in relation to stability, a time-frame of adjustment should be chosen to ensure that the long-term goals of development are not impaired by any short-term loss of output and employment (Dornbusch, 1982). It needs to be reiterated that stabilisation policies should not be equated only with demand management policies. There is an increasing awareness that "... short-term demand-oriented adjustment programs are frequently not well suited to the structural characteristics and problems of developing countries" (Khan and Knight, 1982). The consensus is veering strongly toward policies which would change aggregate real domestic supply. This, of course, presumes the availability of adequate financing to bridge the time during which supply responses can be evoked.

III

In contrast to demand-side policies, supply-side policies are concerned primarily with increasing the domestic supply of real goods and services rather than influencing aggregate nominal domestic demand (Crockett, 1981; Khan and Knight, 1982). Supply-side stabilisation policies have two dimensions. The first relates to augmenting the availability of domestic goods and services through increasing the efficiency of the use of factors of production, while the second relates to enhancing the long-run rate of growth of full capacity output. The distinction between these two aspects of supply-side policies warrants a difference in measures to be adopted in the supply-side oriented stabilisation programmes. The efficiency of the use of factors of production, which is usually reduced by pricing, exchange rate and tax-subsidy policies, can

---

3. For an economy suffering from balance-of-payments deterioration and inflationary pressure, it is necessary to consider the consequences stemming from the absence or postponement of stabilisation policies and to compare those with the effects of the pursuit of stabilisation policies.

be increased by financial measures which do not in essence differ from those adopted in a demand-oriented stabilisation programme. To that extent it is not possible to draw a sharp line between supply-side-oriented and demand-side-oriented stabilisation policies. But there is a qualitative difference in the measures available to stimulate long-run rate of growth of full capacity output; these measures include policies, e.g. to induce saving and investment, raise the supply of skilled labour, and expand the use of technology, which have a more microeconomic character.

While a shift in favour of supply-side policies in stabilisation programmes is to be greatly welcomed, it is necessary to be precise in interpreting supply-side economics, particularly because it means different things to different people. Supply-side economics as currently practised in the United States is overly biased toward a drastic reduction in government expenditure and taxation and restoring the reign of market forces in determining the growth and composition of output (Gilder, 1981). The supply-side policies of the Kennedy era had, however, a different connotation. The marginal rate of taxation on personal income was reduced, but taxes as a proportion of government revenue as well as GNP were, in fact increased. Government expenditure on defence was reduced, but not in the aggregate. As a result, there was a shift in the public savings along with a sharp simultaneous expansion of investment activity in the private sector (Heller, 1981).

When one comes to LDCs, supply-side policies are supposed to have a different connotation. In these economies, private investment and public investment both need to grow together. Indeed, the former is itself heavily dependent on the public investment programme because of the presence of externalities. Public saving in turn is critically dependent on the magnitude of the tax effort, which necessitates a steadily rising ratio of tax receipts to GDP. Unless this fine distinction between measures to be applied in LDCs and advanced countries is properly grasped, ill-conceived supply-side-oriented stabilisation policies in LDCs may entail costs which may more than offset the benefits expected from these applications.

REFERENCES

Brown, W.W. and G.J. Santoni (1981). "Unreal estimates of the real rate of interest", *Federal Reserve Bank of St. Louis Review* (January).

Coates, W. and D. Khatkhate (1980). *Money and Monetary Policy in Less Developed Countries: Survey of Issues and Evidence.* Oxford: Pergamon Press.

Crockett, Andrew D. (1981). "Stabilisation policies in developing countries: some policy considerations". *IMF Staff Papers*, 28(1): 21–38.

Dasgupta, P., A.K. Sen and S. Marglin (1972). *Guidelines for Project Evaluation.* New York: UNIDO.

Dell, Sidney (1980). "The international environment for adjustment in developing countries", *World Development*, Vol. 8 (November).

Dornbusch, R. (1982). "The international environment for adjustment in developing countries", *World development* 10(9): 784–97.

Fry, M.J. (1982). "Models of financially repressed developing economies", *World Development*, 10(9): 761–83.

Galbis, Vicente (1979). "Theoretical aspects of interest rate policies in less developed countries", *IMF* (unpublished).

Gilder, George (1981). *Wealth and Poverty.* New York: Basic Books.

Goldsmith, Raymond W. (1969). *Financial Structure and Development.* New Haven: Yale University.

Guitian, Manuel (1981). "Economic management and Fund conditionality", paper presented at the IMF/ODI Seminar on the Third World and Global Payments Problems.

Heller, Walter (1981). "Kennedy's supply-side economics", *Challenge* 24(2) (May/June).

Khan, Mohsin S. and Malcolm D. Knight (1982). "Some theoretical and empirical issues relating to economic stabilization in developing countries", *World Development* 10(9).

Khatkhate, Deena R. (1982). "Anatomy of financial retardation in a less developed country: the case of Sri Lanka", 1951–1976. *World Development* 10(9).

—————. (1980). "False issues in the debate on interest rate policies in less developed countries", *Banca Nazionale del Lavoro Quarterly Review* (June).

Leite, Sergio Pereira (1982). "Interest rate policies in West Africa", *IMF Staff Papers.* 19(1) (March).

Little, I.M.D. and J.A. Mirrlees (1968). *Manual of Industrial Project Analysis in Developing Countries, Vol. II.* Paris: Development Centre of OECD.

Patrick, Hugh T. (1966). "Financial development and economic growth in underdeveloped countries", *Economic Development and Cultural Change* XIV (January); also appeared in Warren L. Coats, Jr. and Deena R. Khatkhate (eds.) (1980). *Money and Monetary Policy in Less Developed Countries.* Oxford: Pergamon Press.

Porter, Richard C. and Susan I. Ranney (1982). "An eclectic model of recent LDC macroeconomic policy analysis". *World Development* 10(9).

Robichek, Walter E. (1967). "Financial programming exercises of the International Monetary Fund in Latin America", address to a seminar of Brazilian Professors of Economics, Rio de Janeiro, 20 September.

Roe, Alan R. (1982). "High interest rates: a new conventional wisdom for development policy? Some conclusions from Sri Lankan experience", *World Development* 10(3): 211–22 (March).

Tanzi, Vito and Mario I. Blejer (1982). "Inflation, interest rate policy, and currency substitutions in developing economies: some major issues", *World Development* 10(9).

Tobin, James (1978). "Monetary policies and the economy: the Franciscan mechanism", *Cowles Foundation Paper, 462.* New Haven: Yale University.

Published in World Development 10(9): 689–94 (1982).

The author thanks his colleague Charles Collyns, who commented without committing himself to the errors, on an earlier version of this paper.

6

Financial Liberalisation

International and National Perspectives

It gives me great pleasure to address this august body of bank economists on the subject not only of intellectual excitement but also of practical necessity at the present stage of national economic development. For me personally, it is a dream opportunity in more than one sense. As a callow youth on the edge of an uncertain career, I was inducted on the board of the Saraswat Cooperative Bank, which sponsored my presence here today. That accidental beginning into banking domain turned into an enduring, educative and enthralling odyssey, which carried me first to the Reserve Bank and then onto many other institutions in a global space, engaged in the management of finance. A sheer diversity of experiences in different cultural milieus and exposure to the gleaming streams of knowledge and ideas taught me one important lesson that adherence to constancy of views is a veritable infirmity of mind. One must always be on the lookout for 'how many doors are open to me' sort of situations and exploit opportunities that come one's way as a result, to enrich the mind so as to be able to harmonise the disturbing changes flowing from modernity with the noble purpose of traditions. I am emphasising this aspect of my experience not least because my reflections on financial liberalisation might be prejudged as being contaminated by my association with the international financial institutions such as the IMF and the World Bank, which incidentally was adduced by the organisers of this conference as the main justification for inviting me here. There is a widely held view in this country that these international institutions are the finance gnomes out to intellectually enslave the countries to whom they provide resources and the associated policy advice. While one cannot deny that their advice can at times be annoying and sanctimonious, it is necessary to see it in the context of a given country situation. If the advice is different from what needs to be done to take India from its economic dystopia, by all means it should be thrown on a dump hill. But if not, then it is in the country's own interest to accept it without frown and its people should not fret with fury because it came from outside. To do otherwise would be the supreme national hubris, which already has damaged the Indian economic and social progress over the last three decades.

A cynical political commentator once said that what one stands for depends upon where one sits. I hope you would not identify me with that strawman after listening to my thoughts on financial liberalisation and its rationale. For good or evil, my approach to these issues has been evolved both through my work in this area, embracing a large number of developing countries across all continents and the inductive logical process which avoids ideological trappings. If some aspects of it conform to the policies of the international organisations, so be it. But there are many areas where my ideas diverge substantially from received doctrines, wherever they reign. That means I prefer pragmatism in the best sense of the term—that which is useful is real.

The Indian economy today stands at the crossroads of history. The direction it will choose from now on will determine not only its own future but also its locus in the competitive world economy shaped by the technologically advancing economies and the resurgent developing countries in Asia and Latin America which are pulling themselves out of the rut with radical reform policies to get on the high road of economic progress. The year 1991, when India was launched on an economic reform trajectory, marked a watershed in its history in the same way as 1951 did when planning was accepted for achieving the economic goals. Yet, these two watershed years differ significantly from each other. The beginning of the planning era in 1951 was under the most auspicious and euphoric circumstances of firm and visionary political leadership, stable and efficient administrative apparatus, absence of a haunting record of failure of past policies, and a hopeful though uncertain future. In contrast, 1991 was the year when the Indian economy edged to the precipice, with the wages of past failed policies due to be paid, a faltering, feeble and myopic political leadership, loss of moral timbre and social upheaval, all of which made the country hostage to the charity, indulgence and pity of the industrial countries. The change in the format of economic policies in 1991 therefore was not either self-propelled or self-designed. It was a *pisaller* for India in a state of desperation. To the credit of the present government, it must be conceded that the policies it adopted were bold and far-reaching in their implications and showed promise that could well lead to a turnaround in the economy to achieve competitive enterprise and efficiency of production, if only they do not take twists and turns midway, as often happened in the past.

Financial reform, or what is also known as financial liberalisation, is a penumbra of economic reform. Indeed, reform of the economy—its agricultural and industrial sector and the foreign trade sector—cannot progress unless it is leavened by the elixir of financial liberalisation. A hallmark of economic reform is retreat of mindless government intervention in economic activity so that the market forces rather than discretionary and arbitrary bureaucratic decisions dictate the choice of industries, the mode of production, trading activity, and a host of other economic enterprises. The same forces have to prevail in the financial sector, if it is to respond to the liberalised real sectors of the economy. If, for instance, the decisions to lend by the financial institutions are taken on the basis of criteria different from those governing the liberalised real sector, the reforms of the real sector would not deliver. It is for this reason that financial liberalisation or a less interventionist financial system should become an indispensable part of the overall economic reform policy.

However, there is no unanimity about whether a less interventionist financial system can be a panacea for improving the efficiency and growth of the real sectors. It is argued, and not without logic and persuasiveness, that in some of the most successful industrial and developing countries, such as Japan, Korea and Taiwan, intervened financial sectors not only did not stymie the progress of their economies, but promoted them to become economic giants through correcting market failure situations. If these interventions have succeeded there, the argument proceeds, there is no reason why those policies should not be replicated in developing countries like India. This question is certainly not a rhetoric and undeniably contains truth, but it is not the whole truth. Interventionist policies have been tried by almost all developing countries from Argentina, Chile, Mexico and others in Latin America, where economists of the 'structuralist' school held sway until the end of the 1970s, to India, Pakistan, Bangladesh, and Indonesia in Asia, to Tanzania, Zambia and several others in Africa. The question to ask then is why it is that the interventionist policies failed in those countries and succeeded only in Korea, Japan and Taiwan. If one follows a logical method of analysis, one should be able to conclude that in the success or failure of financial policies the presence or absence of government intervention is not a determining factor. There has been something daunting in the situation of Japan, Korea and Taiwan and something missing in other countries with the failed financial systems. And that 'missing link' is none other than the market forces which made the sectors favoured through intervention earn their keep. In the successful countries credit was allocated to the preferred sectors at subsidised rates, interest rates were regulated, but care was taken to see that the favoured sectors were exposed to competition particularly from foreign countries. If they failed in these markets, they were immediately ticked off the list. In countries with the interventioned financial systems which failed, the sectors to which credit was provided at subsidised rates were insulated from the market forces so much so that they continued their cosy existence, draining away the precious resources from the worthy and productive sectors. This raises the question about what should be the real meaning of financial liberalisation. I, for one, would not over emphasise the absence of government intervention as the distinguishing feature of financial liberalisation. Rather, it is the presence of competition, be it in regard to lending or borrowing, which should constitute the main core of financial liberalisation policies. If competitiveness and government intervention could somehow cohabit, all power to government intervention. But if they do not, then wisdom lies in doing away with government intervention in the financial system and in substituting it with policies which will directly create competitive conditions in the credit market, benefiting both the users and lenders of funds.

Recognising this, most of the countries in Asia and Latin America and a few in Africa veered round in recent years to policies directed to release their financial system from the stifling regulations. In order to lend an international perspective to the Indian approach to the problems and policies of the financial system, I would like to take you on a guided tour of some of the important Asian and Latin American countries which embarked on financial liberalisation experiment during the 1980s. Their experiences underscore both the strength and weaknesses of their actions and may help us in India to know the dos and don'ts in pursuit of financial liberalisation policies. There are a large number of countries which have liberalised their financial systems but here I have been selective in picking up eight countries—five Asian countries, Korea, Malaysia, Indonesia, the Philippines, and Sri Lanka, and three Latin American countries, Chile, Argentina and Uruguay. They are representative enough to yield some general lessons which can be learnt by others who want to follow their path now or in future.

A striking fact that emerges from the experiences of these countries is that consequences of financial reform across these countries lacked uniformity and a question is whether their divergence was related to differences in the approach and modality of the reforms undertaken. Of the five countries in Asia, South Korea and Malaysia both exhibit the beneficial impact of financial liberalisation but for different reasons. The main emphasis in South Korea's financial reform policies was on gradualness in the speed of reform; government intervention was made purposive and market-oriented. Furthermore, the thrust of the reform policies was directed toward the non-banking sector, which was relatively late to arrive in South Korea and was much less regulated to begin with. In contrast, liberalisation of the banking sector was much slower. In addition, care was taken to continue the controls on the capital account, which rendered interest rate arbitrage relatively difficult. Consequently, domestic influence on interest rate determination remained much stronger than foreign influences. Progress in orienting the financial sector to competitive conditions without abandoning government intervention was made concurrent with positive macroeconomic developments such as a favourable turn in the terms of trade, stable inflation, a declining deficit in the current account of the balance of payments and a lower fiscal deficit. The interaction between the macro and micro aspects of economic policy strengthened both. One feature of South Korea's financial reform experiment, which contrasts with those in other countries, was what the Korean authorities accomplished in regard to the banking system's non-performing loans. It became apparent in the early part of the 1980s that the already large size of non-performing loans was expanding and threatened the survival of the banking system. The authorities did not force the pace of reform but in fact retracted it by (a) providing low-cost funds through prompt downward adjustment in bank's nominal interest rates as inflation began to decelerate and, (b) taking determined steps toward corporate financial structuring. Thus, the authorities bought time until economic recovery was well on its way. By following this pragmatic approach, South Korea succeeded not only in strengthening the macroeconomic environment which had already benefited from vigorous adjustment policies in force, but also in avoiding unfavourable fallout from the reform.

Malaysia, on the other hand, succeeded in its main object of financial reform, though its approach and its macroeconomic conditions were different. Malaysia's so-called reform, unlike South Korea's, was confined to those banks whose interest rates were freed from prevailing restrictions; there were no controls on interest rates of finance companies, the capital account was free, and competition among banks was intense. Government intervention was minimal and there was pervasive market determination of interest rates and other financial transactions even prior to interest rate deregulation. In a way, the financial reform in Malaysia was only a continuation of the well-established tradition of minimal interference with the financial system. Despite unfavourable macroeconomic developments—here too, the contrast with South Korea is striking—of adverse terms of trade, large fiscal and external accounts deficits, Malaysia maintained the momentum of its financial liberalisation without untoward consequences largely because of a stable inflation rate. It did not escape a rising burden of bad and doubtful debts, a consequence mainly of the severe economic recession which coincided with interest rate deregulation, but they were not as burdensome as in South Korea for a variety of reasons, and the banking system could live with them without much difficulty. For one thing, nominal interest rates did not escalate as much as elsewhere, though real interest rates remained high and even inched up slightly due to the stable inflation rate. Second, the financial structure of the corporate sector was less sensitive to interest rate changes because of a low debt/equity ratio compared to that in South Korea, the Philippines, and Indonesia. Third, the banking system had a very low level of bad and doubtful debts to start with because of the Central Bank's effective supervision and because the banks had autonomy in determining loan allocation before and after the reform. Malaysia, thus, could maintain vigorous expansion of its financial sector, deepening and widening it, with a policy of pronounced market orientation.

The Philippines and Indonesia present quite different visages of reform. The dismantling of interventionist regimes was telescoped and was even more far reaching in the context of capital mobility. At the start of the liberalisation programmes, the Philippine and Indonesian financial sectors reacted well to the phasing out of government intervention, as seen in the attainment of positive real interest rates and faster growth of the financial sector. But macroeconomic developments turned sharply adverse for both countries. The Philippines was enfeebled by the second oil shock at the end of the 1970s, political turmoil, and a balance of payments crisis. In late 1983 the situation deteriorated further with the freezing of foreign credit, severe import compression leading to a decline in investment, and a consequent deep recession. Government intervention became imperative to bail out several banks and to take over some private commercial banks. The situation continued until 1985. A similar pattern of events took place in Indonesia. Because the fiscal and balance of payments deficits remained large, persistent expectations of rupiah depreciation kept domestic real interest rates intolerably high. Thus, both in the Philippines and Indonesia, the high level of real interest rates greatly aggravated the vulnerability of the financial system, particularly due to the highly leveraged corporate financial structure, and the size of non-performing loans ballooned.

In Indonesia, the financial crisis was more or less of the same intensity as in the Philippines. First of all, in the wake of general liberalisation, nominal and real interest rates rose sharply. Though inflation remained stable after reform, expectation of currency depreciation raised the expectation of inflationary pressures, which added to the high level of real interest rates. Naturally, business firms groaned under the heavy burden of high interest rates and the high rates in turn adversely affected the loan portfolios of banks. The profitability of financial institutions was affected in two ways. The magnitude of problem loans reduced the average return on bank assets, and new avenues for lending shrivelled. On the other hand, rapid growth of high-interest deposits raised the banks' costs and squeezed profits. Second, the state banks, which dominated the financial scene and accounted for about 70 per cent of all loans, bore the major brunt of non-performing loans. By virtue of their ownership, they had preferential access to captive deposits from public entities and liquidity credits from Bank Indonesia. This enabled them to wield excessive power in the loan market without having to put in efforts to mobilise deposits. With such monopoly power, there was no compelling need for banks to discard outdated operational practices or improve the management of their loan portfolios. Even where competition prevailed, as in the other sectors of the financial system, it had a deleterious impact on the banking system's soundness because small and average-sized banking units indulged excessively in deposit-mobilising activities by offering very high nominal interest rates even though they could not use those funds for profitable loan operations. Third, one of the offshoots of financial deregulation was that with the shortening of the average maturity of bank's time deposits, presumably because the volatility of interest rates dissuaded depositors from holding long-term deposits, the banks could not continue to extend longer-term credit and starved the economy of investment finance even more than before the financial reform.

Sri Lanka's liberalisation regime was comprehensive and embraced all sectors of the economy, though in contrast to the Philippines and Indonesia deregulation of the financial sector was more limited and gradual. The main reform of the financial sector was the removal of interest rate ceilings and watering down of the selective credit programmes. However, the full effects of liberalisation were not as beneficial as expected because they were offset by external and internal shocks beyond the control of the authorities. But unlike South Korea and Malaysia and far from easing the impact of the shocks through appropriate adjustments in the macroeconomic policies, Sri Lanka in fact thwarted its liberalisation strategy by following a dissonant macroeconomic policy. However, the consequences for the financial system were not as severe as in the Philippines or even Indonesia. Non-performing loans no doubt increased, but they did not reach the relative dimensions seen in the Philippines and Indonesia, owing to Sri Lanka's strict adherence to prudential regulations.

Financial liberalisation in the Southern Cone countries in Latin America—Argentina, Chile and Uruguay—was a different kettle of fish. The experiment, though well intended, went awry for several reasons. First of all, financial liberalisation was initiated in an unstable macroeconomic environment which was made even worse by inconsistencies in macroeconomic policy. In addition, the way financial reforms were designed and implemented contributed to financial disequilibrium and thus magnified macroeconomic disturbances. Second, it was not realised that financial liberalisation in imperfect and oligopolistic financial markets had certain inherent limitations. Therefore, when control on interest rates was eliminated and the operations of financial institutions were freed from government intervention, the outcome was distasteful. Real interest rates were extremely high in relation to marginal rates of return on capital in all the three countries. As a result, firms were involved in financial difficulties which in turn created a crisis in the financial system and engulfed their economies in a crisis. Third, abolition of restrictions on the capital account was clearly premature. With macroeconomic imbalances as severe as ever—Chile was an exception—freedom of capital movement proved to be disequilibrating insofar as it generated expectations of further currency devaluation, which in turn raised domestic interest rates even further. Finally, the crucial importance of supervision of the financial institutions was virtually overlooked. Financial liberalisation was mistakenly equated with elimination of the most essential regulations required to maintain sensitive credit institutions on an even keel. The latitude so given was used by the oligopolistic banking firms to jack up the interest rates and intensify a scramble for new deposits even when loans were failing.

Looking back at the attempts of these countries to liberalise their financial system it is possible for us in India to learn and unlearn about the intricacies of management of micro- and macro-financial policies, unless of course we are 'knowledge proof', as Raj Krishna characterised the Indian intellectuals. The one major outcome in most of the countries was the financial crisis that followed implementation of the policy of financial liberalisation. The question is whether it was endemic in the policy itself. Financial crisis in these countries descended when government intervention in economic activity could not be continued any longer without macroeconomic imbalances. The moment government protection was withdrawn, industry and trade put on respirators so long collapsed, causing all-round insolvency problems. This had ricocheting repercussions on the financial system whose non-performing loans rebounded. Thus, the real cause of the financial crisis was in the prolongation of the inefficient economic policies in general beyond the tolerable limits.

Notwithstanding the overstay of interventionist regime in these countries, which ultimately spawned the financial crises, it is also a well-substantiated observation that the design and sequencing of financial liberalisation strategy in several countries were contributory factors. The rationale for financial reform is based on a valid premise that macroeconomic imbalances can be eliminated over time through operation of a competitive financial system. If that is so, two questions arise: (a) whether financial reform should be initiated when the macroeconomic imbalances predominate or wait for stabilisation before they are unleashed; and (b) whether the financial liberalisation policy itself becomes an instrument to accentuate macroeconomic imbalances. The gravitas of evidence favours the view that the way financial liberalisation was conceptualised in many of these countries adversely affected the macroeconomic outcome and, therefore, brought about financial crises or aggravated their severity.

This implies that gradualism could be a virtue in designing a financial liberalisation policy for several reasons. First, increased freedom of entry into the financial sector and greater latitude to bid for funds through interest rates and new financial instruments could lead to excessive risk taking, and deregulation could facilitate too rapid growth of some financial institutions and allow unqualified persons to enter into financial business. Second, the institutional structure of the banking system emerging from deregulatory changes could lead to a concentration of power in banking, interlocking ownership and lending pattern. Such an environment is particularly vulnerable to market failures. Third, deregulation may well result in excessive increase in interest rates if euphoric expectations coupled with unsound liability structures of firms cause a sharp increase in credit demand: with high debt/equity ratios, an initial increase in real interest rates, among other things, could lead to distress borrowing and hence fairly inelastic demand for credit, which could perpetuate the high interest rates. Its corollary that in the deregulatory environment, the interest rates would find their true equilibrium value or that they would automatically tend to converge to international rates over time is also falsified by the experiences in these countries. All this clearly demonstrates that financial liberalisation policies, though highly desirable and necessary on the ground of efficiency, have no unique path nor do they fall in a neat category of quantity theory dogmata, which has been a favourite hunting ground of economists, particularly of the IMF.

Though what I have been saying about financial liberalisation and financial crisis is largely derived from the experiences of the countries I mentioned earlier, I must caution that these conclusions may not hold good for the financial liberalisation experiment going on in Eastern Europe and the Commonwealth of Independent States. Though overtly the problem of bank solvency, high interest rates and monetary overhang look alike as between the developing countries and the transition economies, it will be a gross mistake to treat them as identical. Otherwise, economic policymakers will reach the same intellectual *cul de sac* as they did in the case of Latin American countries earlier. Bank insolvency in Eastern Europe is not a product of malpractice on the part of bank officials in the past but the result of a radical change in the economic environment in the countries concerned. As two young economists of the IMF, Daniel Hardy and Ashok Lahiri have argued in their stimulating paper,

> Banks in the former Socialist system were relatively large, on-going institutions which provided transaction services centered to household's life cycle savings pattern, and financed investments according to the diktat of the central plan; the past bank contracts were not written to suit the new circumstances. The reforms have generated a situation where the depositor's continuing claims on banks are no longer backed by the repayment capacities of the bank's debtors. Failure to arrive at a comprehensive resolution of this divergence between depositor's claims and bank's payment liabilities over the medium term can jeopardise the system of financial intermediation and may lead to a financial collapse. (From the draft of their paper in 1990, "Bank Insolvency and Stabilization in Eastern Europe", which was subsequently published as *IMF Staff Papers*, 39(4): 229–53.)

One of the most important lessons to be drawn from financial liberalisation across countries is that price stability and, more broadly, macroeconomic stability, is the linchpin of successful liberalisation, not the deregulation of interest rates *per se*, especially when the countries undergoing financial reforms have shallow financial markets. The experiences of the Philippines and Malaysia and the Southern Cone countries underscore the importance of price stability in two different ways. In the first two countries, the level of inflation was a determining factor in attaining positive interest rates. The adjustment in real interest rates lagged when inflation was declining, although the interest rates were fully liberalised. The resulting high interest rates may lead to widespread insolvency of firms with high gearing ratios, as in Indonesia, or to an economy on a downward slope, as in the Philippines. In South Korea, however, although interest rates were administered by the government, interest rates were substantially positive and stable because of price stability and the flexibility with which nominal interest rates were adjusted according to the movement of inflation. At the other extreme, in the Southern Cone countries inconsistent macroeconomic policies rendered their economic system unstable and vulnerable to shocks, and their economies did not prove congenial to the whiff of financial liberalisation policies.

Among the Asian countries, the experiences of Indonesia and the Philippines reflect the two-way effects of the macro environment and financial reforms on each other. Indonesia's macroeconomic imbalances were severe when reforms were initiated, but they were corrected initially after the reform. However, its troubles were later accentuated when continually high domestic interest rates led to an increasing loan default rate. In the Philippines, macro and microeconomic policies combined to accentuate the financial crisis.

When capital movement is completely free in an economy where the financial market is relatively small, liberalisation of domestic interest rates makes them very sensitive to the pressures of expectations of foreign exchange movement. This often leads to volatile and high domestic interest rates, which may significantly diverge from the long-run equilibrium level. On the other hand, if a government attempts to control domestic interest rates, it may risk massive capital flight. The best approach, may be to achieve a stable macroeconomic environment which will eliminate any abrupt changes in expectations about exchange rate movement. When this is not possible, a country with a small and vulnerable financial market may choose a second-best approach of continuing some restrictions on the capital account and maintaining interest rates.

Financial liberalisation centred on the banking system has limitations. These are related to an important feature of banking institutions, i.e. that the banking sector performs both the monetary and the financial intermediation function. These two functions do not work in the same direction, especially when macroeconomic imbalances arise. Often, the growth of liabilities and assets of the banking system is constrained by a tight monetary policy. When the financial liberalisation policy is pursued concurrently with a stabilisation policy, the intended goal of the policy, to enhance the financial intermediation role of banks, is weakened by the monetary policy directed toward containing inflation.

The second feature of the banking system stems from the banks' debt intermediation function whereby short-term fixed-fee liabilities (deposits) are transformed into long-term fixed-fee assets (loans). This function places banks at the risk of runs and insolvencies in the absence of appropriate government supervision and regulation. In addition, the dominance of debt intermediation in the financial markets makes corporate firms when they are highly leveraged vulnerable to economic downturns and increases in interest rates. This has continuously called for some kind of government intervention in bank-oriented financial systems. This should not be taken to imply that a policy of financial liberalisation is not a good policy. The point is that a complete liberalisation of the banking system when inflation is high and variable has severe limitations. The resulting high level of real interest rates, when banks are the only financial intermediaries, leads to adverse selection in the quality of borrowers and in the banks' own behaviour and these problems assume a serious proportion when the monetary authorities attempt to impose a stringent monetary contraction.

Financial liberalisation assumes that the fully liberalised financial system will function optimally. However, it should be recognised that in economies which have a long history of financial repression the participating actors, be they bank managers, borrowers, lenders or public servants, are not trained in new ways of dealing with a liberal and competitive system. In the case of Chile, some of the blame for a disastrous financial crisis resided in little experience existing in the country in the management of a freer financial system. Inability to size up risk and lack of capacity to cope with adverse situations prevented the liberalisation programme from succeeding to the desired extent. If, on the other hand, these policies were unleashed gradually, those at the helm of the financial institutions and others associated with them in some capacity would have adjusted and become familiar with these new tasks over time.

Closely related to the above is the need to set up a well-planned financial infrastructure with provision for information flow, legal and accounting systems and an appropriate regulatory system to monitor it carefully and continuously. Otherwise, financial liberalisation will fail in its main purpose— to orient the financial system toward greater efficiency, competition and effectiveness. In the case of banks, it is not always possible to distinguish a necessary control for monetary stability purposes from a supernumerary regulation affecting credit allocation, but it is imperative that essential regulation be strictly enforced because of the oligopolistic nature of the banking system in several developing countries. It is now generally acknowledged that there is widespread concentration of banking in developing countries. What is more, in some countries like Chile, the bank holding company structure is more prominent and adversely affects competition, in opposition to the avowed objective of financial liberalisation and deregulation. In the presence of such oligopolistic financial and industrial structures, freedom in transactions is often harnessed to increase the market share by price war. Loans are provided to the interlocking firms in which banks have close interest; high interest rates thus do not affect credit demand. This encourages banks to be even more imprudent because they know that the government cannot allow them to go bankrupt without jeopardising the entire monetary system. There is thus a moral hazard which provides incentive to banks to lend at very high interest rates in order to reduce liquidity strains. This underscores the need to strengthen the supervisory apparatus in liberalising countries so that banks are disciplined in mobilising deposit and lending operations.

There is no gainsaying that financial liberalisation is overdue in India as the Indian banking system has been caught in a vice for much too long. While I for one would not denigrate the promotional policies pursued by the government in the early 1950s, which contributed to the diversified banking system as we see today, I would at the same time not overlook the pernicious consequences arising from the overstretching of that policy, which brought the banking system to its present sorry pass, thereby making good an aphorism of 'nothing fails like excess'. If what is seen is taken as real, the Indian banking system could be considered to have made rapid strides since 1969 when it took on a social banking character following the nationalisation of banks. Deposits as a proportion of GDP ballooned from 14.5 per cent to 40 per cent in 1992. The ratio of financial assets to GDP has now reached 47 per cent, which is not attained even by Korea. The level of nominal interest rates, which were negative most of this period 1960–1970s rose to yield positive real interest rates even with the interventionist approach to interest rate determination. In terms of allocation of credit, the priority sectors now account for almost 40 per cent of credit outstanding as compared to barely 10 per cent in 1968. Branch expansion spatially into the rural hinterland, which was one of the avowed objectives of the nationalisation policy, has taken the total number of branches to a staggering figure of over 60,000 as against a mere 2000 in 1968. And yet those responsible for laying the foundations of a financial system may be mistaking age for health. In many ways Indian banking policy is a mirror image of Indian fiscal policy. Both have performed well in the mobilisation of resources, but unless the mobilised resources are utilised with efficiency and prudence not only is the purpose of mobilisation vitiated but the source of expansion of future resources will also dry up. In the case of banking, take first the case of priority sector. Loans to the small-scale industrial sector are bandied about as the hallmark of social banking. But on the Reserve Bank's own reckoning, as many as 200,000 amongst them are sick and many of the others are about to be so sooner or later. These together with the sick non-small industries may well account for as much as around 20 per cent of total outstanding credit.

The precise financial position of a bank is known only to the supervisory department of the Reserve Bank. But one can roughly divine it on the basis of official information from diverse sources. Around 20–22 per cent of the outstanding bank credit has lapsed into non-performing category. In regard to credit to agriculture, which became a target of competitive policies, what with writing off of small loans, about 40–45 per cent of debt service has passed into arrears. If these figures are added up, they would far exceed the capital and reserves of banks, which would normally have spun off into bankruptcy if the Government of India were not their owner. In normal circumstances, banks in India could have offset the losses by building up reserves from profits over the years. However, the return on bank assets has averaged approximately 14–15 per cent, which is about the lowest in Asia and much lower than in the pre-nationalisation period. The way the banking system is allowed to function through the maze of bureaucratic controls and political shenanigans, it is not likely to generate adequate profit now or ever. About 40 per cent of banks' credit or 20 per cent of banks' total assets is assigned to the priority sector involving heavy subsidy and also rising bad debts. The subsidy element of roughly 5 per cent against the average deposit cost of 10 per cent heavily eats into profits. In addition, there is another type of subsidy implicit in the non-recovery of credit, following compromises in lending procedures. The published profits in their books are often a figment of the imagination of bank managers, the Reserve Bank, and the wise men in the banking department of the Government of India. This is because the banks follow 'creative' accounting rather than internationally accepted accounting practices. Thus even when it is claimed that the provisioning is made from profits, the resulting figures are phoney and the published balance sheets are of no more than tinsel value. Furthermore, as much as 53 per cent of bank deposits is locked up in low or non-earning assets such as government bonds and reserve requirements. Had it been possible for banks to make up for low earning on those investments by charging higher rates on non-priority credit, the adverse impact on banks' profitability could have been mitigated. However, there is little scope to raise these rates beyond a point without private sector investment being curtailed.

Slow growth in operating income of banks is only one aspect; the other is the cost escalation on account of increase in staff and its low productivity. India has about 40 per cent more bank employees per million dollars of assets than Pakistan, 150 per cent more than Indonesia, and nearly 300 per cent more than Malaysia. This comparison is only with other developing countries in Asia. If you see India in relation to the industrial countries, India would have the honour of carrying a wooden spoon!

The inefficient banking system in India is also a consequence of the bureaucratisation of bank management. The creation of that bureaucratic monstrosity—the banking department of the Government of India—on the specious ground that the government being the owner has to micro-manage banks has done the greatest disservice to the financial services industry. To begin with, it duplicated the functions which were already being done fairly efficiently until 1969 by the Reserve Bank. With this banking department, the asset management of banks was virtually surrendered to the bureaucrats in Delhi. This resulted in throwing to the winds, all canons of prudent banking. There has been little skill developed to conduct foreign exchange transactions, to deal with consumer banking, and to assess credit-worthiness of bank projects. In the last fifteen years, the banks were made merely to dance to the tune of the banking department. The directors on the bank boards were no more than totems, appointed not for their financial skills or savvy but for their political skulduggery. One of the most pernicious practices that the banking department introduced, was a centralised system of recruitment of staff. Every bank has to absorb the staff selected by the board, over which it has no control. As a consequence, the banker as a professional class has become an extinct species.

With such an inefficient financial system, the government fiddled around for much too long, although it was not unaware of the state of affairs. Its response was to appoint a committee to study the problem when it arises. The Reserve Bank appointed a 'Committee to review the working of the monetary system' in 1983. After expending its labour on investigation, it did not come up with any new insights into the financial system or the concept of deficit financing that were not anticipated in the studies of the Reserve Bank. To cite one example, a major claim of the committee to fame and glory lies in its recommendation that fiscal deficit should be measured as a net Reserve Bank credit to government. But this was no more than reinventing the wheel, as the Reserve Bank's own economists had suggested that concept as far back as 1961 and that too in articles published in the Reserve Bank bulletin. What is galling is that the Chakravarty committee resurrected it two and a half decades later, when its time had long passed with radical changes in the budget arithmetic! Even more amazingly, the committee which was credited with initiating first steps in financial liberalisation put forth as a key recommendation that: "The reliance on the price mechanism should be in addition to and not a substitute for quantitative controls on credit flowing from Plan priorities and the compulsion of demand management." This should truly be applauded as a New Testament on financial liberalisation!

For all the fanfare surrounding the Chakravarty committee, the government almost ignored its recommendations. It scratched here, tinkered there and stretched everywhere but the major domain for banking remained out of its bounds. When new economic reforms were initiated in 1991, the government woke up but instead of formulating an action plan, it reverted to its old habit of appointing a new committee on the financial system to study the same old questions. The committee did not discover new facts or new relations among old facts nor did it come up with logically consistent and economically sound recommendations. While strongly pleading for a competitive banking system driven by market forces, the committee displayed its power of clairvoyance by putting down a precise number of banks the country would have. Thus what it suggested was neither fish of financial liberalisation nor a fowl of a directed financial system. What the committee should have done but did not was to devise a fiscal incentive structure for the financial institutions such that they would be encouraged to move in directions where the broad social objectives of the government could be successfully achieved. This could have ensured real autonomy in the functioning of banks and relinquishing of governmental authority over them. But the committee has shirked the issues. While paying lip service to the doctrine that the government should distance itself from the internal working of banks, it has upheld rather timidly the existing unsavoury practice of nominating government directors on banks' boards. It has not been frank enough to admit that the banking division of the finance ministry is a fifth wheel and should be done away with. On the contrary, the committee justified these practices on the ground of 'proprietary rights'. Surely the committee ought to have realised what the government nominees on the boards end up doing in effect. They do what proprietors are supposed to do—run them as private fiefdoms.

It is high time that the country realises that appointment of committees every time a crisis looms is no solution for its problems. Most of the committee members may be experts but certainly not independent, occupying as they do vantage positions in several financial institutions or the government. Like the communists in India, they cannot forget their past nor stop worrying about their future. If the government and the present finance minister are convinced of the need to liberalise the financial system, they should act and act without any further delay, holding the bull of political opposition and the vested interests by their horns. In broad terms, the authorities should move in three areas with as much speed as possible if the reform in the real sector is not to be thwarted.

First of all, the government should dismantle all the bureaucratic apparatus it has set up for managing the banking system. All regulatory powers should be vested in the Reserve Bank as the pivotal centre of the monetary system. Second, individual banks should be given full autonomy both in regard to management of their assets/liabilities and deployment of their staff. There should be a careful selection of board members drawn from consumer groups, bank depositors, public men of probity and character, and industrialists and traders not tainted with business malpractice. It is for the government to give banks a charter and a detailed one with rights and obligations. If banks are mismanaged, the heads of the chief executives and board members will have to be on the block. Unless the chief executives are involved in fraud or gross negligence of duties, they should be allowed to complete their full term. The banks' management should have full powers to retrench surplus staff, if possible with a golden handshake, to tone up banks' operational efficiency. If this experiment of management accountability within a framework of public ownership fails, the government should be honest enough to speed up privatisation.

The volume of subsidised credit and its misuse have been the real scourge of the banking system. While recognising that elimination of such credit at one fell swoop is politically difficult, the government should take them out from the books of banks and pool them into a special institution. The cost of these credits then would be transparent, and the government's responsibility will be clearly defined.

Thus, the regulations governing allocation of credit and deposits should be liberalised, but in step with the restructuring of the supervisory authority. The buzzword should be that as economic intervention is withdrawn, regulatory intervention should be made to step in. I would draw a sharp distinction between these two kinds of intervention, as they are often confused. Economic intervention and regulatory intervention are based on two different concepts of freedom, which the great philosopher Isaiah Berlin calls a "positive freedom" and a "negative freedom". Under positive freedom, some entity other than the individual decides "what you want or what is good for you". This concept has some virtue but it often leads, as we have seen in a world of interventionist regime, to elimination of choice altogether. Negative freedom does not decide what is good for a member of society but aims at eliminating obstacles to the conditions which ensure that good. But it also permits action to curtail freedom of the individual, if it begins to encroach on the freedom of any other member of society. The regulatory intervention is based on the explicit recognition of Berlin's negative freedom concept. It is not a choice of the banker, depositor, the borrower, or the community at large, but it protects the encroachment by any one of these groups on the freedom of individual choice.

Certain rules of operating a regulatory system without its misdirection can be conceived, both on the basis of practical necessity and economic efficiency. First of all, any policy affecting allocation of resources and regulation of private economic activity needs to be pursued if and only if there is a specified set of procedures or criteria for deciding what fits within the defined scope of the enunciated economic policies as also an administrative apparatus for implementing that policy. Second, it is imperative to limit regulatory intervention to minimum necessary scale because once intervention enters the scene it develops a life of its own, diverting some scarce management skills away from where they have greater comparative advantage. Third, from amongst the available alternative regulatory sets, it is necessary to go in for one which will provide the least scope for rent seeking. Thus the regulatory regime should be such in form, substance, and direction that the fundamental economic determinants of investment are not stifled.

The success or failure of financial reform depends critically on how the Reserve Bank as the head of the banking system would play its leadership role. It is imperative that the Reserve bank's image is radically changed to allow itself to undertake new responsibilities. With its present structure and personnel, it is simply incompetent to do so. It has become flabby and fossilised. It has a staff of some ten thousand people, but the quality of the staff is inversely related to its size. Some of its functions have become superfluous after it shed several of its subsidiaries and yet its higher management continues to be top heavy, involved in make-work projects of one kind or another. Its once hallowed research department has been reduced to a pathetic agency, collecting statistics whose purpose and use are not known to themselves and even this routine task is done unimaginatively. Individually the researchers may be able, but the working environment and the institutional culture are such that it pays them to be routine workers and shirkers.

In terms of new ideas on finance, monetary policy or the exchange rate, the Bank's staff is amazingly unproductive. Though the world outside has changed so much, their thinking has remained insular and opaque. The Bank's supervision department had kept itself abreast in the period prior to 1960 and set some high standards of auditing and integrity. With political interference, these standards have plummeted. The Bank maintains a huge foreign exchange department whose business has dwindled over the years but its chores have multiplied. If the financial liberalisation is set in motion in such a milieu, it will be nothing less than a disaster.

The first step that needs to be taken to reform the Reserve Bank is to give it back its lost pride. The government, in consultation with the opposition, should redefine the Bank's role. The government can assign powers to the Reserve Bank to present an audit to Parliament every quarter, analysing the economic trends and policies in a cohesive and forthright manner and indicating policy options. This would give the Bank enough clout to rein in the irresponsible politicians both in the ruling and opposition parties, while providing full information to the country at large. However, the Reserve Bank cannot undertake this onerous task unless it trims its size, creates a core of high-powered staff and a cost-effective organisational structure.

Three areas are overdue for reforms. First, the focus should be on monetary policy operation and counterpointing of the fiscal policy. With financial liberalisation, there will be growing reliance on the indirect monetary policy instruments and their fine-tuning. The Reserve Bank should have a workable short-term forecasting model, with reference to which it can formulate its policy. Though forecasting is a hazardous task, it is better than mere hunches and second-guessing the politicians' judgement. Second, bank supervision should become the first charge on the Reserve Bank management. The staff should be alert, information system up-to-date and as comprehensive as possible, and action on delinquent banks should be prompt and decisive. Third, the Bank should be asked to simplify foreign exchange controls before they are totally dismantled and pass their administration to the commercial banks; only cases involving policy change could be referred to the Reserve Bank. The Bank would have enough to do about foreign exchange policy and foreign exchange markets.

Most importantly, the Reserve Bank's top-heavy administration should be made lean and efficient. With trimming of functions, the top-heavy administration echelon is a luxury the Reserve Bank can do without. It is time that organisations like the Reserve Bank start giving a chance to the young to have their place in the sun rather than lean on the tired old guard. Experience and age are not necessarily assets. "Experience", as Oscar Wilde said, "is the name they give to their mistakes." Age is the name we give to our follies. The young, who could have a stake in what they do, can think in modern and new ways to face the challenges of the times. Without a thorough reform of the Reserve Bank, the country will only go from regulatory inefficiency to deregulatory incompetence.

Before you come to thinking that the length of my discourse is designed to earn my presence here from a distance of some ten thousand miles, let me hasten to refer to what I consider to be the summum bonum of my talk. Whatever be one's ideological predilections or subjective judgements, the present stark economic reality in India as elsewhere is that it brooks no waffling or hesitancy or pusillanimity when it concerns taking right, prompt and imaginative action. Things are allowed to drift far too long in our country.

Being a nation that revels in talking rather than doing, we allow our past intellectual failings to assail us and our ancient glory to gnaw at us whenever we are required to depart from the path we treaded before. We then postpone action and engage in futile debate. If we find that reform policies have succeeded in other parts of the globe, we promptly proffer one excuse or another to play it down. If Indonesia has achieved startling results through liberalisation, we attribute it to that country having dictatorship, without realising that it had the same type of regime when it was in economic doldrums in the 1960s. If Mexico has emerged triumphant from the labyrinth of economic stagnation through new reform policies, we put it down to its physical proximity to the United States as if the big bang explosion of the universe has taken place in the last ten years to change Mexico's location; if Korea has become a miracle country, we are quick to find its analogue in Punjab which is small sized, without acknowledging that there are scores of small countries in the world still languishing in squalor and poverty. We ascribe our lack of progress to our being the largest democracy as if democracy is antithetical to economic advancement, knowing not that the world's greatest economic power is a democracy with the same pulls and pressures as we experience in India. On the other hand we will point with glee to countries that have failed by adopting policies of economic reform. Here again, we wear blinkers. There have been several failures, but with time and persistence many countries like Argentina, Mexico and Chile have conquered their failures. In short, we as a nation like to invest in failure. I think the time has come for us to learn and unlearn from the successes and failures. The choice before us is a Hobson's choice. We can no longer quibble over whether financial liberalisation is necessary: it is unavoidable in today's world economic environment. When the countries outside are liberating their economic and financial system while we remain staid, we would be the losers. The old regime of trade, industrial and financial regulations has outlived its utility. Capital will flow out through goods and assets arbitrage even if India maintains its old-style economic regulations, as international markets are unified through international and communication technology. We have to see, however, that we do the right things for the right reasons, unlike Captain Queeg of 'The Caine Mutiny' who did all the right things in all the wrong ways. I remember poet T.S. Eliot's delectable line, "The last temptation is the greatest treason: to do the right deed for the wrong reason." It may be the poetic fancy of a great poet but reveals to us a disturbing reality we have ignored for a long time.

Keynote Address at the 16th Bank Economists' Conference on Liberalisation in the Financial Sector, Mumbai, February 1993.

Timing and Sequencing of Financial Sector Reforms
Evidence and Rationale

INTRODUCTION

Financial intermediation refers to the process by which savings of the scattered economic units in an economy are garnered by institutions, often banks in the initial stages of economic development, to make them available to other investing units in the economy. This process becomes necessary and also inevitable when the investing units who use resources to produce output are not always the units which save. Thus, the faster the pace of financial intermediation, the higher the growth potential of the economy.

In the initial stages of growth of the developing countries, it was believed that financial intermediation can be advanced best if governments intervene strongly in the process rather than leave it to market forces, as in the case of several industrial countries. A case for government intervention rested on the presence of 'market failures' in developing economies, which make it difficult for economic agents to take rational decisions to save and to invest. This has led to a multifaceted policy agenda for financial intermediation: interest rates need to be kept lower than market clearing levels; financial institutions have to be necessarily imbued more with social concern than with profit maximisation; credit allocation is to be rather deliberate than market driven; and so on. However, with these measures, financial intermediation, far from advancing, was in fact retarded. They weakened the incentives for savers to hold savings in financial form, as the rate of return was lower than on other non-financial assets. Allocation of resources at the behest of the government rather than in response to profit potential of the projects resulted in inefficiencies in production and dissipation of savings. All these factors created repressed financial systems.

If financial intermediation is to be promoted at a speed, academics as well as policymakers concluded that the best way to accomplish it was to liberalise the financial system from the shackles of government regulations or to eliminate the elements of financial repression. This could be done through vigorous

financial liberalisation policies, first adopted in Latin American countries such as
Chile, Argentina, and Uruguay, and later in East Asian countries such as Korea,
Malaysia, Indonesia, etc. and which now is a universal phenomenon.

The success of countries which have implemented financial reforms has
been uneven, depending upon real sector situations and the financial condition
of the country. Financial liberalisation has many facets: complete deregulation
of interest rates; elimination or softening of directed credits; introduction
of competition through widening the franchise for new domestic or foreign
banks; scaling down of liquidity and reserve ratios; and introduction of
indirect monetary policy instruments. In each of these areas the experiences
of countries which introduced reforms and sustained them have been varied,
and more often quite different from what the theory suggests.

Even countries considered to be shining examples of success, such as South
Korea, Malaysia, Thailand, and Indonesia have come unstuck after a period of
financial development, as evidenced by the sudden eruption of banking and
currency crises in 1997. So much so that there has been a growing tendency to
fasten this crisis to the financial liberalisation policies of the past. This is not
to speak of Latin American countries such as Chile, Argentina, Uruguay, and
Mexico, where the initial impact of financial reforms was totally adverse in
terms of output, inflation, and the financial sector regression.

The question then is whether financial liberalisation should be jettisoned
or a search should be made to identify elements which make for the success of
such policies and to avoid those which contribute to their failure. This question
is crucial for the simple reason that there is no real or effective alternative to
financial liberalisation as repressed financial systems neither promise growth
of the real sector nor facilitate development of financial intermediation. Critics
of financial liberalisation often take shelter under the umbrella of the Stiglitz
and Weiss (1981) theory that it is possible to have efficient credit rationing
and optimal interest rates below the market-clearing level even in the non-
intervened financial system because of the asymmetric information between
lenders and borrowers. But they err in misreading the Stiglitz-Weiss thesis
with its implied but unstated premises. While it is true that optimal interest
rates can remain below market clearing at all time, the rates can be much
lower when the banking system is fragile with a substantial proportion of non-
performing assets; bank supervision is weak or non-existent; macroeconomic
instability is pronounced and persistent; and banks do not have the required
skills to manage their assets and liabilities (Villanueva and Mirakhor, 1990).

If this modification of the Stiglitz-Weiss theory is right—and it has been validated by the work of Caprio and others (1994)—then it throws a different light on financial liberalisation strategy and policy. The success of this strategy depends not so much on its intrinsic worth, which still remains unchallenged, as on how it is implemented. There is a certain order in which various elements of financial reforms have to be introduced. In addition, a careful assessment has to be made of the state and structure of the financial system, the financial position of the borrowers, the fiscal stance of the government, the positing of the economy in the business cycle, the macroeconomic stability, and the nature and effectiveness of the regulatory framework. These building blocks cannot be put in place all at once but in an appropriate sequential order in a mosaic of financial reform. In other words, the sequencing and timing of financial reform are critical to its success or failure.

Section II of this paper presents a brief account of a changing perspective on financial reform as it has evolved since the 1970s both from the implementation of financial reform policies and the theoretical developments in academic literature. Section III outlines the main strands of financial reform experience in a sample of countries—both successful and failed—in so far as they relate to the sequencing of financial reform elements. Section IV will then proceed to focus on the analytical underpinnings of sequencing of the key elements such as interest rate deregulation, phasing out of directed credit introduction of competition, and other related issues. The final section will contain a broad summary, more with an eye on what countries should vice in their financial policy matrix.

CHANGING PERSPECTIVE ON FINANCIAL REFORM

With the growing acceptance of financial reform, not only by itself but also as a part of the overall economic reform, its content and context tended to change gradually. Financial liberalisation policy as modelled by McKinnon (1973) and Shaw (1973) and implemented in several developing countries has undergone profound changes in regard to its connotation, operational mode, approach to sequencing, and above all, its very interpretation in light of the experiences gained. The changes in the perspective of financial reform-related issues can be attributed to several factors, namely, the difference in the institutional and macroeconomic context in which financial liberalisation policies have been initiated and implemented, the instrumentality of financial deregulation, its interpretation, the financial position of banks, degree of macroeconomic stability, the emergence of financial crises, the state of the real economy, and the fiscal deficit. Unless these factors are analysed at a basic level, it will not be evident why financial liberalisation has succeeded in some countries and not in others. The analysis would also throw up implicitly though not overtly, the underlying rationale for sequencing, which will be discussed at length later.

The institutional and macroeconomic policy context, which is country-specific, has been a major factor influencing the outcome of financial reform. This has been dramatized by what happened in the Southern Cone countries of Latin America. When financial reforms were ushered in there, false signals were sent by the disequilibrating relative prices. When wrong exchange rate policies—the predetermined exchange rate adjustments ("tablita")—were adopted in Chile, their exchange rate appreciated with unsustainable capital inflows. Likewise, tighter fiscal policies and easier monetary policies were adopted. All these unravelled the financial reforms.

Being among the first to adopt financial liberalisation policies as theorised by the academics, the Southern Cone countries thus did commit unavoidable mistakes typical to new economic policies which have to go through a trial and error process before they become fully operational. This is nowhere more evident than in the execution of interest rate deregulation. It is now well recognised that the dismantling of interest rate ceilings was implemented without regard to the existing institutional set-up and conditions of the real sector. It came, therefore, as a surprise to the propagators of the policy when the results of interest rate deregulation totally diverged from what was intuitively expected. This hiatus between the ex-ante and ex-post consequences of interest rate deregulation should not, however, be ascribed to the inappropriateness of the policy. Rather, it is closely connected with the sequencing of the different elements of the financial reform (Khatkhate, 1992). It must be remembered that the institutional structure of the banking system that results from regulatory changes can also propel concentration of power in banking, interlocking ownership and lending patterns; an environment which is particularly vulnerable to market failure. Perhaps the most disturbing consequence has been that a full deregulation could culminate in excessive increase in interest rates with inelastic demand for credit. The belief that in the deregulatory environment interest rates would find their true equilibrium level or tend automatically to converge to international rates over time has also been proven wrong by this experience.

These unexpected results came about not only because interest rate deregulation was introduced in the midst of macroeconomic instability—an observation which is now accepted without dissent—but also because of wrong timing, as structural reform aggravates macroeconomic instability which it seeks to eliminate in the first place. This conclusion, which has been derived from a macroeconomic analysis of economic reform process (Cho and Khatkhate, 1989; Lindgren *et al.,* 1996), has been supported by microeconomic analysis of the financial liberalisation policy that if financial reform is pursued when inflation is high or rising, the corporate sector's profitability will be strained, bringing it in serious financial distress (Cho 1994). The learning points here are that: (a) financial deregulation should not be used as an instrument of stabilisation policy; (b) the existing state of the financial system should not be disregarded; and (c) wrong sequencing of financial liberalisation policy will aggravate the macroeconomic imbalances.

Financial liberalisation will be more likely to succeed if the prevailing banking system is generally sound. However, reforms often take place in the context of widespread distortions in the financial system which are a consequence of the previous interventionist policies. These distortions render the banking system generally unsound, with a large amount of non-performing assets. If in such a milieu interest rates are deregulated, the banking system will become more fragile and may ultimately reach a crisis situation. An unsound bank tends to offer higher interest rates or resort to casino ploys to drum up income to meet operating expenses or it may incur higher risk through adverse selection. When a bank finds it difficult to openly declare loans in default lest it hastens to translate illiquidity into insolvency, it may continue to lend to risky borrowers or to capitalise interest on loans to those borrowers. These consequences weaken banks as well as the real economy, thereby pushing them to the brink of financial and economic crisis.

Empirical evidence shows that there are close linkages between financial sector reform and financial crisis (Sundararajan and Balino, 1991). First of all, increased freedom of entry into the financial sectors and freedom to bid for funds through interest rates and other instruments often lead to excessive risk taking, especially in the absence of prudent regulatory control. One of the reasons for this is the lack of credit appraisal skills of bank managers. Second, the institutional structure of the banking system tends to have too much concentration of power, resulting in interlocking ownership and lending pattern. As mentioned earlier, such an environment is particularly vulnerable to market failures caused by factors such as moral hazard, adverse selection, and the inherent oligopolistic pricing of loan. Third, deregulation of interest rates and other controls on bank operations makes possible a sudden splurge in credit expansion which may even exceed deposit growth. Fourth, instability in the credit market could arise not only from an inelastic demand for credit and uncertainty but also from credit rationing. For instance, in tight credit conditions, real interest rates could rise sharply. The lending banks may consider higher loan rates as indicative of enlarging risks and hold back credit, thereby aggravating credit crunch and causing bankruptcies of firms and banks. Finally, a spike in interest rates following their deregulation often affects banks severely, as their long-term loan portfolios which are financed by shorter-term liabilities carry fixed interest rates. This situation could precipitate a crisis for certain segments of the industry (Caprio et al., 1994).

When the credit market which is sought to be reformed is not perfect but one with distortions even prior to government intervention, financial liberalisation takes on a different character (Gertler and Andrews, 1994). In view of the market distortions arising from imperfect information, a rise in interest rates following financial liberalisation results in a drop in borrowers' net worth via a declining value of collateralisable assets and the discounted value of future stream profiles. An erosion of borrowers' net worth raises the premium on external finance, driving down investment below the optimum. Since the borrowers' net worth provides a link between the financial system and the real sector, financial liberalisation tends to shrink economic activity as well.

There is another aspect of the financial institutions which affects the effectiveness of financial reform. The real sector is often found to be weak in countries with financial repression. In these conditions, if financial repression is removed without alleviating the real sector problems, the net worth of the financial institutions tends to decline as well, as a result of growing volume of non-performing assets. Thus there is a double whammy on the borrowers and the real economy.

Since the crucial importance of timing of financial reform was ignored, the financial liberalisation experiments did not meet with expected success in Latin America. The experience was the opposite in Korea. The Korean government initiated financial liberalisation measures like reducing interest rate ceilings, etc. only after a significant deceleration of inflation and the abatement of recessionary tendencies. Thus a realistic set of relative prices and a profit-making corporate sector are ensured (Cho and Khatkhate, 1989; Caprio, 1994). This reinforces the conclusion of Gertler-Andrews that the initial condition of the banking system is crucial in determining the impact of financial reforms.

"Not only the net worth of banks, but their initial composition of assets and liabilities, their information set, or information capital, their endowment of human capital and their internal incentive systems, all reflect the pre-existing set of controls and determine the banks' response to reform."

The implications for a close linkage between fiscal deficit and financial reform are also very important to recognise. There are often two ways to look at the fiscal deficit in the context of financial reform. One of them refers to the difficulties in raising budgetary revenue. Fiscal revenues normally are inelastic with reference to income because of the poor tax administration as well as the nature of taxes. Governments therefore are prone to lean on the indirect taxation of financial intermediation such as very high reserve requirements and below-market interest rates paid on government securities which financial institutions are obligated to hold. In addition, there is often an inflation tax imposed in the developing economies which experience rapid monetary expansion. Initiation of financial reforms requires that all these three sources of taxation are plugged, without any assurance that they would be easily substituted by other sources of budgetary revenue.

The second way of looking at the fiscal deficit is its size. It is often the case that in developing countries the fiscal deficit is large and is mostly monetised. This implies that its size has to be reduced if the financial reform is to get on a steady and sustainable trajectory. Paradoxically enough, a fiscal deficit, far from going down, tends to get worse, as the financial reform gets into swing. Reduction in reserve requirements and the containment of inflationary monetary expansion reduce tax revenue. On the other hand, market-determined interest rates on government loans, being higher than before the financial reform, tend to raise fiscal deficit. In the absence of action on creating alternative sources of revenue, which depends critically on radical reform of the tax system or reducing expenditure, fiscal deficit cannot easily be pared, and in fact is more likely to rise in the wake of financial reform. It is, therefore, quite misleading to assert that financial reform only makes transparent the magnitude of the fiscal balances which is otherwise hidden by the financial repression (Johnston, 1997). It is also crucial that the financial reform will not be sustainable unless fiscal reform proceeds *pari passu* with financial reform or precedes it.

Doubts about the original mode of financial reform are raised by the ambiguity in the interpretation of what constitutes a financial reform or financial liberalisation. The basic tenet of these policies, which equates them with a withdrawal of government intervention in the financial system (such as imposition of interest rate ceilings or direction of credit allocation) has now become suspect by the kind of financial reform policies followed by Korea and Taiwan, Republic of China, which achieved better results (at least until recently) even though the government's presence in the financial system remained substantial.

Therefore, a question is pertinently raised in this connection, whether it is analytically meaningful and operationally relevant to consider that financial repression, as McKinnon-Shaw defined it, is necessarily harmful in all cases. Countries like Japan, Taiwan, Republic of China, and Korea made rapid strides both in regard to GDP growth and the development of their financial systems by permitting their governments to strongly influence the credit allocation and interest rates. This calls for greater precision in defining terms such as government intervention in credit market and financial repression and the specification of the conditions under which the interventionist stance could succeed (Cho and Hellman, 1993). Still, there is a further question whether deregulation should always imply a total absence of government intervention or it could be consistent with a modified and gradually declining government presence. In other words, should a certain degree of financial repression be maintained long enough for bank management to acquire maturity and skills and borrowers to improve their net worth? This issue becomes especially relevant in regard to directed credit. However, on this question the jury is still out. The recent banking and currency crises in East Asia have been interpreted as indicating that loan policies of banks based on non-commercial criteria and cosy relationship with the borrowers have led to both the unsoundness of banks and inefficiencies of the borrowing enterprises (IMF, 1997). In any case, the withdrawal of government intervention and its pace can be legitimately considered as important in designing financial reform policies, especially with respect to the sequencing and timing.

Sequencing of Financial Reforms: Experience of Selected Countries

Financial reforms were undertaken with varying degree of success in several countries. The countries cited as most successful, at least until the South-East and East Asian banking and currency crises, have been Korea, Indonesia, Malaysia, and Thailand. On the other hand, countries like Chile, Argentina and the Philippines were categorised as less successful. Their experiences therefore will provide a part of the answer to the question of the extent to which the timing and sequencing of the various elements of financial liberalisation determine the outcome of these policies. In what follows, the instrumentality of reforms pursued by all these countries would be briefly surveyed and an attempt will be made to discern if there is a pattern regarding the sequencing of reforms.

Indonesia's financial reform of 1983 was far-reaching in both content and coverage. The major reform was in two stages, in June 1983 and in 1984. The June 1983 reform had three principal aspects: (a) elimination of ceilings on bank credit; (b) gradual narrowing of loan categories from access to Bank Indonesia (BI) liquidity credits; and (c) deregulation of state banks' interest rates on most categories of deposits and on all loans except a few priority loans. Two follow-up elements of the subsequent measures were: (a) introduction of rediscount facilities and the BI certificates, called SBI, and (b) the introduction of new money market instruments like SBPU. The second phase of reform in 1984 called for the creation of new instruments to absorb the excess liquidity of banks which otherwise was being directed to foreign assets. Credit ceilings were eliminated, thereby facilitating a switch to indirect regulation of credit through reserve money management. The reform measures did not initially ease barriers to entry until after 1955 when restriction on banks and non-banks on establishing branches were relaxed. Measures to develop money and capital markets came on the scene later in the reform process. Capital account liberalisation, which related to foreign direct investment or portfolio capital, was effected after 1985 and that too gradually (Cho and Khatkhate, 1989; Pill and Pradhan, 1997). It is noteworthy that Indonesia always had to recognise a 'Singapore factor', as it was difficult to maintain strict capital controls due to its close proximity to financial centres such as Singapore (Table 7.1).

The financial reform in Korea was part of a broader economic adjustment policy that included actions on wide fronts such as currency devaluation, fiscal and monetary policy, etc. The pace of the reform was gradual. Interest rates were adjusted upward in 1979 to yield positive real interest rates. In 1982 all preferential lending rates were abolished. The loan rates were unified at 10 per cent. However, preferential access to credit by specific group of borrowers continued in some form or the other. The real deregulation of interest rates was initiated after 1992, when many measures to broaden money market and capital market developments were intensified (Dalla and Khatkhate, 1995). Initially, some sort of competition was introduced both among banks and between banks and non-banks. What is noteworthy about Korea is that capital account opening took place only since 1988 and that too gradually and as a sequel to the development of the domestic money and capital markets. Even today, Korea's capital account cannot be described as liberalised in any sense of the term (Table 7.1).

Malaysia did not have a repressed financial system, though there was an array of administrative controls on the financial system. Even before 1978, commercial banks were free to determine their own interest rates. There was a fairly well functioning financial regulatory and supervisory machinery in place. From 1981 onward what significantly changed was the introduction of market elements on a larger scale in the movement of assets and liabilities of banks. The capital account has been fairly open since the 1970s, though there was administrative overseeing and monitoring of the capital account transactions (Table 7.1).

Thailand's financial liberalisation sequencing differed from the above three countries in a few important aspects. Thailand boasted a liberal capital account since the 1970s through the passage of the Alien Business Law of 1972 and the Investment Promotion Act of 1977. FDI and portfolio investments were treated liberally although exchange controls applied to the repatriation of interest, dividends and principal. Likewise, foreign borrowing was treated liberally, though it excluded registration. One notable exception was the control on capital outflows, which was subsequently liberalised gradually. However, Thailand accepted Article VIII of the IMF to remove all restrictions on the current account only in 1996 (Cho and Khatkhate, 1989; Takatoshi and Kruegert, 1996). Interest rates and other credit controls were relaxed but not removed. Only in 1992 were they completely eliminated. However, Thailand was slow to develop indirect monetary policy instruments. It enhanced the supervision and prudential regulations after the banking crisis that enveloped the financial system in the mid-1980s (Table 7.1).

Table 7.1

Sequencing of Financial Reform in Successful Countries—Indonesia, Korea, Malaysia and Thailand, 1980–1997

Type of Reforms	Prior to 1980	81	82	83	84	85	86	87	88	89	90	91	92	93	94	95	96	97
Indonesia																		
(a) Interest rate				o		o												
(b) Directed credit			o	•	o	o	o	o	o									
(c) Money market instruments					o	o												
(d) Exchange rate regime							o	o	•	•	•				•	•	•	
(e) Exchange market system																		
i. Current account						o			•	o		o						
ii. Capital account				•		•	•	•	•	•		•	•	•	•	•	•	
(f) Competition	o							o										
(g) Supervision and regulation									•	o	o	o	o		o	•		
(h) Capital market								o		o	o	o	o	o	o	o	o	
Korea																		
(a) Interest rate		o	o		o	o			o	o	o	o	o	o	o	o		
(b) Directed credit					o										o	o	o	
(c) Money market instruments		o	o	o	o	o			o	o	o	•	o	o	o	o	o	
(d) Exchange rate regime							o				o			o	o	o	o	

contd...

contd...

Type of Reforms	Prior to 1980	81	82	83	84	85	86	87	88	89	90	91	92	93	94	95	96	97
(e) Exchange market system																		
i. Current account					○	○	○	●	○	○	○	○	○	○	○			
ii. Capital account									○			○	○	○	○			
(f) Competition														○				
(g) Supervision and regulation					○	○	○	○	●	○	○	○	●	○	○	●	○	
(h) Capital market					○	○	○	○	○	○	○	○	○	○	○	○	○	

Malaysia

Type of Reforms	Prior to 1980	81	82	83	84	85	86	87	88	89	90	91	92	93	94	95	96	97
(a) Interest rate	●			○	○													
(b) Directed credit	●			○	○			●		●								
(c) Money market instruments	●				○	○	○	○			○	○						
(d) Exchange rate regime	●																	
(e) Exchange market system																		
i. Current account	●			○	○	○	○											
ii. Capital account	●					○	○											
(f) Competition	●	○	○			●	●			●								
(g) Supervision and regulation										○	○	○						
(h) Capital market							●			●	○							

contd...

contd...

Thailand

Type of Reforms	Prior to 1980	81	82	83	84	85	86	87	88	89	90	91	92	93	94	95	96	97
(a) Interest rate			o		o	o												
(b) Directed credit		•	o	o														
(c) Money market instruments						o	•	o	o	•	•	o	•	o	o	•	•	•
(d) Exchange rate regime				o		o	o											
(e) Exchange market system																		
i. Current account				o						•					o			o
ii. Capital account							o	o		o	o				o	•	o	•
(f) Competition				o	o		o	o		o		o	o	•	o	•		o
(g) Supervision and regulation					•				o	o	•	o	o	•	•	•	o	o
(h) Capital market	o	o			•		o	o	•	•	•	•	o	•	•	o	o	•

Note: o represents change; • represents major change.

Source: Cho and Khatkhate, 1989; Pill and Pradhan, 1997; Bisat *et al.* 1992; Johnston and Echeverria, 1997.

It is interesting to see how the so-called less successful countries like Argentina, Chile, and the Philippines implemented their financial reform policies in contrast to the countries mentioned earlier and whether their performance is affected by the sequencing of their reforms. Argentina's reforms, which were initiated from 1976, were sweeping and of a big bang variety. Interest rates and capital movements were unfettered from restrictions. Interest rates except those on saving deposits were allowed to be determined by market forces. Financial institutions were freed from all restrictions to manage their own assets and liabilities. Directed credit was abolished at the very beginning. Competition was encouraged through elimination of entry restrictions. Exchange rate also was market determined (Cho and Khatkhate, 1989; Pill and Pradhan, 1997; Takatoshi and Kruegert, 1996). Chile's approach to financial liberalisation was almost similar to that of Argentina. Competition was encouraged, interest rates were freed. Capital controls were effectively removed since 1979, though in phases.

The Philippines was the only one amongst the South-East and East Asian countries that experienced financial crisis following financial liberalisation. It started a phased liberalisation of interest rates in 1980, with the removal of interest rate ceilings on deposits with maturities greater than two years. The removal of ceiling on other interest rates followed: on loan rates with maturity greater than two years in 1981; on the remaining deposit rates in 1982; and on other loan rates in 1983. Indirect monetary policy instruments received a boost when the prime rate monitoring system was instituted, the compilation of deposit reference rate (Manila Reference Rate) was initiated and the central bank rediscount rate was brought in line with the 90-day Manila Reference Rate. The capital account was opened even before the financial   form was introduced.

There is one common feature which cuts across the reform experiences of Argentina, Chile and the Philippines. They all had gone through financial crises that severely undermined their financial systems as well as economies. What is more, the causes of those crises were in one way or another related to the financial liberalisation policies. The financial crisis in Argentina threw in bold relief the risks of financial liberalisation, when it is not supported by other structural and macroeconomic reforms. As Johnston (1997) points out:

> At the structural level, the competitiveness and depth of the financial system were not significantly promoted by the reform, which largely resulted in reshuffling of existing institutions and ownership rather than a fundamental reorganisation—consequently, the financial system remained non-competitive and undeveloped, and borrowers continued to rely mainly on bank borrowing. Also prudential controls were not developed, while deposits were guaranteed by the state.

In addition, the inconsistent macroeconomic policies contributed to the failure of the financial liberalisation. The result was that Argentina backtracked on financial reforms and reimposed the administrative controls on banks' assets and liabilities, the removal of which was the essence of financial reform.

The Chilean financial crisis, though it coincided with the financial reforms, was triggered by macroeconomic policy errors which led to an extreme and unsustainable overvaluation of the real exchange rate. This resulted in large-scale speculation against the Chilean currency, which raised the domestic interest rates sky-high. Both the high interest rates and overvalued exchange rates had an adverse impact first on the profitability of the borrowers and through them on the solvency of the banks. In some measure, the financial crisis in Chile was not directly related to the financial liberalisation policy *per se* (Cho and Khatkhate, 1989).

The Philippines had a major financial crisis during 1981–1986, which followed the financial liberalisation. Initially, the crisis was sparked by the excessive credit expansion following deregulation. When the financial system is repressed, the banks follow certain directives to manage their portfolio. When these restraints are suddenly removed, banks tend to misuse the newly acquired freedom to take excessive risk in lending. This is precisely what happened in the Philippines. When the bubble burst, the immediate cause being a large-scale default in the commercial paper market, the banks swung to the other extreme by curtailing credit, causing the real economy to shrink. A contributing factor was also the imperative of a stabilisation policy concurrently pursued, which warranted a restrictive monetary policy. The Philippines is one of those cases where the financial reform policies were rendered nugatory by the demands of the stabilisation policy, thereby precipitating a severe financial crisis.

In the light of the experience of both the successful and unsuccessful countries in implementing financial reforms policies, it is possible to search for a pattern, if any, in sequencing of financial reforms. Tables 7.1 and 7.2, which capture under broad categories the sequencing in seven countries, reveal the following.

Of the successful countries, only in Korea the major reforms like interest rate deregulation, capital account openness and tightening of supervision and prudential controls were ushered in gradually. In fact, interest rates continued to be administratively managed, with a view to keeping them at positive levels in real term. However, this did not prevent the authorities from turning the real interest rates negative when the economy was in downward spiral. Bold steps to remove controls were taken only after 1992, well a decade after financial liberalisation started. The capital account was opened slowly and with circumspection. A different approach was taken in regard to inflow and outflow of capital, adjusting it, depending upon the current account position of the balance of payments. The same degree of caution characterised the directed credit elimination. Among other successful countries, Indonesia presented a contrast to Korea in that it deregulated interest rates early on in the process of financial reform and liberated its capital account in the middle of the process. Meanwhile, directed credit was removed at the very beginning.

Malaysia, another successful country, pursued a different course. To begin with, it had a liberal financial system, which was less repressed and relatively open capital account. Consequently, its deregulatory measures were, in the nature of things, mild. The exception was in regard to directed credit, which survived till 1988. For Malaysia, financial reform meant basically the development of money and capital market, with a fine-tuning in other areas of reform such as competition and bank supervision.

Thailand differed from Indonesia, Korea and Malaysia in sequencing its reforms. The deregulation of interest rates came in the middle of the implementation of financial liberalisation. This was also true of the capital account opening. Table 7.1 shows that the clustering of reforms was towards the tail end of the process.

Turning to the less successful countries—Argentina, Chile and the Philippines—what strikes the eye is that almost all financial reform policies were taken at one go in the beginning of financial liberalisation. The removal of directed credit, ceilings on interest rates, capital account convertibility and exchange rate reform were effected at the very beginning in Argentina and Chile. While the speed of reform was slower in the Philippines, the direction was similar. There is one deviation from this pattern, however. In Chile bank supervision and prudential controls were strengthened and their implementation improved after the advent of financial crisis.

Thus, it is surprising that sequencing of reforms *per se* has little or no bearing on the success or failure of the financial reforms. While Indonesia and the Philippines followed more or less the same sequencing, the Philippines went through a severe financial crisis while Indonesia escaped it, though its banking system became fragile after the financial reform. As a matter of fact, what brought about the crisis in the Philippines was the macroeconomic developments, which sharply turned adverse (Cho and Khatkhate, 1989). The Philippines was enfeebled by the second oil shock at the end of the

1970s, and subsequently by the political turmoil and a balance of payments deterioration. In late 1983, the situation became critical with the freezing of foreign credit and severe import restrictions, leading to a decline in investment and subsequently a deep recession. Government had to bail out several banks and took over some private commercial banks (Sundararajan and Balino, 1991; Johnston *et al.,* 1997).

The sequencing pattern of financial reform in Argentina and Chile also does not adequately explain the failure of financial reforms or the resulting crisis. Their sequencing is similar to that in Malaysia and yet Malaysia's progress through financial reforms was smooth, without any untoward developments marring its financial sector. This means that for financial reform to succeed, it is necessary to turn to some other elements which are missing in the unsuccessful countries undergoing reforms.

The failure of financial reforms is linked to the oligopolistic structure of the banking system, particularly in Chile and to some extent in Argentina, and to market imperfections. When financial liberalisation was going full steam, with the concomitant restoration of the holding company structure to the banking system, groups of industrial and trading firms closely linked with financial institutions constantly exerted strong pressure on the latter to appropriate even larger credit resources to finance their business activities. This raised credit demand and, consequently, interest rates. Banks, for their part, were driven equally to compete for deposits regardless of the price. The profitability of the group's productive operations could not have been sustained for long in the face of high interest rates. Yet, because of the interlinking of ownership, the banks continued to lend at high interest rates to the borrowing groups. This accelerated the accumulation of arrears of bad and doubtful debts but did not deter banks from aggressively competing for deposits at still higher rates following abolition of all controls on their operations. The oligopolistic structure was not as prominent a feature of Argentina's financial system, though the residue of monopoly power which allowed banks to appropriate monopoly rent in the form of higher interest rates was not insignificant. To some extent, the level of interest rates reflected a large risk premium on loans given to newly emerged clients whose credit background was unknown and who, in securing new avenues of profit sharing, were not daunted by the riskiness of projects so long as the expected returns were thought to be high. In the event of bankruptcy such borrowers have nothing more to lose than the collateral against loans if the business fails, but they can claim the entire profit if it succeeds.

Table 7.2

Sequencing of Financial Reform in Successful Countries—Argentina, Chile, the Philippines, 1980–1997

Type of Reforms	Prior to 1980	81	82	83	84	85	86	87	88	89	90	91	92	93	94	95	96	97
Argentina																		
(a) Interest rate	•																	
(b) Directed credit	•																	
(c) Money market instruments	•																	
(d) Exchange rate regime	o																	
(e) Exchange market system	•													•				
i. Current account	o																	
ii. Capital account	•	o	o															
(f) Competition	•																	
(g) Supervision and regulation	•	o																
(h) Capital market	•		o	o	o													
Chile																		
(a) Interest rate	•																	
(b) Directed credit	•																	
(c) Money market instruments	•					o		o				•	o	o		•	o	
(d) Exchange rate regime	o					o			o	o		o	•	o		o		
(e) Exchange market system																		
i. Current account						o					•	o	o	o	o	•	o	

contd...

contd...

Type of Reforms	Prior to 1980	81	82	83	84	85	86	87	88	89	90	91	92	93	94	95	96	97
ii. Capital account							o	•			o	o	o	o				
(f) Competition	o							o				o	o	•		o	o	
(g) Supervision and regulation	o					•	•	o		•					o	o	o	
(h) Capital market	o					o	o	o				o	o	o	o	o	o	

The Philippines

Type of Reforms	Prior to 1980	81	82	83	84	85	86	87	88	89	90	91	92	93	94	95	96	97
(a) Interest rate	•		•	o														
(b) Directed credit	o					•												
(c) Money market instruments	o		o	o		o												
(d) Exchange rate regime					•													
(e) Exchange market system																		
i. Current account	o																	
ii. Capital account	•			o	o			o		o	o		•	o	o			
(f) Competition		o		o	o	o												
(g) Supervision and regulation	•								o	o	o	o						
(h) Capital market				o	o	o			o	o	o							

Note: o represents change: • represents major change.

Source: Same as Table 7.1.

A second explanation about the high level of real interest rates has to do with distress borrowing, implying that the borrowing firms, under financial stress and with serious cash flow problems, will borrow at any interest rate rather than sell assets to meet losses. Distress borrowing was more typical of Argentina. During the late 1970s, firms appear to have substituted dollar debt for peso debt, keeping their overall leverage stable. But beginning in 1980, when earnings began to fall sharply, firms steadily increased their reliance on debt finance. Thus part of the firms' financial riskiness may have been due to distress borrowing. Since the upward leverage trends correspond generally to the emergence of banking sector crises, they may well have been a causal factor.

While it was recognised that the financial crisis in these countries emanated from wrong and inconsistent macro policies, it is also true that the disequilibrium following financial reform adversely affected the macroeconomic outcome. If real interest rate reached intolerable limits because of the oligopolistic banking structure or distress borrowing, they lead to damaging consequences for the financial systems. Therefore, financial liberalisation, far from leading to an equilibrium level of interest rates, had a severe adverse impact on profitability of firms and generated a disastrous financial crisis. This in turn necessitated injection of central bank credit into the system when macroeconomic imbalances were serious. Thus, the inappropriateness of the liberalisation design under an imperfect financial structure reinforced inconsistencies in macroeconomic policies and aggravated the economic and financial disequilibrium.

CETERIS PARIBUS APPROACH TO FINANCIAL REFORM SEQUENCING

What seems to emerge from the varied experiences of financial reforms across countries, with dissimilar financial and economic structures and macroeconomic conditions, is that sequencing of financial liberalisation by itself is not as important and crucial to its success, provided that the reforms take into consideration the prevalent macroeconomic policies and adapt to them. Assume that the real sector is bereft of the usual distortions, which generally characterises the developing countries, and further that macroeconomic policies, fiscal, exchange rate and monetary are well conceived and not mutually inconsistent. Then the question of timing and sequencing of financial reform in that setting becomes highly relevant in ensuring success. In other words, it is necessary to assume the *ceteris paribus* condition and proceed to focus on the sequencing order of the various elements of reform. However, the rationale for sequencing each element is not the same and the policymakers have to make sure that a rationale specific to each is present in the economy before the element of reform is introduced. In this paper, four elements which are considered to constitute the core of financial reform will be singled out for discussion about their sequencing. They are: interest rate deregulation; directed credit; competition; and capital account convertibility.

Interest Rate Deregulation

The main justification for interest rates deregulation, which refers to removal of ceilings and allowing the rates to be solely determined by the market, rests on the assumption that low interest rates and accompanying credit rationing are brought about by financial repression. However, this may not always be the case. The work by Stiglitz and Weiss (1981), by throwing new light on how commercial bank credit markets actually operate, has shown that because of asymmetrical information between lenders and borrowers, optimal interest rates even in the modern, freely operating bank-dominated credit market can be and often are below the market-clearing levels. In a bank credit market the interest rate charged on the loan differs from the expected return to the bank, which equals the product of loan rate charged and the repayment probability of borrowers. This probability is always less than 100 per cent because of imperfect information between lending banks and borrowers as the latter have greater information about their default risk than the former. For this reason, as the interest rates charged on loans increase, there is less probability that the loan will be repaid. It is therefore in the interest of banks that they ration credit even when the borrowers are willing to pay higher interest rates. This means that the actual interest rates, or what may be called the optimal rates from the banks' point of view, may remain below the market-clearing level (Villanueva and Mirakhor, 1990).

Where the economy is riddled with macroeconomic instability, which creates conditions such that a failure of one borrower may lead to a systemic crisis, the optimal interest rate under normal competitive conditions is even further reduced. This is because the authorities force the banks to make provision against probable defaults, which in turn reduces the expected profits of banks at a given loan interest rate. There is a further twist to this phenomenon. The optimal interest rate charged by banks, as seen earlier, is less than what would be determined under competitive credit conditions. It would be even lower than that if the economy suffers from severe macroeconomic imbalance. However, all this assumes that there is a sound and effective prudential and supervision control. When such supervision is absent or inefficient and there is deposit insurance, there is an increasing scope for moral hazard for banks. Banks then are encouraged to lend at an increasing interest rate, which, however, does not deter new borrowers. In other words, a rise in interest rates tends to cause a rise in demand for credit as well. Banks become impervious to this situation as they are certain that in good time they can keep all profits but in bad times they can get away from losses, as deposits are already insured. In these circumstances, the optimal interest rate should be even lower than under unstable macroeconomic conditions with effective prudential and regulatory controls.

What does all this signify for sequencing interest rate deregulation? If the macroeconomic environment is unstable and supervisory and prudential controls are deficient or inoperative, the interest rates should not be liberalised at one go. On the contrary, the ceilings on them should be maintained. As the situation improves, interest rate ceilings should gradually be removed.

In addition, the sequencing interest rate deregulation should take into account two factors. First, the situation in the real sector should be carefully looked into as the sector is often found to be weak in countries with financial repression. If in these conditions interest rates are freed without any actions to alleviate the real sector problems, the net worth of financial institutions will tend to decline as well. Second, the elimination of interest rate controls should be synchronised with the cyclical phase of the economy. If, for instance, the economy is in a cyclical downturn, due to external shock such as adverse terms of trade or high interest rates transmitted from abroad, the borrowers' net worth declines and consequently the cost of external finance goes up. As a result, real investment declines, leading to a fall in net worth of the financial institutions themselves. This linkage between financial reform and the borrowers'/lenders' net worth dictates that governments should move more aggressively on interest rate deregulation in good times and more slowly when the borrowers' net worth is being eroded by negative shocks such as recession or losses due to terms of trade (Caprio et al., 1994).

Directed Credit

Sequencing of regulations on directed credit is also important though not as important as the deregulation of interest rates. Directed credit by definition precludes banks in pre-reform period from lending to certain sectors of the economy which they would have done in view of high expected return. If directed credits are terminated suddenly, banks will tend to rush to these sectors without being well equipped to handle these credits in a prudent manner. One of the results may be asset price bubble. As testified by experience in several countries, banks end up with a large exposure to the real estate sectors after the financial reform. Such widespread portfolio reallocation in a sizeable amount always entails high credit risk. Thailand and Indonesia are notable examples where in the wake of financial reforms there was a rapid increase in bank credit to the real estate sector, which later landed banks into serious problems of non-performing assets.

For this reason, the most prudent policy in regard to directed credit is to avoid abrupt portfolio shifts. It should be phased out in stages and synchronised with the strengthening of the institutions involved and prudential control. This would ensure that banks do not misuse their new freedom to indulge recklessly into lending to particular sectors.

A gradual approach to control on directed credit is also necessary in view of the limited asset–liability management skills amongst the management of banks. As Caprio *et al.* (1994) have pointed out,

> A less recognised and perhaps more crucial initial condition is the banks' stock of human and managerial capital at the time of reform. Reform programmes should take account of the absence, in countries with prolonged financial repression, of incentives for banks to invest in credit assessment, monitoring skills, and risk analysis. Such skills take time to develop, which means that there should be some restraint on banks in the post-reform period in allocation of credit in new areas, until they are ready with necessary skills.

Competition

One of the avowed purposes of financial reform is to introduce competition among banks so as to improve efficiency. However, competition at the very start of reform is fraught with many risks, unless some basic preconditions are met. Banks open business because of high franchise value of new offices. But franchise value may slump in the aftermath of financial reform, if the competition is keen and persistent. Domestic banks being long in business under government intervention, have often low capital base. If they are thrown open to competition from stronger banks both from within or outside the country, they might trigger a systemic crisis as they would surrender profitable avenues to their superior competitors. To force them to raise capital to be viable is risky when profits are down. If they reduce credit, especially when the real economy is on a downward slope, the recession may be aggravated. On the other hand, if banks are allowed to continue in competition with stronger banks, they would be tempted to follow unsound banking practices.

Open entry for banks, desirable though over the long term, creates severe problems of unsoundness, especially when the bank supervision machinery is weak. Besides, most of the banks are not equipped with good accounting standards, making their operations non-transparent. In addition, judicial and legal reforms which can facilitate prompt enforcement of contracts and punish fraudulent activities may not be in place. Competition should come after a sustained effort is made to improve the incentive system for banks. Such incentives, which refer to the regulations to ensure that the institutions are sound, include insistence on high capital requirements so that a certain amount of bad lending would not lead to heavy losses; liability fastened on to bank owners; and adequate debt collecting procedures. Once the incentives are in place, there will be little risk of banks relapsing into a situation where their net worth is negative because they will employ their capital more efficiently, enabling them to face competition with greater confidence. Thus, sequencing of competition should be carefully planned, so that at least the basic preconditions mentioned above are met.

Capital Account Convertibility

It is now generally recognised that capital account convertibility is an integral part of the financial reform. However, what is controversial is its sequencing. At one extreme, several fervent advocates of capital account convertibility stress the need to open the capital account at the very beginning of the financial reform process. At the other end, it is argued that a rapid capital account convertibility would cause severe financial crisis. Though actual country experiences vary, leaving this issue in suspended animation, there are some underlying economic considerations on either side of the debate which need to be analysed in some depth, before taking a decision on the sequencing of capital account convertibility.

The traditional rationale for capital account convertibility in developing countries is at two levels. The first suggests that an open capital account broadens the risk diversification choices for the investors, as it enables them to exploit differences in asset prices in domestic and foreign markets and thus, minimises the risk of their investments. The other argument is that capital inflows following capital account convertibility will permit the country to finance increased investment more cheaply, especially in terms of forgone consumption (Hanson, 1994).

These more basic arguments are supplemented by the practical problem of enforcing capital controls. Experience has shown that it is difficult, if not impossible, to control capital flows. For one thing, most of the capital controls are circumvented, leading to the emergence of unofficial foreign exchange markets. It is further argued that restricting capital account, especially when the current account of the balance of payments is made convertible, is infructuous as capital flows out in a disguised form such as over-invoicing of imports and under-invoicing of exports and several other legal or illegal devices. As such, it is better to liberalise capital account simultaneously with the current account.

Though these arguments appear on the surface to be persuasive, they do not adequately make a case for rapid capital account convertibility. Risk diversification looks plausible in theory but often fails in practice. An economy with open capital account may be sound by any criteria and yet fails to withstand capital outflow, which may be induced by the contagion effect stemming from the structural imbalances in other countries near and far. This is because of the herd instinct of international investors. Any difference in asset prices across countries, reflecting differences in risk, are swamped by the irrational exuberance or gloom of investors.

Similarly, the belief that foreign capital inflows resulting from open capital account could ensure a cheaper financing of domestic investment is often not borne out by experience. The benefit of capital account liberalisation is often much smaller as it is based only on the differences between the inflows and outflows. Besides, the increased inflows of foreign capital may result in the lowering of return on capital and thereby the amount of domestic savings.

Open capital account also reduces the scope for taxation revenue by the fiscal authorities. To the extent domestic financial assets and capital flow out, being easier under open capital account, the government's ability to tax them is constrained. Furthermore, there is less scope for inflation tax with open capital account because inflation or its threat leads to greater use of foreign currency in mediation of transactions. Considering that the budget in developing countries is always under unremitting pressures to raise revenue, the loss of avenue for revenue under open capital account tends to widen fiscal deficit—the factor which often influences increased capital flight.

A hasty capital account liberalisation ahead of complete liberalisation of interest rates, elimination of directed credit, high liquidity ratios, and credit ceilings tends to increase the spread between deposit and lending rates, thereby encouraging borrowing abroad rather than domestically. Such developments could often lead to appreciated exchange rates, both nominal and real, excessive external debt, and a widening of current account deficit. This implies that premature capital account liberalisation or placing it ahead of other domestic financial reforms is counterproductive and slows the pace of financial sector reforms and other structural forms of the real economy.

On balance from both theoretical and empirical standpoints, it seems prudent to hold capital account opening till the tail-end of the financial reforms. Even then, the recent Asian financial and currency crisis has dramatised this problem. Most of the so-called successful countries in financial reform experiment, such as Korea and Indonesia, have seen their banking systems overloaded with non-performing assets. This apart, the enterprises being under the direction of the government were allowed to borrow from banks, often with public guarantees. The consequences of these measures are partly responsible for the over-expansion of the balance sheets of banks, imprudent reliance on foreign exchange loans mainly of short-term maturity, and excessive flow of credit to sectors like real estate and high-cost domestic industry with excess capacity. When the structural imbalances surfaced, and the risks of foreign finance were enlarged in the eyes of the foreign investors, capital flowed out and the currency crisis became unavoidable. Even for a country like Korea, which implemented a limited degree of capital account convertibility, the problem is still severe because of the fragility of the domestic banking system.

CONCLUDING REMARKS

A general conclusion that becomes apparent is that while financial reform is both desirable and inevitable, it has a certain sequencing pattern built into it, which varies according to the characteristics specific to each country. The sequencing of financial reforms which takes into account the institutional imperatives has a better chance to succeed. This is most evident in regard to interest rate deregulation and capital account convertibility. For the former, the preconditions are macroeconomic stability and adequacy of supervision and prudential control. As mentioned earlier, effective supervision and control are crucial in ensuring that freedom for banks to manage their own assets and liabilities immediately after the end of a prolonged period of financial intervention does not go astray, throwing the baby away with the bath water. For capital account convertibility, the preconditions are that internal financial sector reforms like interest rate deregulation and directed credit are completely eliminated and bank monitoring mechanism is firmly established. Further, the banking system, with its inherited weakness in terms of structural, functional and policy related, is restored as fully as possible to its intrinsic soundness. In addition, it is necessary to ensure at least a minimum set of instruments, institutions and markets for the effective management of monetary and exchange rate policies. Since these actions take time, it is always advisable to postpone capital account convertibility till the end of financial liberalisation process.

Even with all the sequencing and timing problems resolved, experience has shown that it does not guarantee the success of financial reform policies. It has to be preceded by real sector reforms, good corporate governance, a firm control of fiscal deficit, as well as consistent macroeconomic policies with exchange rate, fiscal and monetary policies in perfect harmony. In other words, the structural and macroeconomic policies should be delicately balanced and interwoven, with space for adjustment if unanticipated events intervene.

REFERENCES

Bisat, A., B. Johnston and V. Sundararajan (1992). "Issues in managing and sequencing financial sector reform: lessons from experiences in five developing countries", IMF *Working Paper* (mimeo).

Caprio, G. (1994). "Banking on reform? a case of sensitive dependence on initial conditions", Chapter 3 in G. Caprio, A. Atiyas and J. Hanson (eds.), *Financial Reforms: Theory and Experience*. New York: Cambridge University Press.

Caprio, G., A. Atiyas and J. Hanson (1994). "Policy issues in reforming finance: lessons and strategies", Chapter 12 in G. Caprio, A. Atiyas and J. Hanson (eds.), *Financial Reforms: Theory and Experience*. New York: Cambridge University Press.

Cho, Y.J. (1994). *Interest Rate Liberalisation, Inflation and Corporate Profitability: Is financial liberalisation sustainable under high inflation?* Seoul: Korea Tax Institute.

Cho, J.J. and B. Hellman (1993). "Government intervention in credit market: an alternative interpretation of Japanese and Korean experiences from the new institutional perspective", *Working Paper*. Seoul: Korea Tax Institute.

Cho, J.J. and D. Khatkhate (1989). "Lessons of financial liberalisation in Asia: a comparative study", *World Bank Discussion Paper No. 50*. Washington DC: The World Bank.

Cole, David C. (1997). "Sequencing versus practical problem solving in financial sector reform". in A. Harwood and Bruce Smith (eds.), *Sequencing Financial Strategies in Developing Countries*. Washington DC: Brookings Institution Press.

Dalla, I. and D. Khatkhate (1995). "Regulated deregulation of the financial system in Korea", *World Bank Economic Discussion Paper No. 292*. Washington DC: The World Bank.

Gertler, M. and R. Andrews (1994). "Finance, public policy and growth", Chapter 2 in G. Caprio, A. Atiyas and J. Hanson (eds.), *Financial Reforms: Theory and Experience*. New York: Cambridge University Press.

Hanson, J. (1994). "Sequencing of capital account convertibility", in G. Caprio, A. Atiyas and J. Hanson (eds.), *Financial Reforms: Theory and Experience*, New York: Cambridge University Press.

International Monetary Fund (1997). *World Economic Outlook*. December.

Johnston, B. (1997). "Speed of financial sector reform: risks and strategies", in A. Harwood and Bruce Smith (eds.), Sequencing?: *Financial Strategies for Developing Countries*.Washington DC: Brookings Institution Press.

Johnston, B., S. Darbar and C. Echeverria (1997). "Sequencing capital account liberalisation: lessons from experiences in Chile, Indonesia, Korea and Thailand", *IMF Working Paper* (mimeo).

Khatkhate, D. (1997). "Financial liberalisation: a revisionist view", *Economic and Political Weekly* 32(23): 1833-39 (28 June).

——————— . (1992). "Financial liberalisation and financial crises", *Economic and Political Weekly* 27(42): 2017–21.

Lindgren, C., C. Garcia and M. Saal (1996). *Bank Soundness and Macroeconomic Policy*.Washington DC: IMF.

McKinnon, R. (1973). *Money and Capital in Economic Development*. Washington DC: The Brookings Institution.

Pill, M. and M. Pradhan (1997). "Financial liberalisation in Africa and Asia", *Finance and Development* 44(2): 26–9.

Shaw, E. (1973). *Financial Deepening in Economic Development*. New York: Oxford University Press.

Stiglitz, J. and A. Weiss (1981). "Credit rationing in markets with imperfect information", *American Economic Review* 79(2): 47–68.

Sundararajan, V. and T. Balino (1991). *Banking Crises: Causes and Issues*. Washington DC: IMF.

Takatoshi, I. and Anne O. Kruegert (1996). "Financial deregulation and integration in East Asia", *Proceedings of the NBER's Fifth Annual East Asian Seminar in Economics*. Chicago, Ill.: Chicago University Press.

Villanueva, D. and A. Mirakhor (1990). "Strategies for financial reforms: interest rate policies, stabilisation, and bank supervision in developing countries", *IMF Staff Papers* 41(3): 51–67.

Published in the Economic and Political Weekly XXXIII(28): 1831-40 (1998).

8 | Fiscal Deficit and Real Interest Rates*

A rationale for recourse to fiscal deficit to promote economic development particularly in developing countries has a long pedigree in Keynesian economics. There have been two strands of thinking on the fiscal deficit justification. The first is that in the presence of a large amount of unemployment, disguised or open, and excess capacity in the producing sectors, money creation, which is what fiscal deficit in developing countries often implies, would result in new investment without inflationary pressures. This view was propounded by several economists in India and elsewhere in the 1950s (Khatkhate, 1954;[1] Mathur, 1965, among others). However, one of the assumptions on which fiscal deficit was justified, that "... in a consciously developing economy, the central authority could take steps in advance for augmenting capacity in crucial sectors ahead of the envisaged demand" (Mathur, 1965), was falsified in India, but more decisively in the Latin American and African countries because of the State being an irrational entrepreneur and the difficulties involved in solving the principal-agent problem. All that happened as a result of heavy resort to fiscal deficit was inflation, decline in income, saving and investment (Acharya, 2006; Khatkhate, 2006). Undaunted by these dismal experiences, there are still many fiscal deficit hawks, particularly in India, who still harbour the utopia that investment financed by free recourse to fiscal deficit would ensure 'development with dignity' (Bhaduri, 2005; Patnaik, 2006), though there are few takers for their advocacy both among academics and policymakers. Therefore, their proposition has remained more of a curiosum.[2]

The second strand of thinking on this issue has a different slant and is more enduring. It is argued by Patnaik (2001) that, fiscal deficit does not affect

---

*   Revised and extended version of the articles jointly written with Dan Villanueva, originally published in the Economic and Political Weekly of 12 May and 28 July 2001.

1. This article is in a way a mea culpa plea on behalf of one of the authors (Khatkhate), who made a strong case in 1954 for fiscal deficit for development on the basis of a dynamic interpretation of Keynes' multiplier.

2. A little known fact, which would surprise votaries of fiscal deficit and monetary expansion, is that communist China in 1988, when faced with double-digit inflation invited, of all economists, Milton Friedman, to advise on how to get out of the doldrums of high inflation. Needless to say what his advice was.

(i.e. raise) real interest rates and those who think otherwise are, perhaps, in their view "slaves of the defunct economists" (to borrow a phrase of Keynes used in some other context) from the International Monetary Fund (IMF), who are supposed to assume that the Indian economy maintains full employment in the Keynesian sense. The purpose of this article is to subject Patnaik's proposition to scrutiny before it becomes a new *mantra* for critics of the reform policies in India as elsewhere.

Before we embark on this, it is necessary to bear in mind the epistemological nature of economics as a science. One can start with any assumption of one's choice and proceed to derive results which conform to the preconceived notions. Patnaik makes it clear that he is analysing the linkages between fiscal deficits and real interest rates in a closed economy model; exchange rates and the balance of payments figure nowhere in his analytical framework. It is obvious that if his assumptions are replaced with other sets of assumptions closer to reality, the conclusions are apt to be considerably different from those they espouse. We shall remain focused on the reality of the Indian economy to the extent possible insofar as the assumptions are concerned and see, by using Patnaik's analytical construct, if the results which we obtain approximate his to any substantial degree.

Using the main tenets of the Keynesian type of theoretical literature, together with the IS/LM framework, in an economy with capital controls and with either a fixed or floating exchange rate, an increase in the fiscal deficit will raise both income and interest rates. Under a fixed exchange rate, the increase in income triggered by a higher fiscal deficit will raise the demand for and lower the supply of money—the latter via deterioration in the external current account (higher imports) and consequent reduction in the monetary base. The new equilibrium in the money market implies a higher interest rate. The effects on the money stock are indeterminate, depending on the relative shifts (increase) in money demand and (decrease) in money supply. Under a floating exchange rate, the endogeneity of the monetary base is removed and, clearly, the interest rate rises in response to higher money demand; the equilibrium money stock is higher (as interest rates go up, excess reserves are drawn down by banks and the currency deposit ratio declines, resulting in a higher money multiplier). India is a partially open economy (though the capital account is not fully convertible) with a floating exchange rate regime (a managed float, though). Hence, the latter result holds in India's case.

It is one thing to argue that an increase (decrease) in the fiscal deficit will raise (lower) both income and interest rates. It is another to argue that a high level of real interest rates can be caused only by a high fiscal deficit. In the IS-LM framework used by Patnaik, the equilibrium real interest rate is defined by the intersection of the IS and LM curves. Depending on the shift of these two curves, it is possible, as in the case of Thailand mentioned by Patnaik, that a fiscal surplus can co-exist with a high real rate of interest. This would happen, for instance, if the effect of the fiscal surplus, which would tend to lower the interest rate, were more than offset by the outflow of capital, as happened in Thailand (reflecting the reduced confidence of international investors in Thailand's ability to manage its external borrowing, in turn undermined by weak supervision of, and weak asset-liability management by, Thai financial institutions). It is also possible, as is true in the Indian situation, that a fiscal deficit can coexist with a high real interest rate and a recession, if the effect of the fiscal deficit, which would otherwise raise income, is more than offset by capital outflow induced by international investors' concern with the sustainability of the fiscal deficit, or by a lower money multiplier induced by build-up of excess reserves "owing to insufficient demand for credit from worthwhile borrowers."

After convincing himself that fiscal deficits have no bearing on real interest rates, Patnaik tries to explain the cause of high real interest rates in third world countries like India, but this time he switches to the assumption of India being an open economy. In controverting the Mundell-Flemming model he argues, erroneously in our view, that in a world of free capital mobility, rates of interest (he calls them, questionably, rates of return) might be equalised across all industrialised countries but not between industrialised and developing countries on the ground that investors from industrial countries face higher risks and uncertainty in developing countries. This is a most bizarre assertion. The empirical evidence is overwhelmingly against it (Haque *et al.*, 1990). The risks and uncertainty are captured in the expectation about the level of the exchange rate and therefore, interest rates in developing countries adjusted for the expected exchange rate changes (the uncovered interest rate parity condition) tend to be equalised in a world of capital mobility regardless of the distinction between industrial and developing countries.

In this connection, Patnaik imparts a strange twist to the interest rate parity problem—a stratagem that ideologues often resort to. He makes an exception to his thesis that the fiscal deficit does not lead to a rise in real interest rates in a third world country if it permits inflow of foreign capital. His argument is convoluted in its logic. His proposition simply is: for "international finance" (Patnaik's surrogate for capital flows) reduction of the fiscal deficit in developing countries signals a retreat from state intervention and therefore the gnomes of international finance consider it a danger to "their interest" and threaten to withdraw their funds. To propitiate them, the authorities in developing countries are forced to offer "even higher interest rates". This is wrong both in fact and logic. A country can have a high fiscal deficit and a very minimal role for state intervention, as in the US during the 1980s, or it can have a fiscal surplus and large-scale state intervention, as in the East Asian countries. The factual evidence also shows that interest rates can remain higher with a fiscal surplus, depending on other economic variables, than in a situation with a fiscal deficit. In such argumentation economics as a discipline succumbs to ideology.

Patnaik in criticising our analysis set out two propositions, one weak and one strong in his own words (Patnaik, 2001). The weak one suggests "that there is no theoretical justification for cutting the fiscal deficit as a means of lowering the interest rate" as it applies to the Indian situation. In India, which has a partially open economy (some capital controls) and a floating exchange rate regime (a managed float), cutting the fiscal deficit should theoretically lower the interest rate. The transmission mechanism is the following: Given the projected net capital flows, the money supply schedule is fixed by the Reserve Bank through its domestic credit operations and reserve requirements. From an initial equilibrium position, the fiscal deficit reduction lowers real income and the money demand schedule, resulting in excess money supply, which is eliminated by a fall in the interest rate. As the interest rate decreases, the quantity of money supplied goes down (bank excess reserves ratio goes up, leading to a lower money multiplier), while the quantity of money demanded goes up. In the new equilibrium, owing to the decline in the demand for money schedule, both the interest rate and money stock are lower. In clearing the money market, owing to imperfect capital mobility there is a role for the foreign interest rate adjusted for expected exchange rate depreciation. To the extent that a cut in fiscal deficit is substantial and credible to convince international investors of the sustainability of the fiscal deficit and the external current account balance, the reduction in the domestic interest rate is reinforced as part of the money market clearing process. Net capital inflow would shift the money supply schedule further and exert downward pressure on interest rates. Thus, the weak proposition cannot be sustained.

Nor do we concede his 'stronger proposition', which is based, according to him, on "what determines the level of the real interest rate in an economy open to free capital flows". We were somewhat remiss in not being unambiguous and precise, though vaguely right, in not providing sufficient explanation concerning our position on the uncovered interest rate parity problem; and Patnaik has raised some legitimate doubts about our formulation. Instead of stating that risks and uncertainty are captured in the expected exchange rate we should have argued that they, i.e. all risks, principally default risks, are already embedded in the market interest rates—we emphasise market interest rates and not administered interest rates prevailing in a developing country like India. Thus, Patnaik's risk premium, i.e. s, is already reflected in the market interest rate. To obtain the uncovered interest rate parity condition, therefore, we just have to add the expected change in the exchange rate d. This means that Patnaik's equilibrium condition, his equation (1),

$$r_1 - p_1 - s - d = r_2 - p_2$$

includes a redundant term s.

To avoid double counting, the equation should read

$$r_1 - p_1 - d = r_2 - p_2,$$

which is the same as we mentioned in our article. This equilibrium condition holds in the steady state. The dynamic relationship implicit in the steady state is the following:

$$dF/dt = [(r_1 - p_1 - d) - (r_2 - p_2)]F,$$

where F is the (interest-sensitive) stock of net foreign liabilities, $d(.)/dt$ is the differential operator, and the other variables are as defined by Patnaik in his reply. The steady state or equilibrium condition is $dF/dt = 0$, or when $r_1 - p_1 - d = r_2 - p_2$. If $r_1 - p_1 - d \neq r_2 - p_2$ then $dF/dt \neq 0$, and there will be net capital outflows or inflows. When we say that interest rates adjusted for expected exchange rate depreciation tend to be equalised in a world of capital mobility regardless of the distinction between industrial and developing countries, we are stating the steady-state condition when $r_1 - p_1 - d = r_2 - p_2$. Given this condition, $r_1 - p_1$ would necessarily be higher than $r_2 - p_2$ by the amount d. We have to sound a caution that we are only discussing here how the level of real interest rates is determined in an economy open to free capital flows and not advocating a policy of full capital account convertibility for India at the present state of its financial development.

Patnaik wants us to be specific about the propositions of the ideology which has driven him to his conclusion on the relationship between the fiscal deficit and the real interest rates. He believes that international finance is a devil, echoing Joan Robinson's flamboyant phrase of "humbug of finance". He argues that fiscal deficit in a country like India is perceived by international finance as an indicator of dangerous state activism and therefore, it needs to be bribed by the offer of higher interest rates in order to prevent it from moving the funds out of the country. As we argued earlier, if countries have fiscal deficits, it does not necessarily imply that they have state activism. If he were not stuck with this ideological predilection, he could have found a simpler explanation in the interest rate parity theory for why the fiscal deficit in capital-receiving countries leads to higher real interest rates there. A larger fiscal deficit, among others, leads to expectation by investors of exchange rate depreciation, which in turn results in higher interest rates.

His ideological hang-up is revealed in his hyperbolic prediction about what would happen if "a regime of unrestricted capital mobility is accepted". According to him, "the right to strike and agitate" will have to be "abrogated and people's freedom to elect governments of their choice" will have to be "curtailed, all for the sake of lowering the real interest rate". This is more an emotive oration of a fear-mongering and rabble rousing politician than a cool and reasoned argument of a learned academic. Can Patnaik in all seriousness point out one single instance of capital mobility having resulted in denying freedom to vote to the population of any country? Are we then wrong in saying that Patnaik allowed himself to be swayed by ideology?

Both Patnaik and we can go on arguing till kingdom come without arriving at anything new beyond our stated positions. It will be rewarding if others come up with their own critique of the subject we have debated.

REFERENCES

Acharya, Shankar (2006). *Essays on Macroeconomic policy and Growth in India*. New Delhi: Oxford University Press.

Bahaduri, Amit (2005). *Development with Dignity*. New Delhi: National Book Trust.

Haque, Nadeem, Kajal Lahiri and Peter Montiel (1990). "A macroeconometric model for developing countries", *IMF Staff Papers*, Vol. 37(3): 537–59.

Khatkhate, Deena (2006). "Indian economic reform: a philosopher's stone", *Economic and Political Weekly* XLI(22): 2203.

————. (1954). "The multiplier process in developing countries", *Indian Economic Journal* II(2): 1550–60.

Mathur, Ashok (1965). "On throwing the baby away with the bathwater: an essay in the defence of Keynesianism in relation to the underdeveloped countries", *Indian Economic Journal*. VXII(4): 397–416.

Patnaik, Prabhat (2006). "An integrated totality", *Economic and Political Weekly* XLI(11): 1160–6.

————. (2001). "Fiscal deficits and real interest rates", *Economic and Political Weekly* XXXI(18): 1175–83; XXXI(20): 2267–73.

Published in the Economic and Political Weekly XXXVI(19): 1646-47 and XXXVI(30): 2900 (2001).

III

NATIONAL ECONOMY

9 | Oeirolysis of Development?

Politicians play politics, economists fiddle with models, and common men and women dream of better things to come. All these categories of persons had a grand vision of the future of the poor countries immediately after the Second World War. There were no facts but only folklore about the countries aspiring to be developed; there was resentment about what was happening to these countries; there was faith and charity. Now that more than three decades have gone by, even the most optimistic amongst development economists have begun to rethink about the way actual development has taken place in the Third World. Has the dream of development faded or is there, to use the felicitous Koestlerian phrase, an oeirolysis? If the dream has indeed faded, it is ominous, because in that state of mind the sleeper when he awakes "cannot describe in precise verbal terms—except by saying that something reminded him of something but he no longer knows what or why?" (A. Koestler, *Brick to Babel*, New York: Random House, 1980, pp. 365–6). Or is there still a possibility of attaining 'oneiroynthesis' which can lead, after waking, to "the vaguely sensed connections forming nascent analogies which the fertile minds always teem with." This mood of pessimism, alternating occasionally with the mood of optimism seizes one seriously concerned with the problems of development when one comes across a type of book written by one of the best minds in the field of economics. One is referring to *Economic Development: Theory, Policy and International Relations* by Ian M.D. Little (New York: Basic Books, 1982).

Little is, admittedly, a neo-classical economist who strongly believes that the pattern of development has to be justifiable in terms of economic rationality, but he does not follow blindly the tenets of his School. Had it been so, he would have written a book on development like those authored by Baur, Yamey and Gilder. He bends the rules of the neo-classical theory, whenever desirable, recognises the grim reality in the LDCs and the humane aspects of the science he professes. Drawing on Baumol's concept of "magnificent dynamics" which connotes "analysis of functional dependency of the quantities of one period on those of another" with its magnificence embodied in "the sweeping nature of its generalisations and the fact that the subject matter is the development of the whole economy over long periods" (p. 18). Little modifies it to cover, in addition to the normal economic variables, "the institutional, political, cultural and psychological variables in a broad historical context". From this, one thing should at least be crystal clear—that Little's intellectual mould does not differ from that of several development economists of different persuasions: Marxist, dependency theorists, etc. And yet his conclusions and policy prescriptions are devastatingly different in their implications for the paths of development many of the LDCs have chosen or may choose in future. It is not possible to ignore him simply on the ground that a neo-classical theorist's conclusions are predictable. Little has used a clever technique of not disputing in a blunt manner the theories of his opponents nor does he question their motives or broad social commitments. He takes their assumptions in an overtly sympathetic manner and juxtaposes them not to his own but to those of others amongst his opponents. He then reduces their arguments to absurdity with the flourish of a typical British logician. He does this by disgorging facts after facts, generally acceptable even to his opponents. His book is supposed to be a critical survey of development issues but in fact it emerges as a document severely indicting the planners, politicians, economists and the international brigade of 'aidocrats' from LDCs whose sole reason for existence is to be able to mobilise foreign aid by harping, after the fashion of the counting of beads by an Arab, on the woes of the Third World countries.

Whether or not one agrees fully with Little's treatment of the various aspects of development policy and strategy, both on a theoretical level and at their implementation stages, it is possible to admire his style and approach employed in dealing with the subject. This is particularly evident from his discussion on planning. Planning has a chequered history, traceable partly to the experience of Europe in the post-Second World War era, partly to the woolly Fabian socialism in England, but predominantly to the radiating glow of the New Economic Policy of Soviet Russia. He starts with Indian planning, which is in a way proper, India being a pioneer among the LDCs in planning experiments. The usefulness or otherwise of planning is judged in terms of success or failure of Indian planning. Little, though of a neo-classical persuasion, is not averse to planning in principle. In fact, he himself shared during the 1950s many of the aspirations and hopes of Indian planners. What he dislikes is the travesty of planning. Many a plan—and Indian plans were not an exception—was designed to justify the need of foreign aid as rationalised by Rosenstein Rodan, Milikan and others on the basis of a 'two-gap' models of development. This approach to planning naturally precluded the hard choices which the planners and the politicians had to make, and thus ensured its subsequent failure. As Little puts it, "...the apparatus, symbols, and rhetoric of planning were accepted for political reasons" but

> the discipline of a central plan was often rejected, for another set of political reasons. The construction of the plan, and the plan document itself, should in theory be an instrument for rational decision making in economic sphere, especially as far as government expenditure is concerned; and it might, because of its long-term nature, provide continuity in expenditure plans and economic policies when governments change. But these supposed advantages are also disadvantages. The plan may constrain the shorter-term economic choices that are essential in an unstable and uncertain world, choices politicians see as their prerogative... This helps to explain why planning was accepted, and at the same time rejected (pp.56–7).

Who would deny that the present state of planning in India and other LDCs substantiates Little's observations?

Little's comments on the role of economists are equally illuminating, Economists at all times are prone to exaggerate their importance, what with programming models of one type or another, input-output tables, and so on, and in doing so they often lose sight of the institutional, political and administrative imperatives.

> Our account also suggests that those economists who were also planning enthusiasts had little influence on the acceptance of planning. They probably had more influence on the directions it took (though not in India). Planning for growth at the macroeconomic level was their speciality....With these aids they concocted supposedly consistent plans of mainly empty boxes. Sectoral and sub-sectoral investment totals were targeted or projected when there were no projects, no levers to influence their creation, and no analysis to show that investment in that sector would be a good use of scarce funds. Thus economists contributed to the excessive emphasis on central paper planning .... (p.57).

When thus political reality is given a go by and flights in the cloud cuckoo lands are undertaken, is it any wonder that planning should end where it actually did and in the process get discredited? A choice of wrong investment or inefficient investment is not a prerogative of planning as such and Little does concede that inefficient industry and missing of many opportunities for good industrial investments characterise several Latin American countries which did not boast any planning. But the question is, if planning cannot avoid the mistakes which lack of planning permits, how does planning establish its *raison d'être?*

The diminishing importance of planning is because of confusing a planning model on a grand scale with actual planning. If the importance of the latter were recognised, greater emphasis would have been given to project planning and sectoral planning rather than to comprehensive overall planning. This was almost always ignored, and in consequence, cost escalations impaired feasible projects, and lack of profitability of the projects already implemented destroyed new projects. All this led to the shortage of savings in relation to the investment requirements and thus to the emergence of inflation. So the villain of the piece is not planning *per se* but planning of a wrong kind, totally divorced from the prevailing political reality and the efficiency imperatives.

Little makes a strong case against quantitative controls on imports though his critique cannot be considered to be truly in a neo-classical mould. In the context of economic development of a country with imperfections of all kinds characterising it, imports need to be regulated. But the issue is which of the available instruments can do it in the most efficient manner. However, the way import controls have worked in practice in all countries has spawned the very things whose production is sought to be contained. Tariffs and countervailing excise duties can restrict luxury imports better than quantitative controls. As Little argues,

> ...there is a price mechanism way of dealing with luxury imports, which is to tax them heavily by a high tariff while at the same time taxing the domestic production, or potential production of substitutes by excise taxes. This is likely to do more to raise domestic savings, and so permit capital goods imports, for two reasons; first the high tariff on residual imports results directly in government income and savings; and second domestic substitutes or luxury imports often have a high import component....(p. 65).

One should only consider the experience in India and elsewhere in the Third World to see whether this is not true. Import controls restricted import of luxury goods but not inputs which go into the domestic production of luxury goods, which prospered under one sort of incentives or another from the government. This apart, what Little has said does not differ in respect of its core argument from what Kalecki expounded in his celebrated article in *The Economic Weekly* in the 1950s. His thesis was to put in place a graduated scheme of indirect taxation in a developing economy in such a way that only the "essential consumption" as defined by him was encouraged.

Little no doubt stresses now and again the importance of price mechanism in the development process. However, his support to price mechanism is not unqualified. The history of administered prices, even when necessary because of the logic of the situation, is not edifying. In actual operation, the personal judgement of politicians and administrators did not prove itself to be superior to the impersonal judgement of the markets. This is not surprising for the simple reason that the fundamental factors making for imperfect market mechanisms in LDCs have been the same as those which tend to render the administered price system unreliable as a guide to allocation of resources. The main argument against following the market mechanism to have a free reign in LDCs is that asset and income distribution is skewed, that monopoly power rules the markets, and information is scanty and ill distributed. But it is a matter of common knowledge that the prices in these countries are fixed by the politicians and the administrators under the influence of the same economic agents who possess a relatively large proportion of assets and income. Indeed, the latter system is worse because everything is done in secrecy and in conspiratorial fashion, depending upon which of the vested interests, at any point in time, is nearer the seat of political power. The arbitrarily administered prices tainted with political manipulation have little to commend themselves any more than prices determined in the imperfect markets.

Little's support to the market mechanism in LDCs is subject to very many caveats.

> Even where the price mechanism is reasonably undistorted, there remain very large areas where investment budgeting or control is indicated: (1) where the price mechanism is no guide because the product cannot be sold on a market; (2) where there are overriding social reasons against it being marketed (for example, education); (3) where uncoordinated investment decisions might go very wrong; and (4) in the case of very large investments, which would make a noticeable dent in the total amount of investment (p. 33).

Can even a socialist planner disagree with such a modified price mechanism?

In my view, Little's discussion of the dependency theories is the most captivating, apart from being relentless in logic though lampooning in tone but rich in facts. He shows at places how much of the dependency economics is riddled with internal contradictions and how its neo-Marxist garb is far removed from what Marx himself envisaged. For instance, Marx thought that capitalism even when imported by imperial power was a necessary precondition in the stagnant economy of the East because it would in the end lead to the emergence of socialism. The dependency economists just argued against it, emphasising that the links of the periphery with the metropolitan centres, distorted and stymied the whole process of development of the former. If dependency is interpreted as a trading relation or investment relation with any advanced capitalist countries, then it would lead to some of the most absurd conclusions. Does it mean that LDCs should trade only with each other? Or else should they trade with the socialist countries? But then what is the guarantee that the socialist countries will not or do not exploit each other or the LDCs which trade with them? There are too many examples of LDCs' trade with socialist countries resulting in the exploitation of the former by the latter. Even within the socialist camp, trading relations have been unequal, which often culminated in the rupture of diplomatic relations. Dependency as a concept is at best fuzzy and at worst meaningless. Here it is worth recalling Little's very sarcastic remark:

> The dislike of dependency may be that there is expected harm, or risk of harm, as compared with some (difficult to define) independency. Dependency on a certainly benign being, God, perhaps, may be welcome. But some people may resent dependency even if assured that it is benign (p.224).

It is more uncomfortable and inconvenient for the dependency economists to be told that their description of the state of affairs in the so-called dependent economies and the remedies to reduce their dependency are not at all different from the description and prescription suggested by the conventional economists. Dependency economists stress the evil consequences stemming from excessive industrial protection through import controls such as agricultural stagnation, frequent balance of payments crises, non-competitive domestic industrial sector and the urban deterioration, etc. As Little argues on the basis of substantial evidence, it is the policy recommendations of the leftist economists, who were vociferous in advocating pervasive price and import controls, from which the consequences they denounce have emanated. What is even more damaging to the dependency economists is that their policy prescriptions, if derived logically from their diagnosis, would be on all fours with those of the neo-liberal economists. I believe that the time has now come for all those who are deeply interested in economic development not to be bamboozled by the various labels attached to different theories of economic development. The distinction between one socialist country and another is as striking as the distinction between a capitalist country and a socialist country or for that matter between two capitalist countries. This sort of label addiction is a reflection of either total intellectual bankruptcy or rank dishonesty.

Little's handling of the issues of distributive justice in the context of economic development is also quite refreshing. The clamour by all LDCs for distributive justice is often limited to their concern for justice between States, and not justice between people within their sovereign territories. For this reason, the LDC statesmen, irrespective of the nature of the political regimes they represent, are more enthusiastic about the New International Economic Order (NIEO) than about the "basic needs strategy of the World Employment Conference, which was telling them to look after their poor better" (p.320). Nowadays most of the LDCs have even gone to the extent of asserting that "international conferences should make proposals only about inter-State relations" (p.326). If LDCs themselves are callous about their own people, why blame the North for aggravating poverty in the South?

Little's treatment of the trade option for the LDCs is neither as elegant nor relevant as his discussion of other controversial aspects of development. His faith in the export-led strategy is almost absolute. However, he seems to overlook what Arthur Lewis, whose contribution he quotes approvingly at many places in his book, has said about LDCs which opted for external trade rather than domestic agricultural development. Lewis strongly believes that the LDCs by choosing a trade option almost destroyed their domestic growth mainly because of poor performance in labour productivity in agriculture, since agricultural surplus constituted the lynchpin of economic development and the lack of it. Little, of course, does not deny the crucial role of agricultural surpluses but fails to perceive a link between the generation of agricultural, particularly food, surpluses and the trade option.

In the same way, Little takes labour surpluses and agricultural surpluses as two independent phenomena. Even conceding that labour surpluses are low during the busy seasons in LDCs when the demand for agricultural operations is at its peak or that labour surpluses are unrealisable without institutional and social transformation, it is rather farfetched to argue, as Little does, that labour surpluses are a mirage. Furthermore, he is not sufficiently aware that labour surpluses and agricultural surpluses are different sides of the same coin. If agricultural surpluses are generated through increases in labour productivity, which in turn entails the use of new technology, the economy does end up with labour surpluses. Putting it another way, the larger the agricultural surplus, the greater the possibilities of siphoning off surplus labour from agriculture to non-agricultural occupations.

Though Little's book is controversial and provocative it certainly does not write an epitaph on development economics or development policy. It tells its readers that they have either not learnt by doing or only half-learnt what they have sought to do. They, therefore, should start to do by learning from the experiences so far accumulated by LDCs. If certain theories to which some got addicted over the years have now been found to be irrelevant and inadequate, they should not hesitate to cast them away and look at the problems faced by LDCs afresh and with new insights. Economists have survived too long through submergence and it is time that they come out in the open with all their wits and, most importantly, the facts.

Published in the Economic and Political Weekly XIX(8): 337–39 (1984).

10 | Economic Growth *versus* Income Distribution
A Perennial Charade

Who is it who said that economics, for all it esoteric techniques and highfalutin phrases, is the most frustrating of all social sciences? It stridently proclaims to be a scheme of thought, a body of its own rules of the game, but dissolves into a mere manifesto of schism. As a social discipline it stands at the Olympian heights for its achievement of intellectual breakthrough, but when it descends to the lowland of policy making it breaks down, to be classified as no more than an art of the possible. In the realm of practical policies, the same ideas are churned around like the sartorial fashions, though in different nuances and expressed in different lingo.

Nowhere is this description of economics, in its practical ramification, more apt than in the discussion on economic development of the less developed countries (LDCs) in the world of today. Time was when state control of economic activity was considered to be the basic imperative of economic policy, with all the egalitarian connotation in its trail. Then a turnaround came about in the thinking of the earthy politicians and ivory tower economic theorists. The order of priorities in concepts was reversed. State intervention became taboo; income redistribution was good only as a red herring for the social cranks who had somehow to be silenced. Consumer sovereignty and Pareto optimality were the hallowed deities; maximisation of saving and investment was the new epistle. It appeared for a while that economists and policymakers regained their touch and they were truly on 'the track of a solution'.

But this state of bliss hardly lasted before an array of fresh questions assailed the minds of those who were at the helm of policymaking, what with mounting unemployment and growing social inequity. Now it is back to square one, with the early ideas on economic development and income distribution coming back in vogue. Economic policymakers and advisers want to concentrate primarily on the more pressing demands in LDCs for greater equality in income distribution and for more employment.

It is believed that once the desired income distribution is achieved, growth would take care of itself. However, this renewed emphasis on distributive aspects of economic development does not answer one fundamental question of why some of the countries which had avowedly planned along the lines now being advocated under a rubric of 'new strategy' ended up with a path of development substantially different from one embarked upon. Before this question is answered, it may perhaps be helpful if the issues implying an antithetical relationship between growth and income distribution or growth and employment are probed a little more closely.

When the dilemma before LDCs is posed as one between growth and income distribution or growth and employment, its implicit logic is often slurred over. The objective of subordinating growth to income distribution may mean broadly two things. First, it may imply that it is the content of growth rather than its quantum which is of crucial significance from the point of view of welfare of the people in LDCs. Second, it may be taken as suggesting that the desired income redistribution can be attained irrespective of what the rate of growth of the economy is.

Taking the former first, it is true that output is not a homogeneous entity; it can comprise refrigerators, movie cameras for the rich, as well as food, clothing and cheap housing for the masses. Both types of goods are, however, encompassed by that generic term, growth, so that denigrating growth in general is tantamount to ignoring also the growth of essential goods. When such a pattern of output is envisaged, the rate of growth denotes the production of essential consumption goods and investment goods. Thus, there is no contradiction between growth and the need to produce goods of mass consumption.

Many of the planners, when they speak of the rate of growth, have their eyes riveted on this essential aspect of consumption, but things go askew not in conception but in execution, not in lack of proper strategy but in its implementation, not in perception of the situations in LDCs but in the failure of administrative response. To recognise this hiatus between the idea and its working out should not lead one to discarding the main ingredient of influencing income distribution, that is, the rate of growth.

Under the second interpretation of the income distribution as a primary goal of economic policy, it can be easily demonstrated that a country even with an extremely skewed income distribution would be better off with growth than without it. In an economy where living standards are abysmally low, anything that raises the aggregate output is worth having. While the relative income differences would continue to be as uneven as before, absolute level of income of all classes of people would be scaled up; so as to bring the incomes earned in the lowest bracket nearer to the level thought to be reflective of a minimum standard of living. This is even more so when the State makes a conscious effort to redistribute incomes in favour of the poorest segment of population through fiscal and other economic devices, under which incomes of the first five per cent of the earning population—and this is the class which is supposed to corner about 40–50 per cent of the national income in most of the LDCs—are sliced off for transferring to those below the poverty line.

The question that assumes critical importance is whether such income transfers would be smoother than otherwise, when the growth of output is less or it is higher. In a society where democratic institutions prevail for good or evil, such a shift in income from the rich to the poor would be resisted by the middle classes with an effective voting power, let alone the very affluent. But the same classes would be more willing—or, perhaps, a better way of putting it, less resistant—to a portion of their income being diverted to the poor classes if the total income is growing at a certain rate. It is all because of the illusion created by the concept of the average and the marginal. The richer classes would not feel cheated if some proportion of the increased income is taken away than if inroads are made in the existing level of their incomes. It is some such realisation on the part of the planners in India which led them to argue for a higher rate of investment and growth, so that it would benefit the poorest 40 per cent of the people.[1]

Then again, it is necessary to be clear about what exactly is connoted by the concept of income distribution in LDCs. It inspires awe in one's mind to be told that the first five per cent of the population claims, say 40–50 per cent of total income in the country, but this feeling should be tempered by the simultaneous realisation that in the top income brackets are included all organized industrial workers, small agriculturists, very small-sized industrial enterprises, and the lower middle classes, whose average earnings can be compared only with the earnings of the lowest decile in the size distribution of income in many of the developed countries, and it is these classes which have a larger weightage in that income bracket. This is enough to prove that the real problem in LDCs is not so much the skewed income distribution becoming

---

1. "Perspective Development: India 1960-61–1975-76: Implications of plans of minimum level of living", 1962. Planning Commission, Government of India (mimeo).

even more skewed as the one of improving the standard of the whole mass of people, which is possible only with rapid economic growth.

Sources of income can be generated in such economies largely through the creation of jobs for the unemployed or underemployed, which again is a function of investment expenditure. In fact, expansion of investment outlay and the growth of employment, defined appropriately in the context of labour surplus in underdeveloped countries, are intertwined.

One of the intractable problems faced in LDCs is how to measure covert unemployment, which is a more widespread phenomenon. Perhaps, it now seems that the most persuasive definition of underemployment is given by the income-cum-productivity approach, under which productivity aspects of employment are underscored more than its earning aspects *per se*. In that case, the real incomes of the unemployed, who are the lowly ones in the income scale, can be bettered by increasing their productivity either in their existing occupations or by transferring them to the more productive vocations or by transferring the incremental incomes from the rich to the poor.

All those three ingredients form part and parcel of one single approach to development and income distribution. Increase in labour productivity, be it in the existing activity or the newly emerging one, is a direct function of investment, and income transfers are directly dependent on income growth. Hence, change in income distribution is only the reflected image of the main desideratum in these countries, *viz.*, the rate of growth of income.

A step-up in investment rate is but one aspect of a solution to the unemployment problem or income distribution. The other lies in the choice of techniques of production. Here again, as in the other areas of economics, conventional wisdom—whether conventional or not depends on which side one stands of the prevailing controversy on issues of economic policy—throws enough light on how the techniques of production should be chosen.

It was furiously debated in the late 1950s how to cope with the choices open to a labour-surplus economy. With the given techniques of production and given factor price ratio, the planner can aim at solving the problem of underemployment in two ways. First, he may try to maximise the rate of growth of income over a certain time horizon. In this case, the output minus wages over capital will have to be maximised. As relatively greater proportion of wage income is supposed to be consumed rather than saved, in contrast to profit incomes where the reverse is true, the technique chosen will have to be relatively more capital-intensive. But then immediate employment would be small, to be compensated by greater employment in the future. In the second case, the planner may maximise immediately income and employment. This is a case of greater degree of labour intensity in the techniques chosen. However, greater absolute amount of immediate income and employment are offset by a smaller rate of growth in the future. This is because a larger proportion of incomes generated is in the form of wage incomes, where income saved is relatively small.

Can one argue, therefore, that the choice of techniques poses an either-or problem in regard to growth and income distribution? Here again, it is possible to reconcile the two conflicting objectives. Suppose the most capital-intensive techniques are used for all the sectors—industry or agriculture—which use scarce input like capital. After it is fully used up, there would still remain a large pool of unemployed. This labour is going to be idle, consuming the social output without contributing to its production. Now, if this labour is employed together with other non-scarce resources in producing whatever goods and services can be produced, and assuming that the additional consumption of the labour so employed does not exceed their production, the per capita output would increase almost immediately, and over time it would be higher than in the case where the redundant labour is kept idle.

Of course, the rate of growth in this case would be smaller than under the maximisation of rate of growth criterion, as saving/income ratio would be smaller; but the absolute level of incomes as well as employment would be all through higher. It will thus be perfectly rational to use concurrently techniques with utmost degree of labour intensity in certain projects, in conjunction with the most capital-intensive techniques in certain others. The policy indicated by this analysis is that the government should start a well-organised public works programme, to be dovetailed into a general development plan.

This programme would consist of an inventory of projects such as road construction, small irrigation, cheap housing, etc. which would primarily involve expenditure on labour and other non-scarce raw materials. They have to be organised not on an *ad hoc* basis but as a continuing arrangement. They should be distinguished, however, from the 'mere' relief programmes in that they can be an instrument of changing the existing pattern of agricultural employment, that they can provide the surplus labour with an assured source of employment unhampered by the exigencies of agricultural activity.

Aside from the fact that there need not be posted an inverse relationship on a theoretical plane between income distribution, empirically too, there is no strong evidence to support such antithetical relationship. It would indeed be heroic to draw general conclusions in a definitive manner from any statistical series, and even more so in LDCs where the data base is inadequate, and time series are flawed by the difference in concepts. Yet one may allude, rather illustratively, to the quantitative work on India, where more heat is generated than light is shed, to illuminate the trends in income distribution.

Contrary to the general belief, the existing studies fail to indicate a firm trend. In any particular direction in so far as income distribution is concerned, some of them show that concentration ratios which are taken as a measure of inequality of incomes have declined during some years of the planning period, while some others depict the opposite trend. In two studies by the same author, two trends but in opposite directions are noticed in income distribution. All one can say with a reasonable degree of certitude, therefore, is that income distribution in India over the planning period may have moved in favour of the poor only marginally, or one could also argue that but for whatever growth the economy could muster, income distribution could have worsened. In this negative sense at least, the growth of the economy has contributed to arresting further adverse change in income distribution. It is possible to speculate that with the time trend observed in the growth of the Indian economy, which itself was not more than 3–4 per cent, the actual income distribution certainly would have improved only if the population had not increased at the rate it did in fact.

So it seems that there is no valid reason why there should be a contradiction between growth on the one hand and equal income distribution on the other. The choice between the two is no more than a Hobson's choice. Those who are keen on income distribution have to be equally committed to the growth of the national income in the same way as those who lay much store on growth should not fail to seize upon the opportunities to change income distribution in a desired direction. One would do well to remember Robert Solow's sagacious words, though written in a different context:

> I think those who oppose continued growth should in all honesty face up to the implication of their position for distributional equity and the prospects of the world poor. I think those who favour continued growth on the grounds that only thus can we achieve some equity ought to be serious about that. If economic growth with equality is a good thing, it doesn't follow that economic growth with a lot of pious talk about equality is a good thing. In principle, we can have growth with or without equity. An argument about first principles should keep these things separate.[2]

Solow almost suggested that economic theory did pretty well standing firmly on its feet and it is not necessary for it to perform acrobatics by standing on its head!

---

2.   Robert M. Solow, "Is the end of the world at hand?", Challenge 16(1): 39–50.

Even as concepts in economic theory or as the leading elements of economic strategy and policy in LDCs, these ideas give one a feeling of *déjà vu*. At least some countries' planners visualised the inevitability of equity considerations in the planning process; Indian planners were perhaps the pioneers in this development game. The First Five Year Plan, itself a model of clear thinking, lucid exposition and keen awareness of social responsibilities, delineates at great length the issues of income distribution, unemployment and growth; the same logic is carried forward in the subsequent plans. Looking back with hindsight, it was, by any test, a visionary foray into development economics. Yet, these visionary ideals remained unconsummated, despite many achievements to the credit of the planners. These failures are to be ascribed not to the lack of will on the part of the politicians because the will was never weak, not to the absence of political stability, as it was one of the few blessings bestowed on India, but to tardy implementation.

Why is it that the implementation faltered and failed? The priorities in regard to output mix and the corresponding investment volume and pattern, which are derived meticulously through the input-output matrix and iterative exercises, got distorted in the course of their transmission from the manifesto of the political parties to the higher echelons of the government. The distortions took various forms. Goods not to be produced were produced, relegating the production of essential goods to the background; investment not to be encouraged was undertaken, controls designed to prevent meretricious consumption were employed to achieve the very opposite. The public control of economic activity in order to attenuate the concentration of economic power in fact entailed a drain on the public exchequer with its deleterious consequences for income distribution.

The public sector thus presented no more than a different visage of capitalism which it sought to replace; the fiscal devices adopted for bringing about the transfer of income from the affluent to the immiserised mass of people became a haven for the tax dodger. In short, there were seepages of many sorts in the transmission channel through which strategies and ideas of the planners percolated from the board rooms of planners to the floors of the workshops, and the agricultural farms. If, therefore, one has to search for the location of these seepages of ideas, one has to go the whole hog of the political and social processes in these countries.

The implementation of the designed programmes implies a certain transmission process—a channel through which ideas and ideals which the politicians profess and the administrators articulate move up from the political parties to the political government, and move down from the latter to the bureaucracy and further down to the people. It also subsumes a feedback from the lowest layer to the political parties *via* the political government.

In concrete terms, this process can be segmented into the following stages. First the masses, through their voting power, give mandate to the political parties through elected representatives. Second, the party representatives articulate it in the parliamentary forum and leave it to the political government to translate it into action. Third, the political government judges the feasibility of the mandate in terms of its ability on one hand and its responsibility to the electorate on the other. Fourth, the bureaucracy interprets the decision of the political government and then acts on it. The upward feedback is from the masses, to the political parties via the bureaucracy and the political government.

It is obvious that the programme intended would be best actualised only if the upward and downward movements of ideas and ideals are smooth and fast. But it is not so as there are various influences acting on this transmission of programmes, emanating both from within and without. The pressures from within arise because at each stage there is a leakage. Thus the elected representatives, members of the government or the bureaucracy, can snap the strings which bind them to their creators. The pressures from without are generated because of the contradictions prevailing between the interests of various types of groups—between industrial workers and the unemployed, small agriculturists and big ones, agriculturists and landless labour, white-collar lower middle classes and the organised industrial workers, the big industrialists and the small ones, and so on. These contractions do not permit the translation of vague ideas and ideals into effective policies. In a type of society like China's where the ideologically motivated mass movement has integrated the different organs of policymaking—the party, government, the bureaucracy—the severity of the contradictions between the various interest groups has been watered down.

It is, therefore, necessary to seek the causes of the failure of the implementation of egalitarian social and economic programmes in the nature of the political regimes of LDCs described as, to borrow the tantalising phrase of Michel Kalecki, "intermediate regimes". K N. Raj has very perceptively analysed the implications of such regimes, in terms of economics and politics, for the development policies of these countries.[3] It is clear from his thesis that the pressures from within have affected more grievously the "intermediate regimes" insofar as pursuit of egalitarian policies is concerned. And yet, there is no escape from such regimes, in view of the almost total absence of more revolutionary options, either due to the weaknesses of the ideology or the peculiar sociology of radicalism. It follows, therefore, that a solution for amelioration of the social ills has to be found within the framework of the "intermediate regimes", through necessary adaptations.

While Raj has to be lauded for visualising this new dimension to the discussion on development policies, his analysis is short on the directions in which the pressures emanating from the heterogeneity of group interests can be usefully harnessed for the social good. One conceivable way is to devise an institutional arrangement within the compass of the "intermediate regimes", which can decelerate the pressures on decision making. Is it not possible, for instance, to confer the right on the electorate to recall their representatives if they fail to implement the promises within a finite time horizon? Is it beyond human ingenuity to immunise the political government from the pressures or the elected representatives, through tearing down the walls of secrecy surrounding government operations or through open public discussion? May it not be that the government can institute a machinery whereby it issues its specific directives to the bureaucracy, in wide public gaze, as to what it should do in spheres assigned to it and then make it accountable for its failures? Could not the bureaucracy announce to the public when it takes action, the basis on which certain policies are taken, thereby paving the way for those unfavoured to ask for redress of their grievances? There is a world of possibilities open to the "intermediate regimes" if only one feels sufficiently committed to the goal of income equality and social justice.

Economic transformation of the poor societies, thus, is more a non-economic problem, which is not amenable to purely economic nostrums. Adding the trappings to the economic strategy, however well articulated or motivated, if divorced from the nature of the regime which is supposed to make it operational, would only end in a maze of policies, conducive neither to the desired change in income distribution nor to social transformation. In such a situation, to set aside economic growth as an objective of policy on the ground that income distribution is a prior condition to be met is to lose something tangible on the swing without getting anything by way of equality

3. K.N. Raj. "The economics and politics of "intemediate" regimes" (mimeo).

in income distribution on the round-about. It is not growth, but economics as social discipline, which is a 'besieged deity'. It is futile to expect them to follow a system of government and social order of the communist China vintage; the socio-political-cultural history and the deeply entrenched traditions deny them this option. Economists need to digest the lessons of history. Phelps Brown was it who said that "he is not a trained economist if he is not a numerate; neither is he trained if he is not a historiate."

If the role of economics and economists is constrained, so much more is true of the aid policies to influence the developed countries. Aid would contribute to the process only if it were purely a question of resource transfer to fill the gap in domestic saving. But the egalitarian forces have to be internally generated more than externally transplanted. Any persuasion by outside agencies, however gentle, would hone the inner contradictions in these societies which, far from bringing about income redistribution and growth, would only help to destroy them. There is no better alternative to the solution of the problem facing LDCs than to understand the inner core of it.

Published in Commerce 47(3): 27-32 (1978).

11 | Management Accumulation Process

In early discussions about theories of economic development the main interest was focused on capital accumulation as the central theme. Economic progress in terms of the rate of growth of per capita income was assumed to be a consequence of larger quantities of inputs participating, perhaps in different combinations, in the production process. The inadequacies of an exclusive occupation with capital accumulation were soon realised. It is not merely the material agents but also the efficiency with which they are combined and their quality which have an important bearing on growth performance. There has thus been something of a shift in the discussion of development economics away from the quantitative aspects of capital accumulation and toward what is now thought of as 'technological change'.

The efficiency of factor combination may be considered as a function of management and the organisation of productive activity and can be called a third factor of production, no less important than labour and capital. This third factor must itself be considered qualitatively; the growth performance of the economy will not necessarily improve by the mere accumulation of managerial and organisational talent through, say, a spread of general and university education. In a larger number of developing countries in Asia, such as India, Pakistan, Sri Lanka, the Philippines, and in some of the Latin American countries such as Argentina and Brazil, there is no dearth of managerial ability as such, i.e. persons of good natural ability and general education. Yet these potential managers have not been able to contribute to the improvement of their national growth performance as much as they could have if they had been sufficiently oriented toward accomplishing their principal tasks. It is such qualitative aspects of the entrepreneurial organisation in those developing countries already having some management talent that will be discussed here.

Economic development entails a change in the whole gamut of relationships—social, political, production, and psychological—which combine the elements of what John Hicks calls "custom" and "command" based societies (Hicks, 1969: 11–16). They have to be overhauled, at times drastically, to make them approximate to a market organisation. These relationships are not distinct entities, independent of each other. They are all threads in the same economic and social fabric. The organisation of society—that generic term—embraces them all. Societies undergoing economic transformation have to refashion their organisation so as to gear themselves to accomplish what the compulsions of economic growth set before them. It is for this reason that it is "no longer possible to view organisational change as a *de minimis* and to be neglected. In fact, changes in environment and in the way a society chooses to organise itself in various markets may have a major impact on the growth performance of the system as a whole" (Ranis, 1963).

These organisational chores have to be discharged by managers, a term used here in the widest sense, encompassing not only those who are in charge of a particular firm or industry but also those who create administrative infrastructure in the economy as a whole. Attributes required of managers are varied: they include skill in adapting an existing body of knowledge to the conditions in their own economies, inventiveness in choosing those forms of organisation and technique which can get the best results under given circumstances, and the purposiveness in distinguishing the essential from the inessential. Priority, therefore, has to be given to the generation and development of such a body of management knowledge and the organisation of the economy appropriate to it.

For organising production along modern lines, two types of managerial ability are essential. The first type relates to management external to a firm or industry, which is directed toward the efficient conduct of the affairs of the entire national community. This is mainly the area economic policy and public administration. The second type of managerial ability is internal to the producing units. Management of this sort represents those qualities that are necessary to direct, to quote Alfred Marshall, "production so that a given effort may be most effective in supplying wants" under complex conditions of modern life and "to bring together the capital and labour required for the work, to engineer its general plan, and to superintend its minor details" (Marshall, 1936: 334–5).

Because of the conscious direction of the economy, through formulation of either imperative or indicative plans, it is the problems of management external to producing units that have come to the forefront in many developing countries. Both the exigencies of modern technology and an increasing concern with the quality of life have led to a conscious, direct governmental control, albeit within a varying margin, of the economies in the developed countries, and even more so in developing countries. The pervasive intervention of the State in economic activity may in some countries have been rooted in political dogma, but it is based also on a practical sense of the needs of developing countries. For one thing, developing countries have to try to telescope their economic development process to escape the explosive situation created by population pressure. Furthermore, the world many of them live in is altogether different from the world of perfect markets with which economists deal. The market imperfections make the prevailing prices a poor guide to the allocation of resources. The State, in such a situation, is envisaged as having a duty to minimise, if not remove, the severity of market imperfections—though often in practice it does the opposite. Thus, the process of economic growth in less developed countries has to be a socially motivated process.

All this is now doctrine. However, what is not yet well understood is how to make State intervention as effective as possible so as to achieve the desired objectives. The experience in many developing countries over the last decade and a half suggests that achievement of development goals is impeded almost at every stage either because of the faulty judgement of the administrators or at times because of 'over-administering'. There are many examples to show that had appropriate orientation been given to the administrative structure and personnel in these countries and had measures been taken to adapt them to the needs of modernisation, which is what economic development is all about, far more could have been accomplished with the given amount of resources.

What then has been wrong with the administrative structure in the developing countries? It is very difficult, indeed impossible, to generalise on this issue, as the developing countries do not provide a uniform pattern of administrative organisation and abilities. At one extreme are India, Pakistan, Ceylon, Malaysia, and other countries where the former rulers left a fairly well organised administrative apparatus. These countries had an educated elite (including experienced administrators), and small in relation to requirements as this administrative cadre may have been, it also had an established system of procedures and rules on which to work. At the other extreme are countries where the former authorities had failed to provide training in administration and even the general education on which such training must be based. It is this diversity in circumstances which underlies the varying economic performances of these countries. Yet, one can possibly classify in broad categories the causes of their failure in the administration, or management, of the process of economic and social transformation.

The first reason is the lack of what might be called an activist orientation in the administration of these countries, even when the administrative system was well constructed. In India, Pakistan, and elsewhere a class of administrators was left at the time of independence who had generally started their careers as district officers in charge of law and order and revenue collection. Their training and attitudes stressed the importance of acting in accordance with an elaborate set of rules; such attitudes were no doubt well suited to earlier times. In a changed context that called for more creative attitudes, their dependence upon established precedent tended to atrophy their creativity and reduce their practical usefulness. They too frequently attempted to apply the rules and regulations meant for routine administration to the management of economic enterprises in a period of rapid change. Compliance with the rules seemed to people so conditioned more important than getting results in terms of output and profit. Because of this attention to rules rather than to output and profit, to status and seniority rather than to efficiency and initiative, economic growth often faltered and failed. This is also true of countries that have remained tied to the administrative procedures bequeathed by the old rulers, though a new class or new generation of administrator has emerged.

The inadequacy of public administration to cope with the task of economic management is nowhere more evident than in the record of enterprises in the public sector. Backwardness in the public sector betokens not so much an inefficiency of the sector *per se* as the unsuitability of the mental attitudes of the administrators, which are generally not oriented toward profits. It is often supposed that profits in public enterprises are of little consequence; such enterprises may be seen as good because they are an instrument of income distribution and social justice. This attitude, discernible among many administrators in developing countries, is largely a reflection of the prevailing notion in these countries that profit is associated with exploitation.

There is widespread confusion between the accrual of profit as such and its use. In a poor country, the use of profit for luxurious living should of course be discouraged, but it often takes place and even a limited amount of such conspicuous consumption blinds many officials, who have a different ethos, from seeing that profit is also the source of saving, badly needed for financing economic development. Public enterprises with growing surpluses assist the expansion of the entire economy and accelerate the rise in the standard of living. It is highly desirable, therefore, for the administrators to discard their traditional remoteness from profit seeking and to perceive the creative role of profits in the development process. It was this orientation of the administrators in many developed countries, particularly on the European continent, which made the public sector enterprises there a potent instrument of growth and distribution.

When the administrators are trained to accept that economic development involves constant change, it will be easier for them to ensure that their policies are action oriented. Operation of a large number of controls which constitute a staple diet in most of the developing countries should have more positive than negative aspects; the principal objective of the controls should be to achieve something rather than prevent everything. Once administrators are convinced of this, they will be less prone to multiply controls needlessly and more willing to hasten the progress of enterprises, whether in the public or the private sector. This is not mere wishful thinking. In Japan, whose economic achievements so many developing countries would like to emulate, the bureaucracy, though large, is oriented to growth and has a clear notion of the area of its jurisdiction. It is at least in part because Japanese industry and government administration work in tandem that Japan's economic growth has been so spectacular.

If the quality and quantity of the administrative organisation of the government provide external economies needed for rapid growth, it is the management of a firm or industry which helps to internalise those economies for the benefit of that firm or industry and thereby the economy as a whole. The ideal manager in industry is supposed to be a Schumpeterian type of entrepreneur who innovates and carries out new combinations of factors of production and distribution and the organisation that he builds up is one where his creativity and innovating spirit blossom out. It is less necessary to aim at an immediate creation of such a class of entrepreneurs in less developed countries because the process of economic development is essentially an adaptive one which has to draw heavily on known technology in the developed world outside. The entrepreneurial class in the developing countries should perhaps be more assimilative than creative; skilful adaptation rather than bold innovation is what his situation generally demands. This does not imply, however, that the manager in industry should shun any creative activity. All that is suggested is that his creative faculties should be harnessed for adapting known technology to his immediate environment.

It is often said of the industrial organisation in developing countries that it is more dynastic than dynamic. The dynastic element is not surprising; most of the enterprises are started as family-owned concerns. There is nothing basically wrong in perpetuating these traits; the history of industrialised countries is replete with instances of great firms and even industries growing out of small, well-built family enterprises. But when the enterprise begins to stagnate in its family traditions, it is time to break with the past and widen the base of the organisation through the infusion of talent from outside the closed circle of group or family.

This, however, is not easy to do, particularly since there are forces at work in developing countries to attenuate competition and render such drastic steps unnecessary. There is a widely spread regimen of controls and regulations in most of these countries which render the entrepreneur impervious to the prods of competition. Profits often flow in easily, and when they do not, the internal political pressures can be readily built up to create a captive market, thus enabling managers and owners of industry to turn their backs on major organisational problems and persist in their traditional—often antiquated— practices. In the presence of competitive forces, on the other hand, the producers have to strive constantly to reduce cost per unit of output, to make profits, and to survive. In this sense, development of managerial ability in private industry is a function of a properly articulated economic policy.

Management techniques closely correspond to the technology of production. Here the question arises, particularly in the context of the adaptive process of development in less developed countries, whether the management techniques from the developed countries should be imitated with little modification. On the face of it, there might seem to be the same objection to this course as to the importation of capital-intensive technology from the developed countries. There is an intimate association between labour-saving technology and labour-saving management practices. Harbison, for example, notes on the basis of intensive empirical investigation that:

> A thin managerial organisation is usually associated with relatively extensive utilisation of non-managerial labor forces and relatively primitive production methods, whereas a relatively deep managerial organisation is almost always found in enterprises which have the largest investment in technology, particularly in labor-saving machinery (Harbison, 1956).

This perhaps indicates that the managerial approach in the less developed countries should be qualitatively different from that in the developed countries. It should have higher labour intensity to fit into the resource endowment structure in these economies. For instance, it might be argued that where two foremen with intermediate education would suffice for supervising a production process that is labour intensive, no attempt should be made to instil greater depth in management by installing one highly qualified technical manager.

This brings us to research and development. There is a tendency in industry in many developing countries to spend a large amount of money either on development of those processes in which considerable research has already been done in the developed countries or on technology which is not immediately relevant. The first type of expenditure is sheer duplication and the second category of expenditure is unnecessary; both of course are very wasteful. Insofar as the transplantation of the technology of the developed countries is concerned, expenditure on research and development in developing countries should be on 'adaptive and environmental research' so that foreign technology is associated in a manner most suited to the resource endowment in those countries. The main problem is "one of gearing down the scale of production and sophistication of technology to lower levels and to make suitable improvisations to meet the dearth or maintenance and support facilities" (Tarapore, 1970).

This, however, is not to argue that there should be no expenditure on the development of technology which is on the frontiers of knowledge. There are many areas where Western technology, however assimilated, would simply not work in a developing country or geographic group of countries, and there is a need, therefore, for research of a more basic type. There is, for instance, a problem of devising an intermediate technology which is neither highly capital intensive as in the developed countries, nor labour intensive but inefficient, as in many developing countries. Research here would be as welcome as in agricultural techniques, and might lead to results analogous to the discovery of a new miracle rice in the Philippines and a new strain of wheat in Mexico. Moreover, expenditure on basic research does not necessarily mean an expenditure on heavy equipment for research as is common in highly industrialised countries. It is possible to devise low-cost equipment even for fundamental research, as J.B.S. Haldane demonstrated at a little laboratory for biological research in a remote town in Orissa state in India.

To sum up, in the planning strategies of many less developed countries, less importance is attached to the management and organisation of productive activity than to capital and labour. Yet, entrepreneurial organisation is also a resource which has both qualitative attributes and quantitative dimensions. Many of the developing countries, even when endowed with adequate capital and surplus labour, have faltered in their quest for rapid economic growth only because they ran short of the essential ability to use those factors in the most efficient manner possible. This means not only a waste of resources but also of time, which in a country confronted with a growing population and its rising expectations may be disastrous. In order to avoid this, the accumulation of managerial skills and organisational abilities has to be seen in its qualitative aspects. Many of the frustrations of the less developed countries could be avoided if only sufficient thought and attention were devoted to this most vital part of the development process.

REFERENCES

Harbison, F. (1956). "Entrepreneurial organization as a factor in economic development", *The Quarterly Journal of Economics* 70(3): 364–79.

Hicks, John (1969). *A Theory of Economic History.* London: Allen and Unwin.

Marshall, Alfred (1936). *Principles of Economics.* London: Macmillan.

Ranis, Gustav (1963). "Economic growth theory", *International Encyclopedia of the Social Sciences.* New York: Palgrave Press.

Tarapore, S.S. (1970). "Foreign collaboration, indigenous research, and development of Indian consultancy services", *Economic and Political Weekly* XIV(33): 143–8 (Review of Management).

Published in the Finance and Development 8(3): 8–14 (1971).

12 | Self-reliance and All That

It would indeed be a state of bliss if a nation, like an individual, could progress relying on its own saving and ingenuity than on borrowed resources and wisdom. But the world we live in is far from being this ideal state. Historically, no country has ever been able to pull itself up by its own shoestrings and the current world scene is one of country after country incurring foreign indebtedness to survive and to develop, however odious it may seem. Why then do nation states, proud of their heritage and freedom, still allow themselves to slip into a foreign debt trap? I.G. Patel has done well in focusing on this important issue in his Pant Memorial Address. However, his strictures on foreign debt might be read to have double entendre by the unwary unless the nuances of his arguments and the subtlety of his logic are comprehended.

The concept of self-reliance can possibly be defined as sole reliance on domestic savings for investment. If domestic savings could be raised and used efficiently, it is obvious that there will not be any need for foreign loans or investment. India had a remarkable saving rate, which rose from a meagre 7 per cent in 1952 to about 23 per cent some time in the 1970s. Then it declined somewhat to 21.4 per cent, and yet it could be considered by no means low, judging by absolute and relative standards. In fact, during four years, 1975–1978, India's domestic saving rate exceeded its domestic investment rate, which meant that India exported capital in those four years—a state even better than mere self-reliance. We should then ask ourselves why it is that despite such an impressive saving performance, India continued to borrow foreign savings to sustain its economic development. The answer simply is that India did not and could not use its savings efficiently. Instead, India employed its savings in the most unproductive manner, which is reflected in the rising capital-output ratio, Plan after Plan despite the pontification of the planners to reduce it. Import substituting strategy, admirable on the drawing board, ended up not in saving imports and therefore foreign exchange but in ever-expanding imports for feeding the import substituting industries. The resulting industrial structure remained high-cost and non-competitive, which denied the country the possibilities of developing export markets. The country was so much taken in by the bug of export pessimism that it saw glory in the false economic premise that domestic savings are no substitute for foreign exchange sanctified in the 1950s by some Harvard economists like Hollis Chenery. Current account deficit thus became unavoidable and India had to go on a binge of borrowing from wherever it could. The savings that went into public sector went down the drain, when major public sector enterprises incurred heavy losses year after year and the Government financed these losses through burgeoning fiscal deficit, the pernicious effects of which India has still not been able to live down.

Sole dependence on domestic savings may be a necessary condition for self-reliance but not a sufficient one. A condition precedent for translating domestic savings into foreign exchange is setting a policy framework which would ensure penalties for failure and reward for success so that its savings are productively utilised. Thus, the main desideratum is not so much that a country should use its domestic savings and shun foreign resources in whatever form as how efficiently it uses its domestic savings in productive enterprises, which alone guarantees self-reliance.

If a country could have such a policy ensuring efficient use of resources, it is a matter of indifference whether it uses domestic savings or foreign savings for financing its development. It can borrow as much as it could, provided, it can invest it in a manner that cost per unit of output is the lowest possible, assuring an economic rate of return, at least as much as the rate of interest paid on borrowed funds. In that case it will be able to compete in the international markets, to raise exports growth rate to pay for its debt servicing. Issues such as the sources of foreign borrowing, whether private financial markets or governments or international organisations, will not vex our minds nor would there be any hassle about negotiating loan guarantees or special tax benefits to the foreign investors.

In the context of foreign borrowing, the traumatic experience of the Latin American countries caught in the vortex of debt crisis is often adduced to dramatise the adverse consequences of foreign borrowing. However, those events have to be seen in perspective. The Latin American debacle was brought about by the myopic vision of the lending banks and the profligate borrowing countries. The lenders were on the lookout for a quick buck through investing their windfall funds, following the oil price rise, secure in the belief that sovereign governments would not default. The borrowers, harried by the payments deficits induced by their reckless spending for decades, disregarded the risks in access to easy credit. Thus, the economic disaster in these countries was almost preordained. If their experience has any lesson to offer, it is that foreign saving should neither be lent nor borrowed unless the borrowing country puts in place efficiency-laden economic policies, with a balance between incentives and disincentives, penalty for failure and reward for success. So that investor, producer, and a worker all learn to earn their keep.

The bottom line thus is that as long as India pursues economic policies directed toward evolving competitive economic structure, which the present government with all its failings is valiantly striving to do, we should not be skittish about using foreign capital. Indeed, there is no difference in this environment between domestic savings and foreign savings, as the efficiency in resource use would automatically ensure servicing of foreign debt. India was brought to the precipice in 1991 not because it borrowed foreign funds over the years. India simply frittered them away through gross incompetence and it will be condemned to repeat that tragic episode if it persists with the same folly, regardless of its non-dependence on foreign loans.

Unpublished, November 1992, Washington DC.

13 | India's Economic Growth
A Conundrum

India has, perhaps, been the first among developing countries in the post World War II period which became aware of the imperative to develop and devised a strategy accordingly. The efforts were attended with success in many ways. It could raise its saving-investment rate from a low level of 5–6 per cent of GDP to an impressive level of 24–26 per cent of investment over 1951–1996. It could diversify its industrial structure and develop varied human resource skills essential to manage a modern economy. Despite all these achievements, India's performance over the last four and a half decades in terms of efficiency of resource allocation and aggregate and per capita income growth has been lacklustre except during 1991–1996. Viewed in relation to achievements of other developing countries such as Korea, Taiwan, Brazil, Malaysia, Mexico, Thailand, Indonesia, and China, the Indian performance seems to pale even more into insignificance.

Two main explanations have been put forth generally for India's dismal record in growth: economic efficiency and the eradication of poverty. The first of these, advocated in a systematic fashion by Bhagwati and Desai (1970) and Bhagwati and Srinivasan (1975) emphasised the microeconomic distortions introduced by policy instruments such as industrial licensing, foreign trade and exchange restrictions, and pervasive price controls on a wide range of goods— both consumption and investment. In the words of its foremost exponent,

> The regime of controls spawned its own interests. The entire society it yielded, with entrepreneurs enjoying squatter's rights, created a business class that wanted liberalisation in the sense of least hassle, not genuine competition. The bureaucrats, however idealistic at the outset, could not but have noticed that this regime gave them the enormous power that the ability to confer rent generates. The politics of corruption also followed as politicians became addicted to the use of licensing to generate illegal funds for election and then for themselves. The iron triangle of business, bureaucrats and politicians was born around the regime that economists and like-minded ideologues had unwillingly espoused (Bhagwati, 1988).

Bhagwati-Desai-Srinivasan's landmark analysis of the Indian economy set the tone, for the first time, for a spate of critiques of Indian economic policy, which focused on analytical underpinnings rather than vague ideological generalisations. Though their analysis did not ignore political elements and their pernicious influence on the economic interrelationship that stymied India's growth and efficiency, its main accent was on economic theory, though modulated to suit Indian political and economic reality. A missing political dimension was added in a striking way to the discourse on Indian economy by Bardhan (1984) who traced the constraints on growth to the existence of a proprietary coalition of the industrial-capitalist class, white-collar bureaucrats and rich farmers. The adversarial relation among these classes, in Bardhan's view, resulted in the deceleration of public investment and the rise in the capital-output ratio in the economy, which largely accounted for the slowdown of economic growth in India.

While the Bhagwati-Desai-Srinivasan diagnosis of India's inefficient development process and Bardhan's elaboration of its political dimensions explained to a large extent India's lack of progress, both in absolute and relative senses of the term, two riddles remained to be unravelled. The first is why the stabilisation policies which India has pursued with a considerable degree of success and which constituted its indispensable preconditions for sustained growth did not lead to acceleration of India's growth rate until 1990. Scanning Indian economic history since 1951, India by and large impressively maintained macroeconomic stability, whenever it was threatened either by the external shocks such as drought or adverse terms of external trade, by resorting to conventional macroeconomic policies, conceptualised in standard economic literature and prescribed by the multinational institutions such as the International Monetary Fund and the World Bank, while at times mixing them with unconventional policies such as using the food and foreign exchange reserves to stabilise domestic prices. This intriguing phenomenon of stabilisation of the economy unaccompanied by growth assailed the minds of many economists in the past who, however, preferred not to come up with any answer to explain it. The second riddle is why the Indian policymakers shirked from mainlining the momentum of growth through unremitting structural adjustment even when a conspicuous success was achieved in stabilising the economy in the latter half of the 1980s and in stabilisation-cum-structural adjustment since 1996.

Two volumes by Joshi and Little and a monograph by Desai between them have attempted to demystify these two riddles, and in this endeavour they have largely succeeded. Unravelling of the first of these riddles, *viz.*, why macroeconomic stability in India maintained reasonably well could not lead to faster growth and efficiency in resource allocation is the principal focus of Joshi-Little's two impressive and thoroughly researched volumes. Joshi-Little have elaborated this theme in a convincing manner, within the analytic parameters moulded by "economic theory, which is, however, more pragmatic than procrustean" (Joshi and Little, 1994: 1). The conclusions Joshi-Little have drawn from this analysis provide a springboard in their second book for evaluating the Indian reforms unleashed in 1991. Though Joshi-Little have an occasional brush with the political ramification of India's economic policy, they seem to have avoided dealing with the second enigma as a deliberate choice, being concerned mainly with economic explanation of the Indian economic policy. It is here that Desai fills the gap. Desai, like Joshi-Little, does discuss, with his acerbic wit and his close knowledge of policy formulation in India, how the myriad microeconomic distortions have led to deceleration in Indian growth rate over the years, but he traverses a wider ground as he believes that India's poor performance has much to do with our government. It has been a kleptocracy—a government of patronage and spoils. It has taken a large share of national resources and wasted it on special favours (Desai, 1993: 3).

He tries to resolve the riddle about why India, every time that it finds itself in a position to grow faster, falters in its track and he seeks that answer in India's political economy and institutions. For instance, he found, while working for the Government of India in a vantage position that "In the government, I encountered much confusion about what constituted a reform, what needed to be done, what was progress and what regress. The government is run by people, who loyally served the ancien regime. They ask for autonomy, which they would turn into autocracy" (Desai, 1993: 5).

Thus, a combination of academics of the eminence of Joshi and Little, who have studied Indian economy as a part of their scholarly pursuit of macroeconomics in a global space, and an economist-cum-policymaker fiercely wedded to his strong convictions have served a mutually complementary fare, which has illumined some of the unexplored or inadequately explored areas of the Indian economic policy.

Both the volumes of Josh-Little are impressive scholarly tomes, in which vast data, covering a long period, 1964–1995, are well sifted and ingeniously employed to support their a priori judgements. Areas that are singled out for evaluation are the link between microeconomics and macroeconomics where the authors' contribution is most significant, both in terms of economic analysis and policy relevance in retrospect and prospect, and the relationship between stabilisation policy and structural adjustment policy, on which the authors have come up with somewhat novel and unconventional approaches, not often found in the debate on this issue.

Joshi and Little in their first study, "India: Macroeconomic and Political Economy, 1964–1991", have taken as their starting point why India's record of macroeconomic stability has failed to deliver rapid economic growth, and then have built up an impressive analytic edifice, which illuminates our understanding of the complexities and intricacies of India's vast economy, and the anatomy of its growth. The central thesis of Joshi and Little is that:

> ...the style of macroeconomic policy, involving multiple controls, creates large price distortions that are at the heart of the problem of the inefficient use of resources. The link between macroeconomic and microeconomic is thus an important concern in this book. A fashionable view of Indian economic policy is that it was unsound microeconomically but sound macroeconomically, and further that these phenomena were positively linked—in other words, the controls that led to microeconomic inefficiency made it easier to attain macroeconomic balance. In contrast, one of our central conclusions is that India's control system was not only microeconomically inefficient but also macroeconomically perverse.(Joshi and Little, 1994: 3)[1].

The whole superstructure of the book is erected on this basic thesis, and the main macroeconomic policy instrument that emerges as critical is the fiscal policy. Though the authors have discussed in depth other macroeconomic policies, such as trade and payments and monetary and exchange rate policies, these policies are of secondary importance.

LINK BETWEEN MACROECONOMIC MANAGEMENT AND MICROECONOMICS

Indian experience in macroeconomic management since 1952 has certain peculiarities of its own, which has distinguished it from that in several other developing and even developed countries. While the structure of macroeconomic policy has undergone some changes after 1991 with the beginning of economic reforms, it has not been divested of its major feature, which reduced its efficiency in the earlier period. There has been a belief held for long, as Joshi-Little emphasise time and again, that India succeeded by and large in maintaining macroeconomic management until the early 1980s, but this characterisation of the policy holds true in a limited sense of controlling inflation, stemming the output falls and containing the balance of payments deficit within the confines of available official capital inflows. But in a larger

---

1.   One of the two authors, Ian Little, was associated with the OECD project of which the Bhagwati-Desai book was an offshoot, and for that reason, there is considerable similarity in the treatment of microeconomic issues. Joshi-Little have carried the analysis further, however, in so far as they analysed in depth the impact of microeconomic historians on the viability of macroeconomic policy.

context of Indian rate of growth, efficiency of saving-investment, and the avoidance of frequent crises, the macroeconomic policy was inefficient and less effective, and in fact spawned severe adjustment problems throughout the four decades since 1951. Joshi-Little have made this as the centre plank of their analysis of the Indian economic policy. They argue, with a great force of logic and historical support, that:

> ...the simple dichotomy between macroeconomic and microeconomic management cannot be maintained. India's macroeconomic management has involved controls. If controls are bad for efficiency and growth, then India's macroeconomic management was bad for growth, even if reasonably good for stability. Were the controls really needed for macroeconomic management? Perhaps they were not only not needed but actually counterproductive (Joshi and Little, 1994: 342).

The reason why the controls were 'microeconomically inefficient but also macroeconomically perverse' is that they created in India a monster of a severe and stubborn fiscal adjustment problem, which attenuated the efficacy of other instruments of macroeconomic management such as exchange rate and monetary policy. They have also created "...opportunities for corruption, and the resulting payments or kickbacks raise the cost of both public and private economic activities, especially investment" (Joshi and Little, 1994: 343). The macroeconomic consequence of the control regime was most visible in the burgeoning fiscal deficit. Consider first the trade regime. Tight import controls adopted to keep the balance of payments viable proved to be a double whammy. It led to a maintenance of overvalued exchange rate, which militated against export growth. To counter these effects, the government introduced an array of subsidies which impinged on government revenue. This was in addition to the loss of revenue arising from tariffs on imports. The other revenue depressant was the subsidy on fertilisers sold to the farmers and to the domestic fertiliser industry. When import controls resulted in excess demand for fertilisers raising the price, subsidy was provided to farmers to lower the price—the administered price of fertiliser was then below the imported cost. Subsidy was also provided to the domestic fertiliser industry to bring up the price paid to it above the imported price. Both of these took a heavy toll of the fiscal policy.

Similar are the effects on fiscal balance of the industrial policy, which culminated in the existence of large public sector enterprises, again a consequence of the microeconomic management of the economy. Had the public sector been profit generating, the government could have prevented the expenditure from ballooning. In practice, however, the earnings of the public sector were inadequate to meet even the interest cost, with a deleterious impact on the government budget. For a long time it was possible to keep a lid on public sector deficit to a certain level, which could be financed without excessive inflation or creation of debt. This was partly because of concessional foreign aid but largely due to borrowing from domestic banks and other financial institutions at below-market interest rates. This could not be continued, however, on the same scale during the 1980s, first because market foreign borrowing that the government resorted to was at high market-related interest rates, and second because the domestic debt, even when incurred at low interest rates, reached a level constituting as much as 40 per cent of GDP, which in turn led to widening of fiscal deficit on account of large interest payments thereon. Thus, the manner in which India managed its balance of payments, industrial policy and other controls directed toward suppression of inflation, resulted either in reduction of revenue or rise in expenditures or both, thereby leading to perverse macroeconomic policy.

The legacy of fiscal balance or better described as fiscal imbalance has continued, perhaps with more serious consequences in a more liberalised and open economic system which India has created since 1991. The consolidated fiscal deficit of the non-financial public sector has hardly changed since 1987—hovering around 10 per cent of GDP (World Bank, 1996). Unless a serious dent is made on this deficit, India's future structural transformation and the associated growth will be seriously in jeopardy. The centrality of fiscal problem and its macroeconomic consequences, argued threadbare within a coherent analytic frame, have been placed on the front burner of policy discussions in India for the first time by Joshi and Little. The terms of debate on India's economy and policy are no longer the same. As a result, the policy advisors both within and outside India have centred their advice around the solution to the fiscal problem, avoiding peripheral issues.

The question then is how to rein in the fiscal deficit without throwing the economy out of kilter. Here too, Joshi-Little have many interesting thoughts which have been elaborated in great detail in their second volume. In order to answer this question, it is first essential to find out that level of fiscal deficit which is consistent with relative stability of the economy, undisturbed by excessive monetary expansion. It is generally known that some part of fiscal deficit can be and often is financed by base money creation, which can take place at a certain rate without inflationary pressures, as the demand for money increases with GDP. Such a monetary expansion is pure seignorage. The government can extract more revenue from higher seignorage than is warranted by the demand for money, but it would be at the cost of inflationary pressure which the economy could not tolerate. The relevant concept of fiscal deficit in this context is primary deficit, i.e. gross fiscal deficit minus the interest payments. If primary deficit less the part of it financed by seignorage is nil, then it implies that the existing public debt will grow with the interest rate paid, because the government is simply borrowing to pay interest. From this, it follows that if the real interest rate equals the GDP growth rate and there is no primary deficit, then the debt will grow at the same rate as GDP and the debt-to-GDP ratio remains unchanged. If the real interest rate is less than the rate of growth, a primary deficit is sustainable and vice versa if the real rate of interest is higher than GDP growth rate. The World Bank (1996) has made some simulations under alternative assumptions to determine the extent of fiscal adjustment in order to ensure sustainability. If the long-term real interest rate and real growth are at 6 per cent, which approximate the present expectations in India, the primary fiscal deficit will have to be in the neighbourhood of 1.5 per cent of GDP as against 3.1 per cent achieved in 1996. In fact, the reduction of primary deficit will have to be even more if the financial sector reform is to proceed even faster than before. This is because of the implications of the financial reform, particularly its two major planks—cash reserve ratio (CRR) and statutory liquidity ratio (SLR)—for the extent of fiscal consolidation. On the assumption that CRR and SLR are scaled down to 8 per cent and 25 per cent respectively, the primary deficit will have to be brought down to 0.6 per cent of GDP rather than 1.5 per cent (World Bank, 1996). Are the Indian policymakers capable or strong enough to bell the cat of fiscal deficit? Here Joshi-Little are pessimistic, as are other ardent supporters of India. The authors' concern that without any attempt at containing fiscal deficit "India is heading for another major crisis" is quite legitimate (Joshi and Little, 1996: 248).

The causes of their pessimism are rooted not so much in economic impossibility to pare down fiscal deficit as in the binding constraints ingrained in the Indian political system. They are brutally frank about India's future. "It is obviously only the nature of the political system and its balance of forces", they state, "that prevents India from regaining its erstwhile fiscal discipline. We do not know by what combination of political forces this deadlock is to be broken. It may need another crisis" (Joshi and Little, 1996: 249). Here, the authors are reminding us of the second riddle, referred to at the beginning of this article—of why India flatters with short spells of dynamism in economic policy only to disappoint by the subsequent retreat into complacency and timidity in pursuing what has proved to be a boon. Joshi-Little are no doubt aware of the political dimension of the Indian economic policy, but they have refrained from delving into it, being preoccupied with purely economic analysis. To be enlightened on this, it is necessary to turn to Desai who has many provocative and far-reaching nostrums to offer.

STABILISATION POLICIES

There was a time when stabilisation policy was considered, mainly under the influence of the International Monetary Fund on the format and content of stabilisation, to be the end all and be all of policy that the developing countries should formulate and implement. Its orthodox origin in the monetarist doctrines and its short-term adverse impact on output and employment gave it a bad name in developing countries where unemployment has been endemic and supply constraints on output severe. During the last few years, particularly the 1980s, confronted with daunting development problems in Latin America, the narrow interpretation of stabilisation policies was jettisoned and stabilisation was seen as the first but indispensable condition for initiating structural reforms directed toward elimination of microeconomic distortions. Joshi-Little have made a distinction long overdue, between stabilisation and structural reforms as a cornerstone of their analysis, viewing stabilisation as desirable for its own sake, in the sense of holding inflation and balance of payments deficit within bounds, both of which generally originate in the private sector. Joshi-Little in the process have broadened the contours of stabilisation by defining it as

> minimizing in addition to the adverse consequences for output, consumption, and investment of supply-side exogenous shocks such as droughts and changes in the terms of trade. The stabilising role of government also involves the avoidance of policy-induced shocks and this in turn requires close attention to the compatibility of policies with intertemporal constraints (Joshi and Little, 1994: 2).

This is a somewhat unconventional but necessary reinterpretation of stabilisation, which not only has made stabilisation policy more respectable to the countries for which it is prescribed but also has made their growth impact transparent and visible through its links with the structural transformation policies.

The authors' discussion of application of stabilisation policies in India over the years is both refreshing and remedial—refreshing because it is without the usual jarring shibboleths and remedial because it focuses the attention on what was deficient in those policies. One of the two major reasons for the intellectual attractiveness of their analysis is their keenness to search for the origins of the macroeconomic crises India faced and the other is their acceptance of policies such as the use of buffer food and foreign exchange stocks for stabilising the economy, which were different from the conventional monetary, exchange rate and fiscal policies. The four crises they have analysed in this context are: 1965–1967, 1973–1975, 1979–1981, and 1991–1996.[2] In their view, the first three crises were caused by the exogenous shocks, like the drought or adverse terms of trade, viz., oil price rise; the last was induced by misconceived policies. A drought during the first three crises, resulting in severe drop in agricultural, mainly food output accounted for serious inflationary pressures. The national calamities were accompanied by the war and border conflicts, which raised the level of government expenditures very sharply. The second and third crises were induced, in addition to drought, by the rise in the price of imported oil, which gave further impetus to inflation, already ignited by shortage of food output. The initial economic conditions were more or less similar during each of the first three crises, though with minor differences. During the first crisis, food stock and foreign exchange reserves were very low, but in the second, the foreign exchange situation was better but not the food reserve position. By contrast, the Indian economy during the third crisis was in a relatively strong defensive position both in respect of foreign exchange and food availability. The main and also crucial difference between the first three crises and the fourth beginning from 1990 was that it was induced by a policy of indiscriminate borrowing from foreign private sources at high interest rates, and inefficient use of those resources. This was followed by a cut-off of private foreign lending that had become a significant element in the capital account of the balance of payments.

Joshi-Little have analysed the policy response of the Indian authorities during the first three crises in an ingeniously demarcated, explicitly stated framework. First, they distinguish between a temporary and reversible agricultural supply shock and a permanent one. In the first type of situation, which was representative of India during those crises, they suggest that the agricultural supply shocks can best be handled by maintaining investment and running down previously accumulated food and foreign exchange reserves to stabilise food prices, food consumption, and price and availability of industrial raw materials. This meant there was little scope for demand management

---

2.   The first three are discussed in detail in their first volume, while the last one has been extensively commented upon in the second.

of the conventional type. What would be the choice for the policymakers, however, if the economy suffers from overheating and excess liquidity and if there are mechanisms that translate the increase in the relative price of agricultural products into an overall inflationary spiral?

This is a real dilemma. Second, the authors spell out a priori what would be the impact on consumption and investment, if oil price rise—the second of the exogenous factors leading to first three crises—is considered to be permanent. In their view, optimal path of consumption is more determinate. Consumption should fall considerably in the short run and the policies directed to that end should have priority. The optimum path of investment, however, is uncertain. An oil price rise would probably reduce investment but this effect may be counterbalanced by the effect on investment of lower interest rates internationally, following rise in saving in oil-producing countries. In their stabilisation policy discussion, Joshi-Little assume that the first of these Indian crises was a melange of two types of shocks and therefore the policies have to be predicated on that premise. In terms of their policy framework, the verdict of the authors about the efficacy and efficiency of the demand management policies during the first crisis is negative. They argue that

> ...the demand management policy in the first crisis had several shortcomings. It was instituted rather late, it went on long after the agricultural recovery, and it was concentrated on cuts in public investment. This was not very efficient in reducing the demand for food during the crisis and the persistence of the cuts had adverse effects on growth (Joshi and Little, 1994: 212).

During the second crisis of 1973-74, on the other hand, the demand management through monetary and fiscal policy was better, though the fiscal policy was rather more restrictive than warranted. In the third crisis, the inflation in particular was well contained by the demand management policy. Inflation was not accommodated and at the same time, there was no restraint on it.

The discussion of the stabilisation policy is in broad terms, just to give a flavour of the authors' analytical repertoire and the sharpness of their insights into the rather complex economic landscape of India. No attempt is made here to go into details of monetary, fiscal, exchange rate and food buffer stock policies, because they are not germane to understanding and assessing the authors' distinctive approach to stabilisation policies. The overall judgement of the authors succinctly presented is:

> Macroeconomic management was good in the simple sense that in the face of consistently adverse exogenous shocks, primarily caused by droughts and secondarily by oil price rises, both high inflation and very serious recession were avoided without any excessive buildup of debt (until the 1980s). We are not saying that it was perfect; greater stability with less loss of productive investment and output could have been achieved.

We also think that the rate of inflation influenced policy to a rather greater extent that it should have. Not only was there a tendency to overreact to price rises caused by drought, but also, when inflation was low, it tended to be wrongly assumed that everything in the garden was lovely, and so the buildup of debt was ignored. Compared with many other developing countries, reasonably stable progress was sustained... (Joshi and Little, 1994: 342).

The 1990-91 crisis was, as observed earlier, a different kind of animal. It was policy-induced. The stabilisation remedies devised were along standard lines. There was a fiscal retrenchment, credit squeeze and hefty devaluation and tightening of import controls initially. In analysing the effects of stabilisation during this period, the authors have clearly drawn a distinction between stabilisation and structural reform and attributed whatever unavoidable hardships the Indian people suffered to the stabilisation policy. But where the authors have struck a new note is in concluding that the severity of suffering was much less than feared. The suffering in the face of poverty was caused during the fourth crisis, by a drop in agricultural output due to poor harvests and the rise in cereal prices, which was not to be connected with stabilisation policy per se. Rise in poverty could be clearly ascribed to stabilisation, insofar as the latter led to a fall in rural employment following cutback in employment schemes and the reduction in fertiliser subsidies. The adverse impact of stabilisation on poverty and employment was softened, however, by the positive effects of structural reforms on industry, which arrested the fall in urban employment, which, without reform, could have risen. All these salutary consequences of stabilisation were made possible by the structural reforms which removed the economy-wide distortions inherited from the controlled regimes of the period prior to 1990.

For all the excellence of the contribution of Joshi and Little to the understanding of the Indian economy, their message to the readers is not conveyed clearly and effectively because their first volume is marred by some avoidable shortcomings both of style and organisation. The book gives an impression that the authors are overwhelmed by the richness of data they marshalled for their efforts. It is difficult for the readers, even those who are fairly conversant with the Indian economy, to go forward in narrative without stepping backward to catch the missing links in arguments or facts. These difficulties could have been avoided, if the discussion in chapters 12 and 13 had preceded the analysis of stabilisation and other policies. Similarly, chapters 5–8, on four crises, could have been prefaced by a succinct presentation with the help of key statistics of their central thesis of a disjunction between macroeconomic policy and microeconomic distortions. By posting a comprehensive analysis of fiscal, monetary, and trade and payments policies after stabilisation discussion, the authors could not avoid repetitions and at times ambiguities in their narration of stabilisation policies pursued during the four crises. It is also unfortunate that a carefully crafted note on quality of statistics is relegated to an appendix instead of upfront before the policy discussion. After all, the assessment of effectiveness of policies critically depends on the story told by the statistics. In comparison, the second book of Joshi-Little is refreshingly well organised, and it compensates the readers for what they might have missed in the first volume.

Political Element in Indian Economic Policymaking

The second riddle is why the Indian policymakers resile into complacency and apathy once the reforms began to pay off. In normal circumstances, the achievements of reforms could have been paraded at the hustings by the political parties to win votes for their programmes. Curiously enough, the government of Prime Minister Narasimha Rao did not place the reforms at the top of the election manifesto of his party. On the contrary, the party was apologetic about reform and brought to the front-burner the old populist programmes discarded in 1991. The other political parties were no different. The only explanation for the politicians' reluctance to own reforms lies in the dynamics of the political system and the process.

The paralysis of economic policy formulation and its fitful course have their genesis in the inner working of the political system which operates in such a manner that, at one extreme, economic policy has punishment as its basis but without any sanction for enforcing it, and at the other, incentive as its rationale without any built-in mechanism to reward for success. It is this nature of the economic policy, based simultaneously on punishment and incentive, but without any sanction for enforcing penalty or a system for offering reward, which largely explains the frequent gyration in economic policy in India. When the politicians need support of the people, they are readily inclined to proclaim a turn to the left in economic policy. This is generally on the eve of an election, when the votes of the poor are solicited. But once the politicians are firmly saddled in power, the halo of leftism in policy posture slowly begins to wear off. Anxiety to perpetuate themselves in power seizes them and the search is on for funds to meet the expense of the next election. The time is ripe then for a swing to the right in policy stance, which lasts until the coffers of the political party in power are filled. Inherently, therefore, economic policy in India moves cyclically—reminiscent of Michel Kalecki's famous political cycle: "sometimes to the left but not enough to be called leftist and sometimes to the right but not enough to be called rightist" (Khatkhate, 1977). The reason for these opportunistic turns in economic policy lies in the concentration of political power at the centre. The situation can be changed only with a radicalisation of the political process, which can ensure a diffusion of political power among state units or even lower down the ladder among the district units. It also calls for a total restructuring of the bureaucracy, which itself is a vast and impregnable fortress, which prevents the reform process from gathering speed (Khatkhate, 1991; 1992).

At present ideas about how to change the existing political framework are hazy and ill-defined. A blueprint of how to manage political change has been put forth with some daring by Desai, who, until he became Chief Economic Advisor to the Finance Ministry during the initial period of reforms, 1991–1993, was a maverick economist, who thought and wrote in the same mould as that of J. Bhagwati, P. Desai, and T.N. Srinivasan, V. Joshi and I. Little. He did not last long as economic advisor because "...the game of snakes and ladders, which those around played with such ferocity, such guile, such subtlety, such flair, was not the game for which I had joined the government and I left" (Desai, 1993: 3). To be sure, his views on how the political process and bureaucracy should be restructured should carry some weight, both because he witnessed the inner working of economic policy formulation and its execution and has closely observed the political forces at work. He has encased in his book his well thought out but controversial views on Indian economic policy and more importantly on its political ramifications, which have not so far been adequately analysed. His views on economic aspects of policy are similar to those of his worthy predecessors, but his political nostrums deserve more in-depth but a critical analysis. Three aspects of his political manifesto are singled out for some remarks below. These are: electoral system, bureaucracy, and federal issues. Taking the electoral system first, Desai identifies its ills with a disjunction between the monetary contributions to the politicians and the party they stand. In order that financial contributors not go to politicians for the jobs they do or get done but rather to parties for the policies they espouse, Desai suggests:

> ...elections based on lists and proportional representation. Every contesting party would have to put up a list of candidates containing as many names as there are seats in the legislative body. It would win seats in proportion to the number of votes it polls. As many candidates from the top of its list downwards would win as the number of its seats. If a member of a legislative leaves his party, he should automatically lose his seat. If a member loses his seat or dies, the first candidate in the party's list for the previous election who failed to win a seat would be elected (Desai, 1993: 306).

The merit of this scheme, according to Desai, is that every party will have to choose candidates with appeal to the entire country, cutting across sectarian loyalties. In order to avoid a hung parliament, he commends that only the votes obtained by the two parties that poll the largest number of votes should count.

On bureaucracy, he would remould it on the principle that "the numbers should be tailored to the work and work to its numbers" so that the capacity of a bureaucracy would match its task (Desai, 1993: 312). He suggests contractual employment for some fixed period and de-layering. This, he believes, would put the bureaucracy on its feet and make it responsive to public needs.[3] As for federalism, Desai envisages compression of the existing four tiers of administrative units—the centre, the states, districts, and urban-rural bodies. He advocates 50 to 100 provinces centred on majorities, below which may be local authorities centred on smaller cities.

Many of Desai's ideas on political restructuring are breathtaking, because of their sweep and non-conventionality. It is possible that they may appear quixotic to some of his critics and utopian to his friends. If the political restructuring were that easy and attainable, these could have been long accomplished. The policies as well as the parties have resisted simple reforms such as restraining political corruption and preventing defection by elected representatives and to expect these revolutionary ideas to permeate the political arena is to ask or the moon. But Desai has raised the relevant issues which have bedevilled India's quest for rapid and sustained growth. The remedies may appear to be the rumination of a gadfly, but the issues are real and have to be faced sooner or later.

It is possible that if the economic reforms continue, even in their truncated form, without any reversal, they may tear apart the political straitjacket. The essence of economic reforms lies in the transfer of decision making from the top to the bottom. In the Indian context, it may mean that the centre would tend to weaken with economic decision making power shifting first to the states and gradually to district level, and still further down. There are already straws in the

---

3.   Joshi-Little have some interesting observation on how bureaucracy tends to become an impediment to reform.

  .... the political barriers to privatization must again be the bureaucracy and the public sector unions. It has also been suggested that the issues involved in privatization and public enterprise reform are too complex to be solved within the present institutional framework of highly disseminated administrative responsibility and lack of expertise in the modalities of industrial restructuring (Joshi and Little, 1994: 259).

wind. The states have now begun to directly negotiate with the international organisations or foreign private agencies for financing projects or undertaking projects within the macroeconomic framework at state level. Once these tendencies gather momentum, they will have an impact on the political process. Political parties may look to the states as the primary theatre for attaining power, which in turn may lead to competition among states to outperform each other. As a result, the ownership of enterprise is likely to be less important than its efficiency. Furthermore, the distance between the rulers and the electorate will be telescoped, providing greater scope for the voters to judge the economic performance of the parties, which is the ultimate guarantee for their welfare. Perhaps such thinking is, to borrow Oscar Wilde's aphorism, a triumph of hope over experience. It is a widely held belief that economic reform will have a liberating influence on the political system, if the latter proves constricting. In this context, it is interesting to read what Roderick Macfarquhar, professor of history and political science said about Deng.

> ...he mistakenly thought he could adopt Western learning for the purposes of modernisation while preserving the political essence of the Chinese state. Western technology seemed like something peripheral that could be plugged into any political hardware...he failed to realise that the intellectual milieu in which such technology can be elaborated is an integral part of an open political operating system. You cannot travel far down the information superhighway in the political equivalent of a model T. (Macfarquhar, 1997).

REFERENCES

Bardhan, P. (1984). *The Political Economy of Development in India*. Oxford: Basil Blackwell.

Bhagwati, J. (1988). "Poverty and public policy", *World Development* 16(5): 539–56.

Bhagwati, J. and P. Desai (1970). *India: Planning for Industrialization*. Oxford: Oxford University Press.

Bhagwati, J. and T.N. Srinivasan (1975). *Foreign Trade Regime and Economic Development: India*. New York: NBER and Columbia University Press.

Desai, A. (1993). *My Economic Affair*. New Delhi: Wiley Eastern.

Joshi, V. and I. Little (1994). *India: Macroeconomic and Political Economy: 1964–1991*, Washington DC: World Bank, and New Delhi: Oxford University Press.

————. (1996). *India's Economic Reforms: 1991–2001*. Delhi: Oxford University Press.

Khatkhate, D. (1977). "Restructuring of the political process: agenda for the new government", *Economic and Political Weekly* XXII(2): 1057–62.

————. (1992). "India on an economic reform trajectory". In L.A. Gordon and P. Oldenburg (eds.), *India Briefing*. Boulder, CO: Westview Press.

————. (1991). "National economic policies in India". In D. Salvatore (ed.), National *Economic Policies*. New York: Greenwood Press.

Macfarquhar, R. (1997). "Demolition man", The New York Review of Books. XLIV(5).

World Bank (1996). *India: Country Economic Memorandum: Five Years of Stabilisation and Reform: The Challenges Ahead*, August. Washington DC: The World Bank.

Published in World Development 25(9): 1551–9 (1997).

14 | Indian Economic Reform
A Philosopher's Stone

Indian economic policy has for long been a Holy Grail for Indian intellectuals of all persuasions. Since independence, a belief system overlaid by the shambolic thinking of the economists and the immediacy of access to power for politicians consisted of a few basic propositions. These included the ideas that India is bereft of an entrepreneurial class and dominated by traders with a short-term time-horizon; inelasticity of export growth leads to the duality of foreign exchange and domestic saving gaps; and deficit finance, a derivative from the Keynesian economics, is a resource which can be freely resorted to for financing economic development. This set of beliefs gave primacy to the statism, which guided Indian economic policy in the aftermath of independence in 1947. While this was sustained up to a point until 1960, mainly as a counterpoint to the decades of economic stagnation induced by a colonial power insensitive to domestic economic interests, it soon began to yield diminishing returns in terms of economic growth, efficiency of production, and distributive justice. Only when the economy reached a *culdesac* did policymakers wake up to the imperative of emancipating the belief system from this tyranny of statism by the "encroachment of economic reform", to use a felicitous phrase of J.K. Galbraith. It was, however, not easy to usher in alternative policies because of the vested interests in ideas, lust for power of the political class and the easy moolah gained by the private sector from the interventionist regime. Economic reform was therefore gradual, slow and faltering in the initial stages in the decade of the 1980s, but took a quantum jump from the beginning of the 1990s.

The new turns and twists in economic policy were greeted with hostility by the intellectuals inebriated with the old brew of statism. First, they harked back to the East Asian countries, particularly Korea, which, from their perspective, accelerated their development by pursuing statist policies. Second, they predicted dire consequences of reform policies—a huge crisis in foreign exchange, worsening of poverty, and rising inflation (for getting a flavour of this, read the issues of the *Economic and Political Weekly* in the first half of 1990s).

However, they betrayed a lack of understanding of the dynamics of Korean development. The analogy was false. Korea's approach to development was rooted in its institutions, history and genius, which enabled it to devise non-market institutions as complementary and supportive to the market system (Dalla and Khatkhate, 1995).[1] That the charisma of Korea and other East Asian countries as exemplars of statism evaporated after the financial crisis during the late 1990s, is a different matter. As for the second, i.e. a prediction of gloom and doom, time was cruel to them. India, far from languishing, is now on the cusp of a great and enduring economic transformation. Endemic foreign exchange crises have now become episodes in distant memory and the poor have not remained that poor.

Even when the winds have gone out of the sails of the sceptics of reforms, they are loath to give up their never-say-die attitude towards statism.[2] They have now taken a different tack. Performance of the Indian economy during the 1990s is not to be gloated over, they argue, as the real turning point in growth was during 1980–1990 and not in the period beginning from 1991, when radical reforms were unleashed. This apart, it is even argued in all seriousness that a great structural change occurred in the period 1951–1980 as it took India from economic stagnation to growth in a broader social transformation (Nayyar, 2006).[3] Taking the latter first, a comparison of the structural change in 1951–1980 with the pre-independence decades is both fatuous and facetious. During the latter period there was no autonomous economic policy geared to the interests of a nation. The objective functions were different. It was a colonial policy, addressing the interests of the home country. Any policy, statist or otherwise, with India's interests at the centre, would have achieved

1. Critics who often cited Joan Robinson in support of their advocacy of statism conveniently develop amnesia about what she said in her three lectures on her visit to China in the 1950s. These "were remarkable in that they contain a skeleton outline of the policies the Chinese authorities are implementing now—a pragmatic, gradualist, trial and error, mix of the market openness and central control" (Harcourt, 2005: 25).

2. There is a variant of the 1980–1990 turning point view, propounded by David Rodrik and Arvind Subramanian (2005) and Atul Kohli (2006). They attribute it to the pro-business policies of the government. However, the difference between pro-business and pro-market economic policies is one of degree and not substance, as both sets of policies place a premium on profits as incentive, which the market also ensures.

3. It is high time that the statists wake up to learn from the famous communist historian Eric Hobsbawm, who showed rare intellectual courage to jettison his long-held dogma, when faced with the uncontestable reality. "The end of official Marxism of the USSR", he told Jaques Altali, an international banker in a debate, "has liberated Marx from the public identification with Leninism in theory, and with the Leninist regime in practice...the globalised capital world that emerged in the 1990s was in some ways uncannily like the world Marx predicted in 1948 in the communist manifesto...Paradoxically, it was the capitalists who rediscovered Marx, more than others"—The New Globalisation Guru (2006), New Statesman, 13 March.

better results than under a colonial regime. The real question is whether the statist policies were superior to other alternatives, but this question can never be answered for want of counterfactual evidence.

The other plank of argument that the Indian growth rate after the 1999 radical reforms was not as robust or striking as that during 1980–1990 is also equally suspect, as well analysed by Shankar Acharya (2006), Arvind Panagariya (2004) and Arvind Virmani (1997). Table 7.1 on page 208 of Acharya's book presents the average GDP growth during the sub-periods 1951-52 to 1980-81, 1981-82 to 1990-91 and 1992-93 to 1996-97, and 1997-98 to 2001-02. Add to these the growth rates during 2002-03 and 2003-04, and it is clear that the reform period of 1991 onward has been quite spectacular. Acharya also nails down the error of choosing the first year of the post-reform period by the critics, who insist that the post-reform period average growth rate is lower than that attained in the immediate pre-reform period. This criticism, Acharya shows, is sometimes compounded by the elementary error of including the crisis year of 1991-92 within the post-reform period. This clearly makes a difference since the average growth in the three years 1992-93 to 1994-95 was 4.9 per cent, as compared to only 3.9 per cent if 1991-92 is included in the post-reform period (Acharya, 2006: 28). Panagariya (2004) also makes the same point.

Panagariya has reinforced Acharya's insights as well as his statistical analysis by shining the spotlight on the higher variance of growth during the 1980s than during the 1990s—a period of high reform. This variance was due to the sources of the shift in the growth rate, particularly during the sub-period 1988-89 to 1990-91, when growth was 7–6 per cent largely because of substantial, though not systematic, economic reform. This phase was noted for policy reforms like import liberalisation, a wide array of export incentives, exchange rate changes, freeing up of several sectors from investment licensing, etc. However, there was a rather unconscionably high recourse to external and internal borrowing, which eventually hurt the liberalisation programme. So the average rate of growth during the pre-reform period of 1980-81 to 1990-91 was boosted by reform policies, raising both the variance as well as magnitude of the growth rate. This empirical evidence amply bears out that the rudiments of economic reforms were apparent during the pre-reform periods of 1980-81 to 1990-91 and therefore both the periods 1980-81 to 1990-91 and 1991-92 to date should be treated as one continuum, rather than treating them separately for assessing the impact of reforms (Acharya, 2006: 12; also Panagariya, 2004; Virmani, 1997).

Judging by a criterion that is wider in significance than mere growth rate in evaluating the impact of reforms is the change in total factor productivity (TFP), which rose from 5.3 during 1981-82 to 1990-91 to 6.5 during 1991-92 to 1999-2000 (Acharya, 2006: 215, Table 7.1). The direct linkage between TFP growth and policy reform draws additional and convincing support from Panagariya (2004).

Acharya has also effectively answered the critics of Indian reforms, who despite being defied by the evidence on growth and distribution still obsess that Indian reforms did not yield a favourable distributional outcome (Nayyar, 2006). As regards employment,

> the Planning Commission's estimates of annual increments in economy-wide employment indicate strong growth from a low of three million in the crisis year, 1991-92, to an average of six million in each of the next two years and then rising further to 7.2 million in 1994-95. Since labour is the principal asset possessed by the poor, this surge in employment opportunities is likely to be associated with a favourable trend in living standards and poverty (Acharya, 2006: 42).

Not only was unemployment on a downward trend, but real wages have tended to rise too. Though they first declined in the crisis years they "rose by 5.6 per cent in 1992-93 and by 3.6 per cent in 1993-94 as the economy recovered from this crisis in response to reform" (Acharya, 2006: 42).

Acharya's employment data may be considered somewhat out of date. But his findings are amply fortified by the latest quinquennial National Sample Survey, scrutinised carefully by an economist, who is no enthusiast for economic reforms. During 1977-78 to 2000, his conclusions are:

> These figures indicate that unemployment rates are relatively low, tend to be volatile but do not point to any secular deterioration...Of course, given that the size of the population and labour force are increasing, the absolute magnitude of unemployment and underemployment are higher now than 20–25 years ago. But there is no warrant for the concern that the situation is getting progressively worse....The fact is that rural employment opportunities have increased progressively and have been able to absorb practically the entire increase in the labour force. Employment is also getting diversified....Taking a longer view we see a progressive decline in the overall labour force participation rates...This trend reflects the combined effect of changing age composition and...a progressive rise in the proportion of persons in these age groups attending education institutions...these figures should not be interpreted as a deterioration of the employment situation (Vaidyanathan, 2005).

The UPA government's latest report for 2000 and 2003 shows "that the employment growth in India has been a very high, 2.9 per cent per annum and almost triple the anaemic employment growth experienced between 1993 and 1991" (Bhalla, 2006).

Acharya could have strengthened his defence of the impact of reform in regard to poverty reduction since 1991, by drawing on the papers at a workshop on *Poverty Measurement and Evaluation* organised in India by the World Bank together with the Planning Commission. The consensus that emerged from the papers of participants of all ideological hues was that "India recorded one of the developing world's fastest reductions in poverty during the 1990s. According to official estimates, poverty fell from 36 per cent of the population in 1993-94 to nearly 26 per cent at the end of the decade" (*EPW*, 2003). Thus, the post-1991 reforms emphatically showed that the economic growth resulting from reforms was not separated from distributive outcomes.

Assessing the consequences of economic reforms by focusing only on the rate of growth reflects a myopic vision. Since 1991, there have been startling changes in the sphere of the financialisation of saving-investment processes, structure of foreign trade and the balance of payments, the institutional basis of the macroeconomic policy, thereby giving a new tone and direction of monetary and exchange rate policies. Acharya's narrative of the institutional and structural transformation is comprehensive, with insights and sure touch that can come only from his close involvement in policymaking and the grasp of political economy dynamics. Today, India has far more developed money and capital markets that are mobilising savings and mediating them to the most efficient use. All this is done with an appropriate incentive system in place and not with high-handed and discriminatory direct controls. Foreign trade was liberated from the shackles of bureaucratic whims and the results are there for all to see. Exports boomed and exploded the myth of export pessimism, imports increased but without encroaching on domestic industry producing similar products, the current account of the balance of payments remained in deficit, which was financed by the autonomous inflow of private non-debt capital through foreign institutions. External debt indicators (as given in Table 4.4, Acharya, 2006: 139) turned extremely favourable. Thus, the total debt/GDP ratio declined from 28.7 per cent to 22.0 per cent between 1991 and 2000 and short-term debt to foreign reserves from 38.1 per cent to 11.5 per cent. With all this, the government, whether the present UPA or the NDA before it managed the external sector with great skill and dexterity so that the balance of payments position was insulated from the vagaries of global capital flows. Thus, the structural change and turning point in India's quest for development in the period 1991–2004 were far more significant and trailblasing than any time in India's chequered history.

Acharya captures all this in his narrative with scrupulous adherence to details and avoiding ideological postures. However, he should have analysed the balance of payment in a little more depth. It is true that there has been striking growth in invisibles in the balance of payments. However, it is difficult to know how much is invisibles earnings proper, and not capital inflows in the guise of invisibles, because of the way the current balance of payments are currently compiled. It is high time that the Reserve Bank shakes off its complacency and undertakes a thorough revamping of the balance of payments data and its integration with national income accounts.

Acharya has, while applauding the impact of the 1991 reforms, not underestimated the lack of governance. We must never forget that the quality of economic outcomes depends crucially on the quality of economic laws and their administration (Acharya, 2006: 53). But the real question is how governance should be improved in future. The new "transaction cost political perspective" pioneered by Avinash Dixit (2004) implies that economic policy has to be negotiated at each stage—from formulation to implementation—with each concomitant cost being determined by the layers of institutions and procedures. Efforts to reduce these costs can be formidable when the work culture and ethos of existing institutions are at odds with the demands of economic development. The implications of the transaction cost theories are exceedingly well captured in Arun Shourie's (2004) terse and episodic narrative of India's transition from controlled to market economy. A similar view on governance, though articulated differently, is presented by Pranab Bardhan (2005):

> Reforms would have been more popular if the authorities were equally and simultaneously concerned with reforms in the appalling governance structure in the delivery of basic social services for the future....It is anomalous to expect reform to be carried out by an administrative set up that for many years has functioned as an inert, heavy-handed, corrupt, over-centralised and uncoordinated monolith.

Governance in India is absent because of the fractured political process structure. Thus, any schemes delivering social and health services or rural employment, financed through pump-priming as advocated by some economists schooled in bastardised Keynesianism, would only end in more development with deception.

Acharya's essays educe consistency in analytic presentation, concision in thought process, as well as the author's concordant relationship with some of the ablest economic policymakers in the paradigm-shifting epoch of India's economic history.

REFERENCES

Acharya, Shankar (2006). *Essays on Macroeconomic Policy and Growth in India*. New Delhi: Oxford University Press.

Bardhan, P. (2005). "Nature of opposition to economic reforms in India", *Economic and Political Weekly*, 26 November.

Bhalla, Surjit (2006). "It does not matter RIP: Reform, Ideology, Politics", *Business Standard*, 6 April.

Dixit, A. (2004). *Lawlessness and Economics*, Princeton, NJ: Princeton University Press.

Dalla, I. and D. Khatkhate (1995). "Regulated deregulation of the financial system in Korea", *World Bank Discussion Papers*, 291. Washington DC: The World Bank.

EPW (Economic and Political Weekly) (2003). "Poverty measurement, monitoring and evaluation in India: an overview", 25 January.

Harcourt, G.C. (2005). "Joan Robinson and her circle", in Bill Gabson (ed.), Joan Robinson's *Economics: A Centennial Celebration*. Cheltenham: Edward Elgar.

Kohli, A. (2006). "Politics of economic growth in India, 1980–2005, Part I and II", *Economic and Political Weekly*, 21 and 28 April.

Nayyar, D. (2006). "Economic growth in independent India: lumbering elephant or running tiger", *Economic and Political Weekly*, 15 April.

Panagariya, Arvind (2004). "Growth and reform during 1980s and 1990s", *Economic and Political Weekly*, 19 June.

Rodrik, D. and A. Subramanian (2005). "From Hindu growth to productivity surge: the mystery of the Indian growth transition", *IMF Staff Papers*. 52(2).

Shourie, A. (2004). *Governance and the Sclerosis that has set in*, New Delhi: ASA/Rupa.

Vaidyanathan, A., (2005). "Employment guarantee and decentralisation", *Economic and Political Weekly*, 16 April.

Virmani, Arvind (1997). "Economic development and transition in India". Papers presented at the Tokyo Dialogue on Alternatives to the World Bank, IMF Approaches to Reforms and Growth. Tokyo: Economic Planning Agency, 7 November.

Published in the Economic and Political Weekly XLI(2): 2203-05) (2006).

15 | Indian Fiscal Policy
Flogging a Live Horse

So much has changed in the Indian economy since the mid-1980s, particularly 1991 when the economic reform process was firmly entrenched in the policy framework. At the beginning of the Plan era, i.e. 1951–52, the parameters of policy were represented by pervasive intervention in regard to quantity of the resources and its distribution between consumption and investment. Prices served no other purpose than that of accounting devices. Monetary policy was used merely as an instrument to countermand the effects of the fiscal policy, reducing the central bank to a compliant inferior agency. Fiscal policy was designed mainly to raise resources for public sector investment, and on many occasions, a fiscal deficit conjured up as non-inflationary in its impact was sanctified as an accelerator of investment and growth.

All this was radically changed once the economic reforms gathered momentum, what with dismantling of controls, enhancing competition, and liberalising foreign trade from stifling restrictions. As a result, there were more degrees of freedom for policymakers with more instruments at their command. Monetary policy with accent on both interest rate and exchange rate came into its own and began to influence the macroeconomy, especially the private sector in a more liberal economic environment. This meant almost as its logical corollary that fiscal policy should shed its monetary intent and intervene, when the private sector acting alone is ineffective and incapable of achieving the public good, to ensure socially desirable income distribution, and above all, help coordinate macroeconomic management towards maintaining stable and sustainable growth.

The crucial question in a reforming India is how to balance these often conflicting objectives in a rational manner without introducing distortions in the economy and disturbing its long-term growth path. In resource-raising, the government is often tempted to offer incentives to taxpayers in the form of tax exemptions and subsidies, thereby raising tax expenditure and also extend its sphere of activities regardless of any concern for whether necessary financial wherewithal is forthcoming. Partha Shome poses these dilemmas aptly in the Indian context when he critiques Drèze and Sen's plea for spending on education and health that "they absolve themselves of the worry of financing matters even though their monograph deals at length with the role of government, public action and market mechanism" (Drèze and Sen, 2000).

Since these valuable considerations are totally slurred over generally in many developing countries but more in India in the last few years, fiscal policy has gone awry, encouraging the central and state governments to boondoggle with public money, thereby widening fiscal deficits and increasing public debt to unsustainable levels. However, this did not prevent many pseudo Keynesians and wrong-headed Marxists from justifying fiscal profligacy with its concomitant features of fiscal deficit and burgeoning public debt. The argument of the former is that fiscal deficit in the Indian economy with abundant labour and excess capacity (questionable) would promote growth faster through leveraging demand. The Marxists living in their own world of day-dreaming start with the Keynesian premise to suggest that fiscal deficit is benign and does not lead to a rise in real interest rates with adverse impact on the economy. These critics have missed the salient features of the macroeconomic framework of a fiscal policy, which Shome (2002) spells out succinctly at the beginning of his book. In any open economy, if total domestic investment equals total domestic savings and the government incurs budget deficit, there will not be any adverse impact on the current account of the balance of payments, except that the private investment will be crowded out and one can argue that it may affect growth to the extent that government expenditure is wasteful, as is the case in India. If, however, the fiscal deficit is higher than the excess of private savings over private investment, it will result in the widening of deficit in the current account of the balance of payments. In India, the adverse impact of growing fiscal deficit on the balance of payments is avoided by two factors—first, that the excess savings of the private sector financed fiscal deficit almost entirely. This also coincided with a large inflow of foreign portfolio capital and non-resident remittances. But the fact that these consequences are avoided does not mean that fiscal deficit year in and year out can be continued. It creates serious public debt problems and thereby for the sustainability of growth.

Shome places the Indian fiscal policy in all its ramifications at the centre stage of the fiscal policy debate in India. His main thesis is splendidly epitomised in the epigraph from Kautilya, which says, "A wise chancellor is one who collects revenue so as to increase income and reduce expenditure. He shall take remedial measures if income diminishes and expenditure increases." Shome's discourse is an essay which, following Kautilya's sage signpost, presents an in-depth analysis of India's fiscal problems, dilemmas and pitfalls as a prelude to sketching out an exhaustive panoply of solutions, theoretically sound but firmly grounded in the Indian political economy and enforceable with the inevitable political compromises without losing sight of their central rationale.

The Three Pillars of Wisdom

Shome covers such a wide swathe of fiscal policy matters in India—both theoretical and empirical, with a broad-brush discussion of direct and indirect taxes and labyrinthine tax administration interspersed with several country experiences—that many subtle but core ideas are apt to escape a reviewer's eye unless he adheres to an overarching schema of the author's presentation. The author, however, makes this task easier by his design of a fiscal policy

> that is feasible, affordable and sustainable for government to undertake, qualities that were termed the three pillars of a fiscal architecture. An architecture that builds in these properties as basic elements is expected to result in a fiscal strategy that is likely to help move a country to a higher growth path without inflation or intergovernmental transfer of public debt (p.201).

The author is, however, careful to qualify that his strategy based on the three pillars had to reckon with "the initial position and the environment of the economy" (p.202) by which he means that

> if the public sector has spread out in economic activities that would essentially be carried by the private sector, and is assessed to be running inefficiently, then fiscal strategy must incorporate shedding public sector activity whenever recommendable. On the other hand, in an environment where the private sector does not have adequate resources and basic economic infrastructure needs to be developed, wider public sector activity has to be undertaken.

The author has done well in drawing attention to the initial conditions of the economy in the Indian context because it is the crucial factor that has caused fiscal policy woes. The hangover of a large number of public sector projects both at the central and the state level was the main revenue sucker. The public sector's loss-making is proverbial but even when they are breaking even the opportunity cost of their operations is high unless a rate of return yielded by them is at least equal to the rate of interest paid by the government on the public debt raised to capitalise them. Assuming that all the public enterprises yield return commensurate with the rate of interest on the public debt, the fiscal deficit as it stands today would have narrowed approximately to half

MONEY, FINANCE, POLITICAL ECONOMY • DEENA KHATKHATE

210

of its current level, if not more. The author by highlighting the importance of the initial conditions has focused on privatisation with appropriate regulatory mechanism and transparency as a way out for the fiscal consolidation.

While the analytical underpinning of Shome's three pillars is sound, there seems to be some overlapping in substance between feasibility and affordability. What is feasible has to be, *pari passu* affordable. If the government resorts to grandiose projects without any cost-benefit analysis or any consideration of their appropriateness in the public sector when the private sector can do so more efficiently, the feasibility principle will be violated and the time will come when the fiscal policy geared to those projects will no longer be affordable. By the same reasoning, the taxation policy and the tax administration could be considered to be both infeasible and unaffordable if these involve excessively high cost out of all proportion to the value added. The author himself seems to be aware of the thin line separating feasibility from affordability both in regard to revenue raising and public expenditure. He poses a series of pertinent questions:

> Is the fiscal policy architecture feasible given the country's available resources and administrative capacity? Does the government propose budgets that are simply not attainable? Do we need a macro-fiscal model that will clearly delineate why the proposed budget is feasible? .... Are the tax revenue projections based on meaningful collection procedures and capabilities? What element of risk do expenditure projections carry? Are expenditure programmes, such as, say, a nationwide school midday meal programme implementable? (p.15)

Shome's book is a sum of his answers to these troubling questions.

In India, the pillar of the fiscal policy architecture, whether you call it feasibility or affordability, has been made fragile by government policy, despite fundamental changes in overall tax and expenditure policies. As regards the former, the author has tried to show that the tax base has not been expanded over the years as it should have been in a fast changing and reforming economy. He attributes this failing to two factors: '(1) existing tax incentives in the income taxes and the exemptions in the indirect taxes and (2) omission of a feasible expansion of the tax base through the taxation of the consumption services' (p.34). Coupled with this is the poorly designed tax administration system. There are exemptions galore in regard to all taxes ranging from customs tariffs, value added tax, excise, to income and corporate taxes on the specious ground that they promote 'social and economic' goals. The absurdity of the "Exemption Raj", as the Kelkar Task Force termed it, is manifested in the standard publication of the tax authorities. Out of 1150 pages of the publication of the customs tariff structure "there are 406 pages describing

121 general exemptions, some of which are (1) further alphabetised and/or (2) divided into lists" (p.35). Likewise, a "[p]ublication of the central excise (running some 720 pages) as many as 220 pages are devoted to exemptions alone" (p.35). The reach of the exemptions is equally mind-boggling in regard to income and corporate taxes. Shome's description of the "Exemption Raj" is so vivid that one does not have to stretch one's imagination to figure out why tax revenue lagged behind expenditure year in and year out, leading to fiscal chaos. Many of these ideas sound familiar now but they have emanated from Shome himself as the chairman of the advisory group on tax policy and administration for the Tenth Plan, published in 2001.

Expenditure policy is the other aspect of the feasibility or the affordability pillar. Here the author alludes, rightly too, to the various suggestions made in the Expenditure Commission's report and there is nothing new or striking about this. The same could be said about the author's discussion on subsidies. It is now generally accepted that a case could be made for subsidies only if they have positive externalities. Many governments have come and gone but none has held the bull of subsidies by the horns, being hobbled by the fear of an unfavourable political fallout. Therefore, the pillar of feasibility or affordability will never be strong enough in India to hold aloft fiscal policy architecture in the foreseeable future.

The author has shown remarkable insights regarding the pillar of sustainability of the fiscal architecture, pointing to various facets of sustainability. It is possible to interpret this in different ways. In the Indian context, the most troubling policy issue arises in regard to sustainability of the public debt, particularly because of the persistence of fiscal deficits over a prolonged period. Various issues are thrown up. What ratio of debt-GDP should be aimed at? Furthermore, what is the time dimension for achieving the desired ratio? What is the way to reduction of this ratio? Here Shome appropriately quotes the incisive analysis of Amaresh Bagchi, on which a consensus among economists is possible. In a standard theory, scaling down the debt-GDP ratio can be achieved by complying with the condition that ensures that real rate growth is higher than the real interest rate so that the primary budget surplus, i.e. excess of revenue over current expenditure net of interest payments, remains positive. But Bagchi argues that this is not a sufficient condition for sustainability of the debt-GDP ratio unless the initial debt stock is equal to the present discounted value of primary surpluses in the future (Bagchi, 2001). The corollary is that the longer the time horizon for the government to repay the debt the smaller is the primary surplus required. Shome rightly adds a rider that the government should not go on extending the period of debt repayment. He has used three criteria to test the sustainability of India's public debt of both the centre and the states. These are "(1) Debt should be zero at a specified future period, n. (2) The debt to GDP-ratio at·a future period, n, should be reduced to a specified fraction, d, of its present level" (p.57). (3) The debt-GDP ratio for the future is fixed at today's ratio. He has presented different scenarios of this exercise, which are quite fascinating. The upshot of this is that "[i]n realistic scenario of growth rate-interest rate combination in a reasonable timeframe, the primary deficit to GDP ratio has to be reduced or a surplus generated for the sustainability of public debt whether the goal be to amortize it, or reduce it or freeze it" (p.60). This poses a far more formidable task for the central and state governments, if the Indian economy is not to tailspin into a crisis and the unborn future generations are not to pay the price for the folly and irresponsibility of the present generation.

Shome could have but did not add a fourth pillar of decentralisation to the fiscal architecture, though he has discussed extensively the issues of federal finance. But the discussion on these issues should have been woven into his schema of the fiscal architecture. He views decentralisation conceptually— quite an innovative approach—as an extension of Musgrave's classic functional classification of public finance into three functions—allocative, distributive, and macroeconomic stabilisation. The first relates to the extent of decentralisation in regard to taxes, degree of autonomy, choice of taxes and division of expenditure responsibilities. The distributive function refers to how the resources should be distributed among the central and the sub-national governments. The macroeconomic management and stabilisation is concerned with how the sub-national governments manage expenditure and borrowing, which has a bearing on the efficiency of fiscal stabiliser. Shome uses this framework to analyse the centre-state relation in India. His broad conclusion, which need not be controversial, is that

> A balance has to be struck between appropriate decentralization and fiscal consolidation. More tax bases can be passed down, first to the states but their borrowing powers might remain circumscribed especially given the prevailing reality of higher fiscal deficits at the level of the states. Local governments might be given strong taxing powers, but borrowing powers might be confined to those with high credit rating in order not to constrain efficient local governments from developing needed economic and social infrastructure and because their borrowing might not have immediate deleterious effects on a national scale.

While Shome's verdict on decentralisation sounds unexceptional, it is doubtful if it meets adequately the criterion of feasibility, given the social, political and the economic situation in India. If the resources are passed on to the sub-national authorities such as district councils or panchayats, as the new UPA (United Progressive Alliance) government is contemplating to do, there is no guarantee they would reach the right targets. The institutions and the governance are woefully weak at sub-national levels and any resources transfer will be wasted, as experience over the last four decades has shown. The question of how to improve those institutions is complex, entailing economic, sociological, and anthropological dimensions. In traditional societies like India's, which are transiting to higher stages of development, relations-based practices and customs dominate. Making way for rules-based institutions and governance is a slow-moving process (Dixit, 2003). Therefore, a hasty rush to decentralisation of a vintage variety, however commendable, would merely end in failure.

Shome has devoted considerable space to the role of the Planning and Finance Commissions in transferring resources to the states. He fully recognises that there is considerable overlap in the functioning of these two bodies but he seems to be somewhat chary of suggesting their merger. The Planning Commission is a fifth wheel in a liberalising economy and there is no reason why its role as a disburser of funds to the states should not be transferred lock, stock and barrel to the Finance Commission by making it a permanent body and abolishing the distinction between Plan and non-Plan expenditure. The main function of formulating medium-term projections with related policy framework and leading economic indicators can be more appropriately assigned to the Finance Ministry, which will have to undertake this in order to implement the Fiscal Responsibility and Budget Management Act, as rightly suggested by the author.

This book, which is a result of the research carried out by the author at the Indian Council for Research on International Economic Relations (ICRIER), is important as it gives an opportunity to the readers to glean information on inter-country experiences in fiscal matters, particularly the emerging countries like Brazil, Argentina, etc. However, the readers' comprehension of these experiences is rendered difficult by the narrative flip-flop. There is no knowing when one gets into the trenches of the Brazilian and the Argentine experiences and re-enters into the open space of their relevance for India. One aspect of this survey is salient in that India, in many ways, has more to offer to the Latin American countries than to learn from them, but this is not saying much, as all are entangled in a fiscal mess. It would have been better if Shome had discussed the experiences of federations like Canada and Australia, which are more relevant to India.

REFERENCES

Bagchi, Amaresh (2001). "Perspectives on correcting fiscal imbalance in the Indian economy: some comments", *Money and Finance*, ICRA Bulletin, Nos. 4–5. January–June.

Dixit, A. (2003). *Lawlessness and Economics*, Princeton, NJ: Princeton University Press.

Drèze, J. and A. Sen (2000). *India: Economic Development and Social Opportunity*. New Delhi: Oxford University Press.

Shome, Parthasarathi (2002). *India's Fiscal Matters*. New Delhi: Oxford University Press.

Published in the Economic and Political Weekly XXXIX(33): 3705-07 (2004).

IV

GOVERNANCE

16 | Profile of Leadership in a Developing Society

When a society stagnates, when its political institutions become decadent and the whole social fabric is about to give way at the seams, there is often a clamour for a leader who can pull the society back on its tracks. A leader's image is formed partly by the knowledge of great leaders from the distant past and partly by romantic idealisation of what a leader should be. Attributes commonly associated with leadership are charisma, power, and popularity with the masses. One might almost believe that a leader, to be a great leader, is divinely dispensed and without him society would continue to be in the doldrums. However, there is enough evidence that possession of charisma, power and popularity may be a necessary but not sufficient condition for being an effective leader. History may have enabled us to know rather too much about leaders but not enough about leadership *per se*.

Leadership is a constant in any equation of change—be it social, economic or political. But the calibre of leadership need not be the same in all transforming societies. Where compulsions are less severe, conflicts not sharp enough, and immediacy of action not so intensely felt, society may move ahead under a lacklustre leadership. However, developing societies offer a contrast to mature developed societies. Changes in them are not marginal but total, and what is more, they bear on the whole gamut of relationships between various social and economic groups which comprise that society. Furthermore, changes come in quick succession, not permitting any respite for short-term adjustment. It is the challenges in a society in perpetual flux which often confront leaders, and how they deal with these challenges determines their success or failure.

Before defining the main elements of leadership in such societies it is necessary to jettison some pet notions held about leadership. Leadership is a comprehensive idea which has a much wider domain than government. The leader of a government need not be a leader of society. Admittedly, the government has the power to hasten change or hinder it; it possesses a sprawling administrative apparatus to regulate the activities of its citizens. But for all the power wielded by a head of government, he cannot command the loyalty of its members for long if he fails to satisfy the aspirations and cravings of the populace. Nor will his control endure if he remains impervious to the dynamics of change. Power is essential in a leader, but by itself it is insufficient to permit him to lead society or to set a direction for its advance. Power is an instrument used to achieve the larger ends of social organism, and that is why a leader ceases to be a leader and becomes a tyrant, as in totalitarian regimes, when power as an instrument is mistaken for power as an end. All leaders, as James MacGregor Burns points out, wield power, but all power-wielders are not necessarily leaders. It is for this reason that in all democratic societies the power-wielding characteristics of leadership should be clearly weighted and not identified with the essence of leadership.

A great and effective leader must necessarily command popular support, but this should not imply that he should do things or espouse what is popular in order to be popular. It is true that popularity does not emanate from the compromises a leader may make in the course of leading his supporters. Followership has a distinct meaning of its own; it is not the penumbra of leadership but an integral part of it. The connecting link between leadership and followership is not to be discerned in the flexibility of a leader in accommodating to the whims and caprices of the masses who follow him; it is the integrity of the leader and his unswerving commitment to pursue what is in the best interests of his people which cement the bonds between him and his followers. The leader articulates their urges, is perspicacious enough to know what the situation demands, and then formulates his plan of action in order to redeem the prevailing malaise. People follow a leader not because he is handsome, of noble lineage, or for that matter successful in some phase in his immediate past; they follow him because he is committed to the same goals, and holds the same values as they do. Followership is only the other side of leadership. Therefore, leadership without followership in this sense is mere demagogy, just as followership without leadership is anarchy. It follows that for followership a leader need not be popular in the usual sense of the word so long as he does things which the followers would not otherwise do. A leader, without being populist can thus command followership.

History is replete with many such examples: Mahatma Gandhi, who became a leader in his middle age without having any conventionally defined attributes associated with leadership. He was not of aristocratic origin and he developed a presence only as his career progressed. He first came on the scene as an upholder of human rights in South Africa, and subsequently in India. Since his posture and presence stirred something deeper in Indian society, he instantly emerged as a leader with enormous followership, which never deserted him. China's Mao Zedong was an ordinary teacher, but he used the Chinese idiom for his ideology which elicited the innermost loyalties of the Chinese people. For a long time this bond remained unimpaired, but neither of these leaders courted popularity nor did he misuse it for his own immediate gains. Instead, they used it to encourage their people to accomplish what they otherwise would not have been able to do. In fact, there were numerous incidents in their lives—in Gandhi's case the calling off of the Churichaura *satyagraha*, and in Mao's case the cultural revolution—which show how at times they defied popularity at great risk to their future. And yet they retained their touch with reality and the affection of their people. In retrospect it seems that their defiance of popularity was a ploy employed to test the steadfastness of the people in their commitment to the goals.

It is often said that leaders in a modern democracy must balance between various interest groups; they should be able to compromise. In short, a leader gives in return for a consideration. However, this view of leadership (as Burns rightly points out) is transactional leadership, which is of a lower order because the leader is more interested in perpetuating himself at any price. Such leaders are least concerned with commitment to ideology or ideals; common interest is conveniently defined to focus on separate interests of individuals or groups comprising society rather than on its collective welfare. It is this perception of leadership—a transactional leadership—which has demeaned the image of leaders in many countries. Power associated with this type of leader is sought for the sake of power and not for the common good. Nor are the means chosen to achieve and to retain leadership such as to endow it with any halo. It is not the nobler purposes of life that provide the leitmotif for this kind of leadership.

The transforming type of leadership, as distinct from the transactional type, is the need of the hour in today's developing societies. Transforming leadership has an underpinning of idealism and is imbued with a vision of how society should evolve. It is not exogenously planted but grows from within. Though it is influenced by history, culture, and tradition, it does not glory in its past but looks to the future with hope and certain normative judgements on what should steer the society from the existing morass to newer vistas of modernity and satisfying environment. Such leadership spurns dynastic moorings and is charged with dynamic energy. It is firmly on its feet in that it penetrates deeper in the system which it purports to change, remains sensitive to the more enduring and in many ways more fundamental forces of change. Thus transforming leadership can be born and fostered only within a framework of social dynamics of Toynbee's *Challenge and Response*.

Transforming leadership, because of the sustenance it draws from society itself, and because it has a higher purpose, is of necessity a moral leadership. Not for it the higgle-haggle of the marketplace. It would prefer to perish than to thrive when the mission for which it comes into being no longer prevails. The morality that one speaks of is not some abstract concept, difficult to define and even more difficult to practise. It connotes no more than a norm of social behaviour in the conduct of human relations. If the fulfilment of those objectives which provide the sole justification for leadership are aborted for some reason, the leader should abdicate his power with conviction, dignity and honour. This is what de Gaulle did in France when he first came to power and again when he lost it. When he sought power he had a clear vision of what he was to accomplish. He used the support of the military to gain that power but when he found its support would thwart his goal he had no hesitation in spurning it. He liberated Algeria and risked the onslaught of the military, but he weathered the storm with great moral courage and eventually succeeded. He displayed the same qualities when he sensed that his ideals had outlived their utility. He was great while in power and greater still when he relinquished it. His was a truly moral leadership.

For a developing society such as that of India, it is only a transforming type of leadership which is capable of coping with the country's gigantic problems. But the success or failure of that leadership depends on to what extent it is able to assess the objective reality in all its ramifications—historical, political, sociological, religious and economic. Present-day Indian society is a transitional one due to its internal turmoil and it is almost futile to hope for a stable equilibrium, at least in the foreseeable future. For that reason it is likely to be prone to one crisis after another. The putative stability that India experienced in the 1950s and 60s should not be ascribed solely to the leadership of the times so much as to slowness of the pace of change. That has now accelerated due to the surfacing of tensions in the wake of economic and technological transformation of Indian society.

In the early years following independence, the organisation and political institutions in India evolved around the nascent bourgeoisie, the urban middle class, the organised working class, and the backward and disorganised agricultural labour. A compact between the bourgeoisie and the urban middle class was easily forged; organised labour was still in the process of gauging its strength, while the agricultural classes, both landed gentry and the landless labourers were too weak and disorganised to figure in any political calculus.

There was thus harmony of interest among different interest groups. Until a technological breakthrough in agriculture took place, the political stability could be maintained. But when the technological forces and the forces of modernisation tended to be incompatible with the existing institutional relationships, new classes—urban organised labour and the rich peasantry—emerged, and social and political tensions became accentuated, affecting the entire Indian polity. The demands of these two organised classes came into competition with those of the entrenched capitalists and the urban elite. Where the economy is afflicted by scarcity of one kind or another, it is well nigh impossible to satisfy all the demands simultaneously. But such a perfectly understandable logic is slurred over in a situation where access to political power is a coordinate of the ability to draw as much popular support from each of the two main classes as possible. It became the ideology of every political group to play up to the aspirations of these classes with growing political clout. This is a major reason why any change in economic policy over the years under political programmes remained a small change, despite apparent differences in their ideological bases.

With the demographic compulsions, no political party can turn its back on the egalitarian goals of income distribution, poverty amelioration and eradication of unemployment. However, in practice, this preoccupation with redistributive goals has often culminated in supportive action for the organized proletariat and the landed peasantry, who constitute the first 10 per cent of the income distribution scale. The unorganised, unemployed proletariat is left out of the reckoning. In other words, organised labour is equated with the poor. Even devout Marxists persisted with this myth, forgetting the warning of Rosa Luxembourg that the organised proletariat can become "joint exploiters with the capitalist class". If redistributive aims are to be achieved, and if the downtrodden are to receive succour, it is imperative that this unorganised lumpen proletariat have a voice in political action, which has been hitherto denied them.

In the Indian context, the distinction between various types of agitation, whether region related or class related or caste and religion related, is artificial. The root cause lies in the smallness of the cake for which various groups compete among themselves. The current Assam movement basically owes its origin to the discontent of the local population which has been losing influence in the local government. The caste violence has spread in recent years largely because castes, which hitherto were weak, have now grown stronger because of the scarcity of labour generated in the rural hinterland following technological developments in agriculture and the spread of education. Considering that low castes are almost coterminous with the poor classes it is difficult to disentangle the class and caste factors from caste-related agitations.

Anyone wishing to assume the mantle of leadership in India must develop a deeper understanding of the forces of change at work in the system. Isolated episodes, seemingly occurring independently of each other, reveal a pattern, influenced by a variety of socio-economic and political factors. The leader must articulate those forces and direct them in a manner which will clarify the objectives and approach for the governance of the polity. The principal way the system can be made both dynamic and viable in rder to fulfil the needs of the people is to think of a mechanism by which th   of the weaker sections of society, be they landless labourers, Dalits or other religious or regional minorities, can be translated with ease into an effective political and social programme of action. That mechanism may be in the shape of a decentralised administrative and political structure. At the level of small administrative and political units, the so-called weaker sections may no longer remain weak. These classes or castes can make their presence felt to countervail the influence of other competing groups who hitherto exercised the hegemony in decision making. It is such a vision of the political process and not the manipulative skill that should be the hallmark of effective leadership.

Max Weber envisaged three phases of leadership: charismatic, rational-legal, and traditional. However, Weber's description may be relevant more as a biological mutation of leadership than as the characterisation of what leadership should signify in a transforming society. Once a leader holds sway, he develops charisma which carries him through for a while. But then he gets caught up in a legal cobweb and later decays into tradition. The type of leadership with which a transforming society is concerned is not one which resorts to legal casuistry or invokes tradition; legalism and tradition are both binding constraints on development. Charisma which has been laboured in the context of leadership has no existence of its own. Charisma is a function of followership which, in turn, is fashioned by the innate capacity of the leadership to perceive the nature and direction of change, to articulate the dormant feelings of the followers and to transform the prevailing modes of social behaviour and institutions so that society is carried well near its cherished ideals.

Published in the Economic and Political Weekly XXV(47): 2595–6 (1990).

17 | Intellectuals and Indian Polity

Change in any human society has its own underpinning of ideas, spawned and propagated by intellectuals whose mental mould may be fashioned by some exogenous shock such as foreign influence on the culture in which they function and consequent encroachment on their mental processes by some alien system. Or else their apparatus of thought may evolve naturally from the internal dynamics of an autochthonous milieu, conditioned by an amalgam of religion, history, and literature. Intellectuals thus posit themselves at the centre of change. Their ideas are effectuated when transmitted to the social and political arena where practical men and power brokers reign. This makes the influence of the purveyors of ideas greater at times than that of power itself in bringing about social and political transformation of the polity. "The ideas of economists and political philosophers", Keynes ruminated, "both when they are right and when they are wrong, are more powerful than is commonly understood. Indeed the world is ruled by little else. Practical men, who believe themselves to be quite exempt from any intellectual influence, are usually the slaves of some defunct economist .... I am sure that the power of vested interests is vastly exaggerated compared with the gradual encroachment of ideas....Soon or late, it is ideas, not vested interests which are dangerous for good or evil" (Keynes, 1947: 383–4)[1].

Intellectuals, if they are to live up to their true description, must be at the vantage point in guiding and charting the course of human history.

Indian polity has undergone a remarkable transformation during the last one hundred and fifty years. In the main, this has been a transition from great, though archaic, traditions to modernity with its inexorable technological change, leading to a shrivelling of time and space. At first the changes were slow, imperceptible and less pervasive, but since the third decade of the present century these have been rapid and sweeping, embracing all facets of national

---

The author would like to thank, without implicating, A.K. Das Gupta, Arun Shourie, Manu Shroff, Hasan Imam, A. Vaidyanathan, and V.V. Bhatt for their comments on an earlier version of this paper.

1. Keynes' views on the role of intellectuals, like his economic ideas, changed radically in later years. In the 1930s he was less sanguine about the intellectuals when he described his exhortations on economic issues as "the croakings of a Cassandra" (Keynes, 1932: Preface).

life. The influence of intellectuals on these changes has varied according to the degree of their ratiocinative quality, the mainspring of their mental nourishment, and the ambience in which they worked during this time span. It is, therefore, essential to view Indian intellectuals in a historical perspective in order to assess their role in present-day India.

With a powerful cultural encroachment from the West, formation of an intellectual class as well as its mental apparatus have developed in four different directions. The first, and for many years the most dominant, was the imitative type, which borrowed wholesale from Western culture and ideology and transplanted the concepts derived from them to the Indian situation. The second, and in some sense the more enduring, was the assimilative type which drew its inspiration from the main corpus of the hedonistic and Benthamite philosophy of liberalism. The emphasis of this type was on divesting Indian traditional culture of its outmoded features and refurbishing it so that it could be attuned to the needs of the time. On the whole, the leitmotif for intellectuals of the first two categories was provided by exogenous forces, released by a socially, politically, and culturally advanced Western civilisation. The third kind of intellectual activity was asseverative in nature, the underlying basis of which was that unless the Indian value system, almost totally submerged under the British impact, was revived with renewed vigour, the spark necessary for national regeneration and progress could not be ignited. Perhaps the most feeble type of intellectual activity, compared with the other three, was the creative one. During the pre-independence era there was little original thinking, either in the physical or social sciences. Lack of density of the educated elite or the vacuity of educational instruction or even archaic thought processes may have accounted for almost total absence of this type. All four typological distinctions, though separate, should not be necessarily considered as independent of each other. The first could easily fuse with the second and a part of the second with the third. But each has certain distinguishing characteristics whose impact on the social, political, and economic change in Indian society differed according to the medium through which the ideas were transmitted to the field of practical policy.

The imitative type of intellectualism thrived when the foreign-educated elite manned the administrative, judicial, and military establishments of the state. Being trained in modern ways of thinking, it began revamping the prevailing social and political system. The impulse of change came from the top, as it were, and since the intellectual leaders were also the administrators, the change was smooth, though slow (Panikkar, 1963). Gradually, a local counterpart of this elite emerged which, despite being imitative of the 'imitation', was instrumental in effecting a certain feedback of ideas. Intellectual activity of the assimilative kind received impetus with the establishment of local educational institutions and universities, creating a local intelligentsia. As the circle of intellectuals outside the government, particularly at the universities and among the judiciary, began to break out of the narrow cocoon of the imitative kind of intellectual activity, it was realised that if the social system were to be regenerative it should be treated with an elixir compounded of the essential elements of the indigenous cultural heritage and those of Western thought.[2] The assimilative approach of the intellectuals enabled them to align with the ruling power as there was an essential harmony of interests between the two. But this alignment did not function unidirectionally. The intellectuals reserved their right to criticise, to question, and even to challenge certain unsavoury aspects of public policy within the confines of civil responsibility.

With the spread of education and consequent swelling of the ranks of the intelligentsia, the existing system came under more intensive questioning, propelled by frequent contact with resurgent nationalism and associated developments abroad. At this point, a dichotomy between the power-wielders and the intellectuals surfaced for the first time. If confrontation with power was ineluctable, there was no better option than to hark back to the glories of the receding culture, philosophy, and thought, which was what the asseverative type of intellectual activity did.[3] The drift away from the centre of power by the intellectuals changed their role radically from what it had been before. The instruments of change which the assimilative type of intellectuals used were the government and public opinion. Since the first of these was denied to the asseverative intellectuals, they had to fall back entirely on moulding public opinion in defiance of the government. And yet they succeeded because of the inherent tendency in the Indian society to retain its national identity. "India is no home of mestizo civilisation", argued K.M. Panikkar in his survey of modern Indian history, "a new way of life foreign to the soil or unrelated to its past, a mere borrowed thing, which, however showy and brilliant, is alien to the genius of its people" (Panikkar, 1963: 19). These very basic tendencies and

---

2. This was what the intellectual leaders like R.C. Dutt, M.G. Ranade, G.K. Gokhale, D. Nawroji, D.K. Karve, Jyotiba Phule, and Phirozshah Mehta accomplished in the latter half of the nineteenth century and the early part of the twentieth century.

3. Prominent intellectuals of this type were Vivekanand, Ramakrishna, Tilak, and Arabindo Ghosh, who awakened the somnolent masses to the richness of their past.

characteristics were embodied in the asseverative culture of the intellectuals, which ensured the willing support of the masses for their viewpoint.

A creative type of intellectual activity began to take hold of the Indian polity toward the beginning of the twentieth century. Intellectual activity reflected clear and visible signs of originality in many branches of the social and physical sciences, and in literature.[4] Though most intellectuals of the creative type had no overt political affiliations, they derived support from the authority, while essentially working on their own without compromising the basic tenets of their beliefs. A new dimension, and from the point of view of change, the most significant, was added to the activities of the creative intellectuals by Gandhi, who used an idiom which was, though apparently conservative in approach, fundamentally innovative in impact and intellectual in content. It now appears, perhaps in hindsight, that Gandhi's was the most sweepingly revolutionary influence on the Indian social and political system. He at once transformed the particulars of Indian society into a manifesto of universal humanism and emphasised that a change had a wider connotation than the mere transformation of the matter; it also meant liberation of the mind from the old ingrained habits and norms. Gandhi, besides, signified much more for his country and countrymen than what was reflected in his achievements in the political and social spheres. There is some such thing as "ethics of absolute values" as against the "ethics of reflective and responsible action" (Shils, 1961: 97–8). Those who prefer the ethics of absolute values have no easy shortcuts. They have to pursue relentlessly and selflessly what has been enjoined on them, regardless of the consequences for the prevailing power centres or for their own lives or careers. In other words, he underscored the supreme importance of civil non-abdication for intellectuals in a modern society.

It may be broadly generalised that the pre-independence Indian intellectuals of whatever hue did dominate the course of events as a whole and that their ideas not only preceded social and political change, but actually determined its nature in many different ways. There was first what could be described as the 'cascade effect' of the intellectuals. The four different types of intellectuals—imitative, assimilative, asseverative, and creative—represented different stages of intellectual development, each evolving logically from the preceding one, in a society which was moving from tradition to modernity. The

4.   Representatives of this school were Tagore, Iqbal, Ramanujam, Raman, Bhandarkar, Telang, and Ambedkar.

imitative phase laid the foundation of scientific education, which enabled the emerging intelligentsia to imbibe the spirit of modernisation. The assimilative phase oriented Indian society toward congruence with the culture of the power users and hence cooperation with them. With the deepening of the assimilative process, however, the mental horizons of the intelligentsia were expanded to an extent that reassertion of the values descending from a great civilisation and a search for new ideas were unavoidable. There was thus no conflict between any one of them, and, in fact, they were self-reinforcing. Perpetuation of any one type of intellectual activity beyond its time would have only pulverised the forces of change. On the other hand, supersession of the existing type of intellectual activity by succeeding ones kept the momentum of change not only undisturbed, but accelerating.

Second, the channels of transmission of ideas of the intellectuals to the instruments of change were fewer than in a self-governing country. In a period of Macaulayan reforms, the intellectuals and the implementors of ideas were one and the same, so that there was no seepage of ideas in the process of transmission. During the assimilative stage also, the instruments of change and the originators of ideas remained generally intermingled, though public opinion as a distinct category was brought into play. But far from there being any cleavage, public opinion as articulated by the intellectuals, if at all, reinforced the process of change by exerting pressure on the authorities to pursue reforms in various directions. When the asseverative class of intellectuals appeared on the horizon, there emerged a direct conflict with the agents of change. The sharpening of a distinction between the intellectuals and the administrators contributed to rapid change because the concurrence of the Government was replaced by the sanction of the populace. Apart from this, a change was hastened because the leaders of thought happened also to be the leaders of action. This was inevitable when exposure to liberal education from the West impressed Indian intellectuals with the virtues of a representative government which could be achieved only by direct participation in the political process.

Indian intellectuals with such a pedigree, brimming with such traditions of achievement in public policy, were naturally expected, after independence, to become even more vigorous and to contribute significantly to the process of the modernisation of Indian society in a big way. However, Indian history in the last three decades has clearly shown that in post-independence India it is not the ideas nor the activities of the intellectuals which set the pace of change. The Indian polity has marched ahead for good or evil under its own steam, by its own dynamics and along the lines envisaged by its political leaders. It is, therefore, interesting to analyse the transformation of the intellectuals' role in post-independence India and discover what were the underlying causes of their relative insignificance in the Indian political and social development.

In a way, the submergence of the intellectuals poses a paradoxical phenomenon. There has recently been an enormous growth in educational facilities in India. In addition to the few universities which existed up to 1947, almost one hundred more have been established. The annual turnout of university graduates has been around 4,00,000. Though as a proportion of the population and labour force the number of degree-holders has been one of the lowest in the world, in absolute terms India ranks only with the United States and the USSR in the number of university graduates.[5] Such a large educated elite should, if anything, create the most ideal conditions for hectic intellectual activity in any country. Not only in numbers but also in terms of the 'complexity and density' of institutional apparatus, Indian intellectuals have been fortunate, even when compared with some of the moderately developed countries, let alone a large number of the newly merging developing countries. The institutional apparatus, whose rudiments were first established under foreign rule, has now spread far and wide, covering many branches of knowledge such as physics, chemistry, metallurgy, mathematics, engineering, economics, not to mention Indology and other philosophical disciplines.

But creation of an intelligentsia through the extension of educational facilities is not always synonymous with the creation of intellectuals. It is necessary to draw a distinction, as Paul Baran does, between an intellect worker and an intellectual. An intellect worker lives by his wits and works with his mind rather than with his muscles: "...all intellect workers have an interest in common", Baran emphasised, "not to be reduced to the more onerous, less remunerative, and—since they are the ones who set the norms of respectability—less respected manual labour" (Baran, 1961: 4). It is obvious that India has produced a mass of these intellect workers who are able to man the government agencies, which are expanding in the wake of planned development and the faster growth of the private industrial activity than in the

---

5.   By any measure, except expenditure per pupil, higher education in India has expanded at a great rate....Next to the United States, India probably has more students in universities than any other country, though the proportion of university students per 1,000 population is among the lowest...Probably more Indian graduates leave the university to enter the labour force than elsewhere, though again the percentage of graduates in the labour force is very small indeed. Warren F. Ilchman, "People in plenty—educated unemployment in India," Asian Survey. October 1969, p.763.

century and a half of British rule. This proliferating class of intellect workers has gradually made its presence felt in many areas of human knowledge. In the social sciences contributions of Indian scholars have been most conspicuous. In particular, in two branches of development—economics and agriculture— it can be said that Indian scholars have significantly extended the frontiers of knowledge.[6] In social anthropology and sociology new dimensions have certainly been added. The same can be said of natural sciences such as physics, chemistry, and, to some extent, botany. For all this, however, the Indian intelligentsia has fallen short of that signal distinction of being intellectuals who could influence the extent and nature of social and political change in the country.

An intellectual is not merely engaged in the pursuit of knowledge for its own sake. He is cast in a different role of one who perceives prevailing social and political reality in its 'inter-connectedness' or as a part of the 'historical process'. This means that intellectuals have to have "the largest knowledge, the most comprehensive education, and the greatest possibility for exploring and assimilating historical experience, from providing society with such humane orientation and such intelligent guidance as may be obtainable at every concrete junction on its historical journey" (Baran, 1961: 11).[7] This role places an onerous responsibility on the intellectuals to tell the truth as they perceive it and to have the courage of their convictions, a flaming zeal, and unimpeachable honesty. Since truth-seeking is his major profession, the intellectual should be able, in Marx's words, to criticise "everything that exists", and "that the criticism will not shrink either from its own conclusions or from conflict with the powers that be". Unlike the Indian intellectuals of the pre-independence era who possessed many of these qualities, their descendants have failed singularly in their assigned task.

The decline of Indian intellectuals as fearless social critics was, in a way, inevitable. The conditions under which the intelligentsia could sublimate into intellectuals—or what could be described as the culture of the mind—in fact waned. With the education explosion and consequent deterioration in its

---

6. For sheer range of contributions in economics, see Jagdish N. Bhagwati and Sukhamoy Chakravarty, "Contributions to Indian economic analysis: a survey", The American Economic Review, Part 2. September 1969.

7. Baran's perception comes close to Schumpeter's sociological interpretation of the intellectual: "...the intellectual group cannot help nibbling, because it lives on criticism and its whole position depends on criticism that stings; and criticism of persons and of current events will, in a situation in which nothing is sacrosanct, fatally issue in criticism of class and institutions." J.A. Schumpeter, Capitalism, Socialism and Democracy, Fourth Edition, London: George Allen & Unwin 1952, p.151.

quality, a hiatus developed between "the sea of mediocrity" and the "islands of elite". In a country with limited employment opportunities, the best minds gravitated to a few centres of excellence or to non-academic, but remunerative positions in the government, leaving academia in general bereft of the cream of talent. Those who remained continued their miserable existence without any real interest in scholarship or knowledge, constantly humiliated by the treatment they received from the intellectual *brahmins*. The culture of the mind thus languished. The brightest and the best looked for approbation of their contributions to knowledge either to the institutions of learning abroad or to the authorities rather than to their own tribe, which was large and growing but also intellectually diminishing. This not only debased the standards by which the intellectuals' knowledge was evaluated, but it also deprived the intellectuals of their spunk and vigour and motivated them toward an easy reward and acclaim from the wrong quarters.

From this kind of caste distinction within the class of intellectuals emanated a false value system, divorced from the prevailing social and political structure. This occurred in stages and perhaps without the intellectuals realising its full implications. A sociological impulse, inherent in the Indian polity, to be stratified through differentiation of the elite from masses, the superior by birth from the inferior by status, reasserted itself with a vengeance when the number of educated increased. The elite tried to maintain their distinctiveness by imbibing instruction from the foreign universities, a bias toward which was already strong even before independence. The premium thus placed on foreign education was enlarged gradually by the compact of bureaucrats-politicians, many of whom had their gaze fixed westward. This development had several consequences. For one thing, Indian problems and policies were seen in an irrelevant context without any attempt to analyse the local situation in all its aspects. Therefore, when the prescriptions derived from perception of events proved unworkable, the intellectuals—whether bureaucrats, academics, or journalists—became totally demoralised. For another, the insularity of the intellectuals generated by their educational experience rendered them impervious to the aspirations of the masses. And yet, they persisted for public consumption with their animadversions on the undesirability of Western education and culture. The resulting double standards in the intellectuals' public posture eventually attenuated their usefulness for society as a whole.

Even more importantly, the entire psychological make-up of the Indian intellectual was disturbed. In earlier periods the role of the intellectual was both to generate and disseminate ideas, whether original or borrowed, and to engage in public discussions of the issues that had a bearing on the progress of society. Freedom from foreign rule perhaps strengthened the first role of the intellectuals after independence, extending the areas of interest of the intellectual into new and creative directions, but it enfeebled the second role—that of rousing public consciousness through open and dispassionate debate of the questions of civil concern. This was, in some measure, a corollary of some intellectuals' participation in the political process, thereby blurring the line between their prime concern for truth and the seeking of power. Indifference to civil responsibility was also a consequence of the intellectuals' addiction to the ethics of "reflective and responsible action", as Edward Shils put it (Shils, 1961: 97). Their identification with the national movement was so close and their emotional attachment to the reigning philosophy was so abiding that the intellectuals chose a more painless course of being in the mainstream, rather than risking isolation from it through dissemination of divergent interpretations of the truth. Discussion of public policies by the intellectuals, therefore, became merely a ritual to rationalise popular and acceptable ideas, rather than a vehicle for searching analysis or suggesting potential alternatives.

The diminished status of the intellectuals was also due to the alteration in the objective conditions in which they functioned before. An opposition to the alien regime and its intellectualisation were both relatively easy, but propagation of constructive ideas in a heterogeneous, polycentric society, burdened with growing demographic pressures, was indeed a gigantic task, demanding fundamental thinking, perspicacity, vision, and a high degree of responsibility. These qualities, not generally in abundance in any society, were even less so in India, largely because of the prevalence of what Myron Weiner called the "politics of scarcity". Popular aspirations had expanded so much that the ability of the Indian polity to fulfil them was clearly inadequate (Weiner, 1962: 2). All segments of society—peasants, students, politicians, agriculturists, and workers—were seized by this spectre of scarcity to an extent that the government was asked to step in with one kind of financial assurance or another. One perceptive Indian intellectual, closely associated with policymaking for many years, said in despair: "Everyone looks up to the Government." In the kind of democratic set-up which India possessed, the government could not possibly be all things to all groups without going broke. One could understand the highly politicised groups such as the trade unions, agriculturists, or the businessmen clamouring for patronage of one sort or another, but when the intellectuals too considered themselves to be a commodity in the market, to be governed by the laws of demand and supply, the very basis of their independent existence was seriously eroded.

In the process of surviving, the Indian intellectuals could not maintain the detachment necessary for their role as moulders of public opinion. They became, therefore, hardly distinguishable from the practical men of affairs and the politicians. If the intellectuals were to have a feel of history and perceive a prevailing social reality as part of a historical continuum, they must, as Hans Morgenthau prescribed, strive to seek truth and truth alone. The power-seeking, though important in itself from the point of view of social dynamics, has to be left to those who are better equipped to undertake it. This does not imply that the intellectual is a superior specie of the larger genre of the educated elite; public men and politicians are equally important. But what needs to be stressed is that the objects of interest of the intellectuals and the politicians/practical men have to be kept apart. To continue Morgenthau's argument:

> In his search for the truth, the ideal type of intellectual is oblivious to power; in his pursuit of power, the politician at best will use truth as a means to his ends. Yet the two worlds are also potentially intertwined; for truth has a message that is relevant to power and the very existence of power has a bearing both upon the expression and the recognition of truth (Morgenthau, 1970: 14).

Despite the interconnection between the two pursuits, there still remains an area of potential conflict which the intellectuals may decide to overcome either through confrontation or surrender or isolation. The Indian intellectuals fought shy of facing the issues squarely or dissimulated their pusillanimity by underplaying their ideological differences. The areas of potential conflict were delimited by them in two ways. First, the intellectuals pursued their interests in an esoteric fashion, using modern techniques and tools in the study of subjects where the scope for disagreement was less. No doubt they succeeded in elevating the level of economics, sociology, and some physical sciences through their original thinking. With a few exceptions, however, their work could be significant only as a technical treatise, and a testimony to the resurgence of creativity among the Indian intellectuals against a background of sterility in the years before independence. But as a commentary on larger social and political events, and as an interpretation of social changes in the context of a historical process, their contributions were no more than trivia. Second, in order to narrow the area of conflict, the intellectuals went in for a soft option of stealing the clothes of the power-players themselves. They did this either by surviving through submergence with the power elite, in which case they became dysfunctional and outlived their social purpose; or alternatively, they joined the power elite by proxy. They readily found virtue in the *fait accompli* which facilitated their ex-post-facto rationalisations of the issues of public policy, though as intellectuals, their duty was to criticise, to evaluate the issues, and to pinpoint their implications not only for a particular sphere where policy originated or was applied, but to all the areas of social and political action. In either case, they failed to make a meaningful contribution to the improvement of the political process.[8]

One can illustrate the 'self-effacing' nature of the Indian intellectual in a number of ways. Economic policy formulation represented one single area where the intellectuals truly emerged as a fifth wheel. Partly a by-product of the freedom struggle, partly motivated by the universalism of Gandhi and Tagore, to some extent because of the reaction to world revolutionary events, as interpreted by Nehru and other political leaders, but mainly prompted by the character of the Indian polity, public investment, social control of economic activity, income distribution and employment, and the physical controls had come to occupy a pride of place in public debates.[9] On each of these, the intellectuals' contribution, with of course a few notable exceptions, was to reassert in a dogmatic fashion the importance of these objectives even more vigorously than the politicians rather than to analyse their institutional implications and the cost benefits involved. It was taken as axiomatic that public investment meant not only government ownership, but also its bureaucratisation and non-economic orientation. First, it was seriously argued that public investment need not and should not aim at profit-making. When losses from public investment strained public finances, the importance of profits was recognised but without the knowledge of how to achieve them. Vague suggestions were made to the effect that the working of public enterprises should be improved. Given the public policy to promote public investment, and the intellectuals' agreement

8. A.K. Dasgupta has illustrated this in the case of one class of intellectuals, namely, economists. A.K. Dasgupta, "Economists and government", *Economic Weekly*, Special Number. August 1962.

9. It is not factually true that Indian intellectuals and political leaders turned to socialist ideology because of the spell cast on them by what Daniel Moynihan called "the British Revolution". Nor is it historically correct to suggest that the British civil servants carried the socialist doctrine to their colonies, including India. (Daniel P. Moynihan, 'The United States in Opposition', Commentary. March 1975.) If at all, it was the Russian revolution which carried, through Nehru and Tagore, the socialist message to the Indian subcontinent. The more fundamental reason for receptivity to the egalitarian ideas is to be sought partly in politics of scarcity and largely in a sociological phenomenon of the deep-seated prejudices amongst people against profits and the trading classes. In India, the unpopularity of the traders was generated by the way British rule was inaugurated in India, e.g. 'the flag following trade', and by the fact that the traders who operated in most linguistic regions were alien to them, e.g. the Marwaris in Bengal, etc.

with this goal, they could have made themselves useful to the authorities if only they had concretised their thinking on this subject and traced fully the institutional implications.[10]

The same was true of the policies in regard to income distribution and employment. It was Pitambar Pant of the Planning Commission and his band of high-powered and dedicated economists who first crystallised Indian thinking on income redistribution, based on politically accepted premises. Laudable and desirable though this objective was, there was no reference in the discussions of the intellectuals outside to the enormous and almost revolutionary repercussions of the programme. Neither the protagonists of this policy nor its detractors reasoned out in a detached and objective but responsible manner for themselves, the politicians, or the public at large what that policy could mean for the Indian political and social system as a whole.[11]

If the intellectuals in academia misjudged their role, those in the political arena were afflicted by a mental inertia. This was no more evident than in the lack of intellectualisation of the Indian Communist movement. The Communist Party has been in existence in India for almost five decades, but it has been intellectually barren. K.M. Panikkar has attributed this to its reliance on 'the argument by analogies'. If the linguistic states were important in India, it was because in the Soviet Union Russians had recognised different nationalities; if the Congress Party was bad, it was because the Kuomintang to which they compared it was reactionary. They did not realise that the Indian situation was totally different from the Chinese or Russian and no unthinking application of Communist dogma could work in India. There never was an attempt at fundamental reassessment of the Communist doctrine amongst

---

10. What I am trying to suggest is that the responsibility of the intellectuals does not diminish if they are in agreement with the objectives of the authorities; in fact, it increases enormously because it then becomes their task to see that the objectives are efficiently attained. For Paul Sweezy, public investment was an article of faith, but this did not prevent him from coming to the conclusion that "...the juridical form of state property becomes increasingly empty and real power over the means of production, which is the essence of the ownership concept, gravitates into the hands of the managerial elite." Paul Sweezy, "Reply to Charles Bettleheim", Monthly Review. March 1969.

11. One looked in vain for a Lindbeck among the economists of India. Ideologically of socialist persuasion, sympathetic to the objectives of the government of his country, Lindbeck did not feel constrained to draw the logical implications of government policies. In fact, his forthright evaluation helped to avoid obfuscation in the implementation of socialist policies in his country. Assar Lindbeck (1971). The Political Economy of the New Left: An Outsider's View London: Allen and Unwin. A general malaise from which the economists of all persuasions neoclassical as well as Marxist—suffered was their naïve faith in the 'State' to deliver the goods. See, for a serious indictment of economists, Arun Shourie (1975). "Economists and policy-makers: some preliminary hypotheses", Economic and Political Weekly, Special Number X(5, 6, 7): 147–56.

the Communist thinkers, as in the West.[12] The reason for their reliance on the argument by analogies was the perpetuation of the Guru tradition in scholarship by the Indian Communist intellectuals, under which the wisdom of the elders was passed down to the younger generation as gospel truth (Tariq Ali, 1975).[13] They did not, therefore, comprehend the nature of changes that enveloped the Communist theology in recent years nor could they explain how the spirit of nationalism had tended to be a far more pervasive force even in Russia and China, why the Indian labour theory of value has been antithetical to the dynamics of development and in what way the centralisation of power has frustrated the very aims of a Communist society. They were not even aware of the new ferment of ideas which was shaking off the complacency of the Communist theoreticians in Western countries.[14]

The decline and fall of the Indian intellectuals in post-independence India perhaps merit explanation at a more fundamental level. Could it be that the efflorescence in the intellectual activity of the decades before independence was a mere flash in the pan? The challenges of alien rule may have profoundly affected the psyche of the Indian intellectual who, in response, may have sprung up to an ephemeral glory. Once the foreign regime had passed into

---

12. For instance, such Marxist theoreticians as Paul Sweezy and Paul Baran recognised explicitly the risks inherent in a concentration of power in collectivist economies, saying that "militarism and conquest are completely foreign to Marxian theory, and a socialist society contains no class or group which, like the big capitalists of the imperialist countries, stands to gain from the policies of subjugating other nations and peoples", Baran, P. and P. Sweezy (1966). "Monopoly Capital: an essay on the American economic and social order" New York: Monthly Review Press. p. 337. There has been a solitary exception to this general tendency amongst Indian Communist intellectuals. M.N. Roy, a colleague of Lenin and a leader of the Third Communist International, originated a decolonisation theory as far back as 1936, predicting the gradual disappearance of world imperialism. His thesis as an exercise in dialectics was as significant as Lenin's doctrine of imperialism. Roy was expelled from the Communist movement for his heresies — or perhaps his originality.

13. Damodaran in his self-criticism has provided a series of telling facts about the pathetic dependence of Indian Communist intellectuals on the holy Russian scriptures.

14. There were a few attempts, such as the one by K.N. Raj, at renovating the Marxian doctrine for application to the Indian situation. By using Michael Kalecki's categorisation, he drew certain conclusions totally opposed to the usual Communist generalisations. See K.N. Raj. "The politics and economics of intermediate regime", Economic and Political Weekly, VIII(27): 1189–98. The response to this in one of the subsequent issues of the same journal by a leading Communist, E.M.S. Namboodiripad, has shown how the Communist intellectuals still find it difficult to break away from the existing mould of thought.

The sterility of the Communist intellectuals is seen in their analysis of Indian peasants under British rule. Taking their cue from Marx's observations on India, they attributed the immiserisation of Indian peasants only to British exploitation. And it was accepted for many years as a plausible explanation of the poverty of the Indian peasants until a non-Marxist Indian intellectual showed that the poor peasants were generally identical with the low castes such as the untouchables and explained their poverty both in terms of social and economic causes. See Dharma Kumar (1965). Land and Caste in South India: Agricultural Labour in the Madras Presidency during the 19th Century. Cambridge: Cambridge University Press.

limbo, the sense of humiliation abated, the complacency of self-rule ensued, and the depletion of the Indian intellectuals may have resumed its long-term course. The constant invasions and defeats, the memories of the great civilisation, the frustrations of the present, and the uncertainty of the future may have eaten into the very vitals of the intellectuals. What passed off as absorbability was, in fact, intellectual subjugation.[15] Of all India's great leaders, it was Gandhi who warned his countrymen—perhaps in vain—of this danger and tried to emancipate the Indian mind from the dead weight of history.

<h2 style="text-align:center">REFERENCES</h2>

Ali, Tariq (1975). "Memoir of an Indian Communist: an interview with veteran Indian Communist Damodaran", *New Left Review*. September–October.

Baran, Paul A. (1961). "The commitment of the intellectual", *Monthly Review*. May.

Keynes, J.M. (1932). *Essays in Persuasion*. New York: Harcourt Brace.

Keynes, J. M. (1947). *The General Theory of Employment, Interest, and Money*. London: Macmillan, pp. 383-384.

Morgenthau, Hans J. (1970). *Truth and Power: Essays of a Decade, 1960–70*. New York: Praeger.

Panikkar, K.M. (1963). *The Foundations of New India* (London: Allen and Unwin).

Shils, Edward (1961). *The Intellectual Between Tradition and Modernity: The Indian Situation*. The Hague: Mouton.

Weiner, Myron (1962). *The Politics of Scarcity: The Public Pressures and Political Response in India*. Chicago, Ill.: Chicago University Press.

---

15. One is reminded of Naipaul's remark that "India absorbs and outlasts its conquerors, Indians say. But...I wonder whether intellectually for a thousand years, India had not always retreated before the conquerors and whether, in its periods of apparent revival, India hadn't only been making itself archaic again, intellectually smaller, always vulnerable." V.S. Naipaul (1976). "India: a wounded civilization", New York Times Sunday Review of Books, 29 April p. 19.

Published in Asian Survey XVII(3): 251-63 (1977).

18 | Restructuring the Political Process in India

There is something odd about some of the 'odd' years in Indian political history since Independence. The year 1947 marked India's political emancipation; 1969 heralded the split in the Indian National Congress; 1971 saw the ruling party endowed with a majority of votes to enable it to change radically the structure of the Indian constitution; and the climax has now been reached in 1977 when the much maligned, poor and illiterate Indian people, in their own quiet but determined way, have asserted their basic values and aspirations. When hope was forlorn and the apparatus of power had run amok; when social programmes and policies were being used more as a means to force the people into passivity, all of a sudden the whole oppressive machine crashed to the ground.

Refreshing and rejuvenating though the new developments are, a definite warning has also been sounded to the future rulers that something more fundamental is at stake in India than a mere eye-washing economic programme, that commitments and implementation are invariable concomitants of governance in the country, that social justice and economic growth are not correlates of economic policies which gyrate between public ownership of the means of production and unbridled private enterprise but are deeply embedded in the political process. Without transforming the political process, therefore, nothing worthwhile can be attained in the sphere of economic policy. Shibboleths and nostrums, whether of socialist persuasion or formed of capitalist dogma, would fail as surely as they did during the past three decades of freedom.

Admittedly, the Indira Gandhi regime had pulverised, if not destroyed, many an institution which had come to be associated with the form of government the country has had over the years. Freedom of the press was shorn away; the judiciary was diluted to the point where it was hardly distinguishable from the executive arm of the government; the administrative apparatus was suborned, enhancing its capacity for arbitrary rule. But in the wake of nostalgia for these institutions there should not be haste to revive them in their earlier incarnation as if they are sacred and timeless treasures.

Even when these institutions were active, the Indian polity had made barely any progress toward its cherished and much vaunted goals. Economic, political and social problems, far from being solved, piled up, paving the way for the eventual denouement that occurred in June 1975. The thrust of the movement which brought down the Gandhi regime and replaced it with a new one has been, until now, negative—the ruling politicians are to be pulled down, to be replaced by honest public-spirited men. There is a danger, therefore, that such a movement may culminate in easing out one set of politicians and replacing them by another brand of politicians, without any substantive change in social and economic policies. This kind of tweedledum-tweedledeeism is no answer to India's myriad problems. As experience has demonstrated, even when opposition parties achieved power in some states, they went the same way as their predecessors, which only helped the political system to lose its credibility with the masses. The only solution, therefore, is to evolve and to propagate an action programme within a democratic framework, directed at reforming the political system, a broad outline of which is spelled out in this paper.

II

Before sketching the contours of an agenda for the new government certain lessons about the functioning of the Indian democratic structure have to be learnt. Right from the start of the Indian freedom movement, a view, universally held by political leaders of all hues, has been that India must accept centralisation of power if it is to remain a viable nation. This view was grounded in the belief that India embodied within itself several subcultures, diverse and dominant, so that some superstructure over and above the constituent units has to be endowed with binding authority. For the leftist intellectuals, centralisation of power had its own appeal, first because it implied the hegemony of the party of the poor and the underprivileged, and second because it was thought to prevent egalitarian programmes from being challenged by the competing forces. It was hardly expected, much less understood, that centralisation, with overriding powers vested in the Centre, would sooner or later degenerate into autocracy which would neither ensure unity nor social justice. At the beginning, there appeared to be harmony between the Centre and the states; but it was more accidental than inevitable, because the party which ruled at the Centre was the same as that in the states. However, when the political complexion of the parties began to change, this harmony between the states and the Centre was gradually eroded. As has happened time and again, the party in power at the Centre felt threatened by the parties in power in the states, as in Kerala in the 1950s, in West Bengal in the 1960s, and in Tamil Nadu in the 1970s. In 1975 a stage was reached when centralisation meant not concentration of power in one party but in a coterie of a few individuals who then made puppets out of the chief ministers in the states, even when they belonged to their own party.

What was overlooked by the politicians and social scientists was that concentration of political power could come about without concentration of economic power, and once it is consolidated, all other powerful vested interests gravitate toward the political power centre. The parties on the left advocated socialistic measures such as the nationalisation of industry, press control, regulation of industry through licensing, and a host of other restrictive actions to attain their objectives of stifling the greedy capitalists, promoting social justice and raising the standard of living of the starving millions. R.H. Tawney made a powerful case for this 25 years ago: "It is still constantly assumed by privileged classes that when the state holds its hand, what remains as a result of its inaction is liberty. In reality, as far as the mass of mankind is concerned what commonly remains is not liberty but tyranny." The very means by which the State intervened increased enormously the power and patronage of the political operators. And once entrenched, they were joined by a compact of business, land-owning classes and the bureaucracy which sprawled as a result of growing state intervention. Concentration of power, thus, neither served the purpose of the parties on the right with their liberal creed nor that of the parties on the left with their socialistic ideologies. This has been nowhere more evident than in the field of economic policy formulation.

The paralysis of policy formulation and execution has its genesis in the inner working of the political system which operates in such a manner that at one extreme economic policy has punishment as its basis but without any sanction for enforcing it; and at the other, incentive as its basis without any built-in mechanism to penalise failure to accomplish. The omnipresent physical and price controls and the licensing procedures which are supposed to regulate economic activity are motivated by the desire to punish a defaulting individual, but in fact they are so soft in impact that the very sectors to control which the whole paraphernalia is devised escape their network. Instances are numerous which show that those who should not be granted industrial licences are enriched by them: landlords whose land ownership is supposed to be trimmed to size through land laws are the ultimate beneficiaries of this legislation: high income earners who are supposed to be liable for high tax rates end up by evading most, if not all, of their tax obligations. Enunciation of penalties is thus in the nature of a quietus to hold in check the restiveness of the mass of the people.

But the system also occasionally swings to the other extreme where incentives constitute the basis of economic policy. There have been subsidies aplenty of one kind or another. Production of certain commodities is encouraged by tax benefits or depreciation allowances; export of goods is favoured through cash or credit subsidies; so-called small producers, cultivators or traders are promoted through all sorts of bounties. But the system is incapable of penalising the failure to accomplish that for which the initial incentives are bestowed. If an industry producing certain desired goods, while battening on the government financial bonanza, defaults for some reason, it gets off lightly; and if it is pushed to the verge of bankruptcy it is a signal for the ever-indulgent government to rush in and take it over on the specious ground of preventing unemployment or loss of output in a shortage-ridden economy. If production-limiting restrictions are evaded, then the post-facto sanction comes forth very enthusiastically, rather than exemplary penal action; if export targets for which concessions have already been appropriated are unfulfilled, the eye-washing explanation of the defaulter is sufficient proof of innocence.

It is this nature of the economic policy, based on punishment and incentive simultaneously, but without any sanction for enforcing the penalty, which largely explains the frequent gyrations in economic policy since Independence. When the political system needs the support of the mass of the people it is readily inclined to proclaim a turn to the left in economic policy formulation; this is generally on the eve of elections, when the votes of the poor masses are solicited. But once the politicians are firmly entrenched in power, the pay-off of leftism in policy posture slowly begins to dwindle. Anxiety to perpetuate themselves in power seizes them, and the search is on for finance to meet the expenses of the next election; the time then arrives for a swing to the right in policy stance, which lasts until the coffers are filled. Inherently, therefore, economic policy in India moves cyclically—sometimes to the left, but not enough to be called leftist, and sometimes to the right, but not enough to be labelled rightist.

It follows, therefore, that the system which facilitates the concentration of political power also strengthens the concentration of economic power of vested interests of all kinds. If this be so, then it is imperative that the political process, which has made such concentration of power possible, be radically transformed in a way which will prevent other power groups from exerting their influence on the polity by operating from one narrow centre. This implies directly diffusion of political power, leaving greater autonomy to the states, and indirectly, blocking the ways of vested interests whose tentacles are spread over a wide area.

Another lesson is that there is no alternative to the democratic process for changing the Indian political system. If it has not functioned well, it is all the more necessary to reform and revitalise it, making it more responsive to the basic urges of the people and building it into a power centre, which can countervail the authority of the politician, whether he be a minister, elected member of a governing party or opposition party. It is no use planning strategies in terms of the Russian or Chinese interpretation of Communism. It is now realised, even by the Communists, that approach to an egalitarian society can be made through the democratic process and not necessarily through violent revolution. Every process has its own logic, its dynamics and sociology and must be devised to suit the context in which it is to be used. This applies, in no uncertain manner, to India, as is amply borne out by the recent elections.

In the existing system, which derives its power from the poor segment of the population on a platform which is apparently directed towards their amelioration but reneges on these promises when it needs to placate the affluent in order to achieve the seat of power, certain contradictions are inevitable. The system not only survives but thrives because there is a wide communication gap between the politicians and the electorate, which prevents the latter from exerting any pressure on the former once they are installed in power. Elected representatives as well as members of the government can easily snap the strings which bind them to their electors. Politicians are prone to forget their mandate, obtained from the source of power, as they are secure in the knowledge that their position is unassailable until the time of the next election. They can, therefore, turn their attention toward raising the necessary resources to underwrite their next election programme. Paradoxically enough, in this respect, the interests of both the ruling party and the party or parties in opposition tend to converge more than diverge and the reason for this is not difficult to comprehend. For one thing, the opposition members, once elected, also have to perpetuate themselves. Though they are not in the same league as the ruling party insofar as patronage is concerned, they too can distribute favours in a variety of ways in a regime where every little bit of weight thrown about counts. It also suits the convenience of the ruling party to collaborate and coalesce with the opposition parties in order to strengthen a spoils system where the dividing line between the governing and the non-governing parties can be erased by absorbing the opposition. The opposition parties, therefore, oppose, in a harmless sort of way on only the peripheral issues. Thus, at the root of all the present economic and political difficulties lies the political process and unless it is overhauled India cannot hope to emerge from the morass of poverty and stagnation.

III

One can think of setting up a political system which can pursue an economic policy with punishment as its basis, provided it also incorporates a built-in mechanism to enforce it. The first, and perhaps a more fundamental, prerequisite for such a reform is that the communication gap that separates the political authority from the electorate needs to be bridged, if not removed altogether. The communication gap is created by, among others, the size of the political unit which is the state in India. To strengthen public pressure it is essential to have a homogeneous group with a similarity of approach to socio-political economic programmes, a telescoping of the distance between the rulers and the ruled and smoothness of the two-way communication channel, upward from the electorate to the political government and downward from the latter to the former via the bureaucratic ladder. The presently demarcated states are heterogeneous insofar as identification of group interests is concerned. In a large state only one part of it normally tends to benefit from the policies of the government and this acts as a deterrent to political action as the party in power can play off one part against another to its best advantage. Thus the regime is sustained in a parliamentary democracy, regardless of the mandate given and without any fear of being checkmated by the majority public opinion. This immunity is accentuated by the vastness of the geographic distances between the seats of power at the state and central levels on the one hand, and the large mass of people on the other, as also by the lack of communication facilities. It seems, therefore, better to have a larger number of small states—each unit homogeneous in itself with common attitudes to political and economic problems—so that the action of state governments would be watched closely and constantly by those whom they are supposed to affect. Gandhi, in *India of My Dreams*, placed the whole problem of autonomy of the individual unit very succinctly. Though it was in a different context, it is of no less relevance to the creation of small state units: "In the structure composed of innumerable villages there will be ever widening never ascending circles. Life will not be an apex sustained by the bottom. But it will be the individual always ready to perish for the village, the latter ready to perish for the circle of villages till at last the whole becomes one life composed of individuals never aggressive in their arrogance but ever humble sharing the majesty of the oceanic circles of which they are integral units. Therefore, the outermost circumference will not wield power to crush the inner circle but give strength to all within and derive its own from the Centre." Such identifiable homogeneous groups can be easily discerned in some of the larger states. By the same token, it is possible to perceive a dichotomy in interests of the urban and rural populations and to make a plea for the formation of city states, each with problems of its own, such as Calcutta and Bombay. Each state as a political and administrative unit would be large enough for the benign power of the government to be used effectively to attain the largest amount of good for the largest number, and small enough to prevent the generation of any centrifugal forces in the Union. It is often argued that too many states would lead to internecine squabbles and quarrels among the states. This fear is totally unfounded. Splitting of the existing large states would mean several small states, many of which would share the same language which often drives a wedge between states and encourages parochialism. With the creation of many small states, one basic principle, propounded by Ambedkar years ago that "not one language, one state, but one state, one language" in order that the language sub-nationalism should be reined in, would be fully implemented.

The smallness of the size of a political unit has to be accompanied by the decentralisation of economic power. The state government can win the mandate on the programme but it has to be endowed with the necessary authority to implement that mandate. For this, there will have to be far greater autonomy in the pursuit of economic policy which, in the Indian context, means autonomy in the field of industrial development. The state should be in a position to license any industry, either in the public or private sector, provided that it is within the framework of a broad national plan, and that it is capable of raising the necessary resources on its own to finance it. The Centre then would mainly discharge its role of a leveller between states, as in any federation, through the distribution of tax revenue which falls within its jurisdiction, quite apart from its concern with external relations, defence, the financial system, communications, and some other subjects which abut on more than one state.

Taxation is only one aspect of the resource mobilisation by the state. There are other questions about foreign exchange allocations and the access to the financial system which is likely to be under the control of the central government. True enough, foreign exchange would pose a serious constraint on the activities of the states if it is left solely to the decision of the central government. On the other hand, the Centre, being largely responsible for the foreign affairs of the country, including management of external resources, has to be the custodian of foreign exchange. However, this problem could be overcome by the Centre auctioning foreign exchange to the states after setting aside some part of it for the purpose of foreign exchange reserves and distributing some to the extremely small and poor states (such as Nagaland), so that foreign exchange, though limited, could be made available at a price determined by competitive forces. Only those states which have projects viable at a going foreign exchange price would bid for it while others would abstain without any economic loss.

A smaller state as a political, administrative and economic unit has significance far beyond its political connotation. Those who know India will realise fully what the demographic compulsions are such that a private enterprise-based economic system is a non-starter. Because of stark economic inequalities, growing worse with every addition to the population, profit accumulation by individuals irrespective of their beneficial impact on saving and economic growth is anathema to a large number of assetless people. At the other extreme, state intervention, described by one perceptive economist as "reluctant collectivism", inevitable and on some occasions socially necessary to overcome market imperfections, has a tendency to result in proliferation of a bureaucratic jungle with its own rules and regulations, its *raison d'être* lost in such process. The smaller states with a greater degree of independence from the Centre in the industrial and agricultural spheres, and charged with the responsibility of raising their own resources, can get around this dilemma between a private-enterprise-based system and the dirigistic system of economic activity. If intervention must take place it should be confined to the state government: if private enterprise is to prevail, that too would be within the jurisdiction of the state governments. In any case, each state would be judged by its electorate not only by what it does but also by how it compares with other states. The emotive appeal of ideology centred round the presence or absence of state ownership of economic activity would recede. It is as if each state—a distinct economic entity—would compete with others to prove the superiority of its performance. Thus, the social purposiveness of state intervention can be reconciled with the efficiency and dynamism of a profit-dominated private enterprise system. Furthermore, this would help to trim the scale of bureaucracy which has sprawled all over India during the last two decades. Bureaucratic efficiency is scale-determined—the smaller the area of its operation, the greater its efficiency; with a small-sized state as an economic unit, the social control of economic activity would not be accompanied by a bureaucratic sub-state which is dilatory in decision-making, susceptible to political corruption and impervious to the larger public interests.

The state units would also be left with no alibis in regard to their performance. If the state economy tended to falter and fail, it was because it had not stretched itself sufficiently; if resources were not mobilised it was because it was averse to taking harsh steps to tap agriculture, which is at present a sacred cow. With the detachment of the main metropolitan centres as city states, state governments would be denied the soft option of mulcting the urban middle class and industry to finance investment and social expenditure. They would be compelled to make difficult choices such as taxing agriculture for additional resources, which would only be realizable if the *quid* of achievement were demonstrated to the people for the *quo* of pain imposed on them. On the other side, the urban population, which has not so far figured in the vote calculus of the politician, would come to wield power more decisively to its advantage. In short, solid achievements and not sloganeering, deep and abiding commitment to professed goals and policies and not cosmetics of casual pronouncements from the podium of the party conferences, would be the criterion by which the performance of the parties, both in power and in opposition would be judged.

IV

Paring the size of the existing states and creation in their place of numerous smaller states should be only the first step towards the rejuvenation of the political processes in India. The accountability of the parties would undoubtedly be enhanced, but the game of political horse-trading would continue unabated until the patronage which is its basis is knocked out. Political patronage is endemic in the electoral process, as the parties, particularly the one in power, have always to be ready with resources which can be raised only by bestowing favours for their next electoral battles. If this is the rationale of patronage, it is obvious that electoral laws should be amended to enable the State—all state governments—to finance expenditure of the candidates contesting the election, as is widely practised in Germany, some of the Scandinavian countries, and lately in the United States. In order to avoid frivolous individuals seeking candidacy, a condition should be laid down that an individual should contest an election to any assembly or parliament only through membership of a political party which, in case he is elected, he can leave only on penalty of resignation from it. The issue then is whether all parties, regardless of the public support they command, should qualify for state bounty. Here various expedients can be adopted, the most practical of which seems to be the holding of a qualifying election to test the public's support for each party aspiring to contest the election. Only those parties which are backed by a minimum percentage of votes, say 10–15 per cent of the registered voters, would be meeting the test of qualifying for financial support from the State. The primaries, which might also be State financed, would be a once-and-for-all affair as at every subsequent election the percentage of previously polled votes by each of the parties would constitute the basis, except perhaps for any new party that might emerge on the scene. In such a case, the qualifying election could be repeated. The amount involved in such financing of the electoral process would, no doubt, be huge, but its dimensions would appear to be still modest if seen in juxtaposition to what has been currently spent on it in a clandestine manner. This apart, even if the sums involved are large, the economic and political benefits would be enormous with the improvement of economic policies and the banishment of the corrosive and depraved political practices.

Government financing of the elections should be followed by the imposition of a constitutional limit on the size of the cabinet, both at the state and central government levels, and by the initiation of a system of recall of the elected representatives. The limit on the size of the cabinet is necessitated to further reduce the area of manipulative politics, encouraged by the blandishment of office, and can be defined in relation to population. The recall system would exert a salutary influence on those elected representatives who are prone to kick the ladder they climb. In order that the recall system should not generate into idle pastime, a minimum, but high, percentage of votes can be stipulated for recall with the proviso that only one recall for each member in the life of the assembly can be effectuated. Furthermore, recall should be justified either by specific proven charges regarding the character and integrity of the elected person, or by a catalogue of failures on his part to implement what he had committed through the manifesto of his party. Thus the recall would provide a powerful leverage to the voters to discipline their representatives and to prevent them from being corrupted by office.

Reform of the political process outlined above should be followed by specifying certain norms in regard to some important public offices, to prevent the arbitrary use of power in relation to states as well as to the people's rights. At present the office of state Governor is treated as a patronage post which is filled only by the central government. This means that the central government can prey on the state government in an arbitrary fashion through the Governor, who is in debt to it. A better and perhaps more equitable alternative would be to make these appointments through a panel suggested by the ruling party at the Centre and the state concerned together with the opposition party. The same principle may be extended to the appointment of the Supreme Court judges and High Court judges. The final choice may be subjected to scrutiny by Parliament or the legislature concerned with all the facts fully disclosed to the public. Salaries may be fixed high enough in order to make such posts attractive to the best available talent and their pensions may be made equal to their salaries so that they would not succumb to temptation or fall on evil days later in life.

V

Access to the financial system in general and to central bank credit in particular has relevance for any schema of economic autonomy for the states. The financial system, being in central charge, is a unifying force in a federal polity and also a vehicle for coordination of policies of all state units with that of the Centre. But the central direction of a financial system implies a certain restriction on the autonomy of the states and may generate tensions among them. The autonomy of the central bank of the country, for this reason, has to be guaranteed under the Constitution. It should be independent in day-to-day functioning, but would have to adhere to the policy guidelines laid down by the government in power at the Centre in consultation with the state governments. The head of this organ of the credit system would, as in the case of the Supreme Court judges, be selected by the panel agreed upon by the ruling party and the opposition party at the Centre and the corresponding parties at the state level. Before appointment, the Governor of the Bank should be required to be questioned by both the governing and the opposition parties in Parliament. Then again he should have a fixed term, say eight to ten years, and could be removed through a two-thirds majority of the members of both the houses of Parliament and the state assemblies. He should be banned from holding any office, either within the country or outside, after retirement. He would take a dispassionate look at the monetary and economic policies and submit periodically an independent evaluation report of the state of the economy to both Parliament and the state assemblies. In this way all areas of possible friction between the Centre and the states in the realm of finance would be minimised and political interference with the credit system would be avoided.

As has happened in the last few years, the credit system was used by the politicians in power to corrupt and debase the democratic underpinning of the system. Nobody should have any doubts about the desirability of a nationalised banking system, but the way it has been operated has resulted in its becoming an instrument of corruption and bureaucratic arbitrariness. Bank executives have lost their independence and discretion, and have been reduced to the status of minions of the banking department of the government of India through it or the politicians. Nationalisation should not be equated with bureaucratisation. When the Reserve Bank is there as an apex bank, the interloping of the banking department has deflated the role of the Reserve Bank on the one hand, and converted the nationalised banks into a haven for corrupt politicians on the other, thereby shearing it of its legitimate role of catalyst in bringing about economic development and social justice. The best way to ensure a responsive and efficient functioning of the credit system is to immunize it from blatant political interference while placing its policies within an overall framework to which the government is publicly committed. To accomplish this, the first step should be to disband the banking department of the Government of India and restore the hegemony of the Reserve Bank over the credit system. Secondly, the nationalised banks—both commercial and development—whatever their eventual pattern decided upon by the government, should be made as fully autonomous as the Reserve Bank and their Chairman should be chosen in the same manner as the Governor of the Reserve Bank. Chief executives of banks, while being required to observe government directives about broad policy, would then be able to function without fear of the politicians or administrators or favour from them. At the same time, if they failed in their management of a bank to achieve results, they would be automatically held fully accountable and would have to pay the price.

VI

The new government will have to undo early the damage to the Constitution done under the preceding regime. Some of the obnoxious and unsavoury amendments will certainly have to be removed, but the task of the government should not stop at that. Over the years many deficiencies in the political process have surfaced which have rendered the pursuit of democratic and egalitarian policies well nigh impossible. Turns and twists in social, economic, and political policies have been a sort of patchwork without any logic and perception of what is the real desideratum in the Indian polity. This calls for a radical restructuring of the political process which would reflect the aspirations of the people as well as the sanction required to realise them. Decentralisation of power, diffusion of the power of the vested interests, autonomy of states, improvement of communication between politicians and people, and insulation of the democratic system from patronage should constitute the major planks of a programme to revitalise the political process. It is for this reason that these requirements of the political process must be enshrined in the new Constitution. India with its demographic compulsions and democratic commitment can ill afford to turn away from social justice and equality and thrust for freedom. And for that very reason it is not possible on the one hand to pursue a policy of 'let the hounds run', under which the private enterprise can dictate the course of economic development, and on the other hand, to permit the existing State apparatus, with its insensitive bureaucracy and power- and patronage-prone politicians, to have a stranglehold over the economic system. Social justice can be guaranteed when State intervention is on a scale which is small enough to checkmate the concentration of power; economic efficiency, freedom and growth can be ensured if the units in the economy, while animated by social conscience, can compete with each other. It is just this balance which is likely to be attained if India could have numerous small states with better communication with the people in each state. If it is a communist or a socialist ideology it will have its full sway in a smaller unit; if it is the free enterprise approach, it may be experimented with in a small area. If any of the alternatives succeeds, it would then affect other states, without the failure of any one of them doing irreparable and irreversible damage. Social purposiveness can then be dovetailed with the imperatives of economic efficiency and democratic commitment.

Published in the Economic and Political Weekly XII(27): 1057–62 (1977).]

19 | Nehru and the Indian Administration

Few men in history were as fortunate as Jawaharlal Nehru to enjoy undisputed authority and remain at the helm of his country's affairs for so long. Whatever may be the final assessment of Nehru's contribution in his own country as also in the world outside, he was a man of lofty idealism, a philosophical bent of mind and a magnificent vision of human society. His basic philosophy and political and economic thinking had been well articulated by the time Nehru became free India's first prime minister. The impact of his ideology and vision was seen in every aspect of our national life, in national politics and economic programmes in the field of technology and science, and in foreign policy. His powerful and popular personality made the acceptance of his ideas by the majority of Indian people possible. And yet in the translation of his ideals into practical programmes, Nehru was much less effective. The explanation of this paradox has to be sought partly in the fact that the instruments which Nehru could use for the achievement of his goals were very much at variance with the requirements of his ideology. This often led to ridiculous situations in our foreign relations as well as in the implementation of economic policies.

Nehru's main instrument was the existing administration system. To those who recalled Nehru's views on Indian administration and administrators in pre-independence India, it came as a surprise that Nehru should be eulogising the same administration immediately after he took over as prime minister. At the outset, he did this with plenty of reservations. Occasionally, he made public pronouncements to the effect that the old type of 'sunburnt' bureaucrat was out of place in new India and that dynamic changes that were taking place required a new type of administrator, firm yet flexible, forward-looking yet responsible, aware of his duties to the people yet bold enough to incur their wrath if he had to pursue correct yet unpopular policies. However, as he got involved in responsibilities more and more, his attitude to the administration underwent a change. He slowly came to believe in the infallibility and incorruptibility of the administration and at the slightest provocation he would shower panegyric on it. The result was that the administrative machinery, on which devolved the main task of implementing Nehru's policies, remained out of tune with the socialist aspirations of India with its growing public sector and far-reaching obligations in the world outside.

Examination of the adequacy or otherwise of Indian administration during the Nehru era would be beyond the scope of this article as it will have to cover a vast field from administration of the public enterprises to foreign service personnel, and from civil servants in charge of planning at the Centre and state capitals to district collectors and officers who manage and plan projects in the villages or small towns. We shall focus our attention only on one aspect of administration—the agencies and personnel charged with implementing economic policies.

The nature and quality of the administration in the country on the eve of planning is well brought out by Paul Appleby, who was invited to suggest ways and means to reform and reorganise Indian civil administration so as to equip it to undertake new tasks following the inauguration of the five-year plans. We can do no better than quote from his report:

1. I should say, rather, that the government is somewhat unwisely frugal—spending too much energy in penny-pinching and regarding too little the effectiveness and convenience of the conditions in which able men work.

2. The administrative system is generally characterised by requirements for interministerial clearance and an intricate sharing of responsibilities all the way down through the hierarchy.

3. Manuals seem to be far too didactic and confusing, too detailed and unimaginative. They might be expected to contribute to the extreme insistence on following formal channels too literary and invariably they seem to encourage literal mindedness and damp the spirit, imagination and judgement, which are important to good administration. These basic patterns undoubtedly originated in colonial administration.

4. The British did not feel the need to adjust so much to popular sentiment here as they did at home.

5. Civil servants of higher rank are more concerned with coordination than with 'administration' in action terms…there is instead the diluted and incomplete coordination not involving exercise of a real, and continuing power of control, an excess of cross-references and conferences antecedent to action and a delaying of action, responsibilities nominally lodged elsewhere.

Nehru's impact on Indian administration can be judged by comparing the administration today with what Appleby described over a decade ago.

Such comparison would show that the administration underwent virtually no change in a decade and more of planning and became, if anything, more rigid and more impervious to the dynamic changes envisaged in the plans and to the aspirations of the people. Even the changes that did take place and the new characteristics developed by the system made it a greater obstacle to rapid economic development.

The basic framework of the administration, as it was on the eve of independence, tended to perpetuate itself for a variety of reasons, some arising from the inexperience of ministers and some traceable to vested interests among the services. The core of the higher administration was the Indian Civil Service, its members trained in Oxbridge traditions with a good liberal education. This no doubt equipped them to deal with any problem of routine administration with aplomb and sureness of touch. There were, however, many items on the debit side. Their versatility was confined to maintaining law and order and revenue collection and in these limited tasks the distance they kept from their own people was an advantage. Even after the Congress party assumed power, members of this civil service continued to discharge their limited duties with great skill and ability: they initiated the ministerial novices into the intricacies of government. This provided them the opportunity to entrench themselves in the new set-up and become the *de facto* rulers.

Instead of adjusting themselves to the changing economic and political situation, they carried on with the same old philosophy of administration, regarding the various policies initiated by the Congress with cynicism and scepticism. It is no secret that most of the administrators belonging to this tribe paid only lip-service to the socialistic pattern, planned economic development and other policies which emanated from Nehru's broad vision. They treated every problem, whether in management of public enterprises or community development or trade promotion in foreign markets, as if it were a routine administrative matter.

The complete reliance they placed on the 'steel frame' goes to show that the Congress ministers had succumbed to the myth that the administrators were omniscient and could take on any responsibilities. Convinced of their own ability, the latter fanned out into all branches of economic planning and implementation, irrespective of their suitability for the task. Whether it was the State Bank or the Reserve Bank or the various financial institutions or a steel plant, it was only the civil servant who could deliver the goods, that was the belief. Though the myth was partly exploded by the Mundhra affair, its hold was not loosening. The reliance on the old type administration has done incalculable harm to rapid economic development as slow progress in almost every direction can be tracked down to lack of appropriate managerial ability.

Even at the level of district or *taluka* administration, the situation was no different. In a democracy, particularly one with welfare pretensions, the administrative unit at the *taluka* or district level needs to be flexible, responsive to the aspirations of the people in the area, and approachable. It has to be a conduit through which the desires of the people are communicated to the layers above so that policy formulation at the top remains in close touch with the needs of the people. The situation as it obtains is very different. The collector or the subdivisional officer or the *mamlatdar* is in his approach and attitudes, if not geographically, as far removed from the people as the higher administration. He has been able to break away even less from the old habits of thought and the traditions of a law-and-order state.

The other two arms of the civil administration, *viz.*, the Indian Audit and Accounts Service and the Central Secretariat Service are even more conservative, orthodox and unimaginative. Members of the former service were trained in India and thus did not gain even the wider perspective which members of the Indian Civil Service acquired through their liberal education and experience. The functions of the service as envisaged by its originators were narrow, mainly pertaining to management of accounts of government departments. The rules and procedures framed for this purpose were wholly unsuited to the new demands that arose when the government began to make large disbursements for economic development. Elaborate checks and balances, devised to prevent fraud, were no doubt necessary, but when the purposes of expenditure were such that time was of essence these procedures proved to be roadblocks. Members of this service worried about how to save five rupees while crores were going down the drain wasted, being impervious to any suggestion of calculable risk.

To give a minor example, the existing procedure does not permit prepayment of subscriptions to journals without an agreement being entered into between the President of India on the one hand and the publishers on the other, providing, etc. At least one journal is known to have fought hard to get the procedure changed but to no avail. The procedure was modified to the extent that the government department taking out the subscription could dispense with the prior agreement at its discretion. But no government department ever chooses to exercise this discretion. This in is only a small example but it illustrates the addiction to procedures and rules which have no relevance to facts of life.

By their training and experience members of the Audit and Accounts Service are incapable of seeing things in their broad perspective. Their work concerns mostly other government officials, their pay, and leave rules, etc. in a different setting or when called upon to undertake other tasks, in the public sector undertakings, for example, they are at sea and seek to cover up their inadequacies by dilatoriness and recourse to committees. When there is any major policy decision to be taken, it is standard procedure to call a conference which then appoints a committee which in turn delegates the final decision to a working party. While the search for consensus is admirable in principle, the process is ideally suited to retard action.

There is consultation not only laterally among the various ministers or departments but also vertically within a ministry, or among the officials in New Delhi, the state capitals, the district headquarters and so on, further down. Such procedures appeal to the civil services because it enables them to delay and avoid committing themselves to any policy or course of action. It is not that these grave deficiencies went unnoticed by the Congress party or the prime minister but they were slurred over as minor blemishes in an otherwise competent administration.

To come to the third, *viz.*, the Central Secretariat Service, most of its personnel are drawn from the lower cadre of the secretariat. Some of them are able and competent, but the representative type is timid, cringy and conservative. He is timid because of his past, cringy because he knows that his rise depends on his capacity to please his superiors belonging to one of the higher services, and is conservative because he is in constant fear that new ideas and new men may disturb the existing relationship and his vested interests. This type has survived and prospered by mastering minor details of procedure of which the political bosses were often ignorant. He has opposed overtly or covertly every reform or rules and regulations with much success.

This is the administrative structure we inherited and which has continued and even prospered, thanks to expanding State activities. It has a unique knack of proliferating, not always in response to any increase in the amount of work. The tendency to multiply is built into the very structure itself. If there is a promotion block in any department, the solution is to start a new department, and thus remove the block at one stroke. An example is the gold control administration. T.T. Krishnamachari has removed virtually all the control on gold holdings; yet gold control administration has expanded with many regional offices!

Now let us turn to the services which were formed to tackle the problem thrown up by planned economic development—the Indian Economic Service and the Management Pool. The former took formal shape only a few months ago, though it was in *de facto* existence for over a decade. There are, of course, some very able economists in that service whose contribution to planning has been of great significance. They, for the first time, imparted to the government's economic policies scientific precision and objectivity. As a service, however, it does not seem to have any specific function to perform. There are no clearly demarcated spheres and jobs for this service personnel who, being in the government for some time cease to be economists and become indifferent civil servants of a lower category. The position in the Planning Commission or in the Economic Division of the Ministry of Finance is no better. Most of the economists are concerned with preparation of answers to the parliamentary questions or of speeches of ministers and deputy ministers. Little technical work is done there, except in the Perspective Planning Division of the Planning Commission which is, however, outside the pale and a category by itself.

As for the Management Pool, its fate is not known to all. Originally, the pool was formed to draw trained managers from the business world and put them in charge of public sector undertakings. However, the shape it took made it hardly distinguishable from the administrative services. Lured by the prospect of quick promotions, many civil servants joined it, without, however, relinquishing their lien on their permanent jobs. This at once demoralised the permanent incumbents in the Management Pool and sealed its fate.

The question that arises is: what are the implications of all this for planning and economic development? The Economic Service and the administrators clearly have not been equal to the challenge thrown up by the planned development. There may have been many failings in the leadership of Nehru or of the ruling party stemming largely from the vagueness of ideology. But the real cause of failure has been the faulty implementation of policies initiated by Nehru and his government. It could not have been otherwise because the instrument with which those policies were to be implemented was blunt and outmoded. Nehru did try to refashion it here and there but the core of it remained immune to Nehru's efforts or his political and social philosophy. It is mainly because of the inadequacy of the administration that one has reservations about radical policies.

[Published in The Economic Weekly 16(25): 1243–6 (1964)].

V

INTERNATIONAL ECONOMY

20 | Conflict and Cooperation in the International Monetary System

The international monetary system manages the financial interrelations among disparate nation-states in a manner that world trade and growth are promoted harmoniously. However, cooperation among unequal partners, whose interests diverge from each other, being on different levels of power and development, is difficult enough, but it becomes even more precarious when the rules by which the cooperation is effectuated are not applied uniformly and, if applied at all, are not observed in detached and equitable fashion essential for sustaining the international monetary system. Uniform application of the rules of behaviour has little scope when member countries with varying degrees of economic power have different perceptions of what monetary cooperation should mean both in theory and practice. It is hard to distinguish the domestic interests of the economically and politically powerful countries from those of the less powerful who bear the impact of policies of the former group of countries. The rules devised, therefore, have inherent bias towards countries with greater economic clout and this bias is reflected in the procedural and operational guidelines designed for the working of the monetary system.

Although the set of rules evolved was a result of compromises reached among the powerful and weaker members of the international monetary system, the way member states are called upon to pursue policies so that the international monetary arrangements are strengthened to the benefit of all has developed certain asymmetries. However, despite the appearance of removing them over the last four decades, a discriminatory element in treatment by the International Monetary Fund (IMF) of economically weaker countries persisted. Under the Bretton Woods system of par values, those countries which had deficits in their balance of payments were subjected to severe discipline of adjusting their economies through curtailment of credit and constraints on demand, all of which meant shortfall in investment and output, at any rate in the short run. The deficit countries, which were by and large developing countries with their endemic shortage of savings for development, thus bore the brunt of stabilising the international monetary system. However, the adjustment in the deficit countries has been only a part of the overall policy of sustaining the monetary system: the other side of the coin of adjustment has been the policies or the lack of them in the surplus industrial countries. Indeed, from the point of view of the undisturbed functioning of the international monetary system, the domestic policies of the industrial countries were more crucial as those policies had larger international implications (Camadessus, 1988). But these countries were not bound by the same imperative of adjustment since they did not have to rely on resources of the Fund and hence could not be obliged to observe the rules of the game, so carefully crafted by the founding fathers of the IMF. But this sort of asymmetry was confined not only to the surplus industrial countries, but also to the deficit industrial countries which were the sources of reserve currency such as the United States, which could underwrite its payment deficit by issue of its own liabilities. The compulsion for these countries to rectify their payments positions had been much less, which was more damaging to the stability of the international monetary system than the slower adjustment in the deficit countries. The reluctance of the surplus countries to fall in line with the imperative of adjustment clearly does violence not only to other industrial countries, but also accentuates the economic distress of those developing countries which implement domestic policies in spirit and letter to eliminate their macroeconomic imbalances.

The actions and insensitivity of the industrial countries to the problems of the international monetary arrangements belied that an internal stabilising mechanism will overcome pressure on any country whose balance of payments departs from equilibrium in either direction, as expected by Keynes (Keynes, 1980).

ASYMMETRIES IN INTERNATIONAL MONETARY ARRANGEMENTS

An asymmetry in adjustment responsibilities of different groups of countries was always of paramount importance in the past, but it has assumed even greater relevance and has become critical to the functioning of the international monetary system because of the fundamental changes that have occurred in the financial world in recent years (See, for a comprehensive discussion of the international monetary issues, Khatkhate, 1987). Technology and science have revolutionised the financial intermediation process on a global scale what with the emergence of new financial instruments, and the telescoping of time and space in putting through international financial transactions and the universalisation of information networks. Countries, therefore, are no longer insulated from the effects of policies pursued by other countries, which have dominant international ramifications. When this is the case, it is essential to coordinate adjustments in policies of the industrial countries with the adjustment policies of deficit developing countries which resort to credit from the Fund to tide over their payment difficulties.

The United States, for example, is a leading industrial country and a source of liquidity to the rest of the world and, therefore, its monetary and fiscal policies, which determine its inflation rate and interest rates, have a direct and strong impact on the other industrial countries, transmitted through capital movement across countries. If other countries fail to respond to these impulses in the United States or do not adjust on the scale needed, the growth in the industrial world is impeded with adverse impact on the non-industrial countries. Thus, the budget deficit or existence of high interest rates in the United States, unaccompanied by accommodating changes in the fiscal and monetary policies of other industrial countries like West Germany and Japan, would slow down the adjustment policies in the less developed countries. Slow growth in industrial countries would not absorb the exportable surpluses from these countries, while at the same time it would magnify the impact on their debt flowing from the upward movements in the world interest rates. The result is that the adjustment in borrowing developing countries, even when it is implemented with force and commitment, will not come to fruition. On the contrary, unilateral adjustment by developing countries would diminish their growth without redressing their internal and external imbalances which have provided a rationale for the adjustment policies in the first place. It is in this sense that the adjustment policies to be pursued by countries which are members of the international monetary system should be seen to be of one piece and indivisible.

The question then is how to institute an effective and consensual adjustment mechanism which will maintain asymmetric relationship as between the rich industrial countries which do not need resources from the Fund and the poor developing countries which borrow from it to bridge the payments gap and thus attract severe disciplinary regimen required by the Fund. An equally important question is the nature of adjustment policies that need to be imposed on the borrowing countries. The answer to the first question should centre on putting some teeth into the surveillance procedure which the Fund has adopted. Multilateral surveillance is believed to provide a frame of reference, which relies for its effectiveness on the internal parameters with external consequences and the external parameters with internal ramifications (Khatkhate, 1987). It specifies relations and the contours of policies among different economies, derived from meaningful indicators intrinsic to the economies such as saving investment balances, growth rates, inflation rates and so on, and it sets out an alternative path for policy coordination among industrial countries, and facilitates in that context a course of corrective actions by the indebted developing economies. Bilateral surveillance, which has been the main mode for monitoring developments in the economies of member countries, will no doubt continue to retain its central role in the process. However, in the context of multilateral surveillance, bilateral surveillance will be imbued with new insights and power and, as a result, its impact on policy adjustments in industrial countries will be strengthened. When these adjustments occur in countries whose domestic policies cause changes, beneficial or otherwise, in non-industrial countries, the adjustment process in the latter would be smoother, quicker, and also conducive to the growth of their economies, which is the ultimate test of how successful their adjustment policies have been. In this way, the asymmetry in the adjustment policies in member countries would be considerably attenuated, if not removed altogether.

However, a case for international economic coordination has not gone unchallenged. For instance, Martin Feldstein (1988) has argued that "...many of the claimed advantages of cooperation and coordination are wrong, that there are substantial risks and disadvantages to the types of coordination that are envisaged, and that an emphasis on international coordination can distract attention from the necessary changes in domestic policy." Feldstein's objection is embedded more in his analytical distinction between the nominal exchange rate and the real exchange rate. Since it is the former which is supposed to be managed by the international coordination and since the real exchange rate which is crucial for assessing relative competitiveness of the countries is determined by the differences in inflation rates, which in turn depends on domestic policies of the countries concerned, the agreed nominal exchange rate should be totally irrelevant. What is necessary therefore is the determination to pursue the right kind of domestic policies such as the control of budget deficit.

A major flaw in Feldstein's argument against economic coordination is his strong faith in the market mechanism which is believed to stabilise major exchange rates at levels warranted by domestic policies. While this argument has some validity, the crucial point is whether it is prudent to leave domestic policies to be determined by the domestic considerations only, when they have serious implications internationally. Politicians respond to the domestic constituencies more easily than to the foreign constituency and policies which are determined on the basis of the former may run counter to what seems to be essential on the basis of the latter. Furthermore, what is overlooked is the context of underlying structural asymmetry represented by the "great importance of the US economy for the rest of the world on the one hand, and the small effects of economic performance and policies in the OECD partner countries on the United States and the external accounts on the other" (IMF, 1988b: 212). It follows, therefore, that if international coordination is jettisoned on Feldstein's ground, the new type of asymmetry between the policies of the United States and those of the small industrial countries will be superimposed on the prevailing asymmetry as between the industrial countries and the developing countries to the detriment of the smooth functioning of the international monetary system.

Feldstein's alternative approach is therefore counterproductive, relying as it does on the market mechanism for eliminating the imbalances in the world economy. What is even worse is that his alternative scenario would render the adjustment process in the borrowing countries more intractable than at present. The external imbalances in developing countries or, for that matter, in any economy, tend to arise from the interaction between them and the world economy. Just as they emerge from the wrong type of domestic monetary and fiscal policies of the borrowing countries, they could equally stem from changes in the world economy following wrong economic policies by the leading industrial countries, even when the domestic economic policies of the former group of countries are on the right track. The adverse impact of inappropriate economic policies of the industrial countries is often manifested in a fall in commodity prices, rise in interest rates, a decline in capital flows, and a decline in the industrial countries' demand for the products of the developing countries. This sort of changes, as happened during the 1980s, if not reversed would place an excessively heavy burden on the deficit borrowing countries, thereby forcing them to adjust even more severely, with higher level of unemployment, greater output fall, and a consequent depression of the standard of living (Cornia et al., 1987: 133). What is pertinent is that even this adjustment effort would be in vain unless the international conditions which give rise to the imbalances of developing countries are eliminated. The extent and nature of adjustment required at a national level thus depends on how far the industrial countries are willing to conform to the requirements of the world economy, which can be ensured only through the coordination of policies among the leading industrial countries, as a counterpoint to the adjustment policies in the developing countries.

The adjustment policies at the national level, i.e. in countries which have external imbalances and need resources to remove those imbalances, and to finance domestic investment, have two dimensions. One is the nature of the adjustment policies to be adopted in general, and the second relates to the adjustment policies in the context of a large external debt overhang. The latter is the phenomenon dramatised in the 1980s, when Latin American countries were made to meet their debt service obligations. Taking the first dimension, the conditions suggested for providing loans to the borrowing countries by the international organisations, particularly the Fund, have generated, over the years, more heat than light. It has to be recognised that any loan will entail conditions, if the loan proceeds are to be properly used and the security of the loan is to be ensured. A typical Fund requirement for availing use of its resources is: ceilings on credit and money supply, reform of interest rate to bring it to a positive level, exchange rate adjustment, limit on public sector growth, withdrawal of subsidies, and a limit on budget deficit through control of government expenditure. These are all aggregate demand-restraining measures. One need not quarrel with these conditions if the inflationary pressures are severe because of budget deficit, if the balance of payments disequilibria are the product of exchange rate maladjustment, and if the public enterprises run up losses incessantly. However, there are often the extenuating circumstances which require modification of these conditions. One of these, as mentioned earlier, relates to the externally imposed hardships on developing countries. When this is the case, the countries in payment imbalances should not be asked to bear the cost in terms of lower standards of living, and those countries whose policies have caused those imbalances in their payments position should be required to share the part of the burden of adjustment. In regard to the imbalances whose origin lies in the pursuit of inappropriate domestic economic policies by developing countries, what they clamour for is not an unrestrained freedom to be profligate or to default on their repayment obligations. For them softening of conditionality means designing conditions on which they are given access to Fund resources in such a way that they will be able to grow out of imbalances through growth and more employment. On an academic plane, it has been argued that there is always a trade-off between unemployment and inflation. If you control one, you hope to control the other. But in practice this may not automatically follow and, in any case, even if it does, the point is about the level of unemployment at which the trade-off takes place. The stark poverty and chronic unemployment in the developing world can be alleviated only through more investment, which is precisely the casualty when conditionality is applied without due regard to the nature of their economic problems.

The Fund has not remained static in this respect. It has responded, albeit cautiously, to the aspirations of the borrowing countries and their concerns for maintaining adequate growth, while restraining demand pressures. In this context, the development involving the World Bank in structural adjustment loans that took place a few years ago is of great significance. This initiative on the part of the World Bank at once brings it closer to the Fund in terms of functions, thereby nullifying to some extent the unreal distinction so sharply drawn between short-term credit and long-term capital. It also demonstrates why the Bretton Woods twins together should function as the World Central Bank which, like the central banks in most of the developing countries, could undertake promotional activities, in addition to playing a stabilisation role. Stabilisation without development is as sterile as development without stabilisation is futile.

The implications of this change in the attitude of the Fund and the interlinking of operations of the Fund and the World Bank for the nature of conditionality in programmes are of far-reaching importance. First of all, the adjustment has to be viewed over a long term, say 10 to 15 years. Second, the design of the conditions should incorporate within itself this time dimension. For instance, the credit ceilings or budget deficit have to be related to the type of expenditure and the end-use of credit and they need to be implemented over a longer period than one year. Furthermore, monitoring the progress of the domestic policies should also have a unit of time longer than three months or six months. In other words, the deviation from the short-term performance targets should be seen in a medium-term context, so that shortfalls in one time unit could be considered to be offset by the overfulfilment in another time unit. It is not difficult to dovetail these conditionality requirements in a framework of Extended Fund Facility (EFF). It was an innovation of great potentiality, but somehow it was interpreted essentially in terms of the same conditionality idiom as the usual short-term stand-by arrangements. Consequently, its use has been much less than was expected at the time of its creation.

Third, the link between financing and adjustment has to be redefined in a manner that both these aspects should be taken as complementary rather than competitive. Until recently, it was believed that the more the adjustment the lesser the need for financing. However, the competitive relationship between these two can only be rationalised on the ground that there is no limit to output fall, rise in unemployment and a decline in consumption of the people in adjusting countries. There is a wind of change now, which is to be welcomed by developing countries. The *World Economic Outlook* of April 1988 issued by the Fund has sharply focused on the complementary relationship between financing and adjustment. It says that in a scenario in the medium term for fifteen highly indebted countries,

> an additional $10 billion financing a year over the period of 1988–1992, at maturities corresponding to the structure of existing debts, would over time ensure through increased investment…a rise in productive potential and exports, debt service positions moderate, and by 1992, both gross domestic product and gross national product are higher…. (IMF, 1988a: 37).

The latest move by the Fund is one more step in the direction of adapting conditionality to the needs of developing countries, particularly the poorest. With the explosive expansion in arrearage to the Fund, amounting to almost $2 billion, the Fund has taken a highly imaginative step to resolve the arrearage issue. It is now realised that many poor members of the Fund until the end of the 1970s were relying on foreign assistance and capital flows from the private sector in rich countries to assuage the adverse impact on their balance of payments of the external developments and the domestic misdeeds of the borrowing countries. These difficulties will not simply wither away if they could use Fund resources by implementing programmes which do not assure a total financing of the current account deficit in the medium term. All this means is that the commitment to programme implementation would not be strong unless the countries using the Fund's resources have access to financial packages (analogous to what was invented for easing the burden of debt of the Latin American countries), which would maintain a reasonable balance between resources coming from the Fund and other sources of financing, be it the rich countries or the credit institutions in the industrial countries. And this balance cannot be obtained unless the international community braces itself to deal headlong with this troublesome problem through providing substantial resources. Call these bridge loans or rain checks or good Samaritan acts, the cardinal fact is that others who have, will be required to chip in to give to those who have not, in collaboration with the Fund.

The mechanism that the Fund intends to set up for facilitating this collaborative financing package is ingenious. For countries in arrears there will be a shadow programme endorsed by the Fund, which they are supposed to implement even when no fresh resources of the Fund are involved. These shadow programmes have their provenance in what Colombia and Yugoslavia practised a couple of years ago. Sure, the Fund is not directly involved in designing these programmes nor would it permit access to its resources; therefore, there is a certain detachment. The financing is from 'other sources', a part of which will go to liquidate the arrearage to the Fund. It is, in a way, taking from Paul and handing it over to Peter but it has the virtue of maintaining the integrity of the Fund without impinging on the autonomous decision-making process in the borrowing countries. There will be advice without aid rather than aid with advice, which had perturbed the debtor–creditor relationship in the past.

There are two more features with far-reaching consequences. There will be a support group or groups of major money-giving countries, represented by their highest-level representatives with a mandate to define and assess the financing gap of the arrears-affected countries and come up with concrete numbers to help them. For another, it would avoid designing the programmes with projections of foreign resources which never roll in. Any constricting policy, when a country is in economic doldrums, requires that borrowers reduce their level of comfort as a partial compensation for the earlier overindulgence. But there are political and social limits to forgoing consumption when the income distribution is highly skewed. Which means that the reduction in consumption should be a gradual process, which can be made feasible only if the aid from other sources is concurrently forthcoming. If this is what the new initiative of the Fund means, it should be a major advance on the earlier practices. It is then a question of how the borrowing countries spread the burden of adjustment across different income groups.

The countries in arrears to the Fund are some of the poorest in the world and, through their arrearage, they have isolated themselves from the mainstream of international finance. It is not so much the Fund as these poor countries which suffer since they are denied access not only to the Fund resources but also, eventually, to other credit institutions. Most of them cannot afford this financial isolation leading to hardship and collapse. If a solution is based on a truly collaborative approach such as the one contemplated by the Fund, combining the efforts of debtor countries' banks and creditor institutions and creditor country governments and financial agencies, it will usher in a new era of international cooperation between the industrial countries with resources and the developing countries with needs.

So far, the alternative has been focused on adjustment in macro policies, be they demand management, supply oriented, or institutional. But these macro policies by themselves may not be adequate to alleviate the distress of developing countries when they have to pursue adjustment policies. What is required therefore is adjustment policies with a human face, as aptly described by Cornia et al. (1987). In order to invest the adjustment policies with a human element, what has come to be known as meso policies has to be treated as an integral part of the adjustment policies. Meso policies are designed to fulfil the priorities in meeting the needs of the vulnerable groups and promoting economic growth.

> As with macro policies, meso policies also affect demand and supply—in this case demand and supply for priority resource uses in both the private and the public sectors. Institutional reform also has a role—in particular, reform in institutional structures to facilitate measures to improve the position of the vulnerable, including the development and guidance of community initiatives, and more generally, increased participation, especially of women, which is essential to raising incomes and improving services for the vulnerable (Cornia et al., 1987: 135) .

In order that the adjustment policies should have a human dimension two preconditions have to be fulfilled. For one thing, the macroeconomic policies and indicators should allow for expenditure, direct as well as indirect, on the poorest segments of the population to be included in the performance criterion. Furthermore, government expenditure on retraining of workers thrown out of employment as a result of demand restraint will have to be classified as essential growth-promoting expenditure. This may imply even more foreign financing than under the prevailing type of adjustment policies. For another, monitoring of adjustment process has to be broadened to cover indicators for measuring living standards, health, and nutrition of the vulnerable. These indicators, to be meaningful and useful, should be made available as expeditiously as the monetary indicators under the current adjustment policies. This requires a whole gamut of measures directed towards setting up a full statistical infrastructure which will permit gathering timely information relating to the life patterns of the poorest population. It is clear that if the adjustment policies are to be restructured in this way, there will have to be a far closer collaboration between the international lending agencies such as the Fund and the World Bank than prevails at present.

While redesigning the adjustment policies along the lines analysed earlier will help improve the present imbalances and prevent the emergence of future ones, it will not be enough to resolve the serious macroeconomic problems faced by the highly indebted developing countries. The adjustment, even if spread over a longer period, will not relieve them of the pressures on their output and growth. This is particularly so when they are unable to muster adequate exportable surpluses to repay their debt service liabilities, in view of the lukewarm effort on the part of the industrial countries to partake of their share of burden of adjustment. The ballooning of the Third World debt owes its origin to the combined effects of the shortage of liquidity felt by several developing countries, the plethora of short-term liquidity that emerged in the international banking system due to the large surpluses of the oil-producing countries, and the imprudent domestic policies of the debtor countries. Of the three, the first two were the most determining influences on the size of Third World debt. Flush with excess funds, private commercial banks directed liquidity to those developing countries whose demand for it was pressing regardless of whether the borrowers were creditworthy. The alternative before them was loss of revenue by permitting liquid resources to remain unutilised. It was convincing proof that a much-vaunted market mechanism failed to assess the borrowers' domestic policies in relation to their performance. Viewed in a different way, if the international credit markets had not provided access to easy borrowing, developing countries would have relied primarily on official sources, including the Fund, for financing their current account imbalances, and the latter perhaps would have monitored their performance better than the private banks (Khatkhate, 1987). The Third World debt, therefore, could be traced to the failure to redistribute international liquidity through deliberate use of new and innovative techniques in favour of the developing world (Coats, 1987). If adjustment in the highly indebted countries is to be rewarded with success it is imperative that the weight of the debt is reduced through some device or the other.

When the issue of the Third World debt came to a head in 1982, there was, for a while, a loss of nerve on all sides. The storm was weathered through intervention by the IMF, which helped to spread the maturity of Latin American debt via rescheduling and inducing the creditor banks to increase their lending. For a while, the crisis seemed to have abated and there was all-round euphoria that the debt problem was on track of solution. A case-by-case approach was elevated to the high level of sacred doctrine. But soon the world financial scene was overtaken by the shattering crisis in Mexico, Brazil, Argentina and Chile, which were the giant borrowers in the world's money and capital markets. There were signals that the Latin American debtor countries might jointly default. As a consequence, there were stray thoughts about debt forgiveness, which was an alias for discount on debt. However, this talk was discouraged by the spokesmen of the industrial countries and the international organisations, among which the World Bank figured most prominently. Now things are totally reversed. Right from James Baker, the US Secretary of the Treasury, down to the director of a small-town creditor bank, all changed their tune, slowly, cautiously, but unequivocally. There is, as a result, a bandwagon effect. There are now flying around serious proposals by serious and responsible people from the academia, private research institutes, representatives of the creditor banks, and officials of some of the developing countries. The latest to catch the eye are the ones by James D. Robinson III, President of American Express, and Arjun Sengupta (1988). Both these proposals, though built upon other schemes, are carefully thought out, based on sound judgement of the prevailing international economic situation, well related in analytical terms to the working of the international monetary system, and formulated in concrete operational details.

The main principle underlying both these schemes is a shared partnership in discount on loans both by the creditor banks as well as the debtor countries. They have two common features, which make them acceptable to both sides involved. First, there is envisaged a guarantee attached to the debt acquired by an international agency, though the form that guarantee takes is different. In Robinson's scheme, the existing debt of the participating borrowing countries, acquired at discount by the proposed Institute of International Debt and Development, is subordinated to new financing that is projected to be given by the creditor banks after the scheme is implemented. Under Sengupta's proposal, the principal of bonds issued by the agency, which he identifies with the IMF in exchange for loans from the creditor banks, will be fully guaranteed by the industrial countries. Though the shape of guarantee under these two schemes varies, it is underwritten by the industrial countries. Second, the discount on Third World debt will be passed on to the debtor countries, fully under Robinson's scheme and partly under Sengupta's, provided these countries commit themselves to pursuing economic reform policies described as market and growth oriented, whatever that may mean.

The question is whether these institutional arrangements, imaginative and well-intentioned as they are, are workable. Both involve cost sharing by the industrial countries in the event of failure of policies by debtor countries to improve their economies. Until now, the industrial countries avoided sharing the burden that will ensue from coordination of their macroeconomic policies. Will they readily plumb for the schemes which will involve potentially even greater costs? Even assuming that the industrial countries become suddenly altruistic for some reason or the other, will the adjustment policies in borrowing countries, necessitated by their desire to benefit from discounts on their existing debt, succeed to the point that they will maintain their sustained growth and economic viability? It should be clear by now that symmetry in adjustment policies in both borrowing developing countries and the non-borrowing industrial countries is indispensable, more so today when international money and capital markets are well integrated. If adjustment in debtor countries is through liberalisation of policies and market orientation of their economies, the adjustment in surplus industrial countries or reserve currency countries has to be effected through coordination of their macroeconomic policies. If, thus, a symmetrical relationship in adjustment policies is not maintained, economic reform of whatever nature and magnitude in debtor countries will simply not succeed. Adjustment policies in all countries, developed and developing, surplus or deficit, are indivisible, like peace. Though the experience in the last two years shows that the desired coordination in macroeconomic policies is not forthcoming in a degree essential to assist world economic growth and trade, recent developments in the Latin American countries such as Mexico and Argentina may have queered the pitch for a more effective plan for coordination.

The approach to the debt relief strategy is two-pronged, built on the diversity of debt problems faced by different groups of countries. The small low-income countries, which are by and large from Africa, have contracted 85 per cent of their debt with the official creditors. These countries are being helped by the Fund through its structural adjustment facilities (SAF) and enhanced structural adjustment facilities (ESAF) to the tune of about $5 billion (IMF, 1988a). Besides, the Paris Club creditors have agreed to restructure these debts, while a few of them have agreed to grant debt relief in the form of debt forgiveness. But the debt strategy in regard to middle-income developing countries, though not overtly as generous as that in respect of the poorest countries, is tending to converge in its basic elements with that for the latter. This is because it is recognised very explicitly that "the scope for action in the short run, however, is severely constrained by the burden of existing debt, and by the "adjustment fatigue" induced by persistent and yet inadequate adjustment efforts since the early 1980s" (IMF, 1988a). There is, therefore, greater support than before to the 'menu' approach to debt relief. Since its basic objective is to evolve schemes or to support such schemes if in existence, which are "mutually agreed and which permit debtors and creditors to share equitably both the discounts on existing debt and the potential benefits from successful adjustments" (IMF, 1988a).

The financial world, thus, is slowly but surely veering around to the view that the slackness in adjustment policies in debtor developing countries is not purely the fault of the developing countries; it is as much a failure of the creditor industrial countries to come to terms with the stark economic reality. Unless the heavy deadweight of debt on the shoulders of the developing countries is lifted, they will not have the strength to carry out economic adjustments.

Decision-Making in the International Monetary System

Decision-making is a function of how the power emanating from ownership of wealth is distributed in the management board. In the Fund and also in the World Bank, decision-making is determined by a member's voting power, which in turn is related to the size of its quota. Since the inception of the Fund and the World Bank, the decision-making powers are concentrated in the highly industrialised countries, as their quotas are the largest. Since then, however, there has been a sea-change in the world monetary scene. For one thing, the less developed countries have become more vocal in view of their large populations. For another, several of the less developed countries have suddenly become important in terms of wealth, if not development, as a direct consequence of the upsurge in oil prices. They have assumed the role of creditors to the Fund and the World Bank. Since the wealth-related power balance has radically changed, the present decision-making powers have come increasingly under attack from the newly rich countries and also the large-sized less developed countries. There is no permanence attached to the decision-making powers. On the same criterion which provided the rationale for greater weightage to the industrialised countries in the counsels of the Fund and the World Bank, new oil-rich countries deserve a greater share of powers. On a somewhat different criterion, the countries with large populations but with low per capita income need to have a greater say in the deliberation of these bodies. There are three ways of changing this power balance. One is to selectively increase the quotas of member countries to give more basic v   s to them; another is to change the number of basic quotas given to them; and the third, through the basis of quota calculation. Without detracting from what the Fund is doing through selective adjustment of quotas, the other ways to give greater voice to large-sized less developed countries should become a top priority. This means that the basis of quota calculation, which takes into account, among others, GNP, trade and reserves, should be altered so that population and size of the countries should be given greater weight—the latter because in a large-sized country, markets being mainly domestic, external trade is of small dimension. The shifting of decision-making powers is, of course, not an easy task. Many factors—social, economic, and political—are involved. Furthermore, these institutions have to see that their capacity to raise resources from the profit-conscious capital market and the safety-conscious creditor countries is not eroded by a radical restructuring of power equations. What is important, therefore, is not power by itself or who wields it, so much as the perception of the less developed countries of how the power is exercised by those at the helm of these august bodies. The time, perhaps, has come for changing the shareholding concept and replacing it with a system which reflects an interdependent world and the balance of interest between creditors and borrowers and surplus and deficit nations.

Decentralisation in the Structure of the International Monetary System

At present, international monetary policy is implemented by the IMF and its achievements over the years are rather remarkable, but its structure is premised on the belief that international monetary cooperation is world wide in scope. This belief seems to be receding, judging by recent events. The European Monetary System (EMS) has emerged with a bang, with its own sub-regional cooperative framework, exchange arrangements, and its own currency unit, the ECU (European Currency Unit). From the way events are moving, it can be surmised that the EMS would soon grow into a powerful body with an important role in shaping international monetary policy. However, EMS should not be envisaged as a body rivalling the IMF, but as its adjunct to strengthen cooperation among nations and to help carry the message of the Fund more effectively.

The time may soon come for other similarly constructed regional monetary blocks not only among developed countries but also developing ones. There is now a real possibility of trade expansion among less developed countries. Due to the increasing protection practised by the developed countries, and also their slow growth, less developed countries have no alternative but to trade increasingly with each other. Fortunately, the rapid growth of several of the less developed countries since the 1950s has diversified their economies sufficiently to produce an array of capital and consumer goods. By trading with each other, they can earn their foreign exchange to finance domestic investment. The trade thus would lead first to cooperation in production and later to cooperation in finance and monetary arrangements.

If such regional groups come into existence, there will be a need to decentralise the structure of the monetary system by allowing fuller play to regional bodies to explore wider potential for cooperation and to facilitate the IMF to focus more than before on those issues which cannot be solved efficiently on a regional scale. If decentralisation becomes a reality at all, the IMF would be able to improve its present relations with less developed countries because both the decision-making powers would be dispersed widely and the regional monetary blocs would be able to devise criteria for granting credit which are more appropriate to the economies of the region.

References

Camadessus, Michael (1988). "The evolving monetary system: some issues", *C.D. Deshmukh Memorial Lecture*. October. Bombay.

Coats, J. and L. Warren (1987). "On some possible reforms of the SDR" (*mimeo*). Washington DC: IMF.

Cornia, Giovanni, Jolly Richard and Stewart Frances (1987). *Adjustment with a Human Face*. Oxford: Clarendon Press.

S. Dell (ed.) (1987). *The International Monetary System and its Reform*, Parts I, II and III. North Holland.

Feldstein, Martin (1988). "Distinguished lecture on economics in government: thinking about international economic coordination", *Journal of Economic Perspectives* 2(2): 3–13 (Spring).

IMF (International Monetary Fund) (1988a). *World Economic Outlook*. April.

——————. (1988b). *Economic Policy Coordination*.

Keynes, J.M. (1980). *The Collected Writings*. Vol. XXVI, Activities 1941-46 Shaping the Postwar World: Bretton Woods and Reparations. London: Macmillan.

Khatkhate, Deena (1987). "International monetary system: which way?" *Editor's Perspective, World Development* 15(12): vii–xvi.

Sengupta, Arjun (1988). "A proposal for a debt adjustment facility in the IMF", *World Economy*, pp. 155–85, June.

Unpublished, November 1988, Washington DC.

21 | International Monetary System
Which Way?

For well over a decade, international monetary arrangements have clearly shifted away from the anchor of the fixed exchange rate as a source of stability. The overt rigidity of the Bretton Woods system perhaps, warranted some leeway for member countries to make more frequent adjustments in their policies in tune with changes in world trade and growth and disparities in the development experiences of member countries—industrial, non-industrial, and industrialising. For a while it seemed that the loss of the traditional anchor in monetary and financial arrangement was a good thing in providing the impetus to the world economy to grow, without confining it within the straitjacket of predetermined rules of intervention. But the complacency generated in its wake gave way to a serious concern for the functioning of the international monetary system, in light of the frequent and sharp fluctuations in exchange rates, the impact of two oil shocks during the 1970s leading to recession in several leading industrial countries, and the surfacing of debt problems in many developing countries since 1982.

Though the record of the key currency system with its hallmark of fixed exchange rates may appear to shine by contrast with that of the existing monetary arrangements, it is easy to overlook the conjuncture of circumstances prevailing in the world economy between 1945 and 1971 which, fortuitously or otherwise, contributed to that outcome. Prior to 1971, in an era of rapid economic growth and relative price stability in the international economy, world liquidity was provided through unusual means. The foremost was the massive Marshall Plan aid which replaced IMF resources for the war-ravaged industrial countries in Europe, partly because they were redundant but largely because of the US government's embargo on leaning on the IMF for short-term borrowing by countries receiving Marshall Plan aid (Mundell, 1969). For another, a deficit in the balance of payments of the United Kingdom, when sterling was a major reserve asset in the immediate postwar years, became a source of easy liquidity. The United Kingdom was soon after replaced by the United States as a major source of international reserves, with the US dollar becoming the centrepiece of the international monetary system. The

IMF's contribution as a source of liquidity was a minor one, limited to a few developing countries in payment difficulties, and occasionally developed ones like the United Kingdom, France and Canada.

There was, thus, no possible incompatibility problem, known in academic circles as the 'nth country problem'. Under a key currency regime, characterised by fixed exchange rates, the non-n countries' central banks try to maintain exchange parity with the key currency, i.e. the US dollar, through adjustments in their balance of payments, resulting in reserve flows into or out of the domestic money supply. In this kind of situation, the nth country generally remains passive in its policy postures while the other countries are the recipients of reserves from it, according to their preference pattern. By and large, the exchange parities were maintained and were adjusted, when necessary, in discrete stages under the surveillance of the Fund. It was not that the fixed rate system was always immune from shocks, but they were not as severe as experienced since 1971 under the present monetary arrangements. The fixed rate regime was breached in 1951, when Canada began floating its dollar for almost a decade and West Germany did not adjust its exchange rate parity upward with the speed needed to arrest the excessive building up of its reserves, discomforting the sterling and dollar parities (Mundell, 1969). The key currency system broke down, however, when the non-n countries could not accept without resistance the inflationary repercussions of the key currency countries' money supply expansion and the reserve currency country, the United States, could not afford uninterrupted deficit in its balance of payments without adversely affecting its domestic economy (Horne and Masson, 1987).

II

What cascaded from the collapse of the key currency-based fixed exchange rate system is the present one, combining within itself elements of fixed exchange rate parities and floating exchange rates, not totally free but managed through interventions. The hybrid system covers exchange rates fixed against individual currency or baskets of currencies, limited flexibility of exchange rates against a single currency or multiple currencies of the type represented by the European Monetary System, and the managed floating adopted by the major industrial countries like the United States, Japan, Canada and the United Kingdom. Though there are over 42 countries with managed floating exchange rate arrangements, it is these four countries that often call the tune in running the international monetary system in view of their domination in world trade.

A floating exchange rate system, even though its floating aspects are reined in by the dominant industrial countries, emerged more by a concatenation of circumstances. An implicit assumption underlying the floating rates regime is that a free float obviates any need for official reserves and permits each country to determine its target of money supply and the rate of inflation. In reality, however, the prevailing system, which has included a wide spectrum of countries with pegged currencies, far from discouraging, encouraged all countries to focus on their current account balances, the level of their effective exchange rates and the foreign exchange reserves they desired to hold. It is thus imperative to ensure global compatibility in targets set by different countries unless the reserve currency country or the nth country can refrain from having any explicit target (Horne and Masson, 1987). Since the United States has its own target, a close and sustained policy coordination among leading industrial countries becomes unavoidable for creating a favourable environment for stability in the market-determined exchange rates. A freely determined exchange rate may lead to a compatible outcome but it will be far from optimal in the absence of coordination and cooperation among industrial countries in pursuit of their domestic policies having pronounced international connotation.

A less than satisfactory outcome under the fluctuating exchange rate system is generally acknowledged. The industrial countries, better known variously as the Group of 5, 7 or 10, often lauded the 'valuable strength' of the floating exchange rates as reflected in the quicker adjustments in the payment system of most of the countries, insulation of their economies from the inflationary pressures abroad, and the relative independence of monetary policy in coping with a series of external shocks. But they did not hesitate at the same time to underline the pronounced weaknesses of the floating exchange rate, such as a very high degree of nominal exchange rate volatility, untoward changes in the real exchange rate in the medium term, and the dampening impact of the system on international trade (quoted in Crockett and Goldstein, 1987).

On balance, however, the industrial countries are still inclined to persevere with the floating rate system, through amendments, to remove some of its unsavoury features. Developing countries, on the other hand, judge the existing floating exchange rate system as sub-optimal, since it has increased financial

risks of investment and exacerbated a volatility of the capital movement not
related to trade flows. They are greatly concerned with the fact that

> much of the medium-term movement in real exchange rates in recent years reflects not
> the changing pattern of competitiveness but rather the result of differences in fiscal and
> monetary policies, in which industrial countries have chosen macroeconomic policies in-
> dependently, without serious consideration of their impact on the world economy.

and that "exchange rate variability has hurt the developing countries"
(quoted in Crockett and Goldstein, 1987).

Academic opinion, as usual, has been characteristic of the 'two handed'
approach that economists often take while analysing policy issues in all spheres
of the real world. At one extreme, they would consider, on the basis of existing
empirical work (Shafer and Loopesko, 1983; IMF, 1984) that the floating rate
system, being more unpredictable and therefore unreliable as a guide to policy,
did not contribute to clamping down the payment imbalances nor did it
enhance the self-equilibrating properties of exchange rates. On the other hand,
economists have been quick to dismiss the unpalatable aspects of the present
exchange rate system by asserting that fluctuations in exchange rates during
the last fifteen years have not been as sharp as those in prices of other assets
such as national stock market prices, changes in the short-term interest rates,
changes in commodities prices, and the like. They could also rationalise the
volatility of the exchange rates by underscoring the relative ease with which
the risk in uncertain foreign exchange markets can be covered by operating
on forward markets, option markets, etc. (Frenkel and Goldstein, 1986). Such
disputations amongst economists, the recognition, though grudging, of the
inadequacies of the present floating exchange rate regime by the spokesmen of
the industrial countries, and the persistent clamour by the developing countries
for reform of the monetary system throw in bold relief that something is
seriously amiss in the present floating exchange rate arrangements.

A new dimension has been added to the debate on the international
monetary system by the explosion since 1982 of the world debt problem.
Exchange rate flexibility and the level and distribution of international liquidity
constitute two major pillars of the system. With truly market-determined
exchange rates, there should logically be no need for reserves. The situation,
in fact, has been quite the reverse with the prevailing floating exchange rate
regime. Since exchange rate movement is managed discretely, the floating
countries also feel the need for reserves for intervention purposes and several
leading industrial countries have built up reserves as a precautionary balance
to provide for contingencies arising from uncertainties governing payment

disequilibria. They thus have maintained a reserve target in some form or the other, and they could have access to liquidity to the extent desired by taking recourse to the international credit markets. As for developing countries, their demand for liquidity has remained as high as ever. It is determined particularly by the major industrial countries that international liquidity is ample and any increase in it, either by way of SDR allocation or other means, would be inflationary. It is clear that there is some confusion between the aggregate level of world liquidity and its distribution amongst countries and the latter is sought to be resolved by inducing the countries needing liquidity to approach the international money and capital markets, which are considered to respond efficiently and speedily, the assumption being that liquidity distribution in this fashion would be optimal, being determined according to the degree of creditworthiness of the borrowers in a free market environment.

This assumption has been falsified by events. A plethora of short-term capital was generated in the international banking system by the burgeoning surpluses of the oil-producing countries since 1973. Flush with these funds, the private commercial banks directed liquidity to those developing countries whose demand for it was pressing regardless of whether the borrowers were creditworthy. The alternative before them was a loss of revenue by permitting liquid resources to remain unemployed. This has demonstrated that a much-vaunted market mechanism could not assess the borrowers' domestic policies in relation to their performance. Putting it differently, if the international credit markets had not provided access to easy borrowing, developing countries would have relied primarily on official channels, including the Fund, for financing their current account imbalances, and the latter perhaps would have monitored their performance better than private banks. The Third World debt problem therefore could be considered to be a concomitant of the failure to redistribute international liquidity, through deliberate use of new and innovative techniques in favour of the developing world.

The ballooning of the Third World debt is, in no small measure, endemic in the system of floating exchange rates as it has been functioning. When every country, including the reserve currency, has some target or other—be it money supply, inflation rates or foreign exchange reserves—monetary cooperation tends to become a *sine qua non* of the system. However, it is clear from experience over the last few years that the coordination of policies to be pursued in domestic spheres by the industrial countries to ensure compatibility is grossly inadequate. In consequence, both gyrations in exchange rates and the concurrent volatility of interest rates have increased, thus contributing to the growth of world debt. The lack of adequate coordination of policies amongst industrial countries has also accentuated the Third World debt problem by dampening the growth rate in the industrial countries as a whole. The growth rate in leading industrial countries such as Japan and West Germany could not be as high as desired—in order to offset the contractionary impact of the reduced fiscal deficit on the domestic economy of the United States—so that export surpluses, which the borrowing countries would have generated with the industrial countries via trade, could not materialise.

All this leads to the rather sombre conclusion that the international monetary system has been faltering both because of the lack of discipline in the exchange rate market and because exchange rates are not always determined by the 'fundamentals'. There is a certain degree of irrationality in the behaviour of the market participants to be ascribed to political and psychological factors, which tends to take exchange rates beyond the level warranted by the fundamentals. The system did not also allow for adequate supply of world liquidity, particularly its desired distributional pattern, because of the belief that floating exchange rates would eliminate the need for large reserve maintenance and that the market-oriented international banking system would channel liquidity to the sources of demand on the basis of creditworthiness of the borrowers.

III

The foremost question, however, is to know precisely the contours of policies that have to be undertaken to reform or to amend the existing international monetary system. The difficulties arise not because there is no consensus about reforming the system but because of a lack of analytical clarity in identifying the basic elements of the malaise of the system and the want of firm political commitment. Desired policies to readjust the system are like a proverbial philosopher's stone. Everyone is aware that it exists but no one is sure about where it is and what it looks like. In the same way, there are admittedly right policies but there is a divergence of views about what those policies are and how they should be articulated to elicit the necessary political commitment essential for their implementation.

If there is a certain degree of fuzziness in designing policies for reforming the international monetary system, it should be traced to the fundamental changes that have come about in the global financial setting in recent years.

Due to the advancement of financial technology resulting in the emergence of new financial instruments, procedures and practices in the international money and capital markets, revolutions in communication and transport, and computer applications to all aspects of production and services, the world has become far more interdependent than before and, as a consequence, impulses initiated by policies in one country are rapidly transmitted to all others. This means that policies in any one country have to take into account the ricocheting effects of policies being concurrently implemented in other countries in the world. When this is the case, coordinated adjustments in policies, covering all countries, developed and developing, surplus and deficit, can yield superior results over independently chosen policies. The desideratum of maintaining a symmetry in domestic policies in countries constituting the international monetary system has been crucial at all times, though hitherto only homage was paid to it without any serious effort to achieve it. It acquires a new urgency in the changed international economic environment.

Because the United States is a leading industrial power and a source of liquidity to the rest of the world, its monetary and fiscal stances, which determine its inflation rate and interest rate, have a direct and strong impact on other industrial countries, transmitted through capital movement across countries. If other countries fail to respond to these impulses in the United States or do not adjust on the scale needed, the growth in the industrial world is thwarted with deleterious repercussions for the non-industrial countries. Thus, a budget deficit or prevalence of high interest rates in the United States unaccompanied by accommodating changes in the fiscal and monetary policies in other industrial countries like West Germany or Japan would slow down the adjustment policies in the less developed countries (LDCs). Slow growth in industrial countries would not absorb the exportable surpluses from these countries, while at the same time it would magnify the impact on their debt flowing from the upward movement in the world interest rates. A result is that the adjustment in borrowing developing countries, even when it is implemented with determination, will be impeded. In fact, adjustment in such a milieu would pare down growth in these countries without correcting their internal and external imbalances, which have provided a rationale for the adjustment programmes in the first place.

It is in this sense that the adjustment policies to be followed by the countries forming the international monetary system should be seen to be of one piece and indivisible (Dornbusch, 1985). Alteration in policy direction in leading industrial countries has ripple effects in the developing countries engaged in repairing their economies through the use of resources from multilateral organisations such as the IMF or the World Bank. Whatever justification there might have been before for the asymmetry in economic policies across countries, surplus and deficit, industrial and non-industrial, it is no longer valid and the time has come to remove it. Otherwise the international monetary system will only lumber along, often bedevilled by recurrent shocks of one kind or another.

Primarily for this reason multilateral surveillance, a lynchpin of the monetary system, is considered to provide a frame of reference which embraces both the internal parameters with external consequences and the external parameters with domestic ramification. It clarifies relations among different economies, derived from meaningful and basic indicators such as saving investment balances, growth rates, and inflation rates, etc. and it charts possible paths for policy coordination among industrial countries and facilitates in that context a course of corrective actions by the indebted developing economies. Bilateral surveillance, which has been the main mode for monitoring developments in the economies of member countries, will no doubt continue to retain its primacy as well as relevance. But seen from the perspective of multilateral surveillance, bilateral surveillance will acquire a new meaning and force and, as a result, its impact on policy adjustments in industrial countries will be strengthened. Once these adjustments take place in countries whose domestic policies cause changes, beneficial or otherwise, in non-industrial countries, the adjustment process in the latter would be smoother, quicker, and also conducive to the growth of their economies which, in the final analysis, is the litmus test of how successful their adjustment policies have been. In other words, bilateral surveillance integrated with multilateral surveillance will, in one fell swoop, help to remove the asymmetry in the adjustment policies in member countries.

What is argued above is, of course, a first best solution but the realpolitik of the world in which we live tends to deny such a denouement. A solution reached in isolation by different countries, characteristic of the 'prisoners' dilemma', only rarely converges with the result achieved in a group through mutual cooperation. In such cases, a cooperative solution, which undoubtedly will be an optimal solution, can evolve only if the policies arrived at in isolation end in an economic catastrophe like the great depression of the 1930s. So long as this remains a remote possibility, a non-cooperative game of pursuing uncoordinated policies is found to be rewarding by those with greater economic and political clout. Perhaps, this is the main reason for a slow and crawling progress in the field of policy coordination among major industrial countries, despite the persistent urging by the IMF, the hub of the international monetary system.

The more the dilatoriness in coming to grips with the basic international monetary issues, the greater becomes the severity of the problem. The restoration of stable exchange rates, the mechanism of multilateral surveillance, redistribution of international liquidity and resolution of the Third World debt are the four issues where consensus has eluded, in view of the contradictory positions taken by member countries, particularly the dominant industrial countries. It is realised that the floating exchange rate system as it has been operating currently has created turbulence in domestic economic management in several countries. The very fact that the world economic policymakers are seized of the need to strengthen the multilateral surveillance arrangement, directed towards setting stability in exchange rates through ensuring coordination of domestic policies in countries with a large impact on the world economy on the basis of some agreed economic indicators, implies a tacit admission that the functioning of the floating exchange rate regime is flawed.

IV

Advocacy of a target zone for exchange rates emanates from scepticism about both the viability and the benefits of floating rates. It connotes an intermediate regime between free floating at one end and rigidly fixed exchange rates of the pre-1971 vintage (Williamson, 1987) on the other. The targeting of exchange rates within a zone involves a skilful and studied judgement on the part of the authorities as to how the exchange rate should vary, to the advantage of their respective economies. If it crosses either of the ends of the band, it should trigger policy changes so that a desired exchange rate remains within the band. It may also give signals that the band itself may have to be altered. Clearly, this is the kind of situation in which the policymakers have to be constantly vigilant so that they can cooperate with each other to set things right, which is what multilateral surveillance is purported to accomplish. Both in regard to adopting a target zone for exchange rate variability and to strengthening multilateral surveillance, intervention of the authorities is indispensable, unlike in the case of floating exchange rates (Kenen, 1987).

But multilateral surveillance strengthens, if at all, the case for adoption of a target zone which, while being devoid of capricious and speculative elements characteristic of floating rates, involves rational judgement based on some objective criteria similar to those often employed in formulating and adjusting domestic economic policies.

A seeming contrariness in thinking on these issues amongst the industrial countries (as elaborated in the report of the Group of Ten) is evident in their perception of international liquidity and the debt problem of developing countries. While arguing against an increase in overall world liquidity, maldistribution in liquidity amongst member countries and its link with the emergence of the Third World debt problem is often ignored (Sengupta, 1987). As a result the policies mooted towards solution of the debt problem have been ephemeral in nature, directed mainly towards surmounting the immediate crisis. While this strategy succeeded in its immediate objectives, there was full awareness that sooner or later, the root causes of the debt problem have to be addressed. Third World debt amounting to almost $700–800 billion and the way it descended on the world financial scene clearly indicated that adjustment in policies by the borrowing countries alone would not be enough; policy adjustments by debtor countries need to be an integral part of the adjustment process in all countries. If the industrial countries do not conform to the rules of the game, by coordinating their policies—monetary, fiscal and trade—in a desired direction and a mutually consistent framework, the Third World debt would not shrivel, no matter how valiantly the industrial countries try to contain their economic imbalances. World exchange rates movement crucially depends on the variability of key interest rates, which in turn are governed by the domestic fiscal policies of the major industrial countries. Without fiscal balances, the growth rates of these economies tend to slow down and real interest rates shoot up, as happened at a time when borrowing countries were preoccupied with adjusting their policies. This is not to suggest that the borrowing countries' policies were always their 'best effort policies'; there were many acts of commission and omission on their part, which magnified the adverse impact on their economies of the inappropriate policies in the industrial countries.

Though the link between the adjustment policies in the industrial countries and those in the indebted countries has been slurred over, paradoxically enough, the solution offered to resolve the debt problem has been a cooperative one, in contrast to the lack of coordination of policies amongst major industrial countries. Pure self-interest would have dictated absence of rescheduling or fresh lending to the borrowers, which would have undoubtedly culminated in an international financial crisis. However, the self-interests, rational or irrational, were subordinated by cooperative action by the governments of industrial countries whose banks lent the bulk of funds, largely mediated through the IMF. A clue to the contrast in nature of a solution—a cooperative one in respect of world debt and uncooperative one in respect of multilateral surveillance critical to the pursuit of appropriate adjustment policies in the industrial countries—could perhaps be found in the economic homogeneity of the countries with creditor banks, convergence of their political interests, and the commonality of their goals. However, what is overlooked is that the solution to macroeconomic policies in industrial countries through multilateral surveillance and the solution to the Third World debt problem are two sides of the same coin and unless a cooperative game is played in respect of both, neither will exchange and interest rates remain stable nor will the world debt problem dissolve.

The relationship between interest rates on contracted debt and the rate of growth of exports of the debtor countries is critical in any scheme to scale down the size of debt. Since most of the debt is at floating rates, the borrowing countries bear the full brunt of the risk of any changes in interest rates which are governed by the direction in which the macroeconomic policies in the industrial countries are shifted. Thus the size of debt liabilities is determined by forces beyond the control of borrowers. In the same way, the capacity to repay debt is equally subject to changes in the macroeconomic policies of the industrial countries. Other things remaining constant, debt can be repaid only if the rate of growth of exports receipts is higher than the interest rate. Otherwise the debt/export ratios would tend to rise through time. But export growth is a function largely of the growth rate in industrial countries on the one hand and the additional external finance required by the borrowing countries to step up their productive capacity to raise exportable surpluses on the other, given a limit to reduction of domestic consumption. Both of these variables again are heavily influenced by the substance and form of macroeconomic policies in the dominant industrial countries and how much or how little they are coordinated with each other. It follows therefore that the adjustment policies in the indebted countries, desirable and imperative though they undeniably are, will not reach fruition unless the coordinated macroeconomic policies in the industrial countries operate in synchronisation with those of the debtor countries.

V

While the severity of the debt problem will be assuaged by cooperative action in the sphere of adjustment policies on all sides, world debt is not likely to wither away in the foreseeable future unless a more imaginative and far-reaching framework of action is contemplated. A distinction has to be drawn between the stock of debt and its flow; the latter could be contained by improvement in future policies but the stock of debt is a different kind of animal. The borrowing countries who resorted to credit from commercial banks during the heyday of the 1970s, when there was an abundant supply of bank funds awaiting demand for their employment, diverted resources so acquired towards investment in fixed capital or other infrastructure activities of long gestation period. Furthermore, much of it was misallocated in wrongly designed projects yielding poor results. Thus, short-term bank credit was transformed into long-term capital to finance unproductive enterprises. A faulty assessment of creditworthiness by the creditor banks was reflected in the losses of investment, thereby making it difficult for the borrowing countries to repay their debt. It is thus fair that the risks associated with lending should be shared by the borrowers as well as the lenders—the borrowers by foregoing consumption for some length of time and undergoing other hardships and the lenders by forfeiting a part of their loan portfolio.

It is in this context that the Baker initiative was unfolded about two years ago. While the Baker proposal was appealing and imaginative as an idea, it could not make any headway in persuading the banks to increase their new loan commitments to the debtor countries to a degree that the latter could force the pace of their economic growth through structural and policy reform. Fortunately, the Baker idea has not remained staid but is an evolving one, in response to the rapid changes in the economic environment of the indebted countries, the world economy in general and the pragmatic behavioural attitudes of the creditor banks, partly induced by the vigilant regulatory authorities in their respective countries. The Baker plan initially was structured around fresh loan commitments by banks, policy reform in the debtor countries and rescheduling progressed steadily to the 'menu' approach which included, among others, issue of exit bonds and debt-equity swaps—the instruments essentially spawned by the market-enforced negative non-zero sum game type of solution. This change is a measure undoubtedly of the success of the activist role played by the IMF, which salvaged the international banking system from a possible collapse and also provided it a breathing spell for provisioning against loan default. With the building up of these reserves over a period, the creditor banks could move to a position to shed on the market in small doses their default-prone loans at a discount which initially is absorbed by the private investment banks with a view to swapping it for equity participation in debtor countries. Now there have emerged new instruments such as the 'exit bonds' or new ways such as 'buy-back debt' by the debtor countries themselves and a secondary market has begun to develop for these instruments, particularly bonds, though it has so far remained thin and narrow.

The real issue is how to create an environment under which a secondary market for the Third World debt can thrive in a way that it will facilitate disgorging of the undesirable portfolio by the creditor institutions, while at the same time benefiting the debtor countries. It is here that an international financial intermediary can play a creative and catalytic role. Discounted loans from the commercial banks are currently being bought by a large number of investment banks. For this to benefit the debtor countries, it is necessary that the investment banks renegotiate these debt instruments with the debtor countries on new terms as regards interest and principal favourable to both the debtor countries and the investment banks. If the international intermediating institution could be a member of this club of investment banks in holding Third World debt instruments, it would help bring about a translation of the private profit-making motive into the social task of helping debtor countries restructure their economies for faster economic growth. In renegotiating the terms with the debtor countries, the international agency at the helm can help initiate domestic reforms in the indebted countries without appearing to impose 'conditions' which have an overt unsavoury connotation. Insofar as the debtor countries are concerned, the renegotiated debts would imply availability of their own earned foreign exchange resources for investment purposes to the extent that their repayment liabilities would decline (Mistry, 1987). In order to exercise effective leadership, the international agency should have access to adequate resources at any given time, as it will have to hold a substantial portfolio of LDC debt. Over time, this new activity may become the thin end of the wedge of the development of financial markets for not only the existing high risk debt but for issue of future LDC debt. With the huge amounts involved, a secondary market for LDC bonds may develop width and depth, enabling LDCs to approach it to raise new resources on the basis of their credit rating, which in turn would be governed by the nature and content of economic policies they will pursue to manage their economies.

VI

Given these institutional innovations, the orientation in macroeconomic policies on an international scale, and the creative response to the challenges thrown up by the fundamental transformation of the world financial markets, it will take quite a while before the world debt issue passes into limbo. Until then, the international monetary system and those destined to lead it should not display insouciance towards augmenting and, even more importantly, redistributing international liquidity. The architects of the second amendments to the Articles of the IMF were sagacious and prophetic enough to introduce SDR capable of being "the principal reserve asset in the international monetary system." Except in the aftermath of the genesis of this new reserve asset, there has been a retrogression in its development for reasons mainly non-economic in nature. This is all the more unfortunate because an increase in SDR allocations to meet the anticipated growth in demand for foreign exchange reserves would have lowered the cost of reserve accumulation, especially for poorer countries of the world, while at the same time insulating the international monetary system from the vulnerability stemming from recourse to borrowed resources and the contracting effects of countries that have perforce to generate current account surpluses for accumulated reserves (Coats, 1987). It is true that the distribution of demand for SDR is not uniform, as the need of some countries for liquidity is more than that of others. But there are several ingenious ideas floating around, such as allocation of SDRs to those who incur higher costs by adding to their reserves in other ways, which can be fleshed out through debate and discussion. It is also worth exploring the ways to develop a private market for SDRs like any other foreign currency, through establishment of linkages between the private and official SDRs (Coats, 1982, 1983, 1987; Kenen, 1983(a), 1983(b)). However, notwithstanding the apparent as well as real merits of new SDR allocation, the will to act has been faint, mainly because the different aspects of the international monetary system are perceived by different interest groups from divergent perspectives, and in isolation without comprehending their organic unity.

VII

The international monetary system has truly arrived at the turning point in the evolution of its history. The year 1971 has marked a watershed when the Bretton Woods system, which was to be the grand instrument of the time to maintain in a sustained fashion world economic prosperity, met its demise. What followed in its wake was an arrangement which released, in strong torrents, the market forces tethered hitherto by the earlier system. For a while, it appeared that the market forces would bring about an equilibrating outcome in the exchange markets, and in the domestic markets of countries having a large and dominant impact on the rest of the world. Sensing the hazards entailed in the unrestrained pursuit of self-interest, new rules of the game were formulated through re-adoption of the institutional mechanism of the IMF. Though every country is free to determine its exchange rate, its action is brought within a certain orbit of discipline through a carefully crafted exchange rate surveillance exercise. However, sequels to these developments, such as oil shock-generated recession in the industrial countries, divergence in macroeconomic policies leading to volatility of exchange rates and gyration in interest rates, and the bloated world debt highlighted the fragility of the monetary system. It has been recognised universally that the system needs a new direction and some restructuring but there is no consensus about whether a change should be brought through marginalia or a thorough overhaul requiring an alteration in the Articles of Agreement of the IMF and the World Bank. The latter would involve strong political commitments cutting across ideological divides.

Perhaps, the time for a major reform has come. The world has become more interdependent than ever before. The centres of economic power and its analogue of political power have changed. There is no longer one big centre and a vast periphery; there are multiple poles of economic power, dispersed across all continents. In a not too distant future, new centres of power would be added to the existing ones. When China, the Soviet Union and the host of other centrally planned countries which are rapidly being exposed to the winds of change in all spheres of their activities—economic, political, and social- join the comity of nations, international cooperation in economic policy adjustment will acquire a new complexion. It is a formidable task for those concerned with the running of the international monetary system to anticipate these future events, to look into their innards and to relate their significance to the imponderables in international monetary cooperation in an interdependent world.

There is a possibility that the evolving international monetary system may in the future take a different track than the one to which many have become habituated over the years. There is a loud message in the ongoing developments in the international arena that a distinction between the pure monetary character of the IMF and the developmental character of the World Bank may not remain as endurable and clearly definable as in the past. The emergence of the world debt problem has dramatised that international liquidity perhaps needs being transformed, consciously or otherwise, into finance to support investment activities in a major part of the world, like Molière's hero talking prose without knowing it. In that case long-term capital flows and short-term liquidity may have to be constituents of the common pool of one fungible resource. The juridical distinction between the IMF and the World Bank, though narrowing over the years, may tend to be further reduced to a point of almost complete fusion of their functions. Even a great clairvoyant and prophetic economist such as Keynes could go wrong. At the time of the establishment of the Fund, Keynes replied to a critic of his own and the White plans saying, "It is not the purpose of the currency schemes to deal with different rates of capital expansion causing some countries to be long-term borrowers from the rest of the world and others to be long-term lenders....To deal with that problem requires another type of institution..." (quoted in Chandavarkar, 1987). The difference between what Keynes believed then and the prevailing international economic reality only underscores how radically the world has changed.

Thus, the reform of the world's monetary system, not a piecemeal but comprehensive one, should be on the agenda of the world's statesmen, though there could be disagreement about the forum where it should be deliberated, designed and acted upon. But the task ahead is not an easy one because a mere technical virtuosity, pure economic reasoning divorced from its wider political and social context and legal casuistry, will be a poor surrogate for enlightened statesmanship, capacity to interact with each other in pursuit of the collective good and humane concern for other fellow beings. Men of practical affairs should bear in mind Keynes' warning that "the future would not resemble the past" and that "we shall run more risk of jeopardising the future if we are influenced by indefinite fears based on turning to look ahead further than anyone can see..." (quoted in Chandavarkar, 1987). Men of ideas should recognise that their intellectual world knows no boundaries. They should also not ignore the insidious influence of small clubs and coalitions on the process of harmonising the diverse interests of countries which may necessitate an analytical underpinning of a future international monetary system, more in terms of a theory of oligopoly than that of competitive markets (Chandavarkar, 1987). It is said of the historian by J.H. Huizinga, himself a great historian, that "he is a wrestler with the angel" because it is the angel of death who makes his work necessary. If a historian has to wrestle with the angel, the economist and the economic reformers should wrestle with 'the devil' of vested interests who makes it necessary for them to usher in an equitable, just and fair world monetary and economic order.

REFERENCES

Chandavarkar, Anand (1987). "Keynes and the international monetary system revisited (a contextual and conjectural essay)", *World Development* 15(12) (December).

Coats, Warren L. Jr. (1982). "The SDR as a means of payment", *IMF Staff Papers* 29(3): 422–36.

————. (1983). "The SDR as a means of payment": reply to comment by Collier van den Boogaerde and Peter B. Kenen', *IMF Staff Papers*, 30(3): 662–9.

———— (1987). "On some possible reforms of the SDR" (*mimeo*), Washington DC: IMF.

Crockett, Andrew and M. Goldstein (1987). *Strengthening the International Monetary System: Exchange Rates, Surveillance, and Objective Indicators.* Washington DC: IMF.

Dornbusch, R. (1985). "Policy and performance links between LDC debate and industrial nations", *Brookings Institute Paper on Economic Activity*, No. 2. Washington DC: Brookings Institution.

Frenkel, Jacob A. and Morris Goldstein (1986). "Guide to target zones", *IMF Staff Papers* (December).

Horne, J. and P. Masson (1987). "Scope and limits of international economic cooperation and policy coordination" (*mimeo*), Washington DC: IMF.

IMF (International Monetary Fund) (1984). "The exchange rate system: lessons of the past and options for the future", *IMF Occasional Paper* No. 30 (July).

———— (1986). "Exchange rate volatility and world trade", *IMF Occasional Paper* No. 28 (July).

Kenen, Peter B. (1983a). "Uses of the SDR to supplement or substitute for other means of finance", in George M. van Furstenberg (ed.), *International Money and Credit: The Policy Roles*. Washington DC: IMF.

————. (1983b). "SDR as a means of payment: A comment on Coats", *IMF Staff Papers*, 30(3): 656–61.

————. (1987). "What role for IMF surveillance?" *World Development*, 15(12) (December).

Mistry, Percy (1987). "Third world debt beyond the Baker plan", *The Banker.* London, September.

Mundell, Robert A. (1969). "The International Monetary Fund", *Journal of World Trade Law*, vol. 13 (Sept/Oct).

Sengupta, Arjun (1987). "Allocation of Special Drawing Rights linked to the reserve needs of the countries", in UNCTAD, *International Monetary and Financial Issues for the Developing Countries*. New York: United Nations.

Shafer, J.R. and B.E. Loopesko (1983). "Floating exchange rates after ten years", *Brookings Institute Papers on Economic Activity*, Vol.I. Washington, D.C.: Brookings Institute.

Williamson, John (1987). "Exchange rate flexibility, target zones, and policy coordination", *World Development* 15(12), December.

The author would like to thank, without implicating, Anand Chandavarkar, Warren L. Coats, Jr, Hasan Imam, and Saumya Mitra for comments and suggestions on an earlier version of this paper. The views expressed are the author's own and do not represent in any way those of the International Monetary Fund.

Published in *World Development* 15(12): vii–xvi (1987).

22 | Not the Way to Fix What is Broke

Ageing institutions, national and international, are prone to inertia and resist change even when their original purposes and circumstances are no longer extant. The powers that dominate their functioning use them as convenient vehicles for their other goals, not germane to the institutions. If a change becomes ineluctable, all possible diversionary subterfuges are adopted to weaken the institution's structure and role by setting up auxiliary bodies which often usurp its functions—at least the important part of them. Nowhere is this institutional morphology displayed more starkly than in the shaping of the International Monetary Fund (IMF) during the last three decades.

Under the Bretton Woods system of fixed exchange rates, the IMF's remit extended to all member countries, industrialised and developing, regardless of their economic power. Whenever any country's exchange rate was found to be unsustainable, thereby adversely impacting on its balance of payments, the Fund advised a change in its macroeconomic policies including the exchange rate, often with the provision of its resources to relieve financing problems in the short run. The Fund's approach to the macroeconomic policies of member countries had one most important dimension: it concerned itself more with the policies of the industrialised countries as their policies affected not only their own economies but also other economies, directly and indirectly, and therefore had repercussions on the working of the international monetary system's soundness and stability. Since the industrialised countries, except the United States, also resorted to financing facilities from the Fund, it had a certain leverage in influencing their policies. The US being a reserve currency country was, of course, beyond the pale of the Fund's direct influence, though it could not ignore the Fund's advice as it felt the ripple effects of the policies of the other industrialised countries on its official gold holdings. This scenario was radically transformed in 1971, when the US snapped the dollar's link with gold, thus heralding a regime of floating exchange rates. Under this system, there was no need for industrial countries to borrow from the Fund, and if any occasion arose for such an exigency, they could rely on each other under various arrangements. Thus the Fund became a lender of last resort to only the non-industrialised countries.

The upshot of this was that the Fund lost its leadership role in steering the macroeconomic policies of the industrialised countries, thereby eroding its ability to ensure the stability and sustainability of the international monetary system. Montek Ahluwalia (2000) sums up the downgrading of the Fund's power and authority in a telling manner:

> The elimination of the Fund's financing role for industrialised countries inevitably weakened its ability to influence policies in the major economies, even though these policies can have adverse effects on the rest of the world. The surveillance function of the Fund was, at one stage, projected as a possible mechanism for overseeing the consistency of macroeconomic policies of the major industrialised countries, but this has not happened in practice. The Fund was not a significant player in either the Plaza Agreement or the Louvre Accord, with crucial examples of policy coordination among industrialised countries. Its contribution to the process of policy coordination among industrialised countries since then is also limited. (p.53)

In the absence of any direct influence policy, coordination among industrialised countries should have been the kingpin of the Fund's role to ensure the viable and smooth functioning of the international monetary system and yet it was taken away from the Fund's purview by the contraption of a privileged group of industrialised countries, spearheaded by the US. Here again, Ahluwalia's instincts and astute observations serve him well, requiring him to focus on the central issues involved in the reconstruction of the monetary system. The G-7 forum (and before it the G-5) emerged as an "extra-territorial authority", as it was christened by Joseph Gold, a former legal counsellor of the Fund, because of the aversion of the industrialised countries to the Fund getting involved in their internal policies. This undermined the Fund as the custodian of the international monetary system. Ahluwalia does not mince words:

> [T]he consultations are limited to a relatively small group of countries which are both economically more integrated and also much more politically cohesive than other international groupings. The position of these countries on international economic policy issues is usually decided as part of this process and decisions which concern the Fund and the Bank are then presented at Interim and Development Committee meetings, more or less as a *fait accompli*. Since developing countries are excluded from this process during its early and formative stages, and since they do not have the power to force reconsideration at later stage, it is not surprising that they often feel that the G-7 functions, in effect, as the "Directorate of the World (p.53).

The author even describes the agenda of the G-7 as in effect that of drawing attention to the US domination of the Fund's policies.

The exclusion of policy coordination among industrialised countries, from the Fund's deliberations and its location in outside bodies like the G-7, has important implications for the financial crises in emerging and transition countries, which threatened the world financial markets first in the mid-

1980s with debt problems of the Latin American countries, in 1997 with the meltdown in East Asia, and later in Russia and Brazil. These implications remained dormant until the mid-1980s only because many of the emerging and transition countries were insulated from the international capital markets. But the situation vastly changed in the 1990s, when private capital flows to the emerging market economies increased enormously—almost five times from the level in 1989. It is, of course, in the nature of things that capital flows should be subject to volatility due whether to macroeconomic policy efforts or the psychological make-up of investors. Ahluwalia, very meticulously and with pedagogic skills, has encapsulated the cure and cause of the financial crises. And yet he misses the crucial aspect of the failure of the coordination of macroeconomic policies adopted by the industrial countries, particularly the major currency countries like the US, Japan and Germany. When major currencies like dollar, yen and deutsche mark fluctuate, they directly affect countries with a high exposure to capital flows. The foreign exchange traders shift funds across countries for arbitrage gains, which then puts pressure on the domestic monetary, exchange rate and fiscal policies of countries suffering from capital outflows. This is even more so when the capital that flows to emerging countries is almost wholly from the industrialised countries (Khatkhate, 1998b).

What is true of the impact of exchange rate policies of the industrialised countries on capital importing countries is also true of the impact of their monetary and fiscal policies. During the Mexican, the East Asian, and the Brazilian crises, interest rate change in the US and to a lesser extent in some other industrialised countries influenced the financial and monetary policies of the countries with large capital inflows. Banks in Thailand, South Korea and Indonesia, the corporate sector and the public sector had incurred short-term liabilities abroad when interest rate differentials after allowing for the expected changes in the exchange rate turned favourable to them. When these differentials changed with a swing in the internal policies of the capital-exporting countries, there were serious repercussions on the financial system and the private sectors in the borrowing countries. If only coordination of policies of the industrial countries was given central importance as a key element in ensuring a stable international monetary order and a supranational body like the Fund was equipped with the necessary clout to play a role in it, financial crises as experienced in Mexico and East Asia could have been contained in time before they slipped out of control.

The Fund instead imposed programme conditionalities for the crisis countries using its resources, which were out of tune with the financial and economic reality in those countries. Conditionality involved fiscal retrenchment when the fiscal balance in the countries was either mildly negative or in surplus, a sweeping restructuring of banks and the corporate sector, and a severely restrictive monetary policy. As a consequence, there was a virtual collapse of the financial and corporate sectors. The reason often cited for the fiscal control was that the governments of the affected countries would be required to finance restructuring of banks. In fact, to put financial restructuring ahead of staunching the capital outflow to prevent a further depreciation of the currencies was putting the cart before the horse. The reason why the bank and corporate restructuring was given precedence over rescheduling short-term debt (except, of course, in South Korea and Brazil) was the eagerness of the countries, mainly the US and Japan, to facilitate ownership of banks and corporates by their firms, which was resisted for so long by the East Asian countries, particularly South Korea and Indonesia. The crisis countries thus were caught in a double whammy—exchange rates went on depreciating, which in turn exacerbated the bad debt problem of the banks and bankruptcies of bank borrowers, and efforts to restructure the financial system led to further collapse of the firms (Khatkhate, 1998a).

The Fund thus remained a passive spectator to the indifference of the industrialised countries to orchestrate their policies, which unsettled the financial markets, and an active agent to impose conditionality on the countries, which suited more the interests of the industrial countries than the borrowing countries. This is why Martin Feldstein, who by no means could be considered to be anti-American, suspected the Fund's neutrality. He argued that

> the Fund's plans were replays of the policies that Japan and the United States have long been trying to get Korea to adopt. Others saw this aspect of the plan as an abuse of IMF power to force Korea at a time of weakness to accept trade and investment policies it had previously rejected. (Feldstein, 1998).

Jagdish Bhagwati ascribed, with good reason, Fund conditionality to the influence of the 'Treasury complex' in the United States (Bhagwati, 1998).

Contrary to this widely prevalent perception amongst academics and even among majority members on the Meltzer Commission appointed by the US Congress, Ahluwalia bends over backward to soft-pedal the misconceived policies of the Fund during the East Asian crisis. He seems to question that fiscal policy should have been relaxed rather than tightened. The justification for this conclusion is that:

> If a loss of confidence triggers a capital outflow, and if adequate finance is not available to cover the outflow, and capital controls are also to be avoided, then the country has to bring about a turnaround in the current account to accommodate the outflow. Restrictive fiscal policy can be viewed as a legitimate policy intervention aimed at improving the current account ...in order to avoid a collapse in the exchange rate which would impose other costs. (Ahluwalia, 2000: 35)

This statement can be disputed on several counts. First, a tight fiscal policy did not succeed in stemming further depreciation of the currencies. In fact, it led to further depreciation by adversely impacting the business sector of the economies. Second, even conceding that financing from the Fund was inadequate to compensate for the capital outflow, a better solution would have been rescheduling the short-term debt at the very beginning as South Korea did without consulting the Fund and to proceed after stabilising the exchange rate with plans of restructuring the financial system and structural reforms in other areas. There is no need to test the counterfactuals to come to this obvious conclusion.

Ahluwalia is also somewhat confusing on the time sequence and duration of fiscal policy adjustment when he asserts that "The economic contraction which occurred in East Asia therefore cannot be attributed directly to excessively tight fiscal targets as these were never actually implemented" (p.36). In point of fact, a tight fiscal policy was pursued by the crisis countries at the very beginning, though its effects were felt after a lag. The same soft glove treatment is given to the Fund when Ahluwalia explains why the Fund's strategy did not succeed in East Asia. He cites the Fund report by Lane *et al.* published in late 1999, which states that "financing provided in the Fund programmes was sufficient only on the assumption that they would succeed in restoring confidence and halt the capital outflow" (p.36). It is difficult to understand how tight fiscal policy could have been a substitute for adequate financing from the Fund or other sources. As stated earlier, the right thing in those circumstances would have been to somehow reschedule the short-term debt of the crisis countries by involving the creditors to buy time for introduction of more stringent policies later. Not that Ahluwalia is unaware of the policy trade-offs. He is savvy enough to raise doubts about whether "the lack of resources created a situation where there was too much reliance upon adjustment and too little upon financing" (p.36), or whether the Fund overstated "the weaknesses in the financial system as an underlying explanation for the crisis and did in turn deepen the crisis". Having raised these awkward questions, he quickly skirts the embarrassing answers by taking refuge in difficulties in proving the counterfactuals—a common academic tactic pursued when the answers are inconvenient or do not conform to one's prejudices.

The same nimble ratiocination is seen in Ahluwalia's explanatory comments on the Fund's prescription of a hike in interest rates at the beginning of the crises. As against the Fund's rationale, S. Furman and J. Stiglitz argued that higher interest rates could actually aggravate capital outflows, if the investors interpret them as evidence of greater default risks in the economy. While overtly disagreeing with this, Ahluwalia covertly concedes the merit of the Furman-Stiglitz criticism when he emphasizes, "The negative effect is obviously greater where the banking system suffers from a maturity mismatch and is undercapitalised and where corporations are highly leveraged" (p.36). On his own admission on pages 9 and 10, currency crises in emerging countries are overblown into financial crises because of the weak financial system, which is mostly used by the corporations for finance. An initial currency depreciation affects directly the balance sheets of banks and through them the corporates and the real economy. If this is the case, even on a priori grounds higher interest rates are bound to raise default risks for investors. It is splitting hairs to argue that the effects of high interest rates would depend on "the period for which interest rates are hiked". Damage to the financial system can be done even when interest rates remain high for a short duration. It is also not quite true that interest rates in South Korea and Thailand declined quite quickly. In Thailand the rates were raised in the third quarter of 1997 and lasted till mid-1998 and in South Korea from January 1998 to the third quarter of 1998. Considering that the crises lasted only a year, a six-month period of tight fiscal and monetary policy should not be dismissed as very short. It was only when criticism of the Fund's policies became deafening that the Fund retraced its steps. The East Asian economies have no doubt got adjusted but the cost of adjustment turned out to be far too much (Khatkhate, 1998a).

The nature and content of the programmes constituted one aspect of the Fund's policies; the other concerned its surveillance functions. Here Ahluwalia's analysis is candid and does not spare the Fund for its errors of commission and omission. He recognises the failings in surveillance both in regard to the policies of the industrialised countries and the emerging and other developing countries. In the first group of countries, the Fund's surveillance is perfunctory as none of them borrowed from the Fund and their policy is designed and implemented through different institutional arrangements. All that the Fund does in their case is to issue learned and analytically well-grounded reports biannually. But the Fund's record in regard to the emerging and developing countries has been mixed results. The Fund "failed to spot the brewing crisis in Mexico in 1994". Fund surveillance clearly failed to spot the vulnerability of the rest of the region, which led to the spread of the crisis from Thailand. It did not spot the growth of short-term debt, which is viewed as the villain of the piece in retrospect, even though data were available in the Bank for International Settlements (BIS) (Ahluwalia, 2000: 16; see also Khatkhate, 1998a for more details).

It is clear that all is not well with the existing international monetary system and the role of the Fund in guiding it. First of all, it does not have effective jurisdiction over the policies of its industrialised country members, as they are discussed, negotiated in a different forum and the Fund is left to rubber-stamp its decisions. While financial crises are sparked off both by the domestic policies of the crisis countries as well as those of the industrialised countries, the Fund's power to manage crises remains constrained. Second, the power equation in the governance of the Fund is such that the policies that are prescribed for borrowing countries in crisis situations are unduly influenced by the prejudices and the self-interest of the industrialised countries. This asymmetrical power relationship attenuates the capacity of the Fund either to prevent financial crises or to manage them with expediency and effectiveness. Third, the lack of resources at the disposal of the Fund diminishes its ability to contain financial crises. And finally, the Fund's surveillance, which is its main instrument to monitor economic policies and developments in member countries, is weak, and often fails to anticipate events. This is because the Fund relies on governments of countries to update its knowledge of economic events, which is of limited use as compared to what the market can provide.

Any scheme for improvement of the international monetary system thus will have to address each of these areas in which the Fund is involved. Ahluwalia has taken a holistic view on the reform issue, which basically is an amalgam of ideas aired widely within official and non-official circles. The most innovative concept which Ahluwalia can take credit for relates to special issue of SDRs by the Fund to increase the size of the Fund's resources when the financing requirements of the crisis countries far exceed what the Fund on its own or through other arrangements can mobilise. This idea, in novelty and originality, is on par with the aid link which another distinguished Indian, I.G. Patel, proposed in the late 1960s. Ahluwalia has also some alternative suggestions on changing the governance structure of the Fund so that it should reflect the growing importance of the emerging countries in decision-making.

Implicit in his proposal on a new governance structure of the Fund is recognition that the existing power equation in which the industrial countries hold a dominant position should be changed. To this end Ahluwalia proposes the constitution of a group in place of the present International Monetary and Financial Committee (the new incarnation of the old Interim Committee) consisting of "top eight industrialised countries by size of quota in the Fund, plus the top 12 among the other members, which includes oil exporting countries, plus all those countries not already covered by this criterion but which currently represent constituencies in the IMF Board." He would also like to "include the heads of major international institutions concerned with the functions of the international financial system and the world economy in FSF [Financial Stability Forum], WTO, and UNCTAD, BIS, IOSCO [International Organisation of Security Commission]". However, though the purpose of this is laudable, it requires a leap of imagination to believe that the amorphous group could ever achieve anything substantial. Does Ahluwalia really believe that UNCTAD, which has outlived its utility with the arrival of the WTO and whose philosophy does not recognise globalisation, will contribute to the deliberation of the Fund? Nowhere is it mentioned in his proposal that the quotas of members in the Fund should be changed to reflect the growing economic power of the emerging countries. Without this, it will be business as usual in the Fund, and the committee would be no more than a talking shop. Then again, he has little to say about what would happen to the G-7 and a new G-20 (where some of the emerging countries like South Korea, China, India and Brazil are represented), which have undermined the Fund. Would the proposed committee empower the Fund to enforce coordination of policies among the industrialised countries? Instead of providing a solution to the existing problem, it will create new problems. A simpler and a more practical approach is to realign the quotas of the members and the consequent voting power of the emerging countries, so that they would have more influence in regard to the coordination of policies of the industrialised countries and designing of programmes for countries borrowing from the Fund. Under the new order to come, there should not be any place for special interest groups like G-7, or G-20 for that matter. Furthermore, a new forum such as the Financial Stability Forum, with its membership expanded to a wider group of countries, should be institutionally linked with the Fund so that the emerging countries will automatically have a voice in its deliberations.

Far more thought should be given to improving the surveillance apparatus of the Fund. The present arrangements under which the Fund relies only on its own staff to gather economic and statistical information about member countries has been found wanting in many respects. The data that the BIS collects are more reliable as it gets it from market participants. Besides, the World Bank has useful statistical data about the financial systems in several countries. Thus, if the Fund's surveillance is to be a more effective medium of reliable data gathering, a body consisting of the World Bank, BIS, FSF, and IOSCO should be organically aligned with the Fund.

Management of crisis by the Fund in an effective and speedy manner presupposes adequacy of resources at its disposal. However, this issue has aroused a heated controversy. Basically, Ahluwalia's position is that the Fund should strengthen its lender of last resort function and if the resource crunch is an impediment, it should get around it by the issue of SDRs to finance the crisis-ridden countries. Once the crisis is over and the borrowing countries repurchase their currencies from the Fund, the SDRs should be extinguished. Through this simple, innovative device, which can be adopted without amendment of the Fund's Articles of Agreement, the Fund can help countries promptly and effectively without being hamstrung by shortage of resources.

One of the objections often raised against the Fund acting as a lender of last resort is that it will abet moral hazard when most of the creditors are from the private sector. This is a valid criticism and it calls for a mechanism whereby, the private sector could be involved not only when the crisis emerges but also in normal times. Certain countries like Argentina, Mexico and Indonesia and some others have negotiated contingency credit arrangements with commercial banks. But this is purely a private arrangement. There is no doubt that the private sector has to be involved in some capacity so that it is made fully aware of the risks in lending without regard to country risks. Ahluwalia is probably right that contingency credit arrangements may not be the ideal one for associating the private sector. An alternative way to achieve this may be for the Fund to institute a body, along the lines of the market conditions advisory group proposed by Larry Summers, in which major private sector creditors, particularly commercial banks, are represented. This body can meet regularly under the chairmanship of the Fund management for interchange of views on trends in the world capital markets, country risks, and the Fund's perspective on international financial and monetary developments. Through this device, the Fund will be better positioned to acquire a deeper knowledge of market situation. The private sector creditors will then be more amenable to burden-sharing when the time comes.

Ahluwalia is not as convincing, however, in regard to his justification for the Fund's unending lending to the developing countries. He joins issue with the Meltzer Commission's recommendation that long-term financing windows such as EFF and ESAF supporting policy reform, available to the developing countries not exposed to global capital flows, should be closed and instead these countries should approach the World Bank and other regional development banks. It is true that these countries, unlike the emerging market economies, avail of the use of the Fund's resources to tide over temporary pressures on their balance of payments position. But over time, what was considered to be short-term requirement has lapsed into long-term credit, which is hardly repaid. When one loan ends, immediately a new one comes in its place. One telling fact which the Meltzer Commission has spotlighted is that four developing countries have been indebted to the Fund for 40–49 years, 20 countries for 30–39 years, 46 for 20–29 years, and 25 for 10–19 years. The long terms of the loans show that the economic problems of a large number of developing countries are endemic and of long-term nature and unless their political economy is drastically changed and institutional development is placed on a sound footing, no amount of use of the Fund's resources will get them out of the quagmire. They will be better placed as borrowers from the World Bank, which is a developmental institution. This, of course, presumes that the World Bank is reformed radically with a clear focus on development of poor countries and poverty alleviation and a radically different operating structure. The Fund's role in respect of these developing countries will then have to be limited to designing a macroeconomic framework for them, within which the lending policies of the World Bank and other development agencies will be implemented.

Another area that has been generating more heat than light is how the adjustment programme of the Fund could be designed to alleviate their impact on the poor. There is no gainsaying that any adjustment for countries affected either by capital account crisis or the traditional balance of payments problem cannot avoid an adverse impact on the poor. The question, insofar as the Fund's role in this area is concerned, is whether the Fund can do anything at all. The Fund has been populist when it redesignated its ESAF as a poverty reduction facility, with the same substance but laced with soothing lip-service to poverty alleviation. Here Ahluwalia, whose early expertise has been in the field of income distribution and poverty, is forthright and does not mince words, when he says,

> while recognising the importance of protecting the living standards of the poor as far as possible, it must also be recognised that country authorities as well as international organisations will face practical problems if loaded with too many social objectives.

This can distract attention from the immediate task of crisis management and possibly also politicise the design of adjustment programmes. (p.34)

He could have argued, but he does not, that even if the Fund wants to play that role it cannot. Adjustment programmes can be prescribed only when countries can borrow from the Fund. The countries with the largest number of the world's poor are countries such as China, India, Brazil, Mexico, etc. And these will come to the Fund only when they face the crisis in their capital account. This is also true of the other emerging countries in East Asia, where the problem of the poor is not as serious. If the Fund designs the programme for these countries when they face capital outflow contingencies with too many social conditionalities, the main objective of the programme, *viz.*, to staunch the capital outflows and restore balance in the economy, will be side-tracked. As for the other low-income developing countries, poverty can be alleviated through long-term development, which should be the domain of the World Bank, as argued earlier.

Ahluwalia's retrospective view of the latter-day crises, though familiar to those who have studied the developments in the international arena over the last few years, is thorough, except that he does not assign as much importance as warranted to the lack of coordination among industrialised countries as a major cause of the financial crises and the role of the Fund in ensuring it. His discussion of crisis prevention as also crisis resolution is comprehensive but he is tame and rather self-consciously overcautious when he comes to the prospective view of the global financial system. The analytical underpinnings of his retrospective view presage a major restructuring of the monetary system but he seems to pin his faith on the *status quo*. As a result, what he envisages is not a new architecture but renovation of the old one, with alterations at the fringes. Though he suggests an alternative for governance of the Fund and associated institutions, his scheme does not attack the existing power equation in the Fund as a major centre for managing the international order. The basic asymmetry that characterises the relations of the industrialised and the developing countries would persist as before. The Fund would continue to design adjustment programmes for the crisis-ridden countries needing the Fund's resources in a way that subserves the interests of the industrialised countries.

Ahluwalia gives short shrift to the recommendations of the Task Force on the International Financial Architecture sponsored by the Council on Foreign Relations, which makes a distinction between country crisis and systemic crisis. Nor does he recognize the essence of the far-reaching solution, though put in extreme form, offered by the Meltzer Commission, which could have drastically curtailed the influence exerted by the G-7 members. Ahluwalia's monograph, despite its blue cover, thus does not offer a blueprint for the international monetary system, which is broke and is in dire need of fixing.

REFERENCES

Ahluwalia, Montek Singh (2000). *Reforming the Global Financial Architecture*. London: Commonwealth Secretariat.

Bhagwati, J. (1998). "The capital myth: the difference between trade in widgets and trade in dollars", *Foreign Affairs*, 77(3): 7–12.

Feldstein, M. (1998). "Refocusing the IMF", *Foreign Affairs* 77(1): 20–33.

Khatkhate, D. (1998a). "East Asian financial crisis and the IMF: chasing shadows", *Economic and Political Weekly* XXXIII(17): 963–9.

―――. (1998b). 'Impact of volatility of exchange rates of major currencies on foreign exchange management', *Economic and Political Weekly* XXXIII(9): 465–9.

Published in the Economic and Political Weekly XXXV(37): 3309–13 (2000).

23 | Turning the Light Inward
Evaluation of the IMF

The International Monetary Fund (IMF) has been under siege for the last decade or so, with developing countries teetering on the brink of one crisis or another blaming the IMF for their economic malaise. The onslaught on the Fund (and to a lesser degree the World Bank) by economists Joseph Stiglitz, Alan Meltzer, Martin Feldstein, John Taylor and George Schultz, and with equal ferocity by the rank and file of civil societies both in the industrial and developing countries has acquired a new plausibility. Though the rationale and the perspectives of the critics vary depending on where they come from, the end result is the same—the IMF has outlived its mission and the time has come for it to go into oblivion. This is epitomised in a slogan, "Fifty years are long enough."

This animus towards the Fund is prompted by two considerations. First, the developing countries claim that the rigorous conditionalities imposed by the Fund on countries borrowing from it have exacerbated the problems of their economies. Second, its economist and non-economist critics have based their demand for the abolition of the Fund or at least for a drastic diminution of its role in the management of the international monetary order on the argument that the Fund has gone beyond its domain through 'mission creep' and that its policies have created a serious moral hazard problem.

One answer to these criticisms could be to raise the counterfactual. If the Fund were removed from the scene, would the international monetary system function better than it has under the tutelage of the IMF? Secondly, would the developing countries which are the main client group for the use of the Fund's resources be better off without the Fund? If the answers to these two questions were in the affirmative a strong case could be made for dismantling of the IMF.

The Fund was established in the aftermath of the second world war primarily to forestall destabilising forces in the international economic arena and to set up a stable order with well-defined rules of the game. Its other function was to help countries in balance of payments disequilibrium through both lending and non-lending instruments. The difference between these two functions was crucial and that created a schism and disharmony among members of the Fund with the efflux of time. Forces threatening the stability of the international system, such as exchange rate volatility and interest rate changes, emanate from the policies and actions of the industrial countries which, though directed at their internal economies, have wider repercussions on other countries, both industrial and developing. The IMF has acted as a focal point and a central platform from which the domestic policies of industrial countries with international consequences are coordinated. However, of late, particularly during the 1990s the IMF has been sidelined by the policies of the industrial countries which have fostered a parallel centre for managing the coordination issues involved in managing a viable and robust international economic order. Major issues are discussed and policies evolved not in the Fund but in the Group of Seven with close to one-half of the voting power in the IMF (the group may also be called a "Group of One", judging by the enormous influence the US exercises on Fund policies) and its shadow, a Group of Twenty, which includes a sprinkling of some leading emerging countries and some industrial countries in addition to the Group of Seven. That this *de facto* situation is no longer a figment of anyone's imagination is evident from a monograph by a retired secretary of the IMF Board published under the imprimatur of the Fund. It says:

> The major industrial countries, the Group of Seven, ...have exhibited a growing tendency in recent years to act as a self-appointed steering group or 'Directors' of the IMF. Recent reports of the finance ministers to the heads of states and governments at the annual summit meetings have sometimes tended to deal with IMF matters in a manner that raises the question of whether they will leave the Executive Directors representing the Group of Seven countries with the necessary margin for discussion and room for give and take that is essential for consensus building ....' (Van Houtven, 2002).

This means that the first function of the IMF of managing the international system could well be discharged without the IMF as the leverage is with the Group of Seven. The piquancy of the second function is that the member countries of the Fund which are only creditors and not borrowers have greater influence in determining conditionality and all that goes with it in the Fund's programmes, which are of great consequence to the borrowing developing countries. It is this asymmetry in the Fund's governance that often leads civil society critics as well as some academics to assail the Fund and think that the borrowing countries will be better off without the Fund.

Will they be, is the question. Will developing countries which use the conditional lending of the Fund, be better off if the Fund were to fade out? Going over the history of crisis-ridden developing countries over the life of the

Fund, one thing that stands out is that their problems have been home-grown, to begin with, except for a few cases where exogenous forces have intervened. If the Fund were not the lender, they would have gone for resources to the same rich industrial countries whom they chastise for their dominant voice in the Fund's policies. Bilateral borrowing is hardly a blessing and is perhaps a worse option than borrowing from the Fund with all its supposedly pernicious conditionalities. Besides, countries in distress would have to approach a multiplicity of creditor countries, which would involve cross-conditionality. This clearly shows that the clamour for abolition of the Fund by developing countries is empty rhetoric that will not stand a reality check. From the developing countries' point of view, therefore, the Fund has legitimacy; and if it has failed—and there is some truth in that charge—it must be made to succeed.

The issue to be addressed is how to rectify the deficiencies in the Fund's programmes to the benefit of the borrowing countries and to maximise the pay-off of the Fund's programmes. But this cannot be done from outside the Fund. Until recently the Fund's operations have been opaque and have suffered from lack of transparency. Programmes failed times without number and yet the Fund resisted sharing information about the back-room decision-making process and the parameters of its policy frame. Of course, there has been a continuous review of policies within the Fund, but this never went beyond settled modes of thought and remained anchored to the so-called experience of the Fund which, to borrow a phrase from the late Henry Johnson, is "one year's experience multiplied by the number of years." Nor has there been any effort by the Fund to face problems upfront in a manner that did not fall in the groove of the ossified internal thinking processes. Only since 1998 has the Fund woken up to its obligations to its large invisible membership with ineffective voting power. It instituted external evaluation of its Enhanced Structural Adjustment Facility (ESAF) programmes and also of some of its key activities such as research and fiscal and budgetary processes. But the most radical measure, and potentially perhaps the most effective, has been the setting up the Independent Evaluation Office (IEO) for a thorough investigation of the Fund's policies without being contaminated by its internal parochial and often sanctimonious culture.

In September this year, the IEO released its first report directed at analysing the causes of prolonged use of IMF resources by borrowing countries, backed by three case studies—of Pakistan, the Philippines and Senegal. The report delves into the design and the logical basis of Fund programmes and has come up with a forthright critique of the Fund's policies. All this is like a breath of fresh air. Not that there is no room for differences over the analysis or the recommendations based on it. What is heartening is that there is no attempt at white-washing to cover up the Fund management's failures, nor flinching from supporting ideas which may be deemed to be not politically 'correct', nor any effort to be exculpatory in regard to the Fund. This report, to be followed by one on fiscal adjustment in Fund programmes and another on three capital account crises—Korea, Indonesia and Brazil—signals that the Fund is now poised—whether under pressure of public opinion or criticism from the academia or reflecting the changing times—"to enhance the learning culture within the Fund, strengthen the Fund's external credibility...and to draw lessons from its experiences and more quickly integrate improvements into its future work." Even more striking has been the transparent way the IEO has gone about preparing its report. Right from the start it placed its draft terms of reference and other papers about its functioning on the website to elicit criticism and suggestions from the public and incorporated suggestions of merit into the final document. This is unprecedented among not only multilateral institutions but also national governments.

In what follows, the focus will be on the core analysis of the report, which has a bearing on the Fund's policies in programme design and implementation in general and in respect particularly to prolonged users of the Fund's resources. An attempt will be made to look back to the past to identify problems likely to arise in future and to seek solutions to them. So the main findings of the report will be selectively considered. Since improvement of policies depends crucially on governance of the IMF and its institutional culture, the spotlight will be on the implications of prolonged use of the Fund's resources for these two aspects of its functioning.

Before coming to the report proper, it is pertinent to present, albeit in a broad way, the analytical frame of reference for judging the appropriateness or otherwise of the Fund's policies. What has been controversial is the nature, relevance and impact of conditionality in the Fund's programmes because it is often viewed more as a punishment of the borrower administered by the lender. But conditionality has also a positive connotation; it entails reward if the borrowing country fulfils its structural benchmarks and performance criteria. As Avinash Dixit, who has harnessed organisation theory to analyse IMF programmes, argues, under a Fund programme "a country gets rewards or suffers penalties depending on its actions and the outcomes. In other words, IMF programmes are incentive schemes or mechanisms" and "debates concerning IMF programmes can usefully be informed by, and the design and implementation of the programmes can benefit from, viewing them explicitly in this way" (Dixit, 2000). Viewed as incentive schemes or mechanisms, IMF programmes are placed by Dixit in "the framework of the relationship between a principal who lays down the contract or the scheme and the agent whose behaviour it is intended to influence." The principal in this case is the IMF and the borrowing country the agent. However, this formulation encounters, in this specific case, a political problem which has no easy solution. It is true that the IMF is the principal which is owned by sovereign states and therefore remains accountable to them through the Executive Board and the Board of Governors. But this is not as simple as it looks. While member countries, both lenders and borrowers, own the IMF in a technical sense, in practice the borrowing countries have little clout in the governance of the Fund because of their weak voting power, whereas the creditors, who are rarely borrowers, dominate the Fund's policies. Resentment of conditionality arises from the fact that the borrowing countries, despite being owners of the Fund or principals in the parlance of organisation theory, cannot influence the nature of conditionality either as punishment or reward for the borrowers (i.e. themselves) as agents. Perhaps the only way the complexity and political nature of this problem of principal–agent intermingling in the context of Fund programmes can be handled, if not resolved, is by facing the governance issue head on and giving a greater voice in governance to the borrowers as members of the Fund so that they could accept more willingly than at present Fund conditionality as punishment or reward. In short, conditionality should partake the character of self-discipline. The quality, objectivity, ideological neutrality and finally acceptability of the IEO report need to be perceived in this perspective.

The issue of 'prolonged use' of the Fund's resources is central to assessing the Fund's policies in so far as it casts serious doubts on the way the Fund functions, designs its policies and ensures their implementation. At one extreme, prolonged use reflects a negation of the Fund's mandate that use of its resources should be temporary, being confined to coping with balance of payments difficulties. On the other, it supports the general belief that the Fund's programmes are a failure if balance of payments difficulties persist despite use of its resources. There are various intermediate criticisms that the programmes hinder institutional development in the borrowing countries or about these countries' ownership of the programmes, etc. Prolonged use of the Fund's resources need not necessarily be a result of the Fund's errors of commission and omission; it could also be due to the failure of policies of the borrowing countries. The IEO report, however, focuses on the evaluation of the operations of the IMF and "not the policies or actions of country authorities." To the extent the policies of the countries concerned and the operations of the Fund are interconnected, it is unrealistic to expect that the prescriptions suggested by the report would "eliminate all the problems in the countries themselves that have contributed to a sometimes prolonged adjustment process."

Since there is considerable ambiguity about the precise definition of 'prolonged use', the report has put forth its own definition: "countries are defined as prolonged users if they have been under arrangements for at least seven years out of any 10." This is done on the ground that it 'goes to the heart of issues such as programme design, ownership and conditionality'. This definition is applied in two different ways, depending upon the type of analysis undertaken and the nature of the questions being addressed:

> in one, prolonged users are treated as an invariant group that includes all the countries which met the seven out of 10 years criterion at least once over the 1971–2000 period … ; in the other case, the composition of the prolonged user varies each year, as it includes only the countries which met the criterion in that particular year.

Clarity of definition is important because within the Fund prolonged use has not been uniformly defined in different country cases. The report rightly suggests that the Fund should follow a clear definition in future.

There has been a consistent rise since the 1970s in prolonged use in terms of the number of countries, the share of the IMF's membership, and total financial exposure. Out of 128 countries which made use of IMF resources during the 1971–2000 period, 51 countries were prolonged users in terms of the definition used; of these, 44 had actually used the Fund's resources, while the other seven had only precautionary arrangements with the Fund, i.e. the countries had the assurance from the Fund that they would have use of the agreed amounts when the need arose. The prolonged users are predominantly, if not exclusively, low-income countries with little or no access to capital markets. In the group of 44 prolonged users, excluding the seven with precautionary arrangements, 29 are eligible for the IMF's concessional facilities such as the Poverty Reduction and Growth Facility (PRGF). Nearly 40 per cent of prolonged users have resorted to intensive use of the IMF's general resources "in the sense that they had outstanding obligations to the general resources account of over 100 per cent of their quotas for 10 years or more". The prolonged users are slow to 'graduate' from such use. In 2001, arrangements with prolonged users represented about half the number of ongoing IMF-supported programmes, with a total exposure of SDR 24 billion, i.e. about half the total outstanding obligations to the Fund.

The report spells out cogently the causes of prolonged use, which are partly a result of evolving Fund policies but are largely due to lack of clarity in the Fund's approach to the nature of the financial constraint and the design of Fund programmes. Changes in the Fund's policies leading to a rise in prolonged use were based on the premise that many balance of payments problems in low-income countries arose from 'deep-seated structural problems which required a longer timeframe for adjustment'. This was particularly so in the 1990s when the Fund set up a series of concessional financing facilities. The increasing permissiveness in regard to prolonged use was also induced by the nature of financing constraints and the dynamics of the relationship between the Fund and the donor countries. The limited availability of funding for the Fund's concessional facilities constrained its long-term involvement. But the severity of the problem increased when the donors to low-income countries tightened the screws on their aid flows above a level consistent with the intended diminished reliance on the Fund's lending. This meant that "the Fund would either have to remain involved through repeated programmes until a sustainable external situation could be reached or withdraw from the countries concerned midway in the process before external viability could be achieved."

Where the report shows refreshing and unexpected candour is in its well-crafted strictures on the design of Fund programmes and the assumptions on which they are often based as the prime causes of prolonged use. It argues with insight and sapience that the Fund has been often lackadaisical and disingenuous in projecting certain variables such as terms of trade, exports and tax revenue as targets in the programmes and the evidence cited suggests that the over-optimism embodied in such targets "often was a problem in programme design which all led eventually to the prolonged use of the Fund resources." In careful language the report does not shirk from asserting that IMF-supported programmes in prolonged use cases achieved much less than projected. Fund programmes have generally been ineffective in the case of prolonged users. Econometric evidence shows that Fund programmes in respect of countries with prolonged use of the general resources of the Fund tend to be associated with a negative impact on growth "even after controlling for the endogeneity of a country's decision to seek IMF assistance and for other determinants of growth." Oddly, this conclusion does not hold in the case of prolonged users of concessional resources or even temporary users. The extent of fiscal adjustment in multi-year arrangements as also stand-by arrangements was less for prolonged users than for temporary users over the programme period.

The in-depth analysis of the report of the case studies and its judgement on the outcome of Fund programmes are enough to ensure the credibility of the IEO. In its disarmingly frank words,

> The case studies show that during the long period of IMF programme involvement, significant progress towards solving these countries' economic difficulties was eventually achieved in the Philippines and Senegal and even more so in Morocco, although with a mixed record across areas of economic policy and at a much slower pace than originally envisaged. The record in Pakistan and Jamaica was more disappointing. In all cases, substantial challenges remained at the end of the prolonged use period reviewed, especially as regards institutional reforms in tax administration and the broader public sector.

One of the most contentious issues in Fund policies pertains to conditionality because it is often considered to have adversely affected the borrowing developing countries and impoverished them. The report puts on the table all the Fund's cards on conditionality. The analysis based on cross-country data and case studies throws up some surprising results, which may disappoint congenital detractors of Fund policies. They will be hard put to justify their stance in the face of the full range of data revealed in the report. The report classifies conditionality in two ways: hard and soft. The former consists "of prior actions (PA) and performance criteria (PC) both of which are conditions which the country must meet in order to have access to the IMF-resources under a programme." Soft conditionality consists of all the elements which are taken into account by the IMF in forming a judgement about whether or not to complete "a review which triggers the release of a financing tranche. It might include structural benchmarks, indicative targets, or general undertakings in the authorities' letter of intent, sometimes expressly identified as elements that will be subject to reviews." Contrary to what is generally believed and the complaints of the perennial borrowers of the Fund, the cross-country evidence and case studies show convincingly that on average,

> conditionality in arrangements with prolonged users typically had fewer formal structural conditions than arrangements with temporary users, regardless of the type of arrangements. Moreover, most of the cases with very heavy use of structural conditionality did not involve prolonged users; ...only four of the 17 programmes which had more than 10 prior actions per programme-year in the 1990s involved programme users ... .

Then again,

> not only was structural conditionality less extensive in prolonged users, but also that
> it was 'softer'. In prolonged users' (and also the temporary users') arrangements, the
> largest part of structural conditionality was of the soft variety, and fewer prior actions
> particularly in regard to concessional facilities.

Apart from this, "a higher proportion of prolonged users' performance criteria was waived."

The conditionality issues are better crystallised in the case-study analysis. It identifies "a series of problems in the prolonged use countries", which are: discrepancy between the timeframe of programmes and the magnitude of their objectives, insufficient attention to programme ownership and implementation capacity, issues related to the design of conditionality, especially in dealing with core institutional changes, issues related to the financial programming framework, and issues related to the IMF's exit strategy for prolonged users. This identification of issues is disconcerting enough for the Fund's reputation, but potentially explosive and with far-reaching implications for the evolving shape of the Fund is the bold assertion of the report that these weaknesses of the Fund's programmes are imbedded in the Fund's faulty governance mechanism and its uncongenial institutional culture, on both of which the report has come out with some innovative and anti-hegemonistic recommendations. The authors of the report have shown a rare degree of scrupulous care in adding a rider that while the conclusions they have drawn should not be generalised, they "do not just reflect isolated occurrences."

The lessons derived from the analysis of conditionality in the three detailed case studies have application beyond the prolonged users. They are:

(1)   The specific structure of conditionality is much less important than an underlying domestic political commitment to core policy adjustment.

(2)   Excessively detailed conditionality, whether resorted to because of a weak track record, doubts about ownership, or to support reform-minded groups within government, does not appear to have been effective in enhancing implementation.

(3)   There is some evidence from the case studies that conditionality that focused on policy rules or procedures, rather than discretionary, one-time action was ultimately more effective.

(4)   There is no unambiguous evidence as regards the effectiveness of prior actions in Fund programmes. The three cases cast 'light on somewhat counter-intuitive conclusion of several recent studies, according to

which the number of prior actions has not had a significant influence on programme implementation' for the reason that the chosen prior actions were not integrated with the programme design.

(5) Conditionality is especially difficult to apply to complex regulatory and institutional issues that are often critical to achieving longer-term sustainability and avoiding prolonged use. Perhaps use of reviews based on assessment outcomes is a better substitute for splitting the reform into "a detailed timetable of discrete, intermediate steps that are then subject to conditionality."

(6) Finally, it is found that the credibility of conditionality can be eroded by many repeated programmes because the latter spawns an expectation that the borrowers will eventually obtain finance from the Fund even when programmes are interrupted regardless of whether they change policies or not.

In measured language the report adverts to the seriousness of the problems arising from prolonged use, which the Fund failed to anticipate when it mooted its involvement in extended programmes, both from the point of view of the prolonged users and the credibility of the Fund. As regards the former, i.e. borrowers, prolonged use poses serious impediments to robust policy formulation processes over time. There is an 'inherent tension between the quasi-permanent conditionality and the countries taking responsibility for the conduct of their economic policy'. The belief, fostered by the Fund's practice of rolling over programmes through fresh renegotiations, might have been a disincentive to decisive action to deal with some problems. On the other hand, the credibility of the Fund was considerably weakened by prolonged use in some cases, prompted by 'the donor support or debt rescheduling or political pressures'. Apart from this, too much preoccupation of the Fund with prolonged users often tended 'to crowd out' some aspects of its independent surveillance activities, thereby throwing its credibility in doubt. What is even more disconcerting, from the point of view of the Fund's purposive and efficient working, was that its prolonged use activities often did not jibe well with "current internal operational procedures which are still largely built around the relatively short-term framework of programmes."

Even those who have been familiar with the Fund's operations and policies have not been cognisant enough of the impact of the Fund's governance and its institutional culture on policy design and implementation. This report has gone a long way to remove the fog that surrounds the Fund's internal working with all its bureaucratic cross-currents and the intrusion of exogenous political pressures. Two factors are considered by the authors of the report as of crucial importance to the sustainability of the Fund's adjustment efforts. They are institutional change and good governance. Under the present working of the Fund, it is difficult to avoid an overload of the reform agenda which often "resulted in a *de facto* failure to focus on the reforms that were most critical from the perspective of long-term sustainable adjustment and that often depended critically upon institutional development." 'Seemingly intractable' structural problems such as those in areas of tax administration, public enterprises and administered prices that hamper adjustment call for appropriate institutional capability to handle them. Currently, structural problems in adjustment policies governing prolonged users are dealt with by the IMF in cooperation with the World Bank. The Fund approaches these issues "from a narrow angle of their direct macroeconomic implications, while the World Bank concerns itself with the design and implementation or the broader structural reform." But in practice a number of coordination problems arise and they impinge on the effectiveness of the programme. The different timeframes on which the two institutions operate are often blamed for the recurrent difficulties, but the real reasons seem to lie "much deeper than a mere failure of the two staffs to coordinate adequately; they reflect different institutional culture, programme modalities, and objectives." This is a serious institutional failing which should have been addressed long ago when the number of prolonged users was rising and the programmes were causing discontent in the borrowing countries and in civil society everywhere. The suggestion of the report, which appears eminently sensible, is that the IMF and the World Bank should "collaborate effectively in designing the most appropriate strategy for implementing such reform and to monitor their implementation through appropriate, but parsimonious conditionality."

Learning from the case studies, the report also throws into bold relief the fact that ownership and implementation were often the "Achilles' heel" of Fund-supported programmes in prolonged users. The reason cited is the "underestimation by the IMF of the technical and political limits to implementation capacity and the consequent over-optimism about the speed of success." The report pins the technical responsibility on the low 'experience level' of the mission chiefs who negotiate the programmes. But far more important is that the IMF should analyse political factors in a more explicit and systematic way as part of its decision-making procedures or programmes. "This is a different, problematic and intractable area for the Fund." Drawing on an exploratory paper by a political scientist commissioned by the IEO which suggested some tools that could be used in political feasibility assessments, the authors of the report conclude that the application of some of these analytical tools to the Pakistan programmes of 1993-94 and 1997 would have raised significant doubts about the government's ability to implement them. Even then the report recommends, and rightly so, that the management and the staff of the Fund should have in-depth political analysis, from outside if possible, as a prelude to designing Fund programmes.

The report candidly points to the political pressure from influential stakeholders (read the US and the other financially powerful industrial countries) which influences the Fund's decisions and underlies the phenomenon of prolonged use. Recognising on pragmatic grounds that political considerations cannot be banished from the Fund's decisions, the report takes a practical position. It asks whether "a problem arises if political considerations are seen to override technical considerations, leading the IMF to support programmes that have a low probability of success." This would raise concerns that "the principle of uniformity of treatment across countries may not be upheld and it could also encourage a lax approach to implementation by the borrowing country." The report questions, with impeccable logic, the Fund's existing guidelines about programmes under which the Managing Director will recommend that the Executive Board approve a member's request for Fund resources "when it is his judgement that the programme...will be carried out." It is almost impossible, according to the authors of the report, that an absolute judgement can be made on technical grounds. In practice, however, all such judgements "about the likelihood that a programme will be implemented and whether it will achieve its objectives if implemented can only be made in a probabilistic sense, based on clear assessment of the risks and trade-offs for both the member country and the world community." The present procedure does not make a sufficiently sharp distinction between the technical assessment of the risks and the judgements involved in weighing those risks, "which is where any political considerations should presumably enter." That is well said. Once the political factors are well defined, let the chips fall where they would and the whole process of programme formulation, its feasibility, appropriateness and desirability will be transparent, making it easy to establish a line of accountability between the management, the Board and the staff.

The report has provided, for the first time, insights into the thought processes of the staff which formulates the programmes. First, the Fund's organisational structure is such that there is a tendency for the staff comprising the mission to 'over-promise'. The procedures relating to Board approval require the staff to show at least substantial progress towards viability within the programme period, along with net repayments by the member after the expiration of the programme. The report, basing itself on the survey results, states that a majority of the mission chiefs surveyed said that the need of balance of payments viability by the end of the medium-term projection period led to their ex-ante over-optimistic projections or over-ambitious programme objectives. This creates "a cumulative impression of poor implementation on the part of the borrowing countries and also poor programme design on the part of the Fund, eroding credibility of both."

The general perception that Fund conditionality has elements of punishment built into it rather than of reward draws support from the sharp observation of the report that "the internal review process gives a premium to 'toughness' over realism in the setting of programme targets." What is even more disturbing is that most of the mission chiefs surveyed by the IEO "felt somewhat strongly that their individual performance appraisal would be better if they were 'tougher' in negotiations with the authorities of the borrowing countries." It is not for nothing that the Fund has acquired a reputation as being insensitive to the problems of developing countries. The attitude of the staff is seen to be especially egregious when their inadequate knowledge-base and the narrowness of their specialisation are already creating problems in designing programmes, as underlined at various places in the report. The Fund's bureaucracy is averse to learning from experience and to refashioning their operations. The country case studies suggest "that a slow absorption of lessons and broader policy guidance into actual operations on systemic basis contributed to weaknesses in programme effectiveness and hence to prolonged use. However, it is clearly not a phenomenon that is special to prolonged use cases."

Apart from the internal factors ratcheting up the length of programmes, the report has done well to draw attention to the systemic factors, 'the gatekeeper role' of the Fund, in providing signals for other resource flows. Fund financing to countries is considered by other donors as a "seal of approval" of policies adopted by those countries. Given that the Fund's forte is its insistence on a sound economic policy framework and stable macroeconomic environment, which are indispensable for the effective use of aid, donors take the Fund's involvement as signalling that the countries concerned would use other resources as well. While the apparent logic of this signalling role of the Fund is understandable, the basic question which the report pertinently raises is whether the same signal could not be given by the Fund through some other device, such as surveillance, which will not have the features affecting adversely the effectiveness of the programmes which Fund financing has. However, such an alternative is ruled out by the donor countries, particularly the Paris Club members, on the ground of 'burden sharing' and also because of their fear about the large net repayments being made to the Fund. The so-called gatekeeper's role of the Fund in a way indicates the overbearing attitude of the influential member countries and also their presumption that the Fund is an informal guarantor for their lending to the prolonged users. This admittedly distorts the basis of programme design and introduces elements in the Fund's policies extraneous to the main objectives of the Fund.

As against this, the attitude of private creditors has been generally more relaxed in recent years. IMF financing was taken as a signal if the debtor country was negotiating rescheduling or restructuring agreements with private creditors, as in the period after the debt crisis of the early 1980s, and this did contribute to prolonged use at the time—the case of the Philippines, for instance—but now the importance of this factor has substantially diminished. There are many instances of debt restructuring by private creditors that were completed despite Fund-supported programmes having gone off-track. The report concludes that there are better and more effective alternatives to the signalling role of the Fund, provided that (i) the information needs of the donor community are suitably addressed; (ii) they deliver candid analysis of social and economic conditions and prospects; and (iii) they provide a clear assessment that the member's policies are strong enough to be supported. The alternatives that are suggested are the use of strengthened surveillance, reliance on joint staff assessments of Poverty Reduction Strategy Papers (PRSPs), shadow programmes and precautionary arrangements. These alternatives aim at developing a mix of tools that could deliver a seal of approval in different ways, depending on the member's circumstances, in particular its eligibility for the Poverty Reduction and Growth Facility (PRGF) and for the Heavily Indebted Poor Country (HIPC) initiatives, donor/creditor requirements, and the strength of the member's policies and institutions. Such forms of enhanced surveillance may even have an advantage over lending arrangements since they can have a longer-term and broader focus covering all elements of a country's economic strategy.

One would have expected that such a rich analysis of the Fund's policies—relentlessly outspoken, objective, based on a careful sifting of facts and the Fund's policies and procedures and survey of responses from stakeholders, political scientists and borrowing countries, would lead to matching radical recommendations. In that regard, however, the report is something of a let-down. It has made sensible suggestions on procedures, staff orientation and management leadership which, if accepted, would no doubt go a long way to change the image of the Fund and improve its credibility. But on two major issues it has not shown sufficient boldness in recommending changes in the Fund's policies and governance which logically follow from its own elaborate, well-conceived and theoretically sound analysis.

'One of the basic reasons the authors have cited for prolonged use of Fund resources is the intractable structural problem faced by prolonged users. Now, these structural issues are predominantly in respect of poverty reduction programmes and long-term institution building, which form the core of the Fund's programmes such as ESAF (now known as PRGF) and Extended Fund Facility (EFF). The report should have asked itself whether these issues, important as they are, really fall in the Fund's domain and whether the Fund is organisationally equipped to cope with them. The Fund of late has deviated far too much from its originally chosen path by chasing a multiplicity of objectives and in the process has lost its bearings. As Jean Tirole has said,

> ...too many objectives are conferred on the agency within the policy debate on the role of the IMF. These objectives create a lack of focus; furthermore, they are often conflict-ing. A multilateral institution, like any other organisation, should not be a Jack of all trades and master of none...multi-dimensional criteria bode no good economics, and a coherent analysis requires a clearly stated objective function.... (Tirole, 2002).

Tirole specifically refers to the Fund's PRGF in this context: "The refocusing of the IMF should lead...to its abandoning the anti-poverty programmes, leaving them to the World Bank", which "would also gain in focus in the process."

The other issue ignored by the report relates to IMF's governance. It is now well recognised even within the Fund that decision-making in the Fund is dominated by the views of the major industrial countries, especially the US. As a result, the Fund's programmes have not remained purely matters of technical decision-making any more and are directly or indirectly modulated by the powerful members of the Fund. This is put somewhat differently by Tirole:

> More generally, regional, cultural, strategic, or trade considerations imply that a group of powerful countries within the organization have an incentive to lobby for lenient policies when a country fails to abide by its promises. Conversely, powerful countries

with no such vested interests but with high financial stakes in the crisis country may lobby for excessively harsh conditions.

The authors of the report, to their credit, do recognise this problem, as is reflected in the quotation in the report from a Pakistani official that "most IMF-supported programmes primarily served political purposes. Thus it should come as no surprise that they did not achieve much in terms of economic results." However, the report has balked from linking that analysis to the corpus of its recommendations. As argued at the beginning of this essay, most of the criticism of the Fund's programme conditionality is traceable to the influence of the powerful countries in fashioning it, which leaves the voiceless developing countries out in the cold. As a result, governments of these countries find it difficult to sell the hard conditionality imposed on them as borrowers to their constituencies back home, which equate it with loss of sovereignty. Perhaps the IEO may not pull its punches in its forthcoming reports.

All said, this is a landmark report which puts paid to the apprehensions of many sceptics that the IEO would turn out to be a stooge of the Fund's management, providing post-facto rationalisation of the Fund's policies through command performances. These doubts have been set at rest. Though the report may not satisfy all the critics, it is an intellectually and professionally honest effort. Whether it will calm the waters, only time will tell.

REFERENCES

Dixit, Avinash (2000). "IMF programmes as incentive mechanisms", *Princeton University*. June (unpublished).

Van Houtven, Leo (2002). *Governance of the IMF: Decision Making, Institutional Oversight*, Transparency and Accountability. Washington DC: IMF.

Tirole, J. (2002). *Financial Crises: Liquidity and the International Monetary System*. New York: Macmillan.

Published in the Economic and Political Weekly XXXVII(46): 4627–32 (2002).

24 | The Financial Crisis
Chasing Shadows

The East Asian financial and currency crisis has caught everyone on the wrong foot, both because it was totally unanticipated, and it was so severe and pervasive.[1] The International Monetary Fund (IMF), the accredited vigilante of the monetary system, whose principal function is to maintain a close and continuous surveillance over member countries' domestic macroeconomic policies having international consequences, totally missed the mark, even in gauging the short-term foreign exchange liabilities of Korea, Indonesia and Thailand; though it claimed that it warned Thailand confidentially six months before it was enveloped in the turmoil. It put forth a feeble defence that it was denied the necessary information by the countries concerned, without, however, explaining why it failed to evaluate and analyse the information which the Bank for International Settlements (BIS) regularly puts out. Academics, who until recently marvelled at the Asian miracle, came out a cropper in providing a cogent and convincing answer to the issues raised by the crisis, not to speak of those who sought to explain the East Asian growth in terms of political economy. The crisis even eluded the credit rating agencies which are supposed to know the markets well.

Once the Asian financial crisis deepened at around end-1997, threatening not only the economies in the region but also other emerging economies in Latin America and Central Europe, there was no alternative for the affected countries but to approach the IMF for resources to meet foreign exchange liabilities and stabilise their currencies. The IMF response and the policies it packaged were no different from those adopted in respect of Mexico in 1995. The Fund, true to its institutional ethos, emphasised the macroeconomic imbalances, and designed programmes with a heavy accent on fiscal retrenchment, high interest rates, and all that. These macroeconomic policy measures were supplemented by advice on structural reforms, such as restoring

---

(This is a revised and expanded version of the author's lecture at the Bank Negara Malaysia on 22 December, 1997.)

1. Even Paul Krugman, who was perhaps the first to challenge the myth of the East Asian miracle, did not predict the crisis of this proportion and its timing. As he recently said in a Boston meeting of global investors, "I was 90 per cent wrong, while others were 150 per cent wrong."

the banking system to solvency, wholesale restructuring of the corporate sector, and changes in public expenditure pattern, which have now become a new mantra in all Fund programmes. Despite the implementation of these programmes, the turmoil continued with the same fury until end-1997. Only when Thailand and Korea started negotiating for rolling over short-term foreign exchange liabilities for a further three to six months and subsequently arrangement to convert short-term bank loans into medium-term bonds did the severity of the crisis begin to abate. Even the Indonesian imbroglio, made worse by bad politics enmeshed with bad economics, seemed to be getting on track of a solution with a renegotiated Fund programme emphasising more liquidity relief than long-term structural reform.

The East Asian crisis throws up several questions. Was it a crisis deeply embedded into the structural policies and the political economy of the countries? Was the economic appraisal of these countries validated by the information that the IMF had gathered? Could it be that the IMF prescriptions exacerbated the malady and thereby raised the costs of adjustment needlessly higher than they should have been? Was it unambiguous that the Fund's advice was dispassionate and was not biased by the hidden agenda of the foreign economic policy of the US in particular and the OECD in general? In what follows, an attempt will be made to offer explanations for the several riddles, some based on facts now unearthed, some on the recent changes in the Fund programmes, and some on inferential logic. Towards the end, certain issues bearing on the future evolution of the international monetary system will be raised, particularly in the context of new ideas about the reform of the Fund that are currently in the air.

EAST ASIAN FINANCIAL CRISIS: PHANTOM AND REALITY

Early warnings of the impending East Asian debacle were sounded by the mounting pressure on exchange rate of Thailand towards the end of 1996, but the first powerful speculative attack took place during the first quarter of 1997. Several factors, such as high and rising current account deficit, busting of the asset price bubble, and the pursuit of fixed exchange rate parity were cited as the proximate reasons for the speculative attack on the Thai baht. Thailand had an exchange rate regime with baht fixed with US dollar for almost a decade, as it provided an anchor for its non-inflationary monetary policy. This served the Thai economy well for many years. A large current account deficit was also not a new phenomenon. However, the baht-dollar parity and the current account deficit were viewed as unsustainable by the market, when Thai export growth rate reflected a secular decline. This opened the door for huge arbitrage profits from currency speculation. Before it could spill across to other countries, the Thai authorities attempted to fend off the crisis through spot and forward exchange market intervention (IMF, 1997a; Colaco, 1997). However, the success achieved was ephemeral as the basic cause of liquidity shortage was not tackled. The second wave of speculative attack during May–July 1997 soon engulfed the authorities. This time around the Thai crisis proved contagious, spreading to Indonesia, Malaysia, the Philippines, Korea and even to Hong Kong and Singapore. As a result, the currencies of all these countries depreciated sharply in terms of the US dollar.

While other East Asian countries were sucked into the crisis triggered by Thailand, the countries affected most were Korea and Indonesia. Malaysia and the Philippines allowed their currencies to float and Malaysia in particular suspended some of its mega projects, in order to reduce imports and cut expenditure to be accommodated by available foreign exchange resources. Though Malaysia's banking system had similar problems as those faced by Thailand, a better prudential control and supervision could minimise the risk to its banking system at least initially, arising from the depreciated exchange rate and its impact on the quality of bank assets. The Philippines survived the crisis relatively unscathed, first because it had restructured its banking system during the mid-1980s financial crisis and its corporate sector was relatively healthy with a rising rate of exports in contrast to the other crisis-afflicted East Asian countries.

The countries severely damaged were Korea and Indonesia. Once the currency declined their financial sectors and the corporate sectors, as lender and borrower, were involved in losses. The Korean banks had already a high proportion of non-performing assets amounting to as much as 15–20 per cent of the total bank credit (Dalla and Khatkhate, 1995); this ratio climbed further when the corporate sector's liabilities to foreigners in terms of domestic currency increased as a result of currency depreciation. In Indonesia's case the situation deteriorated even more, as the complexities surrounding the Suharto regime supervened in the management of the economy.

Before analysing the causes of the East Asian crisis it is useful to see if it resembles in any way the Mexican crisis of 1995. This is important not only to know the anatomy of financial crisis in East Asia but also to evaluate whether the policy prescriptions of the Fund and other international organisations were appropriate to remedy their ailment. Superficially, similarity is observed between Thailand, Korea and Indonesia on the one hand and Mexico on the other in three respects (IMF, 1997b). First of all, these economies had large inflows of capital. Thus, net foreign capital inflows into Thailand, Korea and Indonesia during 1989–1996 were of the order of $137 billion. Secondly, all the three countries had a current account deficit varying in a range of 2–8 per cent during this period. Note, however, that it was only Thailand which had the higher and growing current account deficit while that of Korea and Indonesia was modest enough to be financed by normal recourse to financing. Thirdly, as in the case of Mexico, all the three countries' nominal and real exchange rates were appreciating, following the US dollar appreciation *vis-à-vis* the Japanese yen, thereby eroding to some extent their export competitiveness. On the other hand, there were sharp differences between Mexico on the one hand and Korea, Thailand, and Indonesia on the other. Unlike Mexico these economies had strong fundamentals—their fiscal position was always in balance often yielding surplus, high investment and saving ratios, large foreign exchange balances, and relative price stability. Capital inflows financed investment rather than consumption, both in the public and private sectors. In Mexico, on the other hand, the large current account deficit was a reflection of a sustained increase in private consumption. As a result, the saving rate of the private sector, which was around 20 per cent of GDP in 1988, plummeted to 17 per cent during 1991–1994. Apart from this, the triggering factor in the Mexico crisis was the sharp rise in the public sector's short-term liabilities to foreigners. When the current account widened and the fiscal deficit increased, foreign investors perceived this as indicating the inability of the authorities to repay their short-term foreign debt. In contrast, in Korea, Indonesia and Thailand, it was the private short-term foreign debt which was the main cause for the investors' panic reaction and consequent currency speculation.

There is no uniformity of views on the causes of the financial and currency crises in East Asia. At one end, they are ascribed to macroeconomic policies of the countries concerned, while at the other end they are sought to be explained by the structural weaknesses of their economies.[2] In the December

2. Jeffrey Sachs (1997) has identified three types of international financial crises. First, the currency crisis is traced to fiscal crisis when the government loses the ability to roll over foreign debts and to attract new loans, forcing it to seek rescheduling or default. Second, the market participants abruptly shift their preferences from domestic currency assets to foreign currency assets in the context of a pegged exchange rate. Third, commercial banks abruptly lose the ability to roll over market instruments (CDS) or to meet a sudden withdrawal of funds from sight deposits, thereby forcing banks into illiquidity. Note that the East Asian crisis does not conform to any of these, except tangentially the second one.

1997 issue of *World Economic Outlook* of the Fund, four sets of factors have been adduced to explain the crisis. They are:

(1) The very success of these economies in attaining high growth through high private saving-investment rates seems to have sowed the seeds of the crisis. Though the rates of private domestic saving were rising, they were outpaced by private domestic investment rates supported by inflows of foreign capital. Thus, the current account deficit was accounted for by the deficit in the private sector balance rather than that of the public sector. The capital flows posed challenges for deploying them in the most efficient manner as well as their prudent intermediation through financial systems, which were neither well developed nor sound in these countries. It was particularly so when the capital inflow was short-term, liable to be reversed at the slightest hint of trouble arising from macroeconomic policy inconsistencies or the vulnerability of the financial systems or inappropriate exchange rate policies.

(2) The second set of factors resided in the international environment. During the first half of the 1990s, when the industrial countries suffered from weak economic performance, necessitating low interest rates and low returns on assets, investors in those countries turned to the emerging markets in Asia and elsewhere in search of higher returns on their savings and for diversification of risks. Such movement of funds has a natural tendency to reverse if the prospect of high returns turns sour. This seems to have happened towards the end of 1997, with a rise in short-term interest rates in the US, resumption of growth both in Europe and Japan, and sustained appreciation of the US dollar in terms of yen, eroding the export competitiveness of East Asia.

(3) The third set of factors contributing to the East Asian crisis is reflected in growing current account deficits, inflation rate higher than in partner countries, and a rise in asset prices. In some cases, such as Korea, a true fiscal deficit was not as tight as it appeared to be on the surface because of extra-budgetary and quasi-fiscal operations. Furthermore, the credit to the private sector accelerated between 1992 and 1995 in the affected East Asian countries and this was troublesome, when much of it was financed by banks incurring foreign exchange liabilities.

(4) The fourth set of factors related to the financial sector weaknesses and other structural weaknesses in the East Asian economies, which made them vulnerable to adverse developments in the international environment.

However, a closer analysis shows that these factors, barring perhaps the appreciated exchange rates of the East Asian currencies, have a poor explanatory power. Most of these factors were present in these economies even when they were booming and persisted over almost a decade, if not longer. If they were the real causes of the crisis, the financial crisis should have come much earlier.

Let us look at each of the four sets of factors which the Fund employed to explain the East Asian crisis. The main focus of the first set of factors is on the excess of private sector investment over its saving that is financed by foreign capital—mainly short term. Since the investment was not efficient, the crisis became inevitable when there were adverse developments in external conditions which either slowed the inflows of foreign capital or spurred the outflows. Figure 4 of the *World Economic Outlook* of the Fund, where the East Asian crisis is analysed, does not seem to support the Fund's conclusion. In none of the countries—Indonesia, Thailand, Malaysia and the Philippines—was private investment lower than private savings since 1989. This phenomenon was always there and in fact was the main pillar of the so-called East Asian miracle. If this provided the main impetus for growth without untoward consequences so long, there was no reason whatsoever to believe that it could suddenly turn a malevolent agent to propel the crisis. There is also no basis to infer that investment turned unproductive or inefficient only since the early 1990s. In Korea's case the excess of investment in private sector over its saving was minuscule and could not have been a determining factor in precipitating the crisis.

The second set of factors, *viz.*, reversal of capital flows to East Asia in view of resumption of growth in Europe and Japan and the rising short-term interest rates in the US, has some merit but it does not explain why it should result in a massive capital flight from East Asia. Furthermore, the ebb and flow of capital characterised the industrial countries even in the past decade but without spawning crisis.

Elsewhere, the Fund has cited persistent adherence to the fixed exchange rate as one of the policy missteps accounting for the crisis (Fischer, 1998). However, the experiences do not unequivocally support the proposition that crisis in emerging markets can be avoided under the flexible exchange rates regime, as the Fund's *World Economic Outlook* of September 1997 had documented. Of the 23 currency crises during 1975–1981, half were under flexible exchange rate arrangements; of the 49 crises during 1982–1989, 19 were under flexible exchange rate regimes; and during 1990–1996, out of 45 crises,

25 were again under flexible exchange rates. This apart, it is arguable whether all the East Asian countries could be considered to boast fixed exchange rate regimes. Korea certainly was not and Indonesia allowed the exchange rate to move in a range. Malaysia was not a rigid follower of the fixed parity. Only Hong Kong and Thailand fell in that category. Even in the case of Thailand the fixed exchange rate was an aggravating rather than an initiating force behind the crises.

Among the third set of factors having a bearing on the East Asian crisis were rising inflation rates, acceleration in bank credit, current account deficits and asset price inflation, all of which were attributed to the burgeoning capital inflows. Table 24.1, again taken from the Fund's December 1997 *World Economic Outlook*, does not quite corroborate this analysis.

The rate of inflation (Table 24.1), never so high in Indonesia, Korea, Malaysia and Thailand, the countries which were prominent hostages to the currency crisis, hardly accelerated except in Thailand and even there an inflation rate at an average of 6 per cent could not be such a cataclysmic event so as to trigger a crisis. It is also difficult to argue, as the Fund seems to do, that though the inflation rate in the crisis-afflicted East Asian countries was modest, it was higher than "the weighted average of trading partners' inflation rates thus contributing to the erosion of competitiveness" (IMF, 1997b). The inflation differential between the East Asian countries and the partner countries such as Japan and even the US does not seem to have increased much (IMF, 1997b: Appendix Table B3 on inflation). Rapid bank expansion, which the Fund identified as the main culprit, was also not so high as to cause any angst to the authorities. In fact, except in Malaysia, bank credit growth during 1995–1997 was much less in Indonesia, Korea, and even Thailand, than during 1983–1990. Only Malaysia recorded a rate of credit growth during 1995–1997 which was almost double that during 1983–1990. The same story can be repeated in respect of current account deficits. Indonesia always ran such deficit since 1983, but it remained modest around 2 per cent and though it reached 3 per cent during 1995–1997, it was by no means unsustainable. However, in Korea's case the average current account surplus of 2.2 per cent of GDP during 1983–90 turned into an average deficit of 1.4 per cent during 1991–1994, which rose to 4 per cent of GDP during 1995–1997. Though Thailand's deficit widened during 1996-97, it was not such as to cause any concern as Thailand always had such deficits in a range of 3–6 per cent over a long period during 1983-84.

Table 24.1

Rates of Inflation, Bank Credit and Current Account Deficit for
Selected East Asian Countries, 1983–1997 (Averages)

	Indonesia			Korea			Malaysia			Thailand		
	1983–90	1991–94	1995–97	1983–90	1991–94	1995–97	1983–90	1991–94	1995–97	1983–90	1991–94	1995–97
Inflation	8	8.7	8.3	4.3	6.6	4.6	2.08	3.6	3.5	3.4	4.6	6
Bank credit expansion (percentage charge)	49.4	19.2	22	23	16.3	17.05	19.6	15.5	29.5	20.5	21.2	14
Current account balance (as per cent of GDP)	–3.1	–2.2	–3.1	2.2	–1.4	–4	–0.8	–6.3	–6.9	–3.7	–5.9	–6.6

Source: The IMF, World Economic Outlook, December 1997.

This brings us to the last of the set of four factors, which is supposed to have been a leading cause of the East Asian crisis. This pertains to the financial sector weaknesses and other structural fragility in the economies (meaning the borrowing corporate sector and its high leverage) which lowered the quality of investment, thereby exposing it to adverse economic developments. The assignment of this factor to the crisis in Indonesia, Korea and Thailand is so befuddled that it is difficult to decipher its logic and reasoning. The Fund's *World Economic Outlook* of December 1997 states,

> As events unfolded, weaknesses in the financial sector became particularly stark in Thailand, Indonesia and Korea, although lack of transparency delayed public realisation of the scale of the problems...Inadequacies in the regulation and supervision of financial institutions—as well as limited experience among financial institutions in the pricing and managing of risk, lack of commercial orientation, poor corporate governance, and lax internal controls—all in the face of movements toward liberalization and increased competitive pressures, had contributed to imprudent lending including lending associated with relationship banking and corrupt practices. The vulnerability of financial institutions in asset quality became clear in 1996-97 as a result of the economic slowdown, tighter financial policies, declines in domestic real estate and equity markets, and eventually currency depreciations that placed in difficulty customers with uncovered foreign currency liabilities. This eventually became apparent in the scale of non-performing loans threatening the institutions' liquidity and solvency. (IMF, 1997b: 22–23).

This extensive quote from the important Fund document is given only to place in bold relief how the underlying reasoning is warped and anachronistic and confuses effect with cause. For one thing, weaknesses in the financial sectors and a lack of transparency in their operations are not a new phenomenon nor are the deficiencies in the regulatory scaffolding of the financial system. These have been in existence, being a part of the hoary but now debased industrial policy, which was credited with bringing about the Asian miracle. These shortcomings, institutional and policy-related, have been in each phase of their economic cycle—upswing and downswing—and though there were minor blips now and then, the countries kept up their progress. The so-called imprudent lending by the banking systems was also a characteristic feature of these economies during their heyday. In fact, it was taken as a part of the virtuous cycle, applauded in the past as an ingenious device of establishing non-market institutions to achieve market-oriented results. All together thus, this explanation does not answer the question why the same benevolent institutional and policy architecture suddenly became an instrument of their downfall.

Similarly, the non-performing assets of the banking systems in Thailand, Korea and Indonesia did not suddenly surface during 1996-97. Those who have been familiar with their financial systems were aware of the balance sheet vulnerability of the banks in Thailand and Korea. In fact, one study (Dalla and Khatkhate, 1995) has pointedly emphasised how the non-performing assets of the Korean banking system were grossly understated, not in 1995 alone but even during the 1980s, when the countries were undergoing financial liberalisation. This implies that the phenomenon of financial system weaknesses was not an immediate or even a distant cause of the East Asian financial and currency crisis, though it assumed ominous dimensions once the currency flight in 1997, prolonged by the ill-designed Fund programmes raised the cost of foreign debt in terms of domestic currency.

Lastly, the argument that "eventually currency depreciations...placed in difficulty customers with uncovered foreign currency liabilities" puts the cart before the horse. The currency depreciation was not caused by the financial sector fragility but was the result of capital flight induced by some other factors. But once the currency depreciated, the woes of the financial system multiplied as an aftermath.

Thus, the Fund's diagnosis of the East Asian malaise is flawed, and though it got some elements right, the overall analytic underpinning is inadequate to explain why the East Asian crisis erupted when it did. Even economists, often the avowed critics of the Fund's policies in regard to the East Asian crisis, seem to have misjudged the proximate causes of the crisis episode. Paul Krugman emphasised the over-guaranteed private sector and over-regulated financial sector that "blew the bubble bound to burst" (Krugman, 1997). This explanation is similar to that of the Fund inasmuch as it overplays the interventionist regimes in Thailand, Korea and Indonesia, which were responsible for their rapid growth until 1996. Radelet and Sachs (1998) suggested that the problem of these economies lay in panic, which albeit rational for each institution, turned what was a necessary and modest adjustment into a catastrophe. Here again, there is no clue in their analysis to the factor which triggered a crisis only in mid-1997, in Thailand, which then spread like a bush-fire to all other countries in the region, but with devastating impact only in Indonesia and Korea.

An alternative rationale for the East Asian crisis is offered below. As noted earlier, the rate of investment in the private sector in Thailand, Korea and Indonesia always exceeded the sector's rates of saving, with the excess being financed by borrowings abroad, and there is no firm evidence to believe that the quality of investment was high even during the 1980s. The low-grade investment was sustained and foreign borrowings supporting it could be repaid because the exports were buoyant during the last two decades of their growth. The weakening of export markets of these countries is well supported by Figure 7 in the *World Economic Outlook* of December 1997. However, the reasons for it go beyond what the Fund has recognised. It is true that the partner countries' imports (i.e. the exports of these countries) started declining because of slackening of activities in the industrial countries and the glut in the global electronics market, but the real cause is in the fact that the East Asian growth was driven mainly by capital and labour inputs rather than by productivity increase (Krugman, 1994). Once a country attains full employment of labour and the capital per worker reaches a highly industrialised country's level, diminishing returns set in. Korea, Thailand and Indonesia thus lost ground in labour-intensive goods to their competitors such as China, Vietnam and other South Asian countries. And because of poor productivity growth, they could not compete with the industrial countries in regard to capital-intensive exports. Once this impetus of exports weakened, the low quality of investment tended to become a drag on their economies, which in turn affected their foreign debt servicing capacity particularly in the context of ballooning of very short-term foreign exchange liabilities of their private sectors (Table 24.2).

Table 24.2

International Bank Lending to Selected East Asian Countries

(Billion US dollars)

China	55.0
Indonesia	55.5
Korea	100.0
Malaysia	22.2
Philippines	13.3
Thailand	70.3

Source: Bank for International Settlements, as reproduced in IMF, *World Economic Outlook*, December 1997.

Except Malaysia and the Philippines, the short-term foreign exchange liabilities were increasing, costing as high as 7–10 per cent of GDP in Thailand but lower at 3–4 per cent of GDP in Korea and Indonesia. A bulk of these liabilities fell due for repayment toward the end of 1997. It is thus clear that large short-term foreign liabilities, together with a weak productivity growth, resulting in declining exports of Korea, Thailand and Indonesia were the real and immediate factors that created apprehension in the minds of foreign investors that these countries would be hard put to meet their repayment commitments when they fall due, particularly in the context that their foreign exchange reserves (assuming that the declared figures were reliable) constituted a small and declining proportion of repayment commitment. This opened a fertile field for speculators to make a killing. Once the speculative frenzy seized the market psychology, the currencies—baht, won and rupiah—had a free fall. Thus, it was the short term liquidity crisis which threatened to transform into a solvency crisis.[3]

ROLE OF THE IMF

Faced with a severe liquidity crisis, all these countries approached the Fund for liquidity support. The Fund came up with the packages in cooperation with the US, European Union, and the East Asian countries to assist them. For Thailand the amount involved was $17 billion, which escalated to $43 billion in respect of Indonesia and $57 billion for Korea. The total assistance was unprecedented in the history of the Fund.

The concept of the Fund as a lender of the first resort is predicated on the assumption that once the Fund makes available its resources with policy strings attached, the economies of the borrowing countries will turn around, though not immediately, paving the way for private investors to reassess the risks. This implies that the conditionality should be such as to help to eliminate the causes of disturbance. The programmes the Fund designed for Thailand, Korea and Indonesia were based on its perception of the problems. As argued earlier, since the Fund's analysis missed the trees for the wood, its programmes were made to stand on their heads, thereby raising the cost of adjustment disproportionately. The programmes were clones of what the Fund had applied to Mexico in 1995, despite the fact that Mexico's crisis and the underlying fundamentals were totally different. In East Asia, the crisis emanated from the private sector debt. However, since the Fund has over the years assisted countries whose problems arose from the public sector deficit, it came naturally to it to design conditions suitable only for disciplining the public sector. This meant retrenchment of public expenditure, fiscal consolidation, and higher interest rates. Added to these were the structural measures of weeding out of weakest banks, restructuring of salvageable banks, improving prudential control, and revamping of the corporate structure, removal of the residue of

---

3. Only Martin Feldstein, of all economists, seems to have put his finger on the right provenance of the East Asian crisis. Citing particularly the Korean case, he argues that its crisis was due to "temporary illiquidity rather than fundamental insolvency" (Feldstein, 1998; see also Tobin and Ranis, 1998).

price controls, etc.[4] With all these measures agreed to and implemented (the exception is Indonesia because of the political dynamics peculiar to it), the currency crisis continued unabated both in Thailand and Korea. With every fall in currencies, the liquidity problems of both the financial systems and corporate sectors cascaded into insolvency problems because the depreciated currencies translated themselves into their rising debt denominated in domestic currencies. Only when Thailand first and Korea next started negotiations with the private foreign creditors, i.e. banks, for roll over of short-term credit for a period of three months until March-end 1998 and to further convert it into medium-term bonds, was the financial crisis tamed.

The Indonesian case stands apart, being clouded by the diverting acrimonious relationship between the Fund, backed up by the US and the European Union on the one hand, and Indonesia on the other. However, the real issues were submerged, by design or accident, in the cacophony of statements on the currency board option floated all round. The currency board was motivated by the concern to staunch the continuous fall in *rupiah*, though there is truth in the insinuation that the Suharto regime had an ulterior motive in backing a currency board. Many of the elements in the Fund's programmes accented on long-term solutions like restructuring of banks and improving corporate governance, which could not have helped to prevent a free fall. The ongoing negotiations between Fund and Indonesian authorities seem to have confronted the liquidity problem and as a result the newly negotiated programme will include up-front a Mexico-type debt-restructuring under which the short-term debt repayment would be at a fixed exchange rate. Structural reforms such as financial system restitution, de-monopolisation of some industries, etc. are likely to be placed on the back burner. These arrangements, in essence, despite the protestation of the Fund and the US government, reflect an entry of the currency board through a backdoor, which is a tacit admission that the Fund's earlier programme was wrongly designed.

---

4. One can argue legitimately for high interest rates to prevent the outflow of foreign and even domestic capital, but the way the IMF formulated the programme increased the cost of adjustment unnecessarily. This has been well put by Feldstein (1998) in the case of Korea.

   Under the IMF plan, the interest rate on won loan is now about 30 per cent, while inflation is only 5 per cent. Because of the high debt typical of most Korean companies, this enormously high real interest rate of 25 percent puts all of them at risk of bankruptcy. Why should Korea be forced to cause widespread bankruptcies by tightening credit when inflation is very low, when the roll over of bank loans and the demand for won depends more on confidence than on Korean won interest rates, when the failures will reduce the prospect of loan repayment, and when a further fall in the won is an alternative to high interest rates as a way to attract non-denominated deposits?

What does this gamesmanship of the Fund indicate? It shows clearly that many ingredients of the Fund's programmes were misconceived and misplaced and the Fund pummelled the East Asian countries needlessly for its own failure to understand the anatomy of the crisis. To bank on fiscal consolidation, closing of banks, etc., the standard Fund programme is to start with the wrong end of the stick. What instead the Fund should have done, but did not, is first to arrange for the roll over of the countries' short-term foreign liabilities in concert with the creditors, subject to the condition that the countries would agree to undertake subsequently structural reform over a defined time period. The Fund's declared support, coming as it does from an international surveillance body, would have calmed the markets, thereby staunching the haemorrhage of the currencies. With currency fall so checked, the flow of new non-performing assets of banks would have been arrested as also new bankruptcies prevented. Negotiating for roll over or lengthening the maturity of short-term liabilities would have forced the creditors to pay the price for their own reckless lending prior to the crisis, insulating the Fund from the charges that it is a willing party to moral hazard. This is not to deny the desirability of elimination of structural deficiencies, but what is disputed is their sequencing in the immediacy of the crisis. To insist on structural reforms at the very beginning of the implementation of programmes only prolonged the agony of the countries. In any case, the structural reforms the Fund advocated are not such as can be implemented in a jiffy, apart from the fact that structural weaknesses existed for a long time without hurting these economies (Feldstein, 1998). By opting for the Fund's resources the countries in distress seemed to have become turkeys voting for Christmas.

By front-loading the programmes with the fiscal-monetary policies together with the heavy accent on structural issues of competition, corporate restructuring and removal of restrictions on foreign ownership of the banking and financial services, the Fund helped its critics to raise serious questions about its credibility and impartiality. The grounds for such questioning were provided also by the close involvement of the US Treasury functionaries at all stages of negotiations with all the three countries, to the point that they appeared to be a joint operation. It is known that the US and other OECD countries have been pressing the East Asian countries to open their markets for foreign ownership in financial services and other segments of their corporate sectors. In Korea's case, such measures have been stipulated as preconditions for entry into OECD. By placing the structural reforms enabling foreign ownership of domestic firms in the East Asian countries ahead of liquidity relieving measures, the Fund played into the hands of its detractors that its advice was not dispassionate and it had its own hidden agenda in designing its programmes for the East Asian countries. Martin Feldstein, a former chairman of the Council of Economic Advisors under the Republican administration, who could not by any stretch of imagination be considered to be anti-American, is persuaded by the Fund's programmes to suspect the Fund's neutrality.

> Several features of the IMF plans are replays of the policies that Japan and the United States have long been trying to get Korea to adopt. These included accelerating the previously agreed upon reductions of trade barriers to specific Japanese products and opening capital market so that foreign investors can have majority ownership of Korean firms, engage in hostile takeovers opposed by local management, and expand direct participation in banking and other financial services. Others saw this aspect of the plan as an abuse of IMF power to force Korea at a time of weakness to accept trade and investment policies it had previously rejected (Feldstein, 1998).

But the Fund's culpability is not confined to its misplaced programme designs and the wrong-headedness in rushing through with their implementation. The way the East Asian crisis unfolded took not only those outside the cloistered chambers of the Fund by surprise but also the Fund management itself, which is supposed to have information on a regular basis to monitor the world economy, and that too after its chastening experience in the Mexican crisis three years earlier. The Fund tried to put a spin on it, saying that in private consultations with Thailand since mid-1996, it had drawn to the attention of the country the stark reality of the impending crisis, and in the case of Korea the managing director had paid an incognito visit in October 1997 to warn the authorities. The Fund was helpless since these countries had no programmes with the Fund for the last several years. Despite the drama and thrills surrounding secret confabulations, the facts revealed subsequently exposed the hollowness of the claim. Thailand had $70 billion short-term liabilities and Korea about $100 billion, which came to light only when the negotiations with the Fund were initiated. The Fund's defence was that it had no source of information other than what the authorities disclosed during the Article IV consultations. This is indeed a very lame and self-serving defence. For one thing, even assuming that the facts were not forthcoming from the official sources, the Fund could have obtained them—at least reasonable estimates—from the market participants which its staff interviews regularly in the course of its annual report on the capital markets as a part of its surveillance. For another, it is covering up its gross failure in doing its main job of surveillance of member countries by drawing a red herring across the trail. It is known to all financial markets and government authorities that the two semi-annual reports of the BIS put out a compressive data on foreign exchange liabilities of most of the countries. It does not reflect well on the competence and efficiency of the Fund's staff if it had not explored these reports thoroughly for the information most vital to the Fund's surveillance activities. Here is what the former highly respected BIS general manager, Alexandre Lamfalussy, has to say on this issue:

> The suggested improvement [that the BIS should speed up publication of its statistics on international bank lending] will surely do no harm but it will not do much good either as long as market-participants and other concerned parties fail to read publicly available information or to draw practical conclusions from it.
>
> In the summer of 1996, the BIS reported in its half-yearly statistics that by end-1995 the total of consolidated bank claims on South Korea, Thailand, Indonesia and Malaysia reached $201.6 billion. It reported in January 1997 that by mid-1996 the figure rose to $226.5 billion and, six months later that by end-1996 it reached $247.8 billion — an increase of 23 per cent in one year. For each of these dates, the maturity breakdown was available. It was therefore known by mid-summer 1996 that bank claims maturing within one year made up 70 per cent of the total for South Korea, 69.4 per cent for Thailand, 61.9 per cent for Indonesia, but 'only' 47.2 per cent for Malaysia.
>
> ...Apart from its sheer size four features characterised bank credit to Asia in 1995. First, two-thirds of the total was in the form of interbank credit lines...this together with the sizeable trade related loans meant that by mid-1995, 64 per cent of the outstanding claims on the region were less than one year. Secondly, Thailand and Korea took up $36.3 billion and $22.3 billion of new funds respectively. By year-end, Thailand had become the largest bank debtor in the developing world (Lamfalussy, 1998).

This quote shows how vacuous were the excuses offered by the Fund. Even worse was the Fund's upbeat certification of Korea's economic performance in its *World Economic Outlook* of September 1997—barely a month before the Fund's top management claims to have had a secret rendezvous with the Korean authorities.

Like the house of Bourbons, the Fund after being forgiven for its lapses in apprehending the approaching crisis in Mexico in 1995 forgot nothing. At least, it had some excuse in 1995 for not having the necessary data from the countries—Mexico being notoriously secretive in regard to data dissemination. The Fund, converting what could have been fatal for its reputation into an opportunity, appointed its retired counsellor to do a post-mortem on the Mexican crisis. The author of the report showed quick footwork by arguing that the nature of the problem the Fund was charged with resolving had changed, as capital accounts of the countries' balance of payments in globalised financial markets have superseded in urgency and importance their current accounts, and the Fund should gear itself to beef up information on it through special effort, as a part of its surveillance activities. With this end in view, the Fund instituted a Special Data Dissemination Standard (SODS), a unit to collect information from all countries. Easy access to information on subscribers' dissemination practices provided through an electronic bulletin board on the Internet's Worldwide Web is a cornerstone of the SODS. This is supposed to ensure that all countries furnish the data on timely basis and if any of them fails to do so the market participants would draw their own conclusions. While newfangled information technology could be an important aid for the Fund's surveillance, it does not absolve the Fund of its responsibility to marshal the available information. On this test, it has not distinguished itself. It is a very serious failure for a body whose major claim for existence is its role in surveillance over the member countries' economies to ensure a smooth working of the international monetary system. It therefore became a butt, and deservingly so, for the attack by academics like Martin Feldstein, the Bundesbank president Tietmeier, leading members of the European Union, and public interest groups at large.

DIVINING THE FUTURE OF THE IMF

With the developments in the international monetary arena since the early 1980s when the Latin American debt crisis emerged with its wide ramifications for the international monetary system, something more fundamental has changed in the nature of monetary and financial transactions amongst countries and within countries. The Bretton Woods system's *raison d'être* was in the effort to eliminate the forces that led to beggar-my-neighbour policies through competitive devaluations. This led to the formulation of certain defined rules for maintaining an order in exchange rates—and by implication the current accounts of the balance of payments of the countries. The IMF-anchored system served the purpose well, despite some hiccups, first in 1971, when the fixed exchange rate system was abandoned, allowing floating rates to replace it. However, the whole gamut of framework was transformed with the dismantling of controls on capital accounts of countries, the process first starting with the industrial countries and now extending to newly industrialised countries and several developing countries. With this the exchange rates no longer depend on merely the current account position of the countries. Even the equilibrium exchange rates consistent with viable and sustainable current accounts are apt to be thrown out of kilter by the swirling around of massive capital flows, not necessarily in response to the economic fundamentals. Such exigencies tend to create first a liquidity crisis of a temporary nature, which degenerates into a severe solvency crisis if prompt action is not taken. Since the magnitude of flows involved is massive, it is not easy even for the highly resource endowed institutions to resolve the crisis. There is besides another dimension, which was not present before the globalisation of the financial markets. The capital flows, whatever their maturity or nature, be it foreign direct investment (FDI) or portfolio capital, are mediated through the banking systems and unless they are sound and solvent, the capital flows cause not only severe problems in the macroeconomy but also lacerate the microeconomy. In other words, the policies needed to cope with the disturbances created by the capital flows have to embrace not only the balance of payments of the countries but also the very structure of their economies.

The issue therefore is whether the Fund as it is envisioned by its founders can deal with the crisis of the dimension of East Asia or any other of even greater magnitude that may emerge in the twenty-first century, if the nature of its functions is not altered and the scope of its activities expanded. Various ideas are being debated. The US as the epicentre of the world's financial markets has already been inching toward "modernising the architecture" of international finance, but its concept of that architecture is at best hazy. Alan Greenspan, the US Federal Reserve Bank chairman, while being content to have the Fund as "an old Tin Lizzie" to take countries to go fishing because walking would not get them there sufficiently quickly, would like to "craft a view of the longer term type of structure that is required". The only concrete suggestions are those of Soros, Henry Kaufman and academic Jeffrey Sachs.

- Soros' proposal is to recognise the necessity of intervention such as that by the Fund but requires the banks to pay for it, when the liquidity crisis takes place as a result of reckless lending by banks. To this end, he visualises a new international credit insurance corporation as an adjunct of the Fund that would charge a small fee on every international bank loan and use the proceeds to finance any rescue. Under this, there will be a ceiling on the amount of lending by any one country and minimum standards for bank regulation in countries receiving insured loans.

- The Kaufman scheme, embodying the essence of Soros' plan, is more grandiose. Its essential ingredient is in the improved global financial architecture. It calls for a new institution along with the Fund to overcome the inadequacies of current national and international structures for supervising and regulating financial institutions and markets. This is because every debt crisis originates from excessive and incompletely disclosed build-up of credit, unwise and at times corrupt lending practices and reckless exposure to foreign currency fluctuations. Its sweep is far reaching in that the body would eventually be required to rate the credit quality of market participants under its authority and would impose sanctions, if the financial institutions fail to abide by the rules. This would enable the Fund to organise funding emergency lending operations as it is doing currently, but without creating more hazard situations.

- Jeffrey Sachs' idea of formulating an international bankruptcy law, analogous to the domestic bankruptcy laws in many countries, is to prevent foreign investors from abandoning it when the confidence in a country weakens. With the bankruptcy law mechanism, the private lenders will not panic and withdraw their funds, knowing that all creditors will be treated equally as part of a negotiated restructuring process.

All these proposals, convincing in their own ways, can be considered to be no more than the building blocks for constructing an edifice of future monetary arrangements. A common thread running through all these proposals is still more power to the elbow of the Fund. It is legitimate to raise a question whether such concentration of power in a single institution is desirable. There can be three reservations about such an outcome. First, the Fund will be the sole repository of information and it will be difficult to know whether that information will be any more reliable than at present. Experience both in regard to the Mexico and East Asian crises shows that the Fund's information was inadequate, unreliable, and not objective. Instead, it is better that there are multiple sources of information, which can provide cross checking to ensure that the information is comprehensive, up to date, and unbiased. There are now three international organisations—the BIS, the World Bank and the Fund—which amongst themselves gather on a regular basis all the relevant statistics together with information on institutional developments on the banking system and capital flows. Though all these institutions are supposed to coordinate their efforts in this field, formally and informally, a more permanent arrangement with greater clout should be instituted. Since the information is likely to be from diverse sources, it is likely to be more reliable. It will also be without the biases, often prevalent, in the country surveillance by the area departments of the Fund, in view of their cosy relationship with the countries concerned. This arrangement is likely to be more cost-effective, to the extent it will avoid duplication of work among organisations and additional layers of bureaucracy.

The second reason for dispersal of surveillance among more than one institution is to insulate the power exercised by the Fund from the Fund's dominant shareholders. It is abundantly clear that the Fund's policy advice both in substance and form was disturbingly influenced by the US, and with the emergence of the European Monetary Union the power of the dominant industrial countries will be further augmented. With such a denouement there is no knowing whether the Fund's programme will serve the foreign economic policy of these countries or the countries in distress.

A third reason for denying all power to one organisation is that a new era of short-term capital flows involves a new architecture of regulatory regime, as Stiglitz (1998) has pointed out:

> It needs to be recognised that while increasing capital flows are a fact of life, a mere good system of information will not be enough to deal with the volatility of flows. However hard one may try to build up information base, it will be impossible to fully incorporate it into market assessments so that markets will respond perfectly to perfect market.

However competent the Fund may be, it will not be able to undertake the task of operating a mechanism to control capital flows as it will have a much wider reach than mere prudential regulation of financial institutions and has to address the issues of corporate governance.

The crafting of a new role for the Fund therefore calls for a thorough and thoughtful debate. Since this debate is not without profound political ramifications, it is imperative for the political authorities of all countries to participate in evolving new monetary arrangements for the 21st century world economy. A new Bretton Woods conference should thus be on the top of the agenda of the world's statesmen.

Concluding Remarks

The East Asian crisis took everyone by surprise because of its suddenness, scale, and the massive rescue operations. The surprise was all the more as East Asia until recently has been a marvel both for the western countries as well as the developing countries, and rightly so. Unlike the Latin American countries drawn into a vortex of financial and currency crisis, the East Asian countries had high saving and investment rates, more egalitarian income distribution, and moderate inflation. Most of the capital flows financed investment rather than consumption. Being dazzled by the sustained good performance of these economies, it was difficult to explain the reasons why they were dragged into turmoil. It was puzzling and no less paradoxical that some of the cognoscenti in the field as well as the international institutions like the Fund rushed to ascribe causes of the crisis to some of the very policies which hitherto served these countries well and came up with remedies to alleviate the crisis based on this perception. However, the crisis worsened with the implementation of these policies. Only later the crisis started to simmer down, once the countries concerned themselves took steps to roll over short-term foreign exchange liabilities and transform them at subsequent stages into medium-term bonds. This implied that the crisis was no more than a short-term liquidity shortage which was allowed to fester into a solvency crisis by wrong policy advice, with mounting but avoidable costs of adjustment.

The East Asian crisis has raised more basic issues about the existing international monetary system's sustainability to deal with the problems of global finance. One thing that became transparent is that a thorough overhaul of the Bretton Woods system—the Fund and the World Bank—should be at the top on the agenda of all countries, if the crisis of the proportion of the East Asian one is not to be a recurring feature of the 21st century world.

REFERENCES

Colaco, Francis (1997). "East Asian currency crises: rogue traders, fundamentals, contagion", *Economic and Political Weekly* XXXII(49): 3129–38.

Dalla, Ismail and Khatkhate, Deena (1995). "Regulated deregulation of the financial system in Korea", *Economic Discussion Papers,* No. 295. Washington D.C.: The World Bank.

Eichengreen, Barry and Poulles, Richards (1997). "Managing financial crises in emerging markets". Paper prepared for the *Federal Reserve Bank of Kansas City's Annual Conference*, Jackson Hole, Wyoming. USA.

Feldstein, Martin (1998). "Refocusing the IMF", *Foreign Affairs*, 77(2): 20–33.

Fischer, Stanley (1998). "The IMF and the Asian crisis" (*mimeo*). *Lecture delivered at the University of California*, Berkeley.

IMF (International Monetary Fund) (1997a). *World Economic Outlook*. Washington DC: IMF, September.

——————. (1997b). *World Economic Outlook*. Washington DC: IMF, December.

Kaufman, Henry, (1998). "Preventing the next global financial crisis", *Washington Post*, 22 February.

Krugman, Paul (1994). "The myth of Asia's miracle", Foreign Affairs 73(6): 62–78.

—————— . (1997). "Will Asia bounce back?" (*mimeo*).

Lamfalussy, Alexandre (1998). "Asian debt: the signs were there for all to see", letter in *Financial Times*. London, 11 February.

Radelet, Steven and Sachs, Jeffrey (1998). "The onset of the East Asian financial crisis" (*mimeo*), *Harvard Institute of International Development*.

Sachs, Jeffrey (1997). "Alternative approaches to financial crises in emerging markets" (*mimeo*), *Harvard Institute for International Development*.

Stiglitz, Joseph (1998). "Boats, planes and capital flows", *Financial Times*, 25 March.

Tobin, James and Ranis Gustav (1998). "Flawed Fund", *The New Republic* (New York) Vol. 218: 16–17 (9 March).

Published in the Economic and Political Weekly (1998) XXXIII(37): pp.963-969.

25 | Impact of Volatility of Exchange Rates of Major Currencies on Foreign Exchange Management

The volatility of the exchange rates of major currencies—US dollar, German deutsche mark, and Japanese yen—has larger implications for the international monetary system and coordination of monetary, fiscal and exchange rate policies of major industrial countries. If, for instance, the US dollar is overvalued or the Japanese yen is undervalued, which is currently the case, the resulting imbalances create a problem for the health of the international monetary system. The Bretton Woods system came into existence to ensure a certain discipline and order in the exchange rates of major currencies, which was marred by competitive devaluation in the pre–Second World War period. However, the Bretton Woods system collapsed because it was too rigid and did not provide an exchange rate tool that permitted flexibility in the adjustment process. After that, there was a long experiment with the unmanaged flexibility of exchange rates between 1973 and 1985 but that too failed. Exchange rates determined solely by market forces responded to 'bandwagon' psychology in the markets (including interest rate differential that may or may not have had much to do with underlying economic relationship). In such circumstances, exchange rates, far from being equilibrium exchange rates, would tend to be misaligned. This happened with excessive dollar and sterling overvaluation and yen and deutsche mark undervaluation, which created tensions in the international monetary system. A remedy for avoiding such disequilibrating exchange rates of major currencies lay in the coordination of economic policies of major industrial countries, so that payments imbalances are moderated, if not eliminated altogether.

The problem of volatility of exchange rates of major currencies is mentioned more as a background and also to indicate that it is a problem by itself for the larger issues of international monetary system. For the purpose of this article what is of importance is that major currencies such as dollar, yen, and deutsche mark, but dollar in particular, have fluctuated often in recent years and they have a significant impact on the developing countries' economies and their foreign exchange management in particular.

Table 25.1 shows how between 1990 and 1996 the exchange rates of three currencies have gyrated. Deutsche mark depreciated *vis-à-vis* US dollar consistently in a range of 1.47 to 6.95 per cent during 1991–93, and appreciated moderately in the next two years before depreciating again. On the other hand, Japanese yen appreciated *vis-à-vis* US dollar between 1991 and 1994, but began depreciating since then. This volatility, or whatever one may call it, has important implications for the developing countries' foreign exchange management, which is our focus. By foreign exchange management, we mean first the foreign exchange reserves held by them and second their exchange rate policies. Though the two are interrelated, we shall discuss them separately.

Table 25.1

Fluctuations in Deutsche Mark/US Dollar and Yen/US Dollar (in Per cent)

	Exchange rates, 1990–96	
	Deutsche Mark/ US Dollar	*Yen/US Dollar*
1991	−1.47	+6.84
1992	−6.46	+0.80
1993	−6.95	+10.30
1994	+10.28	+10.82
1995	+7.4	−3.09
1996	−3.08	−1.58

Note: Depreciation minus, appreciation plus.

Source: IMF (1997). *World Economic Outlook*. May.

Fluctuations in major currencies *per se* do not adversely or beneficially affect the level of foreign exchange reserves held by developing countries as also the East Asian countries. If, say, the foreign reserves measured in US dollar are held in three major currencies, and dollar depreciates *vis-à-vis* other currencies, they will rise in dollar terms, but this signifies little else. However, the impact of major currency volatility will be adverse if a country's payment liabilities are in non-dollar currencies which have appreciated. This is particularly so if a country's trade is denominated in dollar than in other currencies. If that happens, the countries adversely affected will desire, other things remaining the same, higher levels of foreign exchange reserves. The transaction motive of holding reserves for developing countries is more dominant because they have limited access to external borrowing and borrowing to finance current account deficit may be more costly than drawing on reserves.

Countries faced with fluctuations in the major currencies' exchange rates can go for higher level of reserves because of precautionary motive. They may be required to intervene in the exchange market to offset the effects of short-term speculative capital movements which appear to be generated by the instability in the major currency markets.

Looking at the East Asian countries, the volatility of the exchange rates of major currencies will have an impact on the management of their exchange reserves. For one thing, their exchange reserves are mostly held in dollars but their debt is often serviced largely in Japanese yen. Furthermore, they are open economies, in the sense that they have accepted the obligations of Article VIII of the IMF. Thus current account is fairly unrestricted and they are home for a large amount of private capital inflows of all types. As is currently experienced, the unpredicted capital outflows have strained their foreign exchange reserves and, as a result, some of them—Thailand and Indonesia—are forced to approach the IMF for resources to counter the consequences of the currency turmoil and sudden pressure on their foreign reserves.

The problems created by the major currencies for the management of foreign exchange reserves are relatively minor as compared to the impact they have on the exchange rate policies of developing countries. However, it is necessary to remember that the effects of exchange rate volatility of major currency exchange rates on developing countries would depend on what exchange rate regimes they have adopted. If the exchange rate arrangements are such that the exchange rates float independently, or flexibly, though managed, then the consequences of major currency changes will tend to be limited. The exchange rates of these countries will move up or down depending upon their own fundamentals, as well as a reaction to the changes in the exchange rates of major currencies. In fact, if flexible exchange rate policy is operated in the real sense of the term, partly as a response to market signals and partly as a policy instrument, they could as well ignore the fallout of the turbulence in major currencies.

However, most developing countries and also those in East Asia have adopted either explicitly or implicitly fixed exchange rate regimes, even though some of them have given the impression of having floating exchange rate regimes.

Having concluded that the impact of major currency fluctuations on exchange rate will vary according to the type of exchange rate regimes adopted by developing countries, we should turn to see what exchange rate arrangements developing countries have chosen and the rationale underlying them.

Over the past two decades, following the breakdown of the Bretton Woods system of par values, the mix of exchange rate arrangements in developing countries has undergone a sea-change. The immediate response of the industrial countries was a recourse to floating exchange rates determined by the market forces, but the developing countries initially pegged their currencies either to the dominant major currencies like US dollar or French franc or to a basket of currencies, a device used in creation of SDR of the IMF. Table 25.2 sums up the arrangement adopted by developing countries.

Table 25.2

Developing Countries: Officially Reported Exchange Rate Arrangements (in Per cent of Total)

	1976	1981	1986	1991	1996
Pegged	86	75	67	57	45
US dollar	42	32	25	19	15
French franc	13	12	11	11	11
Other	7	4	4	3	4
SDR	12	13	8	5	2
Composite	12	14	18	20	14
Limited flexibility	3	10	5	4	3
Single	3	10	5	4	3
Cooperative	0	0	0	0	0
More flexible	11	15	28	39	52
Set to indicators	6	3	4	4	2
Managed floating	4	9	13	16	21
Independently floating	1	4	11	19	29
Number of countries	100	113	119	123	123

Note: Based on end-of-year classification.

Source: *World Economic Outlook*, May 1997.

Initially, there was a shift away from single currency pegs to pegs defined in terms of baskets of currencies. Since the 1980s most of these countries moved toward flexible exchange rate arrangements of varying degrees. Thus, whereas in 1975, 87 per cent of developing countries had some sort of pegged exchange rates while only 10 per cent of developing countries adopted flexible exchange rates, by the mid-1980s the proportions were 71 per cent and 25 per cent, respectively, and by the 1990s most of them introduced flexible exchange rate regimes. By 1996 developing countries with flexible exchange rate arrangements constituted as many as 70 per cent. However, in interpreting these numbers, it is necessary to add a caveat. These numbers are based on what has been officially declared by the countries. In some countries, an arrangement may have been officially declared as 'managed float' or even 'independently floating', despite the fact that exchange rates continue to be used as a policy instrument, varied by the authorities depending upon the exigencies of the situation. In fact, some of these countries continue to informally peg their exchange rates to one of the major reserve currencies, particularly the US dollar. So that what are declared to be fixed rate arrangements are camouflaged floating exchange rates regimes. Furthermore, the difference between a single-currency pegged exchange rate and a basket of currencies is more apparent than real. The basket peg is justified because fluctuations in the anchor currency imply fluctuations in the effective (trade weighted) exchange rate of the economy, and by pegging it to a currency basket a country can reduce the vulnerability of its economy to fluctuations in the values of the individual currencies in the basket. If the basket is so constructed as to assign excessive weight to one currency like dollar, it amounts to pegging a rate to a single currency than to a basket of currencies. This is particularly evident in the case of the East Asian countries.

Flexible exchange rate regimes, genuine or limited, were favoured when there was a felt need for countering balance of payment difficulties with frequent exchange rate adjustments. More importantly, the flexible exchange rate policy became indispensable in a world with integrated financial markets in the wake of capital flows on a large scale. It is clear that if a flexible exchange regime is in operation, the impact of changes in the major currency alignments on the management of exchange rate policies of developing countries is likely to be very limited. The countries concerned can anticipate the consequences of major currency fluctuations and adjust their own exchange rates to prevent their adverse impact on their economies and financial markets.

However, problems arise when countries adhere to fixed exchange rate regimes. The question is why a large number of developing countries, even those in East Asia, have persisted with the exchange rate arrangements pegged to a single major currency or basket of currencies where one single currency predominates.

The following are the principal reasons given in support of a pegged exchange rate, pegged to a single currency or basket of currencies. When the domestic rate of inflation is very high, a pegged exchange rate by providing a clear and transparent nominal anchor can help establish the credibility of a stabilisation programme. An exchange rate anchor may also be preferable because of instability in money demand as inflation is reduced sharply.

This reason contrasts, however, with a traditional view that the less a country's inflation diverges from that of its main trading partners, the more desirable is a fixed exchange rate. This is because the inflation rate in the anchor currency country determines the inflation rate in the country whose currency is pegged (see Table 25.3). Currency peg imposes a discipline on the country using the peg in regard to monetary policy. If the peg is to be sustained, the country cannot finance fiscal deficits through seigniorage. Consequently, budget deficits either need to be adjusted or financed through the sale of bonds or increased taxes. Since bond financing affects the rate of interest, which in turn strains the peg through changes in capital flows, and since the scope for raising taxes is limited, fiscal policy also needs to be consistent with the peg.

Table 25.3

*Changes in the Exchange Rates of the East Asian Countries
Against US Dollar and Japanese Yen, 1980–1995*

Currency	US Dollar	Japanese Yen
Korean won	0.96	–0.01
Singapore dollar	0.75	0.13
Malaysian ringgit	0.78	0.07
Indonesian rupiah	0.95	0.16
Philippine peso	1.07	–0.01
Thai baht	0.91	0.05

Source: Shingi Takagi, "The yen and its East Asian neighbours, 1980–95: Coooperation or competition?", *NBER Working Paper 5720*, National Bureau of Economic Research. Cambridge, Massachusetts, 1996.

Paradoxically, the very forces that were lying behind the desirability of the exchange rate-based stabilisation programme in reducing inflation and imposing discipline eventually placed an enormous strain on the pegs and ultimately led to their abandonment. In order to signal the authorities' commitment—to disinflate or to sustain a low rate of inflation, the signalling element being central to the approach adopted in the programmes—the nominal exchange rate was either kept fixed or allowed to depreciate at less than the differential between the rate of domestic inflation and the inflation rate of the country to whose currency the exchange rate was pegged. However, this necessarily entailed a real appreciation of the currency over time.

The difficulties of persisting with a pegged exchange rate arise also for two other reasons. For one thing, if the countries are open both in the sense of current account and capital account, capital flows play a large role. While on the whole capital flows help the economy to meet the domestic saving/

investment gap to the advantage of the economy, they also create tension, when capital flows become destabilising for internal and external reasons. Large inflows of capital lead at times to macroeconomic imbalances and sterilised intervention to offset its disturbing impact may be costly. Besides, the nominal exchange rate tends to appreciate, affecting the export competitiveness of the economy. Under these circumstances, frequent adjustment in the nominal exchange rates becomes not only essential but imperative.

Two, in cases where external borrowing by the financial systems or corporations is unrestricted, as in the condition of open economies, the market participants remain complacent about their foreign exchange exposure and do not hedge their foreign exchange risks. When the exchange rate is eventually changed through pressure, the country not only loses foreign exchange reserves but also its financial system's soundness is impaired.

Three, the most serious consequences arise for a country on a fixed exchange rate regime when the exchange rates of major currencies fluctuate. Suppose the currency of a country is pegged to the dollar and the US is its dominant trading partner. If the dollar appreciates *vis-à-vis* say the yen, its effective exchange rate tends to appreciate, but it does not affect its export competitiveness, as it would have done if its trade was with Japan. However, when a significant portion of a country's debt service is denominated in other currencies, the movements in the yen-dollar rate create serious problems for the country with pegged exchange rate.

All this is dramatised by what has happened in the currency markets in East Asia in July 1997. As mentioned earlier, all the East Asian countries except China have pegged exchange rate defined broadly. They have also been the recipients of large capital flows—short term, FDI, and portfolio, both equity and debt (Table 25.4). When the US dollar started appreciating *vis-à-vis* the yen a year and a half ago, their effective exchange rate appreciated, as their trade with East Asia was substantial and growing.

As a result, the current account deficits of their balance of payments started widening, raising questions whether they would be sustainable in the medium term. At the same time, banks and private corporations incurred heavy foreign exchange liabilities. The persistence of a fixed exchange rate regime created an illusion that the uncovered foreign borrowing was safe. When eventually the market perceived that the macroeconomic imbalances would continue, their exchange rates, particularly those of Thailand and Indonesia, came under pressure. The countries could hold the exchange rates for a while.

losing in the process a large amount of foreign exchange reserves. The crunch came when the authorities could not maintain the pegs and allowed the currency to float.

Table 25.4

Net Capital Flows to East Asia, 1991–1996

(in billion US dollars)

	1991	*1992*	*1993*	*1994*	*1995*	*1996**
Total	27.6	43.3	71.5	76.8	92.7	113.3
Public sources	6.7	6.5	8.5	5.8	8.6	4.6
Multilateral	3.0	2.0	3.1	2.3	3.0	2.8
Bilateral	3.8	4.4	5.4	3.5	5.5	1.8
Private flows	20.8	36.9	63.0	71.0	84.1	108.7
Foreign direct investment	12.7	20.9	38.1	44.1	51.8	61.1
Portfolio equity flows	0.7	2.1	14.6	10.1	14.7	12.9
Debt-creating	7.4	13.9	10.2	16.8	17.6	34.7
Commercial banks	5.6	7.8	2.0	2.5	6.9	–
Bonds	0.6	−0.5	4.5	9.8	7.9	11.4
Others	1.3	6.6	3.4	4.6	2.9	–

Note: * 1996 preliminary.

Source: The World Bank, *Global Development Finance*, 1997.

The impact of the currency turmoil was not only on the exchange rates and the exchange reserves; it outreached to the financial sector as well. With capital flows into the economy, bank lending has increased enormously and so their foreign exchange exposure. In Indonesia, for instance, during 1990–94 bank credit expansion was as much as 27 per cent of GDP and in Thailand average bank lending rose to over 80 per cent of GDP in 1988–94 compared with an average of 55 per cent in 1985–87. Euphoria generated by booming bank credit expansion led to rise in asset prices, especially real estate prices. If the banking system is poorly supervised and without adequate prudential regulations, commercial banks, in responding to surges in foreign capital inflows, have ended up with portfolios excessively exposed both to domestic assets with vulnerable values and to foreign currency liabilities. The currency depreciation, and heavy depreciation at that, thus undermined the banking stability, as the banking system bore the brunt of the impact of exchange rate changes.

Published in the Economic and Political Weekly XXXIII(9): 465-67. (1998)

26 | Brain Drain as a Social Safety Valve

Migration of highly educated and qualified people from the less developed countries to the developed world has generated a lively controversy in recent years among the cloistered circles of academics and the more down-to-earth policymakers. The debate has been provoked particularly by the high rate of acceleration of the outflow of talent. During the period 1962–66 alone, for example, emigration of professional and technical workers from the less developed countries to two countries—the United States and Canada—was about 68,500.

At one extreme of this controversy are those who believe in the virtue of unrestricted mobility of the factors of production—including talent and skills—and whose faith in the maximisation doctrine inclines them to conclude that absorption of the educated people from developing countries into the production stream in the developed world will result in raising the world output and welfare. Countering these arguments are those who see the brain drain as an evil, threatening the stability and growth of developing countries by the loss of their most useful citizens. Their argument is that the educated elite and their professional skills are a critical factor in the growth process and hence their transfer through migration, however beneficial for the immigrant countries, is bad for the countries at the losing end.

This wide divergence of views about the brain drain is a reflection of a difference that lies partly in assumptions and partly in value judgements underlying the analysis of the problem. Those who find little to worry about in the brain drain see it as a phenomenon closely related to a nationalistic concept of the world. They see nationalism as "one of the less pleasant mental vices in which mankind indulges itself or as one of the characteristics of childish immaturity."[1] In this view the brain drain becomes no more than an aspect of labour mobility which, if anything, should contribute to world output and welfare. It is then concluded that migration of educated and skilled personnel, being based on a free choice, is a beneficial process, as it helps to make labour

---

1. H.G. Johnson, (1968). "An Internationalist Model", in W. Adams (ed.), The Brain Drain. New York: Random House.

available precisely where it is in short supply and where the potentiality of its marginal product is greater.

Such views can, however, be hardly acceptable, partly because of their unrealistic assumption and partly due to the underplaying of certain elements in underlying economic theory. In the unrealistic assumption, nationalism may indeed be for some a distasteful concept, but it is a fact of life, and policies and problems can usefully be discussed only in the setting of a still highly nationalistic world. One cannot argue that brain drain does not exist in an international context. More specifically, it is inconsistent to postulate free mobility only of the educated and skilled personnel while ignoring the restrictions often imposed on immigration of unskilled labour in developed countries and also on the movement of other factors of production. As for the economic theory, the conclusion that migration of the educated people may contribute to world welfare and output minimises, if it does not ignore, the importance of 'externality' in the context of developing countries, externality being the contribution which an educated person makes to the productivity or welfare of others in his society, over and above what he is paid for doing his own job. It is reflected in such things as enterprise and the capacity for leadership. This implies that in the event of the migration of the skilled personnel the country of emigration would suffer more than the immigrant country would gain.

On the other hand, the assumption of the opponents of brain drain is that the number of educated people is small in relation to the needs of developing countries, and hence reduction of this number through migration removes one of the factors on which the growth of these countries most depends. Therefore, they argue that such a migration not only sets back the growth of the less developed countries but leads to a 'back flow' of aid to the very countries normally considered as donors of aid.

Few participants in the debate accept this view in its pure form. While it is generally true that there is a smaller accumulation of human capital (meaning in this context the highly educated) in developing countries than in developed countries, it does not follow that it is inadequate in relation to their own requirements. Nor (a less committed observer might point out) has it been demonstrated that emigration of the educated personnel largely occurs in those developing countries where it is a critical factor in production; there are no comprehensive data on this point. Yet from such statistics as are available, one important fact seems to stand out. It is seen from Table 26.1, that the bulk of the emigrating population comes from a relatively small group of countries, such as Argentina, India, Israel, Korea, and Pakistan, which collectively account for about 43 per cent of the emigrating population. This might be disputed, however, on the ground that against the population of this small group of developing countries, which accounts for barely 57 per cent of the population of the developing world, emigration of educated people from them may not appear to be large. But the relevant criterion for this is the proportion of the educated people from these countries in the total of educated people from all developing countries. Such statistical information is unfortunately not available in order to reach a more definitive conclusion.

These are precisely the countries which have a large potential capacity to produce more educated manpower, that is, to make good their losses. The Harbison-Myers Index is taken as indicative of a country's capacity to produce graduates of all types. It is an arithmetical summation of, first, the enrolment in secondary education as a percentage of the age group 15–19, adjusted for length of schooling; and second, of enrolment in third level education as a percentage of the age group multiplied by a weight of 5.[2] It is not a very refined index and does not reflect differences in the quality of education, but it is the best that is available. Considering that some of the developed countries, such as Germany and Italy, score as high as 55–85, a score of 20 or above may be taken—of course somewhat arbitrarily—as demonstrating an adequate capacity to produce the educated personnel for developing countries. That emigration takes place mainly from the developing countries with a high capacity to produce graduates implies that the educated personnel are not as crucial a factor in the less developed countries from which the trained personnel are leaving as is suggested by critics of the brain drain, and indeed that emigration from these countries takes place because of the excess supply of the professional and educated personnel.[3]

Now the main question may be raised. Why is it that some of the less developed countries tend to generate an output of graduates in many areas of knowledge far in excess of their own requirements? Ideally, it should be possible for the authorities of these countries to spend that amount on education which would generate the number and types of graduates required by the desired level

---

2. F. Harbison and C Myers (1964). Education, Manpower and Economic Growth: Strategies of Human Resource Development. New York: Oxford University Press, pp. 174–5.

3. Some other countries, such as the Philippines, Hong Kong and Taiwan, have educated people emigrating, and presumably they too have a high capacity to produce them. However, these countries do not figure in the table as there is no Harbison-Myers Index for them.

and pattern of investment in a wider sense of the term. Guidance to this is often obtained from the experience of countries that are now highly developed during the periods when they were reaching this goal; it may also emerge during the technological appraisal of investment projects. Despite this guidance, however, the educational output has been far greater than is needed. There are many complex factors responsible for this phenomenon, and it is to these that one must turn to seek the causes of the brain drain from less developed countries.

Table 26.1

Migration of Educated Manpower to the United States and Canada from Selected Less Developed Countries and their Potential Capacity to Replace this Manpower

Country	Migration During 1962–66	Index of Potential Capacity[a]
Greece	1514	48.5
India	4571	35.2
Iraq	460	31.2
Israel	1254	84.9
Korea, Republic of	1065	55.0
Thailand	–	35.1
Costa Rica	774	47.3
Mexico	3005	33.0
Argentina	3834	82.0
Peru	1127	30.2
Uruguay	10	69.8
Venezuela	402	47.7
United Arab Republic	1600	40.1
Turkey	1405	27.2
Lebanon	658	24.3
Malaysia	177	23.65
Pakistan	682	25.2
Brazil	1475	21.0
Chile	823	51.2
Colombia	3572	22.6
Ecuador	1495	24.4
Paraguay	1122	22.7
Ghana	–	23.15
Total	30,025	
Total migration from developing countries	68,590[b]	

Note: a.   Harbison and Myers Index.

       b.   The coverage of immigrants into Canada is not full. The figures, therefore, should be taken as indicative of broad trends.

Source: Based on Tables I and IV in S. Watanabe, "The brain drain from developing countries to developed countries", *International Labour Review* (April 1969).

If a tendency to overproduce highly educated people is characteristic of those less developed countries that constitute the 'emigration group', this tendency must at large be viewed in the contemporary political setting in which they plan their economic growth. In these countries political awakening preceded economic development, and one of the important consequences of this has been the part played by public opinion in the formulation of government policies. Partly for historical reasons, and partly due to the belief held by many that a college education means more lucrative employment in a modernising economy, the voting populace has come to associate higher education with a higher standard of living. This national urge for expansion of university education is fortified by the effects demonstrated by the achievements in the developed countries by the use of modern technology. On the other side it is strengthened by the failure of young people with high school education to secure employment.

The demand for more education has been further reinforced by certain attitudes formed in many of the developing countries either because of the traditional society where certain tribes or castes are associated with the privilege of higher education, or because of the hierarchical structure of authority based on the level of university education, which originated from the former colonial powers. For instance, in India and Pakistan a university degree is notionally linked to a job with a high status and if it happens to be a degree from a university in the United Kingdom its value tends to increase even further. As a result of this and since the advent of political freedom, the vocal public opinion in these countries has propelled their governments into ambitious projects—they might be called crash programmes—of educational development. For instance, in some countries a typical rate of expansion in the number of university graduates is as high as 10–20 per cent annually. As one perceptive observer has noted: "The driving force behind educational expansion in the underdeveloped countries is very similar to that behind inflation in these countries. As with inflation, few governments of the underdeveloped countries are politically strong enough to check educational expansion once it has got under way."[4]

Is this avidity for education irrational and is the expenditure incurred on it wasteful? Not necessarily. What might be construed as wasteful expenditure, looking at it in narrow terms, might well be a desirable investment in the

---

4. Hla Myint, (1968). "The underdeveloped countries: a less alarmist view", in W. Adams (ed.). The Brain Drain. New York: Random House.

development of the countries concerned when seen in a wider social context. Accumulation of capital does not, by itself, vouch for its efficient utilisation, unless a culture appropriate to the industrial society is created. New capital embodies new technology and knowledge, which can be properly harnessed only if they are accompanied by appropriate orientation in the mental attitudes of men who come in contact with them. For this to be possible, a sort of 'educational density', meaning a depth of various layers of educated manpower, needs to be developed. Expansion of education without an adequate number of trained teachers and necessary equipment, which are limiting factors in developing countries, may perhaps lead to deterioration in the quality of the graduates. While this is true in the short run, over a longer period quality emerges over quantity. With the spread of education and literacy, a new scientific spirit is promoted, and this, in turn, is bound to create a fitting social, economic, and political milieu for innovating and enterprising classes of people.

All this means that it is often necessary to judge the level of educational expenditure not by what it yields in terms of direct output, but by what it contributes to the social productivity of the entire economy. A close parallel to it can be found in the investment in some developing countries, such as India, on the development of atomic energy. The cost per unit of energy produced by alternative techniques—thermal or hydroelectric projects—has proven to be lower than the corresponding cost of atomic energy, and if these costs had been correctly estimated in advance, nuclear plants would never have been set up in India. But their social returns have in fact been immense. They have created a large cadre of scientific personnel and their 'fall out' effects have been wide and pervasive. They sparked off research in a variety of related fields at the Atomic Energy Commission and at the universities. The volume of research undertaken by the atomic scientists, already impressive, is still growing, and it will not be long before its results are fruitfully employed in several other sectors of the Indian economy.

By analogy, the educational expenditure directed at raising the number of graduates may be justified on the larger social benefit criterion even though the private returns are small, and the impact on social return delayed. Since the educational expenditure generates more educated manpower than the domestic economy can absorb, it results in a falling marginal product or, if the limit of existing capacity is reached, in open unemployment. The social return on the other hand takes a great deal of time to be realised. Formation of scientific attitudes and innovating spirits is a slow process and the transmission of their effects to the productivity of physical capital in the various branches of industry is even slower.

The overproduction of skilled manpower as a result of crash educational programmes, however rational, is accentuated further by the artificially created surplus of educated personnel. Even when the supply of university graduates matches the demands of industry, trade, and government in the social and economic systems prevailing in many of the less developed countries, trained manpower is not employed. Whether due to social inertia, prejudice, or conservatism, employers in these countries frequently prefer untrained personnel to the trained ones.

It is then arguable that the brain drain provides a safety valve for the less developed countries which possess surplus university graduates. So long as the tendency to produce these persists—and it is likely to persist for the variety of factors mentioned above—the brain drain is inevitable. And this may not be without advantages. Higher personal incomes are assured when the excess supply of the educated personnel spills over to the developed countries where their marginal product is higher. But their product is not totally lost to the country of emigration. A fairly substantial income flows back from the migrants to the country of origin as invisible earnings, and when it does not take that form, it is spent indirectly on the nationals of the country when the migrants support the education of their relatives abroad or take their families with them.

Even within the emigrating countries, this migration tends to bring about, after a time, a certain desirable social, political, and economic transformation, which not only helps to raise the social product of the educated but also facilitates its quicker realisation. First, when the excess supply of graduates leaves, the tensions begin to ease and a more congenial social and political atmosphere is created. Second, the migration becomes instrumental in breaking the monopsony in the labour market. The employment possibilities within the national boundaries limit the opportunity cost of graduates, but once the employers in the outside world are free to absorb them, the opportunity cost of the educated tends not to be determined only by domestic circumstances but by international ones, and is, therefore, higher than before. This has certain side effects, for once the employers realise that the movement of professional skills is not hampered by lack of alternative avenues of employment, they no longer remain wedded to their traditional modes of operation. The competitive urge begins to seize them. This urge is transmitted to management practices and attitudes toward production, thereby facilitating the institutional transformation of the traditional society which is essential for better use of the educated manpower. The importance of the institutional and social change has been well illustrated by the experience of India where, despite a large number of excellent statisticians, the statistical organisation is relatively weak. As P.C. Mahalanobis has pointed out, the productivity of statisticians in Indian conditions is low because they operate in a social, political, and institutional environment which has stultified their initiative and creativity.

The foregoing analysis should not be taken to mean, however, that the emigrating countries should passively wait, without taking any concrete action to stem the migration of their educated people; the safety valve must be regulated. There are two obvious ways in which this might be done. First, the developed countries might tighten up their immigration laws to make it difficult for the migrants to enter. Even with the best of intentions, this is a course with very limited possibilities. Barring some measures, such as terminating the closed-shop policies in medical education in the United States, there is a point beyond which developed countries will not willingly go in order to enforce their strict immigration laws. The shortage of some kinds of skilled labour is chronic in these economies, which means that curtailment of immigrants would react adversely on their own rate of growth.

The other means of curtailing the brain drain is in the hands of the emigrating countries. They might by law or administrative arrangement stop people from emigrating. But measures of purely preventive nature only compound the difficulties. The growth of modern knowledge and technology needs cross fertilisation of ideas, which is facilitated through constant contact with the more advanced centres of study in developed countries. It is precisely this, however, that would be denied the scientists and educationists in developing countries through negative measures. Imposition of a ban on the migration of educated manpower is as inefficient a policy as rigid import controls with all their harmful consequences.

There is a strong case for removing all existing restrictions—such as permit cards—on the movement of nationals of the less developed countries toward the developed centres of knowledge. Those who desire to pursue their studies abroad would be then left free to do so. As domestic expenditure on education is allowed to exceed what is immediately needed, the same might be done in respect of training and education abroad. As it is, the amount of foreign exchange expended on the education abroad of nationals of the less developed countries is not large.

If, however, the countries could not make enough foreign exchange available for study abroad, they might at least permit their students to travel abroad without it. It is conceivable that the intending student migrant in this case would draw, while abroad, on the earnings of his relatives which otherwise would have accrued to the home country. But by preventing this type of migration, this outflow is far from checked, as is evident from the experience of many less developed countries which have tried it. This is because what is not spent on education is diverted in a variety of ways toward other goods. It is then a choice between the use of potential foreign exchange earnings on education or on other less essential goods, and there is little doubt about where the choice should eventually fall.

It might also be rewarding for these countries to permit those highly trained personnel in domestic universities and industries to go abroad periodically—say, every three or four years—to acquaint themselves with new developments in their fields of specialisation. Here such visits would constitute a sort of 'inducement goods' for the consumption of the intelligentsia, and their fruits would accrue to their countries on their return. It would also tend to remove the fear that if those who might emigrate do not in fact settle abroad the opportunities of intellectual advancement would be permanently denied to them.

A policy that may be profitably followed is that the country losing educated people should create such conditions domestically as would facilitate temporary reflux of its existing emigrants for a year or two. A great deal of talent from developing countries has been employed in the universities and industry in the developed countries. If some of these are induced to come back for a short period, even if it means preferential emoluments in their own country, it might eventually help to create a proper atmosphere for a later permanent return. On returning to their home country, some of their prejudices might be discarded and a hearty welcome might be accorded to them from within once their usefulness is driven home to their employers.

In addition to all this, a determined attempt could be made in developing countries to institutionalise the arrangements for broadening the base of the educational programme. It is possible, for instance, for governments of developing countries to set aside a foreign exchange fund to send abroad for educating their most talented young people. Conversely, the programme should permit the import of high-quality foreign personnel for building up the centres of knowledge and training for those people who do not receive the benefits of foreign education. In this way intellectual development would receive a much needed impetus and a body of research-oriented personnel and institutions would be built up. There is good precedent for such a course. It is what Japan did during the last decade of the 19th century and the early years of the present century in order to stem the outflow of its educated personnel without denying to them the advantage of the advanced knowledge and technological development in the richer countries.

The phenomenon of brain drain is a consequence partly of the prevailing tendency in some of the less developed countries to overproduce graduates and partly of the social inertia in these societies preventing a full use of the available trained manpower. Unavoidable though it is, it may not—in the view I have suggested—be harmful, at any rate in the long run, as it hastens the social, psychological, and attitudinal changes in the economies of the emigrating countries, which can be conducive to more productive use of skilled manpower and other resources.

[Published in Finance and Development 18(1): 34-39. (1971)

27 | Trade Policies and Business Opportunities in South Asia

The whole essence of a link between trade policies and business opportunities is epitomised in the classic phrase of Dennis Robertson that "trade is an engine of growth". Since growth and the markets for goods and services which ensue from it are closely related, the whole focus has shifted to a design of trade policies which can maximise the growth of economies and the consequent expansion of markets. In the early post–Second World War years it was widely believed that developing countries could not grow because of a secularly adverse change in their terms of trade, following declining prices of their primary products (Prebisch, 1952). This sombre assessment of trade prospects for developing countries was supplemented by the different kind of elasticity pessimism of Nurkse, which implied that the markets of industrial countries would not be able to absorb the developing countries' goods because of low income elasticity of demand for them (Nurkse, 1953). These doomsday predictions have been convincingly falsified by events over the last 25 years. World trade not only expanded rapidly between the 1950s and 1960s, but it exceeded the growth of world income (Bhagwati, 1988). Coincidentally, the autarchic policies, concentrating on import substituting type of development, particularly in Latin American and also in South Asian countries, unravelled precisely at a time when the spectacular success that the newly industrialising countries (NICs) such as Korea, Taiwan, Hong Kong and Singapore had achieved in promoting manufacturing exports on a large scale became evident. This cast a serious doubt on elasticity pessimism as an economic concept as also on the policies which many developing countries had pursued and their economic underpinning. It is clear that growth of countries, market for goods, technology transfer through foreign investment and non-parochial trade policies constitute a sure prescription for widening the scope for world-wide business opportunities.

Before proceeding to the trade policy issues in the context of South Asia, it seems necessary to clarify certain notions about trade policies. A market promoting or expanding trade policy has two sides. One relates to what the country aspiring to grow has to accomplish on its own in the field of its internal production and distribution structure by designing a trade regime which would be optimal in terms of maximisation of its output, whether exportables or importables. But it has also another aspect which is that the countries constituting major markets for the goods of developing countries should reciprocate by pursuing complementary or non-contradictory trade policies so as not to negate the efforts of the country following trade promoting policies. It is not uncommon to see that these two aspects of trade policies—the policies adopted by the exporting developing countries and those followed by the importing industrial countries like the US—are often confused in the discussion on appropriate trade strategy by developing countries. For instance, it is argued that protectionist or managed trade policies by some of the industrial countries are the real villain of the piece impeding the trade of developing countries, regardless of whether the latter have put in place efficient trade promoting policies (Bagchi, 1990). While there is some truth in this view, it does not follow that the right trade policies would not yield right results, even though a part of the trade gains resulting from the right trade policies is whittled down by the protectionist policies of the industrial countries. In this paper, for the sake of analytical presentation, attention is focused, to begin with, on what policies developing countries should follow if they need to grow fast through trade expansion. The performance of countries in the Asian regions such as Korea, Taiwan, Hong Kong and Singapore pursuing such policies is then analysed before turning to the trade policies of South Asian countries such as India, Pakistan, Nepal, Sri Lanka, etc.

II

An ideal trade strategy is one which offers incentives that are neutral as between domestic and foreign markets. It neither favours exports nor disfavours them; nor does it discriminate in favour of imports or against them. Thus, whatever is efficiently produced is the one that needs to be produced. The prime condition prescribed for this kind of trade policy is that effective exchange rate (EER) for imports is equal to the effective exchange rate for imports. That is to say, EERex = EERim. In other words, trade policy should be such that the structure of incentives it gives rise to should be neutral between importables and exportables. Whether this policy is called an export-oriented trade strategy or import substituting trade strategy is simply not relevant, so long as what is produced is produced in the most efficient manner, using both capital and labour in optimal combination, given their prices (Bhagwati, 1988; World Bank, 1987). It does not necessarily favour exports, even though rapid expansion of exports is a more likely outcome. At the same time, it does not impede import substitution so long as what is domestically produced can compete with imports at international prices.

A trade policy, usually called outward-oriented strategy, is invariant with reference to the size of the country or to the degree of government intervention. It should work equally efficiently in a continental type of country such as India or China and in a small resource-poor country like Korea or Hong Kong, so long as its incentive structure remains neutral between domestic and foreign markets. If such a policy does not work for some reason in a large-sized country, the cause of its failure may lie elsewhere in misconceived macroeconomic policies, particularly in serious fiscal imbalances.

Outward-oriented trade policy, likewise, should not be equated with the absence of government intervention or a completely free trade policy. Government non-intervention is not a necessary condition for an outward-oriented trade strategy, as is borne out by the experiences of NICs such as Korea, Taiwan, Hong Kong, etc. In fact, as Bhagwati (1988) has underscored,

> government intervention can be of great value and almost certainly has been so, in making the neutral incentive trade strategy work successfully when the governments can bend in some cases toward ultra-export promotion and generate enough confidence in investors to undertake costly investments and programmes in order to take advantage of a shift in such a trade policy.

Under the neutral incentive structure of trade policy, there is a greater incentive to undertake new investment which can contribute to faster growth in output produced under competitive conditions. There is thus greater scope for expanding business opportunities not only in countries adopting such policies but also others which come in contact with them through growth in trade.

III

Outward-oriented trade policy implies that trade controls are either non-existent or low in the sense that any disincentives resulting from import barriers are more or less counter-balanced by export incentives. This policy is also characterised by the absence of direct controls and licensing arrangements and by the equivalence between the effective exchange rates on imports and exports. The real issue is what should be the criteria by which the success or otherwise of a trade policy with neutral incentive structure can be judged. One, and the obvious, way is to compare, following the procedure adopted in the World Bank's *World Development Report* 1987, the economic performance, particularly export performance, of countries adopting outward-oriented trade policies (OO) and those which pursue inward-oriented trade policies (IO). This procedure is particularly apt for the purpose of this paper—that is, to analyse the trade policy orientation of the South Asian countries and the impact on their growth performance—because the NICs which are located in the same geographical area have adopted a set of trade policies diametrically opposite to those adopted in the South Asian countries chosen here, such as Bangladesh, Nepal, India, Pakistan, and Sri Lanka. For convenience, the countries in Asia are grouped under three categories—outward-oriented trade policy countries (OOCs); moderately outward-oriented trade policy countries (MOCs) and inward-oriented trade policy countries (IOCs)—so that the contrast between these trade policies should be seen in bold relief.

OOCs: South Korea, Hong Kong, Singapore, Taiwan.

MOCs: China, Indonesia, Malaysia, the Philippines, Thailand.

IOCs: Bangladesh, Nepal, India, Pakistan, Sri Lanka.

It will be seen from Table 27.1 that per capita GNP in OOCs is way above that in MOCs and IOCs. That also holds true in respect of average GNP growth rate during 1965–87. Only in the Philippines in the MOCs category, GNP growth rate was as low as in the IO group of countries, largely due to the political upheaval in that country. The growth rate of industry and, within industry that of manufacturing, was also higher, generally with a few exceptions in the OOCs group.

The contrast becomes even sharper when the statistics relating to exports, imports and their composition are dissected (Table 27.2). During 1965–1980, the rate of growth of exports was on an average much higher in the OOCs group, followed by the MOC group. The laggard was again the IOCs group, in which the highest rate of growth of exports at 4.3 per cent was in Pakistan. During 1980–1987, export growth in the OOCs slackened somewhat because the base level of exports became larger. As far as the other two groups of countries were concerned, export growth rates picked up mainly because trade reforms in MOCs were speeded up and in IOCs there was some relaxation in their controlled trade regimes, particularly in India and Pakistan.

Table 27.1

Economic Indicators—East and South Asian Countries

| | | Population (Millions) 1987 | Per Capita GNP 1987 | Growth rate | | | |
				GNP per capita 1965–1987	Agriculture 1980–1987	Industry 1980–1989	Manufacturing 1980–1987
Group I: Outward Oriented Countries (OOCs)	South Korea	42.1	2690	6.4	4.4	10.8	10.6
	Taiwan	18.2	2729	7.5	3.2	13.2	14.1
	Hong Kong	5.6	8070	6.2	–	6.8*	6.3*
	Singapore	2.6	7940	7.2	-3.9	4.0	3.3
Group II: Moderately Outward Oriented Countries (MOCs)	China	1068.5	290	5.2	7.4	13.2	12.6
	Indonesia	171.4	450	4.5	3.0	2.1	7.8
	Malaysia	16.5	1810	4.1	3.4	5.8	6.3
	Philippines	58.4	590	1.7	1.8	-2.8	-1.1
	Thailand	53.6	850	3.9			
Group III: Inward Oriented Countries (IOCs)	Bangladesh	106.1	160	0.3	2.4	4.7	2.4
	Nepal	17.6	160	0.5	4.2	–	–
	India	797.5	300	1.8	0.8	7.2	8.3
	Pakistan	102.5	350	2.5	3.4	9.1	8.9
	Sri Lanka	16.4	405	3.0	3.1	4.2	6.2

Note: * Figures relate to 1970–77, as data for later years are not available.

Source: World Development Report, 1989. Washington, DC: The World Bank.

The same picture emerges with regard to manufacturing exports, which are considered to be the most dynamic element in international trade. In two of the OOCs almost all exports—about 92 per cent—comprised manufacturing exports. The same is believed to be true of Taiwan, though no data could be cited for want of necessary information. What is even more striking is the shift in composition of exports in MOCs which began to move, albeit moderately, towards outward-oriented trade strategy during the 1980s. The share of manufacturing exports in total exports in China rose from 46 per cent to 70 per cent between 1965 and 1987. In Indonesia, this ratio rebounded from a mere 4 per cent to 27 per cent, in Malaysia from 6 per cent to 40 per cent, in Thailand from 4 per cent to 53 per cent, and in the Philippines from 6 per cent to 62 per cent in the same period. In contrast, the shift in export composition in the IOCs group was moderate except in Bangladesh and Sri Lanka, but these could not be considered to be typical because the export base from which these countries started was very small to begin with.

Imports in all three groups of countries reveal a divergent pattern. By and large, in OOCs and MOCs the rates of import growth were higher than in IOCs, and apparently their trade balances, instead of deteriorating in fact improved. These observations contradict the widely held belief that with outward-oriented trade policies the balance of payments situation tends to deteriorate. This is, of course, not to suggest that trade policy is the only determinant of a country's current account balance of payments. It also depends on the type of macroeconomic policies, including fiscal and monetary, which it pursues. However, it so turned out that the countries with OO and MO trade policies could maintain reasonably good macroeconomic balances, which reinforced their trade policies and other liberalisation measures.

The first two groups of countries—OOCs and MOCs—dominated the export trade of all developing countries, which is evidenced in Table 27.3. Between 1965 and 1986 the share of all developing countries in total world manufactured export rose from 7.8 per cent to 17.1 per cent. The share of East Asian and Pacific countries, which include OOC and MOC, in world manufactured exports increased during the period from 3.0 per cent to 10.8 per cent. This means that a little less than two-thirds of developing countries' manufactured exports came from nine countries from the East Asian and Pacific region. Looking at it differently, these nine countries also claimed 78 per cent of manufacturing exports by all developing countries to each other. Thus, the OOCs and MOCs have occupied a pride of place in exports to the industrial as well as developing countries, which was made possible only because of their outward-oriented trade strategies.

Table 27.2

Imports, Exports, and their Composition

		Exports ($ mn) 1987	Annual Growth Rate		Share of Manufactures in Exports (%)		Imports ($ mn) 1987	Annual Average Growth Rate		Share of Manufactures in Imports (%)	
			1965–1980	1980–1987	1965	1987		1965–1980	1980–1987	1965	1987
Group I: Outward Oriented Countries (OOCs)	South Korea	47,172	27.2	14.3	59	92	40,934	15.2	9.6	51	62
	Taiwan	–	–	–	–	–	–	–	–	–	–
	Hong Kong	48,475	9.5	11.4	87	92	48,462	8.3	9.1	59	84
	Singapore	28,592	4.7	6.1	35	72	32,480	7.0	9.1	44	69
Group II: Moderately Outward Oriented Countries (MOCs)	China	39,542	5.5	11.7	46	70	43,392	7.9	14.2	39	85
	Indonesia	17,206	9.6	2.7	4	27	14,453	14.2	-2.2	89	78
	Malaysia	17,865	4.4	9.7	6	40	12,506	2.9	-0.7	54	80
	Philippines	5,649	4.7	-0.4	6	62	7,144	2.9	-0.4	63	68
	Thailand	11,659	8.5	10.2	4	53	12,955	4.1	3.4	80	72
Group III: Inward Oriented Countries (IOCs)	Bangladesh	1,074	–	6.2	–	50	2,620	–	2.3	–	70
	Nepal	151	-2.3	5.1	22	72	569	3.0	6.4	59	79
	India	12,548	3.7	3.6	49	69	18,985	1.6	4.7	59	72
	Pakistan	4,172	4.3	8.4	36	67	5,822	0.4	3.4	72	58
	Sri Lanka	1,393	0.5	6.5	1	40	2,085	-1.2	3.2	46	64

Note: Figures for Taiwan are not available.

Source: *World Development Report*, 1989. Washington DC: The World Bank.

Table 27.3

Share in Manufactured Exports

	Share in world exports				Share in developing country exports			
	1965	1970	1980	1986	1965	1970	1980	1986
All developing countries	7.8	7.9	13.9	17.1	100.0	100.0	100.0	100.0
East Asia and Pacific[a]	3.0	3.5	7.4	10.8	49.1	44.0	53.6	78.0
East Asian NICs[b]	1.8	2.7	5.9	8.3	22.8	34.5	42.7	63.4
China	1.1	0.6	0.8	1.4	13.9	7.3	6.1	8.4
Indonesia	–	–	0.1	0.2	0.4	0.1	0.4	1.3
Korea	0.2	0.4	1.5	2.3	2.0	4.6	10.8	13.4
Malaysia	0.1	0.1	0.2	0.4	1.0	0.9	1.7	2.1
Philippines	0.1	0.1	0.2	0.2	0.6	0.6	1.5	1.2
Thailand	–	–	0.2	0.3	0.4	0.5	1.3	1.6

Note: a. East Asian NICs and China, Indonesia, Malaysia, the Philippines and Thailand.

b. Hong Kong, Korea, Singapore and Taiwan Province (China).

Source: A. Bhattacharya and J. Linn (1988). "Trade and industrial policies in the developing countries of East Asia", *World Bank Discussion Paper No. 27*. Washington DC: The World Bank, p.12.

Though the relationship between exports, economic growth, and other variables and policy instruments is complex and therefore is not easily amenable to definitive analytical conclusions, some broad generalisations could be made. First of all, all of the OOCs and MOCs maintained realistic and real exchange rates along with sound fiscal and monetary policies. Particularly during the 1980s, Korea, Indonesia, Malaysia and Thailand depreciated steadily their real exchange rates (Bhattacharya and Linn, 1988: 42). Second, the countries in the region buttressed domestic investment by generally favourable policies toward foreign investment and technology transfer. It is now generally accepted that foreign investment has played an instrumental role in the emergence of Asian NICs as the world's leading exporters of electric and electronic goods. These countries also supplemented acquisition of foreign technology with an active programme to promote domestic science and technology. Thus, the East Asian economies have been relatively less distorted by trade and other economic policies. This facilitated more efficient investment and production, reduced the degree of 'rent seeking' activities in the economy and moderated the anti-export bias that would have resulted from highly protective trade regimes. Third, the incentive structure evolved through various policies was such as to remove the anti-export bias of the production structure. Finally, the very export success of the East Asian countries gave them a greater exposure to the world market, which in turn allowed for a more flexible and creative response to the changing circumstances and produced important dynamic benefits in terms of learning, technology acquisition, and productivity growth.

IV

Various explanations are cited, perhaps as an apology for the failure of the South Asian countries, in emulating the East Asian countries, particularly the NICs. First of all, the protection in the industrial countries is held responsible for justifying the poor export performance of the South Asian countries. Second, it is argued that the size of the country is important. What a small country like Korea or Taiwan or a city-state like Singapore can accomplish may not be possible in a larger continental-size country like India. Third, the South East Asian countries, though recording spectacular successes in export promotion and growth, are not really the countries which pursue free trade policies. However, none of these apologetic explanations provides a clue to the lagging economic performance of the South Asian countries.

Taking the first argument of tariff and non-tariff discrimination against imports from developing countries by industrial countries, it is true that the barriers posed are formidable. Having said this, however, it must also be realised that this discrimination is against all developing countries, including the East Asian and Pacific countries. In that case, the protectionist measures by industrial countries should have adversely affected the East Asian and Pacific countries as well. The study by Bhattacharya and Linn (1988) summarised the pattern of non-tariff protectionism succinctly. Its conclusions are:

> (a) like other LDCs, East Asian countries are subject to more NTBs [non-tariff barriers] than industrial countries; (b) agricultural exports from the regions tend to face a higher degree of trade restriction than manufactured exports; (c) NTBs on manufactured exports tend to be the greatest for the EEC, and surprisingly low for Japan. China and Korea appear to be the most affected by the prevailing NTBs, as they have a relatively high share of textiles and garment exports. Manufactured exports from Thailand and Philippines also face a considerable level of NTBs, whereas Indonesia and Malaysia appear to have so far encountered less NTBs on manufactured produce than the average for developing countries.

However, despite all these restrictions, the East Asian and Pacific countries, which include NICs, exported more to the developed countries, as evidenced in Table 27.4. The share of developing countries as a whole in three industrial markets, the US, Japan and EEC, in 1984 was 28.5 per cent, 27.8 per cent and 11.4 per cent respectively. The corresponding percentages for the East Asian and Pacific countries were 19.5 per cent, 24.9 per cent and 4.2 per cent. This means that in the US market the East Asian and Pacific countries' share accounted for a little less than two-thirds of total developing countries' exports of manufacture to the US, more than three-fourths in Japan and about one-third in EEC. Thus, despite the protective measures, the East Asian and Pacific countries did much better in the industrial countries' markets by

Table 27.4

Share in Imports of Manufactures of Key Markets (1984)

	US	Japan	EEC	Developing countries
China	1.4	4.5	0.5	4.8
Indonesia	0.3	0.6	0.1	0.2
Korea	4.5	8.5	0.8	1.7
Malaysia	0.7	0.7	0.2	1.0
Philippines	0.5	0.4	0.1	0.3
Thailand	0.4	0.7	0.2	0.5
East Asian NICs	16.2	18.0	3.1	7.1
East Asia and Pacific	19.5	24.9	4.2	13.9
All developing countries	28.5	27.8	11.4	15.8
Developed countries	71.1	67.3	88.2	74.3

Source: Bhattacharya and Linn, 1988.

surmounting protectionist barriers than other developing countries, including South Asia. The same conclusion follows if the data on market penetration in major industrial countries for manufacturing and selected sub-sectors by developing countries groups and East Asian NICs are analysed. The NICs and China have performed much better than the South Asian countries or other developing countries (Table 27.5). Thus, the protectionist policies of the industrial countries, however distasteful they may have been, do not explain the poor performance of the South Asian or other developing countries in regard to market shares in world exports. The protectionist barriers affect all developing countries, and despite them if some countries have done better than the others, the explanation must lie elsewhere.

The size of a country is also not a relevant consideration in explaining the divergent trade performances of the South Asian countries. As S. Rajpatirana (1987) has argued, whether a country is an island or a continental economy has no relevance to the outward- or inward-oriented trade policies, since the emphasis is on neutral incentive structure which does not discriminate between domestic and foreign markets. In that situation a continental-size country can and should achieve the same degree of success, if not more, as a very small-sized country, land-locked or island. This can be illustrated by the relative experience of some countries in the Asian region. India's share of total world merchandise exports in manufactures and textiles is lower since 1980 than the shares of Korea, Taiwan, Singapore and Hong Kong (Table 27.6). Even the absolute level of Indian exports in these three categories is lower than that of these four countries (Table 27.7). Considering that India in the 1980s was far ahead of the NICs in terms of manufacturing output, production capacity and exports, the decline in India's shares could only be due to India's misconceived trade and production policies. That India could be so advanced before also shows that India's size was, far from being a disadvantage, the most favourable factor in her industrialisation and that factor could well have been harnessed to raise India's export potential. Thus, the size factor has been of no consequence or relevance in explaining India's not adopting an outward-oriented trade strategy. This point is well dramatised by the Indonesian performance since 1983. Indonesia is not a small-sized country nor is it sparsely populated. Since 1983, when the oil price decline led to a sharp fall in its oil exports, it oriented its trade, exchange rate and monetary policies in such a determined way that the incentive structure that stemmed from it favoured efficient export promotion. As a result non-oil exports, amounting to only about $450 million in 1983, forming about 15 per cent of its total exports, rebounded to $13 billion in 1989, thereby reducing the share of oil exports in total exports from 80 per cent in 1983 to 40 per cent in 1989. All this clearly indicates that size does not impose any constraint on any country adopting an outward-oriented trade strategy.

An outward-oriented trade policy also has nothing to do with whether the country pursuing that policy pursues a market economy or free trade policy. An outward-oriented policy can coexist with government intervention or can do without it. If, however, a need for government intervention is felt, it should be ensured that intervention does not distort the incentive structure discriminating against one sector for the other. In fact, those who laud the Korean or Taiwanese experience in trade policy have never claimed that they boast market economies in the general sense of the term or they pursue free trade policies. Bhagwati (1988) put a case for outward-oriented trade policy succinctly:

> The *laissefaire* model does not quite capture this aspect of trade policy since governments, except in the models of Friedman and Bukanin, fail to abstain or self-destruct; they will invariably find something, indeed much, to do. Therefore, explicit commitment to one activist, supportive role in pursuit of the export promotion strategy, providing the assurance that it will be protected from inroads in pursuit of numerous other objectives in the near future would appear to constitute a definite advantage in reaping the benefits of this strategy.

The relative stagnation of the South Asian countries, in terms of trade opportunities, growth, etc. is thus to be attributed to their wrongly conceived policies, which remained anchored to inwardness. Under this, the overall impact was adverse to exports; the average rate of effective protection for

Table 27.5

Market Penetration in Major Industrial Countries for Manufacturing and Selected Sub-sectors* (Per cent)

		Total Manufacturing		Garments		Footwear		Non-Electrical Machinery		Electrical Machinery	
		1975	1983	1975	1983	1975	1983	1975	1983	1975	1983
United States	World	7.01	10.28	9.80	20.27	23.82	43.31	7.26	11.78	9.09	16.59
	Developing countries	2.01	3.44	7.73	17.82	9.05	29.78	0.46	2.27	3.60	7.82
	East Asia NICs	0.53	1.45	5.61	12.33	4.41	19.62	0.18	1.79	2.02	4.26
	Korea	0.14	0.38	1.49	3.56	2.73	10.50	0.03	0.18	0.38	1.09
	China	0.01	0.11	0.04	1.62	0.03	0.41	0	0.02	0	0.01
	South-East Asia	0.18	0.28	0.41	1.26	0.02	0.54	0.03	0.04	0.37	1.55
Japan	World	4.94	5.26	8.32	13.04	6.31	9.95	5.48	4.25	3.21	3.64
	Developing countries	1.68	1.89	6.20	10.08	4.10	7.45	0.41	0.32	0.87	0.91
	East Asia NICs	0.56	0.74	5.13	7.47	3.67	6.24	0.16	0.20	0.80	0.74
	Korea	0.26	0.29	2.93	3.47	2.31	2.97	0.05	0.06	0.49	0.34
	China	0.11	0.22	0.86	2.22	0.22	0.84	0	0	0	0.01
	South-East Asia	0.37	0.31	0.11	0.20	0.03	0.19	0.04	0.01	0.05	0.14
France	World	17.91	26.21	16.57	33.10	16.80	33.53	30.04	33.74	18.88	30.38
	Developing countries	1.34	2.74	3.33	9.30	1.79	5.45	0.24	0.55	0.65	–
	East Asia NICs	0.11	0.39	0.68	2.21	0.43	1.65	0.11	0.27	0.44	1.63
	Korea	0.02	0.09	0.29	0.99	0.18	1.03	0.01	0.02	0.05	0.30
	China	0.07	0.13	0.10	0.68	0.38	0.93	0	0.01	0	0.01
	South-East Asia	0.07	0.18	0.21	0.69	0.18	0.02	0.01	0.02	0.02	0.50
Germany	World	24.25	35.11	44.91	73.17	43.26	61.07	30.36	39.64	24.40	47.31
	Developing countries	2.42	4.02	14.68	28.70	3.46	9.51	0.93	1.20	1.63	5.10
	East Asia NICs	0.68	1.08	9.24	15.02	1.59	4.24	0.46	0.67	1.11	3.44
	Korea	0.13	0.26	1.80	4.51	0.15	0.66	0.03	0.04	0.16	0.53
	China	0.08	0.20	0.20	2.00	0.05	0.37	0	0.01	0	0.01
	South-East Asia	0.16	0.38	0.18	1.52	0.02	0.08	0.06	0.03	0.09	0.95
United Kingdom	World	21.95	29.32	27.48	39.97	19.51	35.97	33.49	48.36	20.77	43.81
	Developing countries	2.57	3.12	13.70	17.41	3.82	8.71	0.43	1.45	1.31	4.30
	East Asia NICs	0.63	1.13	12.38	13.29	2.08	5.09	0.20	0.68	0.90	3.01
	Korea	0.08	0.23	1.74	2.91	0.50	2.03	0.01	0.03	0.09	0.42
	China	0.05	0.09	0.05	0.46	0.02	0.06	0	0.01	0.01	0.02
	South-East Asia	0.18	0.26	0.07	1.04	0.37	0.61	0.01	0.04	0.11	0.68

Note: • Imports penetration ratio is defined as the share of imports of the item in the 'apparent' domestic consumption of the country, or as Mij / (P$_i$ + M$_j$ - X$_j$) where Mij is imports of j from country i, P$_j$ is production of ij, M$_j$ is total imports of j and X$_j$ is exports of j.

Source: OECD, Compatible Trade and Production Data Base, 1986.

Table 27.6

Share in World Exports

		Merchandise Exports as Per cent of World Merchandise Exports					Textile Exports as Per cent of World Textile Exports					Manufacture Exports as Per cent of World Manufacture Exports				
		1970	1975	1980	1985	1988	1970	1975	1980	1985	1988	1970	1975	1980	1985	1988
Group I	Korea	0.29	0.61	0.92	1.68	2.27	0.73	2.63	4.29	5.33	–	0.36	0.88	1.48	2.49	3.89*
	Taiwan	0.49	0.64	1.04	1.71	2.26	1.70	2.63	3.46	5.26	12.52	0.62	0.91	1.64	2.49	4.95
	Singapore	0.54	0.65	1.02	1.27	1.47	0.47	0.53	0.72	0.75	1.89	0.27	0.49	0.98	1.20	2.60
	Hong Kong	0.87	0.73	1.04	1.68	2.36	1.82	1.75	1.78	2.11	5.46	1.33	1.19	1.71	2.50	2.40
Group II	Thailand	0.25	0.26	0.34	0.40	0.59	0.07	0.32	0.64	0.88	–	0.04	0.08	0.18	0.25	0.38*
	Indonesia	0.36	0.86	1.15	1.04	0.73	0.02	0.01	0.09	0.51	–	0.01	0.02	0.05	0.22	0.63*
	Malaysia	0.58	0.46	0.68	0.87	0.79	0.05	0.14	0.31	0.36	–	0.07	0.15	0.23	0.38	0.63*
	Philippines	0.37	0.27	0.31	0.26	0.26	0.05	0.09	0.15	0.08	0.19	0.05	0.08	0.20	0.24	0.39
Group III	India	0.70	0.53	0.44	0.53	0.50	3.98	2.42	2.23	2.18	–	0.60	0.42	0.49	0.55	0.77*
	Pakistan	0.25	0.13	0.14	0.15	0.17	2.76	1.53	1.71	2.05	–	0.24	0.12	0.12	0.16	0.25*
	Sri Lanka	0.12	0.07	0.06	0.07	0.06	0	0	0.01	0.02	1.23	0	0.01	0.02	0.04	0.05*
	Nepal	0.02	0.01	0.01	0.01	0.01	0	0.01	0.04	0.06	–	0	0	0	0.01	0.01*
World exports (US $ mn)		2,89,700	8,29,500	18,97,600	18,00,200	26,79,600	11,574	24,688	51,199	47,304	36,293	1,75,948	4,72,765	10,62,798	11,12,088	11,21,619

Note: * Estimate for 1987.

Source: The World Bank, World Tables; IMF, IFS.

Table 27.7

Level of Exports (in US$ mn)

		Merchandise Exports: Total					Merchandise Exports: Manufactures					Merchandise Exports: Textiles				
		1970	1975	1980	1985	1988	1970	1975	1980	1985	1988	1970	1975	1980	1985	1988
Group I	Korea	835	5081	17483	30283	60697	641	4147	15722	27669	43579	85	649	2197	2523	–
	Taiwan	1428	5302	19786	30696	60502	1087	4315	17441	27703	55535	197	650	1771	2490	4545
	Singapore	1554	5377	19376	22815	39306	474	2331	10452	13317	29123	54	130	367	353	686
	Hong Kong	2514	6019	19703	30185	63163	2336	5611	18208	27758	26919	211	433	909	998	1980
Group II	Thailand	710	2195	6505	7121	15830	76	397	1886	2800	4300	8	80	330	416	–
	Indonesia	1055	7130	21909	18711	19465	15	88	533	2461	4826	2	2	46	239	–
	Malaysia	1687	3847	12939	15632	21110	125	689	2464	4271	7069	6	34	161	170	–
	Philippines	1060	2218	5788	4629	7032	81	394	2141	2644	4322	5	22	74	39	69
Group III	India	2026	4365	8332	9465	13313	1061	1972	5175	6066	8658	461	597	1141	1033	–
	Pakistan	723	1049	2618	2739	4522	425	585	1285	1731	2801	320	378	876	970	–
	Sri Lanka	338	559	1049	1333	1479	6	65	198	462	560	0	1	3	11	448
	Myanmar	108	173	472	303	147	2	5	34	–	–	–	0	0	–	–
	Nepal	48	100	109	160	190	7	10	33	94	109	–	3	21	28	–
World exports		2,89,700	8,29,500	18,97,600	18,00,200	26,79,600	1,75,948	4,72,765	10,62,798	11,12,088	11,21,619	11,574	24,688	51,199	47,304	36,293

Source. The World Bank, World Tables, 1988-89 edition; IMF, IFS.

home markets was high and the range of effective protection rates relatively wide. Direct controls and licensing disincentives to the traditional exports are pervasive, positive incentives to non-traditional exports are few or non-existent, and the exchange rate is generally overvalued. These policies are also accompanied by the restrictive policies regarding foreign investment in most of the South Asian countries (IMF, 1985). As a result, direct foreign investment, which could have imparted dynamism to their economies, was minuscule in the South Asian countries (World Bank, 1989). Inevitably, both the trade and foreign investment policies combined to deny them the fruits of modern technology and infusion of dynamic entrepreneurial talent. As a result, they remained insular, and outside the mainstream of international economy which could have been a source of new opportunities for business growth and the use of modern technology.

V

Business opportunities tend to multiply in economies which are open in the sense not only of liberal trade and exchange rate policies but also liberal internal economic policies under which saving and investment decisions are unhampered by government regulations; freedom to undertake any economic activity in response to profit potentiality is unrestricted, of course, within the usual parameters of the countries' social and political goals; and the innovative spirit and entrepreneurial leadership are given free play. However, it has to be recognised that the internal liberalisation can hardly progress unless it is accompanied by external liberalisation. In fact, one cannot function without the other. Nevertheless, liberalisation of either trade or industrial policy does not necessarily imply that the government plays a passive role in the domestic economy. What is suggested is a true partnership between the government, the private sector, and the international trading community which is guided by the market indicators in decisions to invest and to produce. The South Asian countries have been slow to move in this direction, though there is now a wind of change in some countries such as India, Pakistan and Sri Lanka. But if they have to be benefited by the dynamic international business sector, they will have to move not only faster than in the past but faster than their other Asian competitors in the international market.

REFERENCES

Bagchi, A. (1990). "Economic policy for the new government", *Economic and Political Weekly*. 10 February.

Bhagwati, Jagdish (1988). "Export-promoting trade strategy: issues and evidence", *Research Observer* 3(1): 27-39.

Bhattacharya, A. and Johannes F. Linn (1988). "Trade and industrial policies in the developing countries of East Asia", *World Bnk Discussions Papers* , 27.

IMF (International Monetary Fund) (1985). Foreign Private Investment in Developing Countries, *Otlamand Paper 3* . Washington DC: IMF.

Nurkse, R. (1953). *Prolems of Capital Formation in Uderdeveloped Countries* . Oxford: Basil Blackwell.

Rajpatirana, Sarath (1987). "Do outward oriented policies really favour growth?", *Finance and Development*. December.

Prebisch, R. (1952). "Problems Teoricus y Praccticus del Crecimiento Economico". United Nations, Economic Communities for Latin America.

World Bank (1987). *World Development Report* 1987 and 1989. Washington DC: The World Bank.

Published in the Economic and Political Weekly XXVI(49): 2815-20 (1991)

Index